THE GULF WAR READER

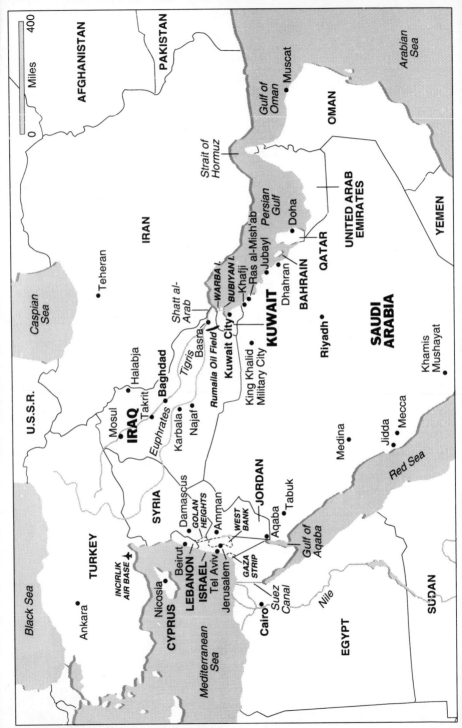

Steve Hadermayer, *The New York Times*, 1991

THE GULF WAR READER

History, Documents, Opinions

EDITED BY

Micah L. Sifry and Christopher Cerf

TIMES BOOKS

RANDOM HOUSE

Owing to space limitations, permission
acknowledgments for previously published material can
be found on pages 504–509.

Library of Congress Cataloging-in-Publication Data

The Gulf war reader : history, documents, opinions /
edited by Micah L. Sifry and Christopher Cerf. — 1st ed.
          p.   cm.
Included bibliographical references and index.
ISBN 0-812-91947-5
1. Persian Gulf War, 1991.   I. Sifry, Micah L.   II. Cerf,
Christopher.
DS79.72.G85   1991
956.704′3—dc20   91-3205

Manufactured in the United States of America
9 8 7 6 5 4 3 2
First Edition

An Introductory Note

THE UNITED STATES and the Middle East are at a critical moment in their individual and common histories. The first international crisis of the post–Cold War era culminated in war. But despite the flood of instant information and analysis provided by television and the press during the course of the Gulf War, most Americans remain ill informed about the history of the region, the policies that brought Iraq, Kuwait, and the U.S.-led coalition to confrontation, and the complex problems that will shape the postwar Middle East. The United States has embarked upon a qualitatively new involvement with the region—a commitment that raises important questions: What is the proper role of U.S. power in the world today? Can it be guided by moral precepts, or is realpolitik and the balance of power the only choice for policymakers? What are the root causes of instability and discontent in the Middle East? Can lasting peace be brought to that tormented part of the world by the forcible intervention of outside powers? Are there other, less violent ways of resolving the disputes among the countries and peoples of the region? Can America's foreign policy be more tightly tethered to democratic debate and control? And what about the "peace dividend" and the pressing priorities back home?

Such questions (and many others besides) suggest that there are numerous lessons to be learned. The passions, interests, and acts that led—directly and indirectly—to the Gulf War will continue to haunt not only those future historians who will ponder whether this war was necessary or inevitable, but also those policymakers and citizens who wish to prevent such crises from occurring again. Moreover, we have yet to know just how many Iraqis—civilian and military—were killed, and the full extent of the Gulf War's political, economic, and environmental repercussions. Now that the great military confrontation has ended with the shattering defeat of Iraq's military forces, the temptation to avoid sober contemplation of the causes and consequences of the Gulf War will be great. A revival of American hubris may be upon us. It is our hope that this book will enrich and deepen the debates that are to come.

PUTTING TOGETHER a reader such as this would have been impossible without the cooperation and hard work of many people. We should like to take this opportunity to thank especially our mutual friend Victor Navasky who was instrumental in bringing us together. Christopher Hitchens and Lewis Lapham also played seminal roles, for which we are grateful. We also would like to thank Eric Alterman, William Arkin (and his colleagues at Greenpeace who issued daily "Situation Reports" on the war), George Black, Tom Burgess, Steve Cobble, David Corn, Elsa Dixler, Deborah Foley, Robert I. Friedman, Josh Goren, Mitchell Ivers, Andrew Kopkind, Carolyn Lee, Suzanne Levine, Susan Luke, John McGhee, Rich McKerrow, Peter Osnos, Naomi Osnos, Tony Platt, David Rosenthal, Stanley Sheinbaum, Virginia Sherry, Jamie Sims, Della Smith, Geoff Stephens, Joe Stork and Martha Wenger (and the editorial staff of the indispensable *Middle East Report*), Jon Wiener, Janet Wygal, and JoAnn Wypijewski for their friendship, encouragement, and advice.

Special thanks are due to Linda Amster and Bill Effros—as well as Andrew Cohen, Adlai Hardin, Matt Hern and the other long-suffering *Nation* interns—who helped enormously with the research; to Sydney Wolfe Cohen, who has turned indexing into an art form; to Cheryl Moch, who masterminded our permissions blitzkrieg; and to Nancy Inglis, our production editor, and Andy Ambraziejus, our copy editor, whose speed and precision made the timely publication of this book possible.

The writers included here are, of course, the real creators of this book; we wish to thank them all for their kindness and cooperation. We would also like to take this opportunity to recommend to interested readers several essays we sought to include, but for which we were unable to obtain permission: Alexander Cockburn's "The Press and the 'Just War'" (*The Nation*, February 18, 1991), William Pfaff's "Islam and the West" (*The New Yorker*, January 28, 1991), and Milton Viorst's "The House of Hashem" (*The New Yorker*, January 7, 1991). We want also to acknowledge our debt to Marcus Raskin and the late Bernard Fall, editors of *The Vietnam Reader*, and to Marvin Gettleman, who edited *Vietnam: History, Documents, and Opinions on a Major World Crisis;* their works, published a generation ago, were the inspiration for this Reader.

We are especially grateful to Ed Victor, our literary agent, who negotiated our contract in only slightly more time than it took General Norman Schwarzkopf to obliterate the Iraqi army; to Andrew Shapiro and Karen Larsen Meizels, who contributed selflessly, and sleeplessly, to every stage of the editorial process; and to Leslie Lieman-Sifry, without whose love and support one of us, at least, might never have undertaken this project.

And finally, our heartfelt thanks to Steve Wasserman, editorial director of Times Books, who saw merit in our project, who skillfully guided us through the unenviable task of trimming 800 pages of "uncuttable" manuscript down to a manageable size, and whose vision, unflagging energy, and unerring editorial skill improved our book immeasurably.

Micah L. Sifry and Christopher Cerf
New York City
March 4, 1991

Contents

Contents · xi

Pax Americana Redux

ROOTS
OF CONFLICT

IMPERIAL LEGACY

Phillip Knightley

THE NEW crusaders from the United States and Europe, along with their Arab auxiliaries, are gathered again in the Middle East. But their chances of a lasting victory are slim. No matter what happens to Iraq and its leader, Saddam Hussein, there will be no peace in the area until the world faces up to these historical facts: the West lied to the Arabs in the First World War; it promised them independence but then imposed imperial mandates; this ensured Arab disunity at the very moment when the West created the state of Israel.

In January 1919, Paris was a city of pomp and splendor. The most ghastly war in history had ended two months earlier in triumph for the Allies: Britain, France, and the United States. Now diplomats from these countries, grave, impressive men flanked by their military advisers, had arrived for the peace conference that would decide the fate of Germany and divide the spoils of victory.

Each night the best Paris hotels, ablaze with light from their grand chandeliers, buzzed with conversation and laughter as the delegates relaxed after their duties. In this colorful, cosmopolitan gathering, one delegate stood out. Restaurants grew quiet when he entered, and there was much behind-the-scenes jostling to meet him. For this was Lawrence of Arabia, the young Englishman who had helped persuade the Arabs to revolt against their Turkish masters, who were allies of Germany. This was the brilliant intelligence officer who had welded the warring tribes of the Middle East into a formidable guerrilla force.

Phillip Knightley, a journalist, is author of *The Secret Lives of Lawrence of Arabia* and *The First Casualty,* a history of war reporting and propaganda. This article appeared in the November 1990, issue of *M Inc.* magazine, under the title "Desert Warriors."

This sounded sufficiently romantic in itself, but it emerged that Lawrence had appeared destined almost from birth to become the Imperial Hero. The illegitimate son of an Anglo-Irish landowner and the family governess, he became interested in archaeology as a boy and at Jesus College, Oxford, and came under the influence of D. G. Hogarth, a leading archaeologist of his time.

Hogarth imbued Lawrence with the ideals of enlightened imperialism, which, Hogarth believed, could lead to a new era of the British empire. Lawrence began to study medieval history and military tactics and to train his body to resist pain and exhaustion. He would walk his bicycle downhill and ride it up, fast; take long cross-country walks, fording streams even in the coldest weather; and spend long, lonely evenings on the Cadet Force pistol range until he became an adept shot with either hand.

During a break from Oxford, Lawrence embarked on a 1,000-mile walking tour of Syria and became fascinated by the Arabs. The Crusades became the subject of his special interest, and he dreamed of becoming a modern-day crusading knight—clean, strong, just, and completely chaste.

Just before the outbreak of war in 1914 Lawrence did a secret mapping survey of the Sinai Desert for British military intelligence, working under the cover of a historical group called the Palestine Exploration Fund. It was no surprise then that Hogarth was able to get him a wartime job with military intelligence in Cairo, where he was soon running his own agents.

But it was when the Arab revolt broke out in June 1916 that Lawrence came into his own. As Lawrence later described in his book, *Seven Pillars of Wisdom,* one of the most widely read works in the English language (and the inspiration for the film *Lawrence of Arabia*), he led his Arabs on daring raids against Turkish supply trains on the Damascus–Medina railway. They would blow up the line, derailing the engine, then charge from the hills on their camels—brave, unspoiled primitives against trained troops with machine guns.

As word of the exploits of this blue-eyed young man from Oxford spread across the desert, the Arab tribes put aside their differences. Under Lawrence, they captured the vital port of Aqaba with one glorious charge, then went on to Damascus in triumph. If the war had not ended and the politicians had not betrayed him, the story went, Lawrence might well have conquered Constantinople with half the tribes of Asia Minor at his side. Small wonder Paris was entranced.

As James T. Shotwell, a former professor of history at Columbia

University and a member of the American delegation, described it, "The scene at dinner was the most remarkable I have ever witnessed. . . . Next to the Canadian table was a large dinner party discussing the fate of Arabia and the East with two American guests. . . . Between them sat that young successor of Muhammad, Colonel [T. E.] Lawrence, the twenty-eight-year-old conqueror of Damascus, with his boyish face and almost constant smile—the most winning figure, so everyone says, at the whole peace conference."

Shotwell did not know it, but Lawrence, dressed in the robes of an Arab prince, gold dagger across his chest, had dubious official status at the conference. Although usually seen in the company of Emir Faisal— who was the third son of Hussein, sharif of Mecca, a direct descendant of Muhammad and guardian of the holy places in Mecca and Medina—no one quite knew who Lawrence represented.

FAISAL, THE military leader of the revolt started by Hussein, thought Lawrence represented him. He thought that Lawrence was there to make certain that the Allies kept the promises made to the Arabs in return for their help in defeating Turkey—promises of freedom and self-government.

The British Foreign Office thought that Lawrence was there to keep Faisal amenable and to calm him down when he learned the bitter truth —that Britain and France planned to divide the Middle East between them and turn Palestine into a national home for the Jews.

Britain's India Office thought that Lawrence was there to frustrate their plan to make Iraq into a province of India, populated by Indian farmers and run from Delhi. This would be the ultimate act of revenge against the British Foreign Office for having backed Hussein during the war rather than the India Office's candidate for leader of the Arabs, King ibn Saud of Saudi Arabia.

As a British political intelligence officer, Lawrence's job had been to find the Arab leaders most suited to run the revolt against the Turks, to keep them loyal to Britain by promises of freedom that he knew Britain would never keep and to risk this fraud "on my conviction that Arab help was necessary to our cheap and speedy victory in the East and that better we win and break our word than lose."

Lawrence salved his conscience at this deception by creating a romantic notion of his own. This was that he would be able to convince his political superiors—and the Arabs—that the best compromise would be for the Arabs to become "brown citizens" within the British empire, inhabitants of a dominion entitled to a measure of self-government but owing allegiance to the British king emperor—something like Canada.

With everyone pursuing his own goal and no one really interested in what the Arabs themselves wanted, the victorious European powers proceeded to carve up the Middle East.

Did they realize that their broken promises and cynical disposition of other peoples' countries would one day bring a reckoning? Did they not recall the words of that great Arabist Gertrude Bell, who once warned that the catchwords of revolution, "fraternity" and "equality," would always have great appeal in the Middle East because they challenged a world order in which Europeans were supreme or in which those Europeans—and their client Arab leaders—treated ordinary Arabs as inferior beings? Do the ghosts of those delegates at the Paris Peace Conference —and the "tidying up" meetings that followed—now shiver as the United States and Europe gear up to impose another settlement on the Middle East?

The past will haunt the new Crusades because the Arabs have never forgotten the promises of freedom made to them in the First World War by the likes of Lawrence and President Woodrow Wilson, and the subsequent betrayal of them at Paris. It will haunt them because history in the Middle East never favors the foreigner and always takes its revenge on those who insist on seeing the region through their own eyes.

THE MESS began soon after the turn of the century. Until then the Middle East had been under 400 years of domination by the Ottoman empire, a vast and powerful hegemony extending over northern Africa, Asia, and Europe. At one stage it had stretched from the Adriatic to Aden and from Morocco to the Persian Gulf, and the skill of its generals and the bravery of its soldiers once pushed its reach into Europe as far as the outskirts of Vienna.

But by the mid-nineteenth century the impact of Western technology had started to make itself felt, and the great empire began to flake at the edges. When in 1853 Czar Nicholas called Turkey "a sick man," Britain became worried. If Turkey collapsed, Britain would have a duty to protect her own military and economic lines of communication with India, where half the British army was stationed and which was unquestionably Britain's best customer.

Others also looked to their interests. Germany wanted to turn Iraq into "a German India"; France longed for Syria, a sentiment that dated back to the Crusades; and Russia yearned to dominate Constantinople, a terminus for all caravan routes in the Middle East.

By the early 1900s all these countries were pursuing their aims by covert action. In the regions now known as Afghanistan, Iran, Iraq, Syria, and the Persian Gulf, networks of Western intelligence agents— ostensibly consuls, travelers, merchants and archaeologists—were busy influencing chieftains, winning over tribes, settling disputes, and disparaging their rivals in the hope that they would benefit from the eventual disintegration of the Ottoman empire.

When the First World War broke out in August 1914, Turkey dithered and then chose the wrong side by joining Germany. Lawrence, working for the Arab Bureau in Cairo, was part of a plan to use Arab nationalism in the service of British war aims.

The scheme was simple. The British would encourage the Arabs to revolt against their Turkish masters by the promise of independence when Turkey was defeated. How firm were these promises? Let us charitably discount those made in the heat of battle, when victory over Germany and Turkey was by no means certain, and consider only two—one made in June 1918 to seven Arab nationalist leaders in Cairo, the other part of the Anglo-French declaration made just before Germany surrendered.

The first promise was that Arab territories that were free before the war would remain so, and that in territories liberated by the Arabs themselves, the British government would recognize "the complete and sovereign independence of the inhabitants"; elsewhere governments would be based on the consent of the governed. The Anglo-French declaration promised to set up governments chosen by the Arabs themselves—in short, a clear pledge of self-determination.

The more worldly Arab nationalists warned that helping France and Britain achieve victory over Turkey might well lead merely to an exchange of one form of foreign domination for another. But these words of warning went unheeded because the hopes of the Arab masses were raised by the United States' entry into the war in April 1917.

THE ARABS thought that the American government might be more receptive than the British to their demands for self-determination. After all, the Americans knew what it was like to be under the thumb of a colonial power, and President Wilson's Fourteen Points, which advocated freedom and self-determination for races under the domination of the old multinational empires, was highly encouraging.

But the Arab skeptics turned out to be right. The Allies did not keep their promises. The Arabs did exchange one imperial ruler for another. There were forces at work of which they were ignorant. The two most powerful of these were oil and the Zionist hunger for a national home in Palestine.

The automobile had in 1919 not yet become the twentieth-century's most desirable object, but the war had made everyone realize the strategic importance of oil. Germany's oil-fired navy had been immobilized in port after the Battle of Jutland in May 1916, largely because the British blockade caused a shortage of fuel. German industrial production was hindered by a lack of lubricants, and its civilian transport almost came to a halt.

It was clear, then, that in any future conflict oil would be an essential weapon. Britain already had one source: British Petroleum, owned in part by the British government, had been pumping oil at Masjid-i-Salaman in Iran's Zagros Mountains since 1908. But it was not enough.

Even before the 1919 peace conference began to divide up the Middle East between Britain and France, some horse trading had taken place, making it unlikely that the promises made to the Arabs would be respected. France, for example, gave Britain the oil-rich area around Mosul, Iraq, in exchange for a share of the oil and a free hand in Syria. Unfortunately, Britain had already promised Syria to the Arabs. St. John Philby, the eccentric but perceptive English adviser to ibn Saud—and the man who eventually introduced American oil interests to Saudi Arabia—understood that British explanations were mere pieties: "The real crux is oil."

At the peace conference, private oil concerns pushed their governments (in the national interest, of course) to renounce all wartime promises to the Arabs. For the oilmen saw only too well that oil concessions and royalties would be easier to negotiate with a series of rival Arab states lacking any sense of unity, than with a powerful independent Arab state in the Middle East.

These old imperialist prerogatives, salted with new commercial pressures, raised few eyebrows in Europe. Sir Mark Sykes, the British side of the partnership with François Georges-Picot that in 1916 drew up the secret Sykes-Picot agreement dividing the Middle East between Britain and France, believed Arab independence would mean "Persia, poverty, and chaos."

Across the Atlantic, President Wilson looked on "the whole disgusting scramble for the Middle East" with horror. It offended everything he believed the United States stood for, and the British establishment became worried about Wilson's views. They could imperil British policy for the area. The question became, therefore, how could Britain's imperialist designs on the Middle East be reconciled with President Wilson's commitment to Middle Eastern independence? One school of thought was that Lawrence of Arabia might provide the link.

LAWRENCE OF Arabia was the creation of an American: Lowell Thomas, onetime newspaperman and lecturer in English at Princeton. When the United States entered the war in April 1917, the American people showed a marked reluctance to take up arms, so to inspire the nation to fight, President Wilson set up the Committee on Public Information under the chairmanship of a journalist, George Creel.

One of his first acts was to propose sending Thomas to gather stirring stories in Europe to stimulate enthusiasm for the war. It did not take long for Thomas to realize that there was nothing heartening or uplifting to be found in the mud and mechanized slaughter on the Western Front, so the British Department of Information guided him toward the Middle East where the British army was about to capture Jerusalem.

There Thomas found a story with powerful emotional appeal for an American audience. The war in the Middle East, militarily only a sideshow, could be presented as a modern crusade for the liberation of the Holy Land and the emancipation of its Arab, Jewish, and Armenian communities. Thomas called Lawrence "Britain's modern Coeur de Lion."

Thomas and an American newsreel photographer, Harry Chase, sought out Lawrence and did stories about this new Richard the Lionhearted. Chase's newsreel footage was a part of Thomas's lecture on the Middle Eastern campaign, which opened at New York's Century Theatre in March 1919. Its success inspired a British impresario, Percy Burton, to bring Thomas to London, where he opened at the Royal Opera House, Covent Garden.

Thomas had refined his presentation with the help of Dale Carnegie, who later wrote *How to Win Friends and Influence People.* It was now more an extravaganza than a lecture, complete with a theater set featuring moonlight on the Nile and pyramids in the background, the Dance of the Seven Veils, the muezzin's call to prayer (adapted and sung by Mrs. Thomas), slides, newsreel footage and Thomas's commentary, accompanied by music from the band of the Welsh Guards and clouds of eastern incense wafting from glowing braziers.

Chase had devised a projection technique that used three arc-light projectors simultaneously, and a fade and dissolve facility that heightened the drama of the presentation. Thomas began by saying, "Come with me to lands of history, mystery, and romance," and referred to

Lawrence as "the uncrowned king of Arabia," who had been welcomed by the Arabs for delivering them from 400 years of oppression.

It was an enormous success, later toured the world, was seen by an estimated four million people and made Thomas—whom Lawrence referred to as "the American who made my vulgar reputation, a well-intentioned, intensely crude, and pushful fellow"—into a millionaire.

But there was more to the whole business than was realized at the time. The impresario Burton was encouraged to produce the show by the English-Speaking Union, of which Thomas was a member and whose committee included such notables as Winston Churchill and the newspaper proprietor Lord Northcliffe.

The union's aim was to emphasize the common heritage of Britain and the United States, to draw the two countries closer together and forge a common sense of future destiny. If Lawrence were portrayed as an old-style British hero and, more important, a representative of the new benevolent British imperialism, then American misgivings about Britain as a greedy, oppressive power in the Middle East might be dispelled.

According to Thomas, the Arabs did not regard the fall of the Turks and the arrival of the British as a simple exchange of one ruler for another but rather as a liberation, and they were delighted when Britain agreed to run their affairs for them.

Britain's aims went further. The United States should not leave the entire burden of running the region to Britain and France. It should accept the challenge of this new imperialism and take on its own responsibilities in the Middle East. At the Paris Peace Conference Lawrence himself suggested that the United States run Constantinople and Armenia as its own mandates. The Americans were more interested, however, in what was to become of Palestine.

The second force that helped frustrate Arab aspirations was Zionism. While the European powers had seen the war with Turkey as an opportunity to divide the Ottoman empire and thus extend their imperial ambitions in the Middle East, the Zionists quickly realized that the future of Palestine was now open and that they might be able to play a large part in its future.

THE BRITISH Zionists were led by Dr. Chaim Weizmann, a brilliant chemist who contributed to the war effort by discovering a new process for manufacturing acetone, a substance vital for TNT that was until then produced only in Germany. Weizmann saw a historic opening for Zionism and began to lobby influential British politicians.

He found support from Herbert Samuel, then under secretary at the

Home Office, who put the Zionist case before the cabinet in a secret memorandum. He said that the Zionists would welcome an annexation of Palestine by Britain, which "would enable England to fulfill in yet another sphere her historic part as civilizer of the backward countries."

There was not much sympathy in the cabinet at first, but the Zionists did not let the matter lapse. Early in their talks with British politicians it became clear to them that the British government felt that only a British Palestine would be a reliable buffer for the Suez Canal. Weizmann therefore assured Britain that in exchange for its support, Zionists would work for the establishment of a British protectorate there. This suited Britain better than the agreement it had already made with France for an *international* administration for Palestine.

So on November 2, 1917, Foreign Secretary Arthur Balfour made his famous and deeply ambiguous declaration that Britain would "view with favor the establishment in Palestine of a national home for the Jewish people. . . ." * How did the pledge to the Zionists square with what had already been promised to the Arabs in return for their support in the war against the Turks?

THIS HAS been a matter of continuing controversy, but has never been satisfactorily resolved. The first agreement between the Arabs and the British was in correspondence between the British high commissioner in Egypt and King Hussein in Mecca. The Arabs say that these letters included Palestine in the area in which Britain promised to uphold Arab independence.

The Zionists deny this. The denial has also been the official British attitude, and it was endorsed by the Palestine Royal Commission report in 1937. But an Arab Bureau report, never rescinded or corrected, puts Palestine firmly in the area promised to the Arabs.

By the time of the peace conference, with a Zionist lobby led by Weizmann and Harvard Law School professor Felix Frankfurter (later a U.S. Supreme Court justice) actively working for a national home in Palestine, the Arabs realized that they had been outmaneuvered. President Wilson, trying to be fair, insisted that a commission be dispatched to find out the wishes of the people in the whole area.

Their report made blunt reading: While there could be mandates for Palestine, Syria, and Iraq, they should only be for a limited term—

---

* Editors' note: Balfour qualified his promise with the assurance that "nothing shall be done which may prejudice the civic and religious rights of the existing non-Jewish communities or the rights and political status enjoyed by Jews in any other country."

independence was to be granted as soon as possible. The idea of making Palestine into a Jewish commonwealth should be dropped. This suggestion that the Zionists should forget about Palestine must have seemed quite unrealistic—their aims were too close to realization for them to be abandoned—so it surprised only the Arabs when the report was ignored, even in Washington.

It took a further two years for the Allies to tidy up the arrangements they had made for the division of the Middle East. In April 1920, there was another conference, at San Remo, Italy, to ratify earlier agreements. The whole Arab rectangle lying between the Mediterranean and the Persian frontier, including Palestine, was placed under mandates allotted to suit the imperialist ambitions of Britain and France.

There was an outburst of bitter anger. The Arabs began raiding British establishments in Iraq and striking at the French in Syria. Both insurrections were ruthlessly put down. In Iraq the British army burnt any village from which an attack had been mounted, but the Iraqis were not deterred. Lawrence weighed in from Oxford, where he was now a fellow of All Souls College, suggesting with heavy irony that burning villages was not very efficient: "By gas attacks the whole population of offending districts could be wiped out neatly; and as a method of government it would be no more immoral than the present system."

The grim truth was that something along these lines was actually being considered. Churchill, then secretary of state for war and air, asked the chief of air staff, Sir Hugh Trenchard, if he would be prepared to take over control of Iraq because the army had estimated it would need 80,000 troops and £21.5 million a year, "which is considered to be more than the country is worth." Churchill suggested that if the RAF were to take on the job, "it would . . . entail the provision of some kind of asphyxiating bombs calculated to cause disablement of some kind but not death . . . for use in preliminary operations against turbulent tribes." In the end the air force stuck to conventional high-explosive bombs, a method Britain used to control the Middle East well into the 1950s.

ARAB NATIONALIST leaders waited for American protests at this suppression in Iraq and Syria but nothing happened. What the Arabs failed to see was that with the Zionists already in the ascendancy in Palestine, America had lost interest in the sordid struggle of imperial powers in the Middle East.

The humiliation suffered by those Arabs who had allied themselves with the imperial powers was encapsulated by the experiences of Faisal, the Arab leader Lawrence had "created" and then abandoned, the Arab he had chosen as military leader of the revolt, the man to whom he had conveyed all Britain's promises. When the French kicked Faisal out of Syria, an embarrassed delegation of British officials waited on him as he passed through Palestine. One described the incident: "We mounted him a guard of honor a hundred strong. He carried himself with the dignity and the noble resignation of Islam . . . though tears stood in his eyes and he was wounded to the soul. The Egyptian sultanate did not 'recognize' him, and at Quantara station, he awaited his train sitting on his luggage."

And where was Lawrence during all this? He was at his mother's home in Oxford undergoing a major crisis of conscience. He was depressed, and according to his mother, would sometimes sit between breakfast and lunch "in the same position, without moving, and with the same expression on his face." It seems reasonable to assume that Lawrence felt guilty over the betrayal of the Arabs, both on a personal and a national level.

This would explain why he jumped at the chance to join Churchill, who had by this time moved to the Colonial Office, and was determined to do something about the Middle East. Lawrence's first job was to make amends to Faisal by offering to make him king of Iraq.

The problem was that it was not clear that the Iraqis wanted Faisal. There were other popular claimants, including ibn Saud of Saudi Arabia, whom Churchill had rejected for fear that "he would plunge the whole country into religious pandemonium." Another candidate, the nationalist leader Sayid Taleb, gained enormous popular support after threatening to revolt if the British did not allow the Iraqis to choose their leader freely.

EVER RESOURCEFUL, the British sabotaged Taleb's candidacy by arranging for an armored car to pick him up as he left the British high commissioner's house in Baghdad following afternoon tea. He was then whisked on board a British ship and sent for a long holiday in Ceylon. With Sayid Taleb out of the way, Faisal was elected king by a suspiciously large majority—96.8 percent.

Because the British desired a quiet, stable state in Jordan to protect Palestine, Faisal's brother Abdullah was made king and provided with money and troops in return for his promise to suppress local anti-French and anti-Zionist activity. Their father, Hussein, the sharif of Mecca, the man who had started the Arab revolt, was offered £100,000 a year not to make a nuisance of himself, and ibn Saud received the same amount (as the strictures of the cynical Cairo accord advised, "to pay one more than the other causes jealousy") to accept the whole settlement and not attack Hussein.

And that was that. Lawrence regarded this as redemption in full of Britain's promises to the Arabs. Unfortunately, the Arabs did not see it this way and have, in one way or another, been in revolt ever since.

In Iraq, Faisal managed to obtain some measure of independence by the time of his death in 1932. But British forces intervened again in 1942 to overthrow the pro-German nationalist government of Rashid Ali and restore the monarchy. Faisal's kingdom fell for the last time in 1958, a belated casualty of the Anglo-French invasion of Egypt two years earlier.

France hung on to Syria and Lebanon until 1946 before grudgingly evacuating its forces. In the same year Britain—then coming to terms with her diminished postwar status—gave up her claim on Jordan. Abdullah reigned until 1951 when he was shot dead while entering the mosque of El Aqsa in Jerusalem in the company of his grandson, the present King Hussein. The assassin was a follower of the ex-Mufti of Jerusalem, who had accused Abdullah of having betrayed the Arabs over Palestine.

In 1958 the American Sixth Fleet stood by to save Hussein from a repetition of the coup that had just ousted his cousin, Faisal II, in Iraq. Hussein and his kingdom, shorn of the West Bank, have survived—the lasting legacy of Lawrence.

IN PALESTINE, Jewish immigration increased rapidly in the 1930s as many fled from Hitler's Europe. This influx, in turn, led in 1936—less than a year after Lawrence's death—to an Arab revolt, which was crushed by the British Army in 1938. Unable to cope with a Jewish revolt, Britain relinquished her mandate in 1947.* In 1948, the state of Israel was established, and immediately afterward the first Arab-Israeli war occurred.

The United States held aloof from the area until oil finally locked it in. There had been some prospecting on the Saudi's eastern seaboard since 1923, but the first swallow to herald Saudi Arabia's long summer of revenue from oil was the American Charles R. Crane, who in 1931 brought in a mining engineer, Karl Twitchell, to make some mineral and water surveys.

The following year Twitchell interested the Standard Oil Company of California (SOCAL) in exploring for oil in Saudi Arabia. Socal negoti-

---

* Editors' note: In November of 1947, the U.N. voted to partition Palestine into two states— one Jewish and one Arab—but the Arab states rejected the plan.

ated a deal using St. John Philby as an intermediary and achieved commercial production in March 1938. The United States now had a strategic interest in the region.

If the new crusaders defeat and occupy Iraq, what then? A United Nations mandate, something like that imposed on the country after the First World War, allowing the victorious army to remain in control of the conquered land? Perhaps a new "Faisal" inserted as token ruler of a reluctant population? And so a new cycle of anger, frustration and bloodshed will begin because 800 years after the Crusades there will still be foreigners in Arab lands.

And Lawrence himself? Everything after his experiences in the Middle East was an anticlimax for him. He wrote *Seven Pillars of Wisdom*, undoubtedly a masterpiece, but found little further in life that really gripped him. He was consumed with guilt over the way the Arabs had been treated, had a mental breakdown and embarked on a series of homosexual sadomasochistic experiences.

He changed his name, first to John Hume Ross when he joined the Royal Air Force, and later to Thomas Edward Shaw when he joined the tank corps. He eventually went back into the RAF again and, not long after retiring, crashed his motorcycle near his home in Dorset. Six days later, on May 19, 1935, his injuries proved fatal.

Lawrence's role in the Arab revolt and his deceit on behalf of Britain left him an emotionally damaged man. He was, as one sympathetic American biographer wrote, "a prince of our disorder." But the conclusion must be that the continuing tragic history of the Middle East is largely due to the likes of Lawrence, servants in the imperial mold.

An incident during the Cairo Conference in 1921 sums up the Arab attitude toward Western intervention in their affairs—one which may not have changed over the years. One day while Lawrence and Churchill were touring Palestine their party got caught up in an anti-Zionist riot. Lawrence, in his neat suit and Homburg hat, conducted Churchill through the crowd of gesticulating Arabs. "I say, Lawrence," Churchill offered, looking rather worried, "are these people dangerous? They don't seem too pleased to see us."

LINES IN THE SAND

Glenn Frankel

To MAKE sense of Iraqi President Saddam Hussein's claims that Kuwait is really part of Iraq, it helps to go back nearly seventy years to a meeting in a tent in the Arabian desert, where a British high commissioner named Sir Percy Cox drew what became the Kuwait-Iraq border.

The meeting had gone on for five grueling days with no compromise in sight. So one night in late November 1922, Cox, Britain's representative in Baghdad, summoned to his tent Sheikh Abdul-Aziz ibn Saud, soon to become ruler of Saudi Arabia, to explain the facts of life as the British carved up the remnants of the defeated Ottoman empire.

"It was astonishing to see [ibn Saud] being reprimanded like a naughty schoolboy by His Majesty's High Commissioner and being told sharply that he, Sir Percy Cox, would himself decide on the type and general line of the frontier," recalled Lt. Harold Dickson, the British military attache to the region, in his memoirs.

"This ended the impasse. Ibn Saud almost broke down and pathetically remarked that Sir Percy was his father and mother who made him and raised him from nothing to the position he held and that he would surrender half his kingdom, nay the whole, if Sir Percy ordered."

Within two days, the deal was done. The modern borders of Iraq, Saudi Arabia, and Kuwait were established by British imperial fiat at what became known as the Uqair conference. Britain had won, and all the others believed they had lost.

Glenn Frankel is a staff writer for *The Washington Post*. This article appeared in the September 10–16, 1990, issue of *The Washington Post National Weekly Edition*, under the title "How Lines in the Sand in 1922 Sketched the Invasion of 1990."

In time, Saudi Arabia and Kuwait swallowed their pride and acceded. But for Iraq, denied a viable outlet to the Persian Gulf, the sense of injustice festered over three generations and was a major factor in the eight-year Iran-Iraq War and the Iraqi invasion of Kuwait.

Iraqi President Saddam Hussein offered many, sometimes contradictory rationales for the August 2 invasion. But the one that resonated most deeply in the hearts and minds both of his own people and of the Arab world in general is his claim to have redressed a wrong inflicted by British imperialism.

"The foreigner entered their lands, and Western colonialism divided and established weak states ruled by families that offered him services that facilitated his mission," he stated in an August 10 address. "The colonialists, to ensure their petroleum interests . . . set up those disfigured petroleum states. Through this, they kept the wealth away from the masses of this nation."

One irony of Hussein's argument is that Iraq's borders, too, were drawn by the "colonialists."

Hussein issued a decree declaring Kuwait to be Iraq's nineteenth province, renaming Kuwait City as Kadhima and naming a new district of northeast Kuwait after himself. "The branch has been returned to the tree trunk," he declared.

Although there is no consensus on the issue, many historians and analysts say Hussein technically got it about half right. They say Iraq's legal claim to all of Kuwait, which is of dubious historical validity, was renounced by Hussein's own Arab Baath Socialist Party during its first brief spell in power in 1963. But Iraq never acceded to a specific borderline, and some believe it has valid historic and strategic reasons for claiming a small portion of northeast Kuwait.

But beyond the technicalities, Hussein staked out what for many Arabs is very powerful emotional ground. They look upon Kuwait and the other tiny Gulf sheikhdoms as the most blatant products of a European imperialism that ultimately dismembered the Arab world, creating the strife-torn, artificial states of dubious legitimacy that today dominate the region.

"In the Iraqi subconscious, Kuwait is part of Basra province, and the bloody British took it away from them," says Sir Anthony Parsons, a former British ambassador to the United Nations who spent thirty years as a diplomat in the Middle East. "We protected our strategic interests rather successfully, but in doing so we didn't worry too much about the people living there. We created a situation where people felt they had been wronged."

Britain's ties to the Gulf date back to the eighteenth century, when the British began setting up trading posts and strategic alliances along the coastal route to India. One of those places was Kuwait, an impoverished and obscure seaport that had been under the control of the sprawling Ottoman empire but gradually had become the feudal domain of the nomadic Sabah clan.

For generations, the Sabahs skillfully played off the British against the Turks, seeking the protection of one or the other in times of trouble. Then in 1899, a new sheikh, Mubarak Sabah, who took the throne after killing his two half brothers, agreed to make Kuwait a formal protectorate of Britain in return for 15,000 pounds a year. The Ottoman empire never gave up its claim of suzerainty over Kuwait but treated it as a semi-autonomous district and the Sabahs as Ottoman governors.

After World War I, Britain and France divided the spoils of the defunct Ottoman empire, drawing new borders and installing ruling families loyal to the two European countries. One of the new states was Iraq, an amalgam that included three ethnically or religiously distinct former Turkish provinces—Kurdish-dominated Mosul, Sunni Moslem Baghdad and Shiite Moslem Basra—created in 1922.

"Woodrow Wilson had disappeared by then, and there wasn't much rubbish about self-determination," Parsons recalls. "We, the British, cobbled Iraq together. It was always an artificial state; it had nothing to do with the people who lived there."

Even before the discovery of oil, the new Iraq was the wealthiest, most politically sophisticated of the new Arab nations. What it lacked was access to the sea, something the British War Office deliberately had chosen to deny the new country to limit its influence in the Gulf and keep it dependent on Britain.

"It was intentional, not by accident," says a London-based Iraqi political scientist who has studied British historical records on the making of Iraq. "It was British policy to prevent Iraq from becoming a Gulf state because Britain thought Iraq would be a threat to its own domination of the Gulf."

The issue was virtually ignored at the 1922 Uqair conference where the major dispute was over Saudi Arabia's borders with Iraq and Kuwait. Iraq was represented by a junior cabinet minister, Kuwait by a British political agent. Neither had much to say once Sir Percy decided where to put the markers, according to Dickson's account.

Still, Iraq never dropped the matter. Iraqi King Ghazi ibn Faisal proposed a union with Kuwait in the 1930s but was rejected by the Sabahs and their British protectors.

Two decades later, after the Iraqi monarchy was overthrown in a bloody 1958 coup, Baghdad tried again. When Kuwait declared its independence in 1961 and British troops withdrew, Iraqi military ruler Abdul Karim Qassim massed troops on the Kuwaiti border in a dress rehearsal of the present conflict. The Iraqi troops pulled back after British troops rushed to the sheikhdom, later to be replaced by Arab League forces.

Qassim blocked Kuwait's entry into the United Nations and the Arab League for two years. But when he was overthrown in 1963, the new ruling Baath Party—forerunners of Hussein's regime—came to terms with Kuwait, recognizing its independence and generally acknowledging its frontiers, although not a specific border line. Part of the deal, according to British Gulf scholar J. B. Kelly, was an $85 million "loan" to Iraq from Kuwait, the first of many Kuwaiti attempts to buy Iraqi goodwill.

The new border never got settled, in part because Kuwait was reluctant to risk its ownership of the South Rumaila oil field, which extends across the frontier that existed until the August 2 invasion. Iraq massed troops on the border again in 1973, and even seized some of northeast Kuwait, although it withdrew under the demand of the Arab League.

The Iraqi political scientist, who wants to remain anonymous because he has relatives in Iraq, says that even those at home who bitterly oppose Hussein's rule believe in the country's claim to part of Kuwait. "It's not Saddam's problem or Saddam's cause; it's every Iraqi's cause, even those who, like myself, are against Saddam and believe the invasion was totally wrong."

The scholar believes Saddam's goal in invading Kuwait was to gain control of a northeast strip plus two strategic islands of Bubiyan and Warba. By seizing the entire country, Saddam thought he would have Kuwait under his thumb and force its rulers to agree to cede the northern area, according to this analysis. But the Iraqi ruler badly miscalculated Western reaction.

Depending on the outcome of the present crisis, the issue of Iraq's access to the sea could again go unresolved—making yet another conflict with Kuwait or Iran inevitable, according to the scholar. "Iraq has to export oil to live, and to export oil we must have a port," he says. "Even if Saddam died today, the source of the problem would not end. It will arise again and again and again until there is a settlement."

By invoking the colonial past, Saddam raised a much deeper issue of legitimacy. For if, as he claims, Kuwait is not really a country, then neither are the other British creations in the Gulf—Oman, Qatar, United Arab Emirates, Bahrain, and Saudi Arabia itself.

"The underlying problem is that six families, put in place by British imperialism and propped up by the West, control thirty-four percent of the world's oil reserves," says Dilip Hiro, a veteran Middle East author. "That's the real colonial legacy, and it's one that won't go away even if Saddam is put in his place."

OIL: THE STRATEGIC PRIZE

Daniel Yergin

WINSTON CHURCHILL changed his mind almost overnight. Until the summer of 1911, the young Churchill, Home Secretary, was one of the leaders of the "economists," the Cabinet members critical of the increased military spending that was being promoted by some to keep ahead in the Anglo-German naval race. That competition had become the most rancorous element in the growing antagonism between the two nations. But Churchill argued emphatically that war with Germany was not inevitable, that Germany's intentions were not necessarily aggressive. The money would be better spent, he insisted, on domestic social programs than on extra battleships.

Then on July 1, 1911, Kaiser Wilhelm sent a German naval vessel, the *Panther*, steaming into the harbor at Agadir, on the Atlantic coast of Morocco. His aim was to check French influence in Africa and carve out a position for Germany. While the *Panther* was only a gunboat and Agadir was a port city of only secondary importance, the arrival of the ship ignited a severe international crisis. The buildup of the German Army was already causing unease among its European neighbors; now Germany, in its drive for its "place in the sun," seemed to be directly challenging France and Britain's global positions. For several weeks, war fear gripped Europe. By the end of July, however, the tension had eased —as Churchill declared, "the bully is climbing down." But the crisis had transformed Churchill's outlook. Contrary to his earlier assessment of German intentions, he was now convinced that Germany sought hegem-

Daniel Yergin is president of Cambridge Energy Research Associates, a leading energy consulting firm, and best-selling author of *The Prize: The Epic Quest for Oil, Money, and Power.* This article is excerpted from Yergin's prologue to *The Prize.*

ony and would exert its military muscle to gain it. War, he now concluded, was virtually inevitable, only a matter of time.

Appointed first lord of the Admiralty immediately after Agadir, Churchill vowed to do everything he could to prepare Britain militarily for the inescapable day of reckoning. His charge was to ensure that the Royal Navy, the symbol and very embodiment of Britain's imperial power, was ready to meet the German challenge on the high seas. One of the most important and contentious questions he faced was seemingly technical in nature, but would in fact have vast implications for the twentieth century. The issue was whether to convert the British Navy to oil for its power source, in place of coal, which was the traditional fuel. Many thought that such a conversion was pure folly, for it meant that the Navy could no longer rely on safe, secure Welsh coal, but rather would have to depend on distant and insecure oil supplies from Persia, as Iran was then known. "To commit the Navy irrevocably to oil was indeed 'to take arms against a sea of troubles,' " said Churchill. But the strategic benefits—greater speed and more efficient use of manpower—were so obvious to him that he did not dally. He decided that Britain would have to base its "naval supremacy upon oil" and, thereupon, committed himself, with all his driving energy and enthusiasm, to achieving that objective.

There was no choice—in Churchill's words, "Mastery itself was the prize of the venture."

With that, Churchill, on the eve of World War I, had captured a fundamental truth, and one applicable not only to the conflagration that followed, but to the many decades ahead. For oil has meant mastery throughout the twentieth century.

At the beginning of the 1990s—almost eighty years after Churchill made the commitment to petroleum, after two world wars and a long Cold War, and in what was supposed to be the beginning of a new, more peaceful era—oil once again became the focus of global conflict. On August 2, 1990, yet another of the century's dictators, Saddam Hussein of Iraq, invaded the neighboring country of Kuwait. His goal was not only conquest of a sovereign state, but also the capture of its riches. The prize was enormous. If successful, Iraq would become the world's leading oil power, and it would dominate both the Arab world and the Persian Gulf, where the bulk of the planet's oil reserves is concentrated. Its new strength and wealth and control of oil would force the rest of the world to pay court to the ambitions of Saddam Hussein. In short, mastery itself was once more the prize.

But the stakes were so obviously large that the invasion of Kuwait was not accepted by the rest of the world as a fait accompli, as Saddam

Hussein had expected. It was not received with the passivity that had met Hitler's militarization of the Rhineland and Mussolini's assault on Ethiopia. Instead, the United Nations instituted an embargo against Iraq, and many nations of the Western and Arab worlds dramatically mustered military force to defend neighboring Saudi Arabia against Iraq and to resist Saddam Hussein's ambitions. There was no precedent for either the cooperation between the United States and the Soviet Union or for the rapid and massive deployment of forces into the region. Over the previous several years, it had become almost fashionable to say that oil was no longer "important." Indeed, in the spring of 1990, just a few months before the Iraqi invasion, the senior officers of America's Central Command, which would be the linchpin of the U.S. mobilization, found themselves lectured to the effect that oil had lost its strategic significance. But the invasion of Kuwait stripped away the illusion. At the end of the twentieth century, oil was still central to security, prosperity, and the very nature of civilization.

Though the modern history of oil begins in the latter half of the nineteenth century, it is the twentieth century that has been completely transformed by the advent of petroleum. In particular, three great themes underlie the story of oil.

The first is the rise and development of capitalism and modern business. Oil is the world's biggest and most pervasive business, the greatest of the great industries that arose in the last decades of the nineteenth century. Standard Oil, which thoroughly dominated the American petroleum industry by the end of that century, was among the world's very first and largest multinational enterprises. The expansion of the business in the twentieth century—encompassing everything from wildcat drillers, smooth-talking promoters, and domineering entrepreneurs to great corporate bureaucracies and state-owned companies—embodies the twentieth-century evolution of business, of corporate strategy, of technological change and market development, and indeed of both national and international economies. Throughout the history of oil, deals have been done and momentous decisions have been made—among men, companies, and nations—sometimes with great calculation and sometimes almost by accident. No other business so starkly and extremely defines the meaning of risk and reward—and the profound impact of chance and fate.

As we look toward the twenty-first century, it is clear that mastery will certainly come as much from a computer chip as from a barrel of oil. Yet the petroleum industry continues to have enormous impact. Of the top twenty companies in the Fortune 500, seven are oil companies. Until some alternative source of energy is found, oil will still have far-reaching effects on the global economy; major price movements can fuel economic growth or, contrarily, drive inflation and kick off recessions. Today, oil is the only commodity whose doings and controversies are to be found regularly not only on the business page but also on the front page. And, as in the past, it is a massive generator of wealth—for individuals, companies, and entire nations. In the words of one tycoon, "Oil *is* almost like money."

The second theme is that of oil as a commodity intimately intertwined with national strategies and global politics and power. The battlefields of World War I established the importance of petroleum as an element of national power when the internal combustion machine overtook the horse and the coal-powered locomotive. Petroleum was central to the course and outcome of World War II in both the Far East and Europe. The Japanese attacked Pearl Harbor to protect their flank as they grabbed for the petroleum resources of the East Indies. Among Hitler's most important strategic objectives in the invasion of the Soviet Union was the capture of the oil fields in the Caucasus. But America's predominance in oil proved decisive, and by the end of the war German and Japanese fuel tanks were empty. In the Cold War years, the battle for control of oil between international companies and developing countries was a major part of the great drama of decolonization and emergent nationalism. The Suez Crisis of 1956, which truly marked the end of the road for the old European imperial powers, was as much about oil as about anything else. "Oil power" loomed very large in the 1970s, catapulting states heretofore peripheral to international politics into positions of great wealth and influence, and creating a deep crisis of confidence in the industrial nations that had based their economic growth upon oil. And oil was at the heart of the first post–Cold War crisis of the 1990s—Iraq's invasion of Kuwait.

Yet oil has also proved that it can be fool's gold. The shah of Iran was granted his most fervent wish, oil wealth, and it destroyed him. Oil built up Mexico's economy, only to undermine it. The Soviet Union—the world's second-largest exporter—squandered its enormous oil earnings in the 1970s and 1980s in a military buildup and a series of useless and, in some cases, disastrous international adventures. And the United States, once the world's largest producer and still its largest consumer, must import half of its oil supply, weakening its overall strategic position and adding greatly to an already burdensome trade deficit—a precarious position for a great power.

With the end of the Cold War, a new world order is taking shape.

Economic competition, regional struggles, and ethnic rivalries may replace ideology as the focus of international—and national—conflict, aided and abetted by the proliferation of modern weaponry. But whatever the evolution of this new international order, oil will remain the strategic commodity, critical to national strategies and international politics.

A third theme in the history of oil illuminates how ours has become a "Hydrocarbon Society" and we, in the language of anthropologists, "Hydrocarbon Man." In its first decades, the oil business provided an industrializing world with a product called by the made-up name of "kerosene" and known as the "new light," which pushed back the night and extended the working day. At the end of the nineteenth century, John D. Rockefeller had become the richest man in the United States, mostly from the sale of kerosene. Gasoline was then only an almost useless by-product, which sometimes managed to be sold for as much as two cents a gallon, and, when it could not be sold at all, was run out into rivers at night. But just as the invention of the incandescent light bulb seemed to signal the obsolescence of the oil industry, a new era opened with the development of the internal combustion engine powered by gasoline. The oil industry had a new market, and a new civilization was born.

In the twentieth century, oil, supplemented by natural gas, toppled King Coal from his throne as the power source for the industrial world. Oil also became the basis of the great postwar suburbanization movement that transformed both the contemporary landscape and our modern way of life. Today, we are so dependent on oil, and oil is so embedded in our daily doings, that we hardly stop to comprehend its pervasive significance. It is oil that makes possible where we live, how we live, how we commute to work, how we travel—even where we conduct our courtships. It is the lifeblood of suburban communities. Oil (and natural gas) are the essential components in the fertilizer on which world agriculture depends; oil makes it possible to transport food to the totally non–self-sufficient megacities of the world. Oil also provides the plastics and chemicals that are the bricks and mortar of contemporary civilization, a civilization that would collapse if the world's oil wells suddenly went dry.

For most of this century, growing reliance on petroleum was almost universally celebrated as a good, a symbol of human progress. But no longer. With the rise of the environmental movement, the basic tenets of industrial society are being challenged; and the oil industry in all its dimensions is at the top of the list to be scrutinized, criticized, and opposed. Efforts are mounting around the world to curtail the combustion of all fossil fuels—oil, coal, and natural gas—because of the resultant smog and air pollution, acid rain, and ozone depletion, and because of the specter of climate change. Oil, which is so central a feature of the world as we know it, is now accused of fueling environmental degradation; and the oil industry, proud of its technological prowess and its contribution to shaping the modern world, finds itself on the defensive, charged with being a threat to present and future generations.

Yet Hydrocarbon Man shows little inclination to give up his cars, his suburban home, and what he takes to be not only the conveniences but the essentials of his way of life. The peoples of the developing world give no indication that they want to deny themselves the benefits of an oil-powered economy, whatever the environmental questions. And any notion of scaling back the world's consumption of oil will be influenced by the extraordinary population growth ahead. In the 1990s, the world's population is expected to grow by one billion people—twenty percent more people at the end of this decade than at the beginning—with most of the world's people demanding the "right" to consume. The global environmental agendas of the industrial world will be measured against the magnitude of that growth. In the meantime, the stage has been set for one of the great and intractable clashes of the 1990s between, on the one hand, the powerful and increasing support for greater environmental protection and, on the other, a commitment to economic growth and the benefits of Hydrocarbon Society, and apprehensions about energy security.

U.S. INTERVENTION IN THE MIDDLE EAST:
A CASE STUDY

Micah L. Sifry

WHY IS the United States in the Persian Gulf? "What is at stake is far more than a matter of economics or oil," President Bush insists. "What is at stake is whether the nations of the world can take a common stand against aggression . . . whether we live in a world governed by the rule of law or by the law of the jungle." We will probably not learn the real reasons for this intervention for years, until some future Daniel Ellsberg comes forward or when the classified documents and cables revealing the administration's thinking are released.

But this isn't the first time the United States moved thousands of troops and the machines of war into the Middle East in response to events in Iraq. Nor is this the first time national security planners contemplated using force to defend Kuwait. In the summer of 1958 they did all of those things. At that time, the deployment of 14,000 troops to Beirut to shore up its pro-Western government was viewed as another episode in the ongoing Cold War; the operation was triggered by an anti-Western coup in Iraq and supposedly focused on blocking Communist designs on Lebanon. But as recently released high-level documents show, the United States' real reasons for intervening had no more to do with the rights of small nations, opposition to aggression, dictators on the loose, or a new world order than we suspect they do now.

On July 14, 1958, a group of Communists, nationalists, and Nasserists overthrew the British-installed Iraqi regime of Premier Nuri Said, setting off tremors throughout the region and calls for assistance from the pro-

Micah L. Sifry is Middle East editor of *The Nation*. This article is adapted from "Iraq, 1958 to the Present: America, Oil and Intervention," which was published in the March 11, 1991, issue of *The Nation*.

Western governments of Lebanon and Jordan. In *The New York Times,* Iraq was described as an "irreplaceable source of oil," the "keystone of the Baghdad Pact" (a British-inspired alliance of Turkey, Pakistan, Iraq, Iran, and Britain) and "the last bastion of Western influence" in the region. Indeed, Said had been an eager and active participant in a covert British-American effort to depose the left-leaning government of Syria that had been foiled the year before. The coup was deemed a "severe blow" to U.S. prestige, and it was assumed that Nasser or the Russians, or both, were behind it. Furthermore, it was reported that the British were worried about "the possibility of a coup in the oil-rich Sheikhdom of Kuwait" and were discussing "armed intervention in Iraq." How did the United States react?

When news of the takeover reached Washington on the morning of the 14th, a group led by Secretary of State John Foster Dulles, General Nathan Twining, chair of the Joint Chiefs of Staff, and Director of Central Intelligence Allen Dulles met at the State Department to discuss their options before briefing President Eisenhower. According to a Memorandum for the Record titled "Meeting re Iraq," the group agreed that if the United States did nothing

(1) [Egyptian leader Gamal Abdel] Nasser would take over the whole area;

(2) the United States would lose influence not only in the Arab States of the Middle East but in the area generally, and our bases throughout the area would be in jeopardy;

(3) the dependability of United States commitments for assistance in the event of need would be brought into question throughout the world.

The memo continues, "General Twining felt that in these circumstances we had no alternative but to go in." The rest of that paragraph was deleted, but according to William Quandt, a senior staff member of the National Security Council, who has written a careful analysis of the Lebanon episode in the Brookings Institution book *Force Without War,* Twining had proposed an "area-wide counteroffensive" that would have sent the United States into Lebanon, Britain into Iraq and Kuwait, Israel into the West Bank of Jordan and Turkey into Syria. The memo further reports that "Mr. [Donald] Quarles [Acting Secretary of Defense] attached great importance to having a United Nations or other 'umbrella' under which to operate so as to give adequate moral sanction to our action." And it concludes with the assessment that "intervention involves the risk of general war" with the Soviet Union, but "that we should face the risk now as well as any time."

Fortunately, Eisenhower did not rush to embrace General Twining's proposal, even though British Prime Minister Harold MacMillan was urging similar action. Fears of a pro-Nasser wave sweeping the region were certainly real among the Western leaders. Aside from the loss of bases and credibility, the West stood to lose control over some very important oil concessions. And access to oil was the crucial factor in deciding the course of both world wars. In 1958 Kuwait was the leading Middle East oil producer, at about 1.15 million barrels a day (mbd). There the concession was shared equally by British Petroleum and Gulf Oil. Saudi Arabian oil, pumped by the Arab American Oil Company (ARAMCO), a consortium of four American oil companies, accounted for another 1 mbd. An international group divided Iran's output of .85 mbd. In Iraq the British and French governments both owned close to one-quarter of the Iraq Petroleum Corporation, which produced .7 mbd. At the time, oil companies shared their profits on a fifty-fifty basis with their host governments. The $200 million that Iraq received from the I.P.C. amounted to half its annual revenues. Indeed, popular resentment against Britain's exploitation of Iraq's resources fueled the coup against Said's regime.

When Eisenhower met with his advisers at noon on the 14th, his first concern was how to respond to an urgent plea from Camille Chamoun, the Christian President of Lebanon—though the Persian Gulf was very much on his mind, as we shall see. Early in 1957, the United States had announced that it would defend any country in the Middle East "requesting assistance against armed aggression from any country controlled by international Communism," a step it took to counter potential radical gains in the wake of the British-French reversal the United States had engineered at Suez the year before. Chamoun had been the only Middle Eastern leader to endorse what became known as the Eisenhower Doctrine, and he had been quietly calling for help for months. Ever since Chamoun had won an overwhelming victory in the 1957 Lebanese legislative elections—thanks in good part to suitcases of money delivered by CIA operative Wilbur Crane Eveland—he had been under attack by Muslim and Druse leaders for having tipped Lebanon too far to the West. In the spring of 1958, this dissent began to spill into the streets, in a dress rehearsal for the civil war that tore Lebanon apart seventeen years later. Even before the July 14 coup in Iraq, Eisenhower had been inclined to move into Lebanon to show U.S. resolve, despite the lack of evidence of international Communist subversion. Now, as he wrote in his memoir *Waging Peace,* "the time had come to act."

There were two prongs to Eisenhower's intervention: the very public landing of 14,000 troops to defend the "integrity and independence" of a small nation, Lebanon, in tandem with a British deployment of several thousand troops into Jordan, and some serious saber rattling in the Persian Gulf to impress the Iraqis, Soviets, and Egyptians, as well as the British, that the United States meant business.

In his message to Congress, Eisenhower justified the U.S. action by claiming that "events in Iraq demonstrate a ruthlessness of aggressive purpose which tiny Lebanon cannot combat without further evidence of support from friendly nations." At the United Nations, U.S. ambassador Henry Cabot Lodge declared that Lebanon was the victim of "indirect aggression," and he drew parallels to Italy's invasion of Ethiopia, Germany's annexation of Austria, and the Communist takeover of Czechoslovakia. As Quandt puts it, "Nothing was said of broad concerns with Iraq, oil, or the Arab-Israeli conflict. For public purposes this was a Lebanese crisis, behind which communism's malign influence could be detected." The Soviet Union and the non-aligned countries were quick to condemn the American and British moves as Western imperialism, and a banner headline in *The New York Times* ominously reported, SOVIET CHARGES MOVE THREATENS NEW WAR.

Until the makeup and intentions of the new Republic of Iraq became clear, "general war" was a real possibility. Eisenhower ordered a worldwide military alert of U.S. forces and the Strategic Air Command. The *Times* reported that an "atomic unit" based in Germany had been dispatched to Lebanon, and the Russians began large-scale maneuvers along their border with Turkey and Iran. Historians disagree on whether the Lebanon and Jordan deployments were intended to give the West the ability to take further action in Iraq or in the Persian Gulf. While Quandt argues that the intervention was always meant to be a limited one, Harvard scholar Nadav Safran writes in *Saudi Arabia: The Ceaseless Quest for Security* that the troops were moved "to be in a position to intervene in Iraq if the opportunity arose."

Certainly, Iraq's threat to the oil-rich sheikhdoms of the Gulf was taken very seriously. On the first day of the crisis, Eisenhower ordered a Marine Corps regimental combat team based in Okinawa to the Gulf "to guard against a possible Iraqi move into Kuwait," he writes in *Waging Peace*. In addition, he recalls, "I instructed General Twining to be prepared to employ, subject to my personal approval, *whatever* means might become necessary to prevent any unfriendly forces from moving into Kuwait." [Emphasis in original.] According to Quandt, who interviewed several of the American principals, "It seems clear that Eisenhower was referring to the possible use of nuclear weapons, an issue that was discussed several times during the crisis."

Newly uncovered documents from the British Public Records Office and the National Security Council give undeniable evidence of what was behind the British and American actions. Here is an excerpt from a July 19, 1958, cable sent by Foreign Secretary Selwyn Lloyd from the British Embassy in Washington back to London:

> They [the U.S. government] are assuming that we will take firm action to maintain our position in Kuwait. They themselves are disposed to act with similar resolution in relations to the Aramco oilfields in the area of Dahran. . . . They assume that we will also hold Bahrain and Qatar, come what may. They agree that at all costs these oilfields must be kept in Western hands.

In an undated but contemporaneous N.S.C. report on "Issues Arising Out of the Situation in the Near East," American security planners carefully assessed the pros and cons of military action:

> Should the United States be prepared to support, or if necessary assist, the British in using force to retain control of Kuwait and the Persian Gulf?
>
> 1. *The argument for such action:* An assured source of oil is essential to the continued economic viability of Western Europe. . . . If Nasser obtains dominant influence over the Persian Gulf oil producing areas, Western access to this oil might be seriously threatened. The only way to guarantee continued access to Persian Gulf oil on acceptable terms is to insist on maintaining the current concessions.
>
> 2. *The argument against such action:* If armed force must be used to help retain this area (or even if there is a public indication of willingness to use force), the benefits of any actions in the direction of accommodation with radical pan-Arab nationalism will be largely lost and U.S. relations with neutral countries elsewhere would be adversely affected. Such accommodation would better provide the basis for continued assurance of access to Kuwait and Persian Gulf oil.

Note the focus on quelling or controlling the forces of Arab nationalism, and the absence of the Soviet bogyman. At that stage of the Cold War, the United States had an overwhelming edge over the Soviet Union. For all his threatening bluster, Soviet leader Nikita Khrushchev had done little to help Egypt during the Suez crisis. Apparently Eisenhower understood that, and after some angry speeches at the U.N., the superpower confrontation generated by the Lebanon deployment rapidly cooled down.

The Iraqis also understood, then, the limits of their revolution. On July 18, 1958, a *Times* headline announced, WEST TO KEEP OUT OF IRAQ UNLESS OIL IS THREATENED. Eisenhower and Lloyd had met and, as Dana Adams Schmidt reported in the paper of record, decided that "for the time being . . . intervention will not be extended to Iraq as long as the revolutionary government in Iraq respects Western oil interests." Dutifully, later that day Baghdad Radio announced Iraq's intentions to "respect its obligations." Once the feared move on the West's oil was averted, the supposed threat to the Chamoun government shrank in importance. Eisenhower sent Robert Murphy, a career diplomat, to Beirut, where he "quickly concluded that communism had nothing to do with the crisis in Lebanon," writes Quandt. A successor to Chamoun acceptable to all sides was found in the person of General Fuad Chehab, head of the Lebanese Army. Ironically, in a communication to the U.S. government months earlier, Nasser had proposed precisely this solution to Lebanon's internal political crisis.*

Thus what followed the coup in Iraq and the landing of troops in Beirut was a new understanding of the rules of the Middle East game: Political changes were possible as long as economic interests were safeguarded. And the United States—not Great Britain—would decide which moves were acceptable and which should be blocked. An N.S.C. report dated November 4, 1958, neatly encapsulates official thinking on the region:

> Be prepared, when required, to come forward with formulas designed to reconcile vital Free World interests in the area's petroleum resources with the rising tide of nationalism in the area. . . . Be prepared to use force, but only as a last resort . . . to insure that the quantity of oil available from the Near East on reasonable terms is sufficient, together with oil from other sources, to meet Western Europe's requirements, recognizing that this course will cut across the courses of action envisioned above toward Arab nationalism and could not be indefinitely pursued.

---

* In *Ropes of Sand*, ex-CIA man Wilbur Crane Eveland tells how an offhand remark by Eisenhower that he hoped "the Nasser problem could be eliminated" had led to the dispatch of assassination teams. "Later," writes Eveland, "finding that Eisenhower had merely meant 'improved U.S.-Egyptian relations,' Foster Dulles ordered his brother to bring the CIA's operation to a halt."

In a parenthetical remark buried in a footnote, our anonymous N.S.C. planner adds that a study was being done on the "feasibility over the longer term" of reducing the "dependence" of the West on Middle Eastern oil.

In the thirty-three years since this episode, the United States has tried a variety of "formulas" aimed at protecting its interests in the region while "accommodating" Arab nationalism. The leaders of Jordan, Egypt, Morocco, and Lebanon have been protected (and spied upon) by CIA-trained security units, as Bob Woodward revealed in *Veil;* for twenty years Jordan's King Hussein even received annual stipends from the agency. Surrogates for U.S. power, like the shah of Iran and the Israelis, have been armed and given broad latitude. Practically everybody else with money—regardless of their despotic ways—was sold weapons as well so long as they stayed out of the Soviet orbit. U.S. efforts to bar Soviet influence from the region combined with tilts toward favored clients had the effect of spurring deadly arms races and outbreaks of Arab-Israeli conflict. A peace agreement that removed the major threat of another Arab-Israeli war was brokered between Egypt and Israel, but only at the expense of the indefinite deferral of Palestinian aspirations.

For a good part of the 1980s, Saddam Hussein was seen as "our" strongman and functioned as such in fighting the Ayatollah. Presumably, had Saddam done as expected and taken only a nibble out of Kuwait, the United States would now merely be bolstering Saudi Arabia as its latest surrogate. But the actual seizure of Kuwait—an indefensible act of aggression—was a bold and undeniable affront to America's domain that summoned an inevitable and crushing military response. The sad fact is that instead of ending America's dependence on oil and encouraging democratic movements for self-determination across the Middle East, Washington has simply relied on one unstable formula after another to maintain its dominance. And to that deadly pattern, there seems no end in sight.

FROM RAPID DEPLOYMENT TO
MASSIVE DEPLOYMENT

Joe Stork and Martha Wenger

T HE SCALE of the U.S. military deployment in the Persian Gulf—
half of all U.S. combat forces worldwide—is something of a shock,
even to the Pentagon. "Nobody ever thought they'd be free to commit
all those forces," one military official said.

Washington's decision to send those forces, though, should come as
no surprise. "The defense of Saudi Arabia is vital to the defense of the
United States," declared President Franklin D. Roosevelt in 1943. All of
the subsequent presidential doctrines of intervention—from the Truman Doctrine to the Carter Doctrine—have had the Persian Gulf and its
oil at the center of their sights. In 1958, President Eisenhower actually
sent U.S. Marines into Lebanon in response to a revolution in Iraq
against the British-installed monarchy there.

In 1969, domestic U.S. opposition to the Vietnam War forced President Nixon to design an intervention doctrine that would "change the
color of the corpses," in the words of one high official. Instead of sending U.S. troops, the U.S. would arm local powers to police Third World
regions critical to U.S. interests. The most important of these regions
was the Persian Gulf, where the Nixon Doctrine designated Iran to play
this surrogate role.

For much of the 1970s, even as the Persian Gulf came to occupy a
larger place among U.S. policy concerns, the surrogate strategy of the
Nixon Doctrine appeared to be adequate to serve U.S. interests. Wash-

Joe Stork and Martha Wenger are editor and assistant editor, respectively, of *Middle East
Report*. This piece is excerpted from an article that appeared in the January–February 1991
issue of the magazine.

ington encouraged U.S. weapons manufacturers to sell $8.3 billion worth of arms to the shah of Iran between 1970 and 1979, and some 50,000 U.S. advisers helped expand and train his army and secret police. Beginning in 1972, with U.S. encouragement and support, Iran provided arms, funds, and sanctuary to Iraqi Kurdish rebels fighting against Baghdad. In December 1973, the shah sent 3,000 of his U.S.-equipped troops to put down a longstanding insurgency against the sultan of Oman.

The revolution which overthrew the shah in 1979 radically changed the strategic equation in the region. Sparsely populated Saudi Arabia was never a serious candidate to play a role comparable to Iran. The real "second pillar" of U.S. strategy in the Middle East was Israel, but Israel's political liabilities severely limited its usefulness in the Gulf. The Iranian revolution, coupled with other developments such as the Soviet intervention in Afghanistan in December 1979, upheavals that year in Saudi Arabia itself, and armed conflict between North and South Yemen, compelled Washington to devise once again more costly strategies of direct U.S. military intervention.

Soon after President Carter took office in 1977, his national security adviser, Zbigniew Brzezinski, dusted off an idea that had been around at least since the Vietnam War: that the U.S. should develop a military force which could be dispatched rapidly to the Persian Gulf or elsewhere in the Third World. Nothing much happened with the Rapid Deployment Force, though, until the events in Iran and Afghanistan commanded Washington's undivided attention.

President Carter marked the transition to the new era of rapid deployment in his last State of the Union address, in January 1980. "An attempt by any outside force to gain control of the Persian Gulf region will be regarded as an assault on the vital interests of the United States," he declared, "and such an assault will be repelled by any means necessary, including military force."

When Carter spoke these words, the Rapid Deployment Force was more a state of mind than a reality. It had no equipment and its troops would have to be requisitioned from U.S. forces assigned to other commands. Perhaps most critically, no country in the Gulf was willing to host its headquarters, which set up operations at Florida's McDill Air Force Base in March 1980. Top Pentagon and State Department officials toured the region to line up "host country support" in and around the region.

While Saudi Arabia could not aspire to be a major Nixon Doctrine player, it did assume a key role under the Carter Doctrine, which required not armies but bases in the Persian Gulf region. Saudi Arabia had already purchased $3.2 billion worth of U.S. weapons and military services between 1970 and 1979, and imported troops from Pakistan and military advisers from Jordan and the West. By 1978, some 675 U.S. military personnel and 10,000 civilian employees of U.S. defense contractors were building military installations in Saudi Arabia.

The Pentagon's search for airfields, ports, barracks, and support facilities to host a U.S. interventionary force took two tracks. Publicly, the U.S. came up against the reluctance of Arab rulers to link themselves openly with the chief Western power and the main ally of Israel. A more discreet approach was required. Egypt, Oman, and Bahrain allowed U.S. air and naval forces limited use of military "facilities." Other bases were more distant—Kenya and Diego Garcia, for instance.

The key was Saudi Arabia itself. Iraq's invasion of Iran in September 1980 and Saudi fears of an expanded war gave the U.S. leverage to extract more intimate Saudi collaboration with U.S. military plans. The centerpiece of this effort was the sale of five AWACS planes and a system of bases with stocks of fuel, parts, and munitions. "No conceivable improvements in U.S. airlift or USAF rapid deployment and 'bare-basing' capability could come close to giving the U.S. this rapid and effective reinforcement capability," wrote military analyst Anthony Cordesman. An added advantage was that the Saudis paid for it all.

Over the course of the decade, Saudi Arabia poured nearly $50 billion into building a Gulf-wide air defense system to U.S. and NATO specifications, and ready for U.S. forces to use in a crisis. By 1988, the U.S. Army Corps of Engineers had designed and constructed a $14 billion network of military facilities across Saudi Arabia, including military cantonments at Khamis Mushayat, Tabuk and King Khalid Military City, port facilities at Ras al-Mish'ab, Jidda and Jubayl, three military schools, headquarters complexes for the air force, the ministry of defense and aviation and the navy, support facilities for F-15 and F-16 fighter planes, and headquarters and training facilities for the Saudi National Guard. (Facilities at Jubayl have been especially critical to accommodate the enormous deployment of the past several months. In August 1990, the Corps returned to construct additional buildings and facilities for the U.S. troops based there, since the original scenarios had not anticipated such a large deployment of ground forces.)

American strategists made the best of the Saudi reluctance to acknowledge publicly its military relationship with the U.S. or to provide advance guarantees of access. Some acknowledged that too close an identity with the U.S. could undermine rather than enhance regime security. "I don't believe that American bases as such in that area are the right way to go," said Carter's Secretary of Defense Harold Brown in late 1979. "A number of countries in the area can maintain bases which, in an emergency in which they asked our help, we could then come in and use." Brown's successor, Caspar Weinberger, made clear in his classified 1984–1988 Defense Guidance report that U.S., not Saudi forces, would be the first-line forces in any crisis. "Whatever the circumstances," he wrote, "we should be prepared to introduce American forces directly into the region should it appear that the security of access to Persian Gulf oil is threatened."

Nevertheless, efforts to improve terms of U.S. access continued. In early 1984, at the height of a major Iranian offensive against Iraq, Assistant Secretary of State Richard Murphy and National Security Council staff member John Poindexter travelled to the Gulf to tell the ruling families that any military intervention on their behalf would require a public invitation and full U.S. access. In 1985, a classified State Department study prepared for congressional leaders by Murphy was leaked to *The New York Times* (September 5). "Although the Saudis have steadfastly resisted formal access agreements," it read, "they have stated that access will be forthcoming for United States forces as necessary to counter Soviet aggression or in regional crises they cannot manage on their own."

In 1983 the Pentagon elevated Persian Gulf contingency planning by transforming the Rapid Deployment Force into a separate military command—Central Command, or CENTCOM. Seventeen ships loaded with supplies for an intervention force—food, ammunition, fuel and drinking water—were stationed off Diego Garcia in the Indian Ocean. Central Command now had the authority to requisition 300,000–350,000 troops, and budget allocations for "power projection" shot up.

U.S. naval intervention became a reality in July 1987, when the Reagan administration responded to a Kuwaiti request to place its oil tankers under U.S. protection, and sent an armada that grew to nearly fifty ships in and around the Persian Gulf. Over the course of a year, the U.S. Navy had several confrontations with Iranian forces, providing the Pentagon with valuable battle experience with many sophisticated but untested new weapons, including the missile system that shot down an Iranian civilian airliner, killing 291 people. This naval deployment was the final step in the steadily growing U.S. efforts to support Iraq in the war against Iran, and helped bring about a cease-fire, on Iraqi terms, in August 1988.

President Bush inherited both the apparatus and the mission for U.S. military intervention in the Gulf from his predecessors, but the circumstances of this present intervention and its scale were hardly anticipated. U.S. cooperation with Iraq from the mid-1980s through early 1990 appeared secure: Saddam Hussein's regime in Baghdad seemed to be a reliable junior partner in preserving the status quo in the region. Iraq's invasion of Kuwait required a reversal of policy gears.

U.S. contingency scenarios, moreover, had initially been based on the premise that military intervention would most likely be required to counter a Soviet offensive into Iran, or to launch offensive strikes against the Soviet Union in the context of a general war between the two superpowers. The sophistication of the airbases in Saudi Arabia is a function of these tasks. Subsequent developments led to planning for a need to stop Iranian advances in the event that Iraq might have been defeated in the Iran-Iraq conflict. There is no evidence that the U.S. anticipated a need to plan against Iraqi aggression.

Nor does it seem that U.S. military planners anticipated such a huge buildup of ground forces. Such a scenario is in many ways a product of the radical changes in the Soviet Union and Eastern Europe: Deployment of upwards of half a million troops to Saudi Arabia is only possible because the rationale (the "Soviet threat") for a large U.S. troop presence in Europe has evaporated.

There is no evidence that Iraq planned to invade Saudi Arabia. The Bush administration intervened militarily in order to offset Iraq's ability to dominate the Gulf politically following a successful and unchallenged conquest of Kuwait.

Now that the troops are there, the Bush administration and the Pentagon confront a new set of questions. This enormous deployment will probably help to undermine the legitimacy of the monarchies it aims to protect, which will only increase pressure for further intervention. Secretary of State Baker and Defense Secretary Cheney have spoken of the need for U.S. troops to stay "as long as it takes." U.S. military officers are advocating that the Pentagon keep at least 10,000 troops in Saudi Arabia "indefinitely."

In a real sense, this costly and dangerous intervention can be traced back to the CIA's successful covert intervention in Iran in 1953 that overthrew the elected regime of Muhammad Mossadegh and brought the shah back to power. One intervention led to another, as Iran was used against Iraq in the 1970s and Iraq against Iran in the 1980s. Each intervention required a more substantial investment and greater risk than the one before it. The Bush administration will find this political dilemma far more intractable than the logistical ones that have obsessed military planners for years. Getting the troops there is one thing. Getting them out again may prove to be the most difficult task of all.

AMERICAN HUBRIS

Theodore Draper

T HE DEADLY incident on May 17, 1987, in the Persian Gulf in which thirty-seven American sailors were killed and the Navy frigate *Stark* was disabled by an Iraqi missile has again raised the question: What is happening to American foreign policy? Is it merely that we have suffered a series of unlucky mishaps—in Korea, Cuba, Vietnam, Lebanon, and now the Persian Gulf? Or is something seriously at fault with the doctrine that has governed our actions ever since the end of the Second World War?

A series of costly misadventures over several decades cannot be considered a string of aberrations. Something deeper and more troublesome must be at work to account for them. They cannot be blamed on one party or the other; they have afflicted Democratic as well as Republican administrations. Former U.N. Ambassador Jeane Kirkpatrick is not wrong to call herself a Truman Republican; the so-called Reagan Doctrine is a variant of the Truman Doctrine—if there is any real difference between them.

This doctrine has been the source of American hubris for forty years and shows no sign of being retired. It is time to reexamine it and to assess what its consequences have been. How did the Truman Doctrine come about in the first place? Where has it led us?

• • •

Theodore Draper is a fellow of the American Academy of Arts and Sciences. He is the author of numerous books, including the forthcoming *A Very Thin Line: The Iran-Contra Affairs*. This abridged essay is excerpted from *A Present of Things Past: Selected Essays*. It was originally published in *The New York Review of Books*, July 16, 1987.

THE TRUMAN Doctrine was the original codification of the Pax Americana illusion. The policy was enunciated in reaction to a specific, local situation and took shape in response to a vision of universal ascendancy.

Greece had traditionally been a British client state. As a result of the black winter of 1946, the British in February 1947 decided that they could no longer afford to subsidize Greece. To make matters worse, Communist-led guerrillas were threatening to come down from the north. The imminent British withdrawal from the country set the stage for the Truman Doctrine.

In March and April 1947, Under Secretary of State Dean Acheson testified before the Senate Committee on Foreign Relations on the need for the United States to replace Great Britain in Greece. Unfortunately, this testimony was not made public for twenty-six years and was then virtually ignored. The inner history of the Truman Doctrine cannot be understood without it.

Acheson made clear that by 1947 the Truman administration had effectively given up all hope of "liberating" Eastern Europe. "It is true that there are parts of the world to which we have no access," he said. "It would be silly to believe that we can do anything effective in Romania, Bulgaria, or Poland. You cannot do that. That is within the Russian area of physical force. We are excluded from that."[1] None of the senators present, headed by the Republican chairman, Arthur H. Vandenberg, demurred at this stark presentation of the facts of life in Eastern Europe.

Acheson also explained that Americans were going to take the place of the British in Greece but on a far larger scale. To the Americans at the time, it made no sense to put money, matériel, and manpower into a country that they knew was run by a chaotic and corrupt government and administration. It made sense to see that the money was well spent— which meant to them that Americans had to oversee the spending. So Acheson told the senators that it would be necessary to put Americans "into the essential key [Greek] ministries which are necessary to control the basic factors."

We need not go into the rights and wrongs of this policy; it seemed necessary at the time. Whatever the rationale, several things are striking about it.

There was no precedent outside the Western Hemisphere for putting

---

[1]"Legislative Origins of the Truman Doctrine," *Hearings Held in Executive Session Before the Committee on Foreign Relations, U.S. Senate, 80th Congress, 1st Session* (Historical Series), made public January 12, 1973, p. 22.

Americans directly or indirectly in charge of a foreign administration. If the British had been able to maintain their position in Greece, the occasion for making such a leap in American policy would not have arisen and would not have forced a sudden, improvised escalation of American responsibilities. It was an example of how little time the Americans had to prepare for and think through their new responsibilities as a world power.

They succeeded, as Acheson testified and events proved, in arriving at a workable postwar foreign policy only after separating the problems of Eastern and Western Europe. If the Truman administration had actively tried to re-create both halves of Europe, the attempt would almost surely have been doomed to failure—or war. The Marshall Plan the following year settled for less and accomplished what is still the greatest postwar success of American policy.

But something else haunted and continues to haunt American policy. The practical policy was limited to a region where it could work successfully—Western Europe. Yet the terms used by President Truman to justify that policy were universal. The limitations of the policy could not or in any case would not be admitted publicly. The mixture of a universal doctrine with limited means of action created a dangerous mixture of illusion and reality which we have yet to rid ourselves of. It has long been puzzling why the Truman Doctrine was cast in universal terms.

The immediate problem for Truman was to get Congress to appropriate $250 million for Greece and $150 million for Turkey, which was also considered to be endangered. He might have been content to explain why the two countries needed the money desperately and why they could get it only from the United States. The State Department drafted a message from him to Congress in this vein, which he later contemptuously described as sounding like "an investment prospectus." Truman returned it with instructions that he wanted more emphasis on "a declaration of general policy."[2] In effect, he wanted to universalize a local, particular condition.

The metamorphosis of Greece into the universe was accomplished by the "domino," or, as it might have been called, the "rotten-apple," principle. Its author was Acheson. The scene of the transformation was the closed meeting of the Senate committee at which the request for aid was presented. According to his own account, Acheson was dissatisfied with the presentation made by Secretary of State Marshall. He injected himself into the discussion to say the following:

[2]Harry S. Truman, *Memoirs*, Vol. 2: *Years of Trial and Hope* (Doubleday, 1956), p. 105.

In the past eighteen months, Soviet pressure on the Straits, on Iran, and on northern Greece had brought the Balkans to the point where a highly possible Soviet breakthrough might open three continents to Soviet penetration. Like apples in a barrel infected by one rotten one, the corruption of Greece would infect Iran and all to the east. It would also carry infection to Africa through Asia Minor and Egypt, and to Europe through Italy and France, already threatened by the strongest domestic communist parties in Western Europe.[3]

Acheson says that this argument persuaded the senators to go along. He swayed them by extending the crisis from Greece—which Stalin had previously awarded to the British sphere of influence in return for British acquiescence in Soviet domination of most of Eastern Europe—to three continents, to all of the Middle East, and much of the West. Iran was then as now one of the endangered species. President Eisenhower later substituted dominoes for rotten apples, but the reasoning was the same. The universalization of American policy needed the universalization of the communist threat.

By the time Acheson's reasoning was echoed by Senator Vandenberg, the process had taken on the character of a fatality. To a correspondent Vandenberg soon wrote: "Greece must be helped or Greece sinks permanently into the communist order. Turkey inevitably follows. Then comes the chain reaction which might sweep from the Dardanelles to the China sea."[4]

That something genuinely new had entered American policy was recognized at that time by the sponsors of this legislation. The new element was not so much aid to another country as the enunciation of a general doctrine that could be applied automatically everywhere.[5] It was on this ground that the language of the president's message to Congress was criticized by George F. Kennan, its most thoughtful critic from within the State Department. Kennan accepted the necessity "to stiffen the backs of the non-communist elements in Greece," though he saw no reason to treat Turkey the same way. As he later explained, he objected to the passage in the speech that gave it the character of an indeterminate doctrine—that "it must be the policy of the United States to support free

[3]Dean Acheson, *Present at the Creation: My Years in the State Department* (Norton, 1969), p. 219.
[4]*The Private Papers of Senator Vandenberg* (Houghton Mifflin, 1952), p. 342.
[5]In his memoirs, President Truman interpreted his new doctrine to mean that American foreign policy had "now declared that wherever aggression, direct or indirect, threatened the peace, the security of the United States was involved" (*Memoirs*, Vol. 2, p. 106).

peoples who are resisting subjugation by armed minorities or by outside pressures."

Kennan's criticism was just as basic as the doctrine itself:

> This passage, and others as well, placed our aid to Greece in the framework of a universal policy rather than in that of a specific decision addressed to a specific set of circumstances . . . It seemed to me highly uncertain that we would invariably find it in our interest or within our means to extend assistance to countries that found themselves in this extremity. The mere fact of their being in such a plight was only one of the criteria that had to be taken into account in determining our action.[6]

A doctrine of this sort could easily become a substitute for thought. It gave the United States a license to intervene anywhere and everywhere at any time in any way, if only the right formula was used to justify the move.

A SURE SIGN that the doctrine is being applied mechanically, with a minimum of discrimination, is the language used to put it into effect. It is always necessary to use the words "vital interest," "national security," "free world," "peace is at stake," and, above all, some version of the "Soviet threat." If these phrases were not employed, it might be necessary to do some thinking and explain the policy in less simplistic and apocalyptic terms. In that case, it is hard to know whose intelligence would be strained the most—our policymakers' or the general public's.

When President Reagan undertook to explain his policy of sending U.S. ships into the Persian Gulf, he repeated or played variations on all of these themes. Five days after the *Stark* was struck on May 17, he said: "Peace is at stake here; and so too is our own nation's security, and our freedom." Peace in the Gulf, surely; our own security, dubiously; and our freedom, absurdly. Twelve days later, he played at full blast the whole doctrinal organ music—"national security," "economic disaster," "freedom of navigation," "commitment" to the "peace and welfare" of "our friends and allies," preservation of "peace."

A perfectly mindless expression of the doctrine was contributed by Secretary of Defense Weinberger on June 9. "The fundamental issue is leadership," he told the House Armed Services Committee, "the leadership of the free world to resist the forces of anarchy and tyranny." One

[6]George F. Kennan, *Memoirs: 1925–1950* (Little, Brown, 1967), p. 320.

would imagine from this hyperbolic verbiage that we were about to get into a war of epic proportions, worth any cost or sacrifice. These incantations have become so routine that the words will not be meaningful if they are really needed.

One wonders whether the policy could have been put over on the American people if the president had told them how Iraq and Kuwait had manipulated the United States with the aim of getting us into the middle of the Iran-Iraq war.

Kuwait is little more than a gigantic oil well. It has been independent only since 1961, before which time it was a British protectorate. It has the population of Houston and an area two-thirds that of Vermont.[7] Thanks to its oil, which provides over ninety-four percent of its revenue, its per capita income is close to a phenomenal $11,500 a year, with no need for anyone to pay taxes. This cornucopia of oil is ruled by the hereditary al-Sabah dynasty, with close ties to a similar ruling caste in Saudi Arabia.

Kuwait and Iraq, its northern neighbor, were not always so friendly. As soon as the British protectorate in Kuwait came to an end in 1961, Iraq's ruler at the time, General Abdul Karim Qassim, announced that Kuwait was really Iraqi territory; British troops had to come back hastily to prevent him from taking possession. Kuwait was not recognized by Iraq until after General Qassim was overthrown in 1963, but frontier fighting between the two went on for years. Iraq, in fact, temporarily seized adjoining Kuwaiti territory in 1973 and has long used threats of territorial aggression to extort vast sums from the overflowing Kuwaiti exchequer. This is not a region of fastidious diplomatic relationships.

Kuwait's relations with the United States have also been checkered. For years its press was one of the most anti-American in the region, largely because of Kuwait's fiercely anti-Israel policy. Kuwait cut off oil shipments to the United States after the Six-Day War in 1967, an action suggesting that we can hardly depend on Kuwait in all circumstances. In 1983, Kuwait refused to accept as ambassador a veteran U.S. diplomat, Brandon H. Grove, Jr., because he had served as U.S. consul general in East Jerusalem. The *Washington Post* correspondent in Kuwait, David B. Ottaway, observed as late as June 24, 1984, that Kuwait was "accustomed to blaming the United States for all the ills afflicting the Arab world, and the gulf in particular." Kuwait modulated its anti-American line in that year because Iran had begun attacking Kuwaiti tankers and had taken the place of the United States as the main enemy.

---

[7]Area: 6,880 square miles; population: 1,710,000 (1985).

In 1980, President Carter's State of the Union message pledged that the United States would go to war, if necessary, to prevent "any outside force" from gaining control of the Gulf region. At that time, ironically, the Kuwaiti minister of foreign affairs objected to the U.S. commitment on the ground that "the people of this region are perfectly capable of preserving their own security and stability."[8]

The predicament of Kuwait in 1987 arose from its increasingly close ties with its former bugaboo, Iraq, dating from the reckless attack on Iran by the present Iraqi dictator, Saddam Hussein, in 1980. Kuwait mortgaged its fate to Iraq by supporting it to the tune of billions of dollars and by acting as its receiving and transshipment point for war matériel, much of it from the Soviet Union. The pretense that Kuwait was neutral was sheer humbug; Kuwait was Iraq's foremost ally.[9]

The Iran-Iraq war has been one of the most savage in modern times. Iraq's Saddam Hussein has resorted to chemical weapons, Iran's Khomeini to the mass sacrifice of children on the battlefield. In 1984, since the fighting was stalemated on the ground, a war against tankers, in which Iran was most vulnerable, broke out. The tanker war was started by Iraq, just as it had started the entire war. Iraq uses a pipeline through Turkey and Saudi Arabia; Iran must transport its oil by sea in tankers from many foreign countries and companies. More than three hundred tankers and freighters had been hit by both sides, with the loss of about two hundred lives, but only one tanker had been sunk. In 1985, three-quarters of the attacks were Iraqi; in 1986, sixty percent. More recently, Iran has concentrated its fire on Kuwaiti tankers, though no Kuwaiti ship has been hit since October 22, 1986. There were no Kuwaiti losses for eight months before the Reagan administration decided to get agitated about the threat to Kuwaiti shipping.

Yet the October incident was soon followed by a change in Kuwaiti policy. A decision was made to entangle the great powers instead of

[8] *Political Handbook of the World: 1986,* edited by Arthur S. Banks (CSA Publications, 1986), p. 314.
[9] Since the United States gave a pledge of neutrality in the Iran-Iraq war, it seems to be essential to the U.S. case that Kuwait should also be considered to be "neutral." When Assistant Secretary of Defense for Public Affairs Robert B. Sims was asked whether the United States would be living up to its neutrality pledge if it escorted Kuwaiti tankers, he answered, "Absolutely," and explained: "The fact is, Kuwait is not a belligerent in the war. The war is between Iran and Iraq" *(The Washington Post,* June 5, 1987). National Security Adviser Frank C. Carlucci has also pretended that Kuwait is "a neutral state" *(The Washington Post,* June 16, 1987). The fact also is that Kuwait is an active ally of a belligerent and doing everything in its power for one side against the other. The dictionary says that neutral means "not engaged on either side." Kuwait is not technically a belligerent, but neither is it neutral.

keeping them out. But Kuwait did not appeal first to the United States. That distinction was reserved for the Soviet Union.

Despite the evident political disparities between Kuwait and the Soviet Union, their relations had been remarkably close for some years. In 1979, Kuwait made known that it was receiving Soviet arms, including ground-to-air missiles. Deputy Prime Minister Sabah al-Ahmad al-Jabir al-Sabah of the ruling family visited the Soviet Union in April 1981 and the Eastern-bloc countries of Bulgaria, Hungary, and Romania the following September. The East German head of state, Erich Honecker, came to Kuwait in October 1982. Then, in August 1984, Kuwait signed a far-reaching agreement for the purchase of more arms from the Soviet Union. This deal is of particular interest because it was virtually a dress rehearsal for the tanker operation.

First, Kuwait wanted "Stinger" anti-aircraft missile weapons and F-16 jet fighters from the United States, but these requests were turned down. Instead, Washington offered a different $82 million air-defense package. Then Kuwait went to the Soviet Union and arranged for the purchase of arms reported to be worth $327 million. With the arms came Soviet technicians and advisers. After this, the Reagan administration relented and sold more military equipment to Kuwait, the total officially reported to be worth $1.5 billion by 1985.

Kuwait, in short, had some practice playing the United States off against the Soviet Union. Its foreign policy had long been one of nonalignment, which it still professes. Its problem has been that it is too rich to be left alone and too weak to defend itself. The West may adopt Kuwait, but Kuwait does not choose the West.

Iraq had also managed to achieve exceptionally close relations with the Soviet Union. Increased Soviet support for Iraq seems to have come in 1983 when Iran cracked down on the Tudeh (Communist) Party of Iran. The Soviet Union has been Iraq's main arms supplier, at least since 1983,[10] with Kuwait the intermediary between the two countries. Saddam Hussein succeeded in getting the backing of a most peculiar combination, including the Soviet Union, France, Saudi Arabia, and the United States. Communist China had become one of Iran's major arms merchants.

H O W   T I N Y Kuwait managed to enlist the support of both the United States and the Soviet Union is one of the most extraordinary feats of modern diplomacy.

---

[10]*Military Review* (an official Defense Department publication), December 1983, p. 10.

According to the best available information, the government-owned Kuwait Oil Tanker Company informed the U.S. Coast Guard on December 10, 1986, that it wished to put the U.S. flag on its ships to gain them U.S. protection. During that same month, Kuwaiti officials went to Moscow and worked out an agreement with the Soviet Union. It provided for Kuwait to charter three Soviet tankers on a renewable one-year lease, with the additional stipulation that two more might be added on "short notice." It also permitted Kuwait to lease to the Soviet Union an unspecified number of additional tankers "to be rechartered to the Kuwait side thereafter whenever the government of Kuwait so requests."

These provisions were worked out to enable Kuwait to increase its Soviet-protected tankers if the United States did not come across. When the United States did not quickly grab at the bait, Kuwait's oil minister, Ali al-Khalifa al-Athbi al-Sabah, formally requested that the United States agree to the "reflagging" of some Kuwaiti ships on January 13, 1987. Still, no American reply was forthcoming until a report was received in Washington on March 2 that a deal had been struck between Kuwait and the Soviet Union for the protection of Kuwaiti tankers. Five days later, the United States decided to outbid the Soviets by offering to put the U.S. flag on eleven Kuwaiti tankers. Kuwait now had both powers on its string; the agreement with the Soviet Union was signed on April 1. All this attracted very little attention until the *Stark* was hit on May 17.[11] Kuwait is so ecumenical politically that it subsequently invited Communist China to join in protecting Kuwait's capitalistic oil trade. In effect, Kuwait did not wish to be beholden to any one of the great powers and preferred to have them compete for the privilege of serving its interests.

It thus appears that Kuwait hooked our guardians in Washington by confronting the United States with a Soviet-Kuwaiti deal. However, the Senate Foreign Relations Committee was also told on May 9 by Assistant Secretary of State for Near Eastern and South Asian Affairs Richard W. Murphy that the Kuwaiti decision to seek Soviet protection had come in November 1986, a month before the Kuwaiti oil company had first turned to the United States and the Soviet Union. Murphy interpreted this Kuwaiti overture to the Soviets as having been inspired by the news that same month that the Reagan administration had secretly sold mis-

[11]This chronology is based on the articles by Don Oberdorfer and Jonathan C. Randal in *The Washington Post*, May 31 and June 5, 1987.

siles to Iran. If so, Kuwait took the initiative to bring in the Soviets in order to punish the United States for arming Iran.[12]

Let us recall: The "tanker war" had been going on, more and more ferociously, for over three years. In all these years, only seven Kuwaiti-owned tankers had been hit by Iran.[13] Well over ninety-five percent of the Gulf's oil had been reaching customers around the world. No U.S. ship had been touched before the attack on the *Stark*. Secretary of State Shultz affirmed that Iran had "respected" the "American presence." All this time no one in Washington had thought that the shipment of oil from Kuwait was so endangered that it was necessary to do anything to protect our "vital interests" or "national security," or to save us from the "Soviet threat."

The rest is hallucinatory. On May 17 the U.S. frigate *Stark* was hit by an Iraqi missile in the Persian Gulf. But this shot was heard in Washington as if it had come from an Iranian missile. Not so long ago the Reagan administration had sold missiles to Iran for use against Iraq. Now it was Iraq's turn to be protected against Iran. By some political prestidigitation, an Iraqi missile provided the occasion for a hasty decision to plunge the United States into the midst of the conflict on the side of Iraq—in fact if not in name.

That the decision was precipitous there can be no doubt. First it was decided to put the American flag on eleven tankers of Iraq's ally, Kuwait —originally a Kuwaiti idea, not an American one. This step led to the next one—protection of the tankers by a much stronger U.S. military "presence" in the region. Only after these decisions were made was any thought given to what the risks were, what methods should be employed, and whether the whole enterprise was practicable at all.

WITHOUT ANY practical policy in sight, we were fed dubious statistical propaganda about the indispensability of Gulf oil. Senator Daniel Patrick Moynihan wrote luridly that "the West risks losing control of two-thirds of the world's oil reserves. The great geo-political prize of the twentieth century is now in their [the Soviets'] grasp."[14] Another Persian Gulf warrior, former National Security Adviser Zbigniew Brzezinski, obviously used a similar source: "Access to Persian Gulf oil reserves,

[12]The source of this information is Senator Daniel Patrick Moynihan, *The New York Times,* June 7, 1987.
[13]*The Washington Post,* June 5, 1987.
[14]*The New York Times,* June 7, 1987.

which contain two-thirds of the free world's proven reserves, is the principal stake in southwest Asia."[15]

The emphasis on "reserves" implied that we were supposed to be worrying about the distant future, as if we could do anything about it by putting the American flag on eleven Kuwaiti tankers. If there was an immediate risk, we were meeting it with ridiculously picayune means. Our leaders were, in effect, playing the old game of dominoes to scare us half to death in order to put across a policy that did not begin to face the horrendous crisis that allegedly awaits us.

Gulf oil is useful but hardly a matter of life or death now. It is least vital to the United States, which gets only four percent of its oil through the Strait of Hormuz at the entrance to the Persian Gulf. But even if the Strait of Hormuz were closed, the cutback in oil shipments could be readily compensated for by another of our friends in the area—none other than Saudi Arabia. A recent study of the Gulf states pointed out:

> A cut-off of Gulf oil that did not include Saudi production would be ineffective, because, due to the enormous Saudi production capacity, that country alone could match most current Gulf petroleum exports. More important, Saudi Arabia is the one Arab Gulf producer that has alternative routes (i.e., non-Gulf routes) for the export of petroleum. (Saudi Arabia has opened one pipeline on the Red Sea, and will soon have a second ready for operation.) Indeed, one of the Saudi pipelines also carries Iraqi crude.[16]

Another authority on the world supply of oil, Professor S. Fred Singer, pointed out:

> With about one-eighth of Free World oil in gulf tanker traffic, as much as one-half of that traffic would have to be interrupted on a steady basis to make a strong impact on the price. That translates to about twenty supertanker sinkings a week! Any lesser interruption can be made up by existing pipelines and from the excess production capacity of other suppliers—and they'll be glad to do it.

[15] *The Washington Post*, June 7, 1987.
[16] Mazher A. Hameed, *Arabia Imperilled: The Security Imperatives of the Arab Gulf States* (Middle East Assessments Group, 1986), p. xv.

Professor Singer went on:

> The bottom line on the benefits of avoiding modest oil-supply disloca-
> tions: hardly any for the U.S. or its allies. The question then becomes:
> Is it worth risking American lives in order to lower insurance premi-
> ums for Kuwait and other gulf producers?[17]

If there is an acute long-term problem of oil reserves, it will have to be
met in a long-term way. Much can change in the use of oil before the
problem becomes acute. In any case, that is no present problem, even
with the Iran-Iraq war; the long-term problem was not going to be met
by reflagging eleven Kuwaiti tankers or by getting enmeshed in the war.
The alarm about oil reserves in the distant future was a cover for taking
some immediate action that had little or no bearing on the long-term
problem.

The technique of the scaremongers is to suggest that something awful
is about to happen and to use veiled language that stops short of saying
what they really mean—that the Persian Gulf must be made an American
monopoly by any means including that of force. Senator Moynihan put it
this way:

> All the more reason, then, that Congress should be seen to support the
> policy of every American President back to Harry S. Truman. We have
> no choice. The Persian Gulf is vital to American interests. It is not vital
> to Soviet interests. We cannot accept their intrusion.[18]

What must we do if "we cannot accept their intrusion"? Clearly, we must
expel them. And how, if we are not going to use force? Leaving aside the
determination of what a "vital interest" is in these circumstances, countries have a right to use an international waterway even if they have no
"vital interest" there. Incidentally, it is interesting to note how the ghost
of Harry S. Truman hovers over this entire affair.

Brzezinski also used the same semantic cover-up:

> Consequently, the United States has no choice but to stand firm
> against any challenges in the defense of Western interests in the Per-
> sian Gulf . . .
>
> The major beneficiary of a U.S. retreat would be the Soviet
> Union . . .

[17] *The Wall Street Journal,* June 9, 1987.
[18] *The New York Times,* June 7, 1987.

The United States must do whatever is necessary to assert Western interests in the Persian Gulf—alone, if necessary. If Iran strikes American forces engaged in protecting third-party shipping in the Gulf, the United States should retaliate against Iranian military facilities and do it in a way that will be militarily decisive.[19]

These are weasel words for the forcible control by the United States of the Persian Gulf. The chosen enemies are both the Soviet Union and Iran. Just what "standing firm" against the Soviet Union means is left to the imagination of the reader. Since the Soviet Union has shown no signs of threatening the United States militarily in the Gulf, Brzezinski must mean that the very presence of three Soviet naval vessels in the Gulf is threatening. How he thinks it is possible to get rid of them without the use of force defies understanding. He is clearer on Iran, but only if it strikes American forces protecting third-party shipping. If non-American shipping should be struck, he fails to enlighten us on what to do about it. By the very nature of the Iranian regime and its popular support, a "militarily decisive" retaliation is not easy to envisage. It would certainly entail more than taking out missile batteries.

But oil was covering up the real issue. Kuwait, acting for Iraq and Saudi Arabia, was really interested in something else. All three had in mind luring the Soviet Union and the United States into intervening in the Iran-Iraq war in order to get the great powers to stop it. Iraq and its allies needed Soviet-American collaboration for their intrigue to have any chance of succeeding. Ironically, the anti-Soviet twist that the Reagan administration and its fellow travelers gave the Kuwait-Iraq-Saudi Arabia scenario was not according to their script.

IF THE free passage of tankers had been the real issue, it would have had to be faced long ago. It was not faced when the "tanker war" was raging, because the Iran-Iraq war was still considered to be a local quagmire that could only get worse if the great powers got into it with their own military forces. The important thing was to isolate it, until both sides dropped out from exhaustion, not to transform it into a contest between world powers. Such exhaustion was what actually brought Khomeini around by 1988, not the maneuvers of the superpowers.

But a number of other things had injected themselves. One was the U.S. withdrawal from Lebanon, which alarmed the Arab states because it indicated to them that the staying power of the United States in the

---

[19] *The Washington Post,* June 7, 1987.

region was limited.[20] The revelations of the Reagan administration's secret sale of missiles to Iran were even more demoralizing, because the Arab regimes under Sunni leadership were terrified by the threatened conflagration from Iran's militant Shiite fanaticism. There was also the inability of the U.N.'s Security Council to pass a resolution calling for a cease-fire and arms embargo owing to the resistance of Iran's ally, Communist China. Iraq, now chastened by its losses and the recognition that it could not possibly win the war, was entirely willing to accept such a resolution, leaving Iran as the real object of the arms embargo.

In these circumstances, the obvious way out for Iraq and its paymasters, Kuwait and Saudi Arabia, was through the intervention of the great powers. The hopeless war, together with the oil glut, had caused a dangerous drain on their resources. From trying to keep the great powers out, Iraq-Kuwait-Saudi Arabia policy had shifted to dragging them in. The Kuwaitis made no secret of their strategy. The *New York Times* correspondent in Kuwait, John Kifner, was told by Under Secretary Suleiman Majid al-Shaheen of the Kuwaiti Foreign Ministry:

> We have approached all our friends. We don't want any country to have an upper hand with Kuwait. The Soviet Union is ready to cooperate, and it is the right of any country to increase its economic activities.

Kifner added: "Mr. Shaheen, a key strategist in the Foreign Ministry, which is headed by Sheikh Sabah al-Ahmed al-Sabah, a member of the ruling family, confirmed that a main goal of the Kuwaiti strategy was to seek an end to the war between Iran and Iraq by involving the superpowers."[21]

The same Kuwaiti strategy was reported by *The Washington Post*'s Jonathan C. Randal on June 14, 1987. The tanker war, he noted, was "a manageable side-show" of far less significance than "Kuwait's gamble that its ingenuity in seeking superpower protection for perhaps a third of its oil exports will force Moscow and Washington to impose an end to the nearly seven-year-old war."

Most opportunely, an Iraqi attack on a U.S. naval vessel gave the Reagan administration the occasion for doing what Iraq and Kuwait had long wanted it to do. The president's major statement of May 29, 1987, did not even mention Iraq, as if it were the innocent party in the war in

---

[20]If a Fatuity Prize were given, it would certainly have been won in 1987 by Norman Podhoretz, who attributed our fiasco in Lebanon to "squeamishness" (*New York Post*, May 26, 1987).

[21]*The New York Times*, June 8, 1987.

the Persian Gulf. Instead, the only two countries mentioned with hostility were Iran and the Soviet Union, on the assumption that they had to be prevented from imposing "their will upon the friendly Arab states of the Persian Gulf" and Iran had to be deterred from blocking "the free passage of neutral shipping."[22]

Here was Iraq, which had not only been at least as guilty as Iran in blocking the free passage of shipping in the Gulf, but had declared a "free-fire" or "exclusion" zone on the Iranian side of the Persian Gulf in which it felt free to attack any vessel, even a U.S. warship. The Iraqi pilot who had attacked the frigate *Stark* was proudly said to be a veteran who had to his credit fifteen successful missile attacks on Iranian tankers. Kuwait, the most active ally of Iraq, was now, however, reclassified by the United States as "neutral." In effect, President Reagan implicitly put the United States on the side of Iraq and its Kuwait–Saudi Arabia allies.

One of the typically doctrinal aspects of this whole affair was the buildup of the Soviet threat. There surely have been Soviet threats, but this one was not like any other. When Secretary Shultz said, "We don't have any desire to see the Soviets assume a role in the Persian Gulf," he was apparently oblivious to or willing to ignore the fact that the Soviets had assumed a role at the behest of our present associates. After all, our latest ward, Kuwait, had brought in the Soviets by getting them to lease it tankers. Iraq had brought in the Soviets by making them one of its major arms suppliers. The entire game played by Iraq and Kuwait had depended on getting Soviet aid in order to inveigle the United States to do the same things for them—or more.

THE ENTIRE U.S. policy in the Persian Gulf was bedeviled by an infernal confusion of motives.

One was that we wished to protect Kuwaiti tankers with the U.S. flag and warships. Another was that we wished to ensure "free navigation" in the Gulf for all ships of all nations because it is an international waterway. A third was that we wished to prevent Soviet domination of the Gulf

---

[22]Yet it should be noted that President Reagan later appeared to cut the ground from under his own anti-Soviet assumptions. On June 11, 1987, he granted that the Soviets "have a stake, too, in peaceful shipping and the openness of the international waters," and were as a result eligible to be asked to take part in a peaceful settlement of the Gulf war. On June 15, 1987, he reverted to his previous anti-Soviet line with the words: "If we don't do the job, the Soviets will," to the jeopardy of "our own national security and that of our allies." This gyration is typical of a policy that has not been thought through and veers crazily from one side to the other.

and, in an even more extreme version of this aim, to exclude the Soviets from the Gulf altogether.

The first aim, to protect Kuwaiti tankers, would be accomplished if we succeeded in the second—to ensure the free passage of all shipping of all nations. Ironically, we would also protect the tankers of Iran, which needed protection the most. These aims were specific and limited, and they depended above all on the cooperation of all interested nations, including the Soviets, for which reason we had been seeking agreement with them at the United Nations. These aims did not involve a struggle for power in the Persian Gulf between the United States and the Soviet Union. The third aim, however, was very different in kind. It implied that only the United States had the right to send warships into the Persian Gulf or play a "role" in it.

The third aim was a sure recipe for disaster. The Soviet Union could not be expelled from the Gulf without the use of force, which had been ruled out by the president and our highest officials. No other nation could support us in an effort to make an international waterway into an American or even Western military lake. Yet by turning an incident brought about by an Iraqi missile into an anti-Soviet crusade, we were heading into the wrong confrontation at the wrong place at the wrong time for the wrong reason.

It will not help to remind us that we are a "world power," as Professor Brzezinski did. To persuade us that the United States should "assert Western interests in the Persian Gulf—alone, if necessary," he instructed us: "We must recognize that the United States holds the status of a world power, and our allies are simply regional powers."[23] This distinction is not original with Brzezinski; it should have been copyrighted by his predecessor, Henry Kissinger.[24]

The term "world power" is a snare and a delusion if it is taken to mean that the United States has the power to decide matters all over the world. We are obviously stronger in some places than in others, and in some places we are not strong at all. North Vietnam was a tenth-rate "regional power," but it was in the right place with the right strength at the right time. Our European allies are much closer to the Persian Gulf; they have a much greater stake in Middle East oil. They refused to get embroiled with us not because they are "regional powers" and do not have suffi-

---

[23] *The Washington Post,* June 7, 1987.

[24] "The United States has global interests and responsibilities. Our European allies have regional interests" (*Department of State Bulletin,* May 14, 1973, p. 594). This statement in his "Year of Europe" speech created an angry furor in Europe at the time.

cient military strength to act but because it makes no sense to them to intervene in the Iran-Iraq war or seek a showdown with the Soviet Union in the Persian Gulf. What separated us from them was policy, not power.

The words "Truman Doctrine" and "world power" seem to have a hypnotic effect. They resemble the slogan about "standing tall," which made voters for Reagan feel better, stronger, and more patriotic, no matter that the words are almost empty of political content and no guide to what the country's real problems and capabilities are.

Until the *Stark* was hit, our policy was based on ensuring free passage of the waterway with the cooperation of the Soviet Union. We were not interested in taking sides in the Iran-Iraq war or using force to gain our ends. We did not whip up a storm of anxiety about the threat to our security, our peace, and our freedom. We understood that the war was between two regimes that had nothing in common with us and were almost equally detestable. We did not expect that it would be easy or quick to achieve our ends in these unpleasant circumstances, but there was no reason to believe that Western civilization hung in the balance in this struggle to the death between Saddam Hussein and Khomeini.

As soon as the *Stark* was hit, this policy gave way to one virtually its opposite. We began to take the side of Iraq against Iran—without, of course, admitting it. Our very security, peace, and freedom were said to be endangered. We cast about for a quick fix for a nasty little war. We suddenly made the Soviet Union the enemy—or at least the obstacle—in the Persian Gulf. Our secretary of state permitted himself to rule out any Soviet "role" in the Gulf. Supporters of the new line took to accusing the Soviets of unacceptable "intrusion" in an international waterway, as if it were necessary to expel them. Suddenly, acts of war such as preemptive strikes—defensive or otherwise—were on front pages.

There was no need to make this bewildering flip-flop. If we are a "world power," we should have enough staying power to outlast the temporary damage that these unpleasant belligerents may inflict.

IRAQ VS. KUWAIT:
CLAIMS AND COUNTERCLAIMS

Walid Khalidi

T HE BRITISH historian A. J. P. Taylor (who, alas, has recently died) said in analyzing the causes of World War II that wars are much like road accidents: They have profound causes and particular causes. In the last resort every road accident is caused by the discovery of the combustion engine and the human propensity for movement from one place to another. But city authorities, policemen, and judges are not interested in these profound causes and look instead into the particular ones: the conduct of the driver, his state of mind, the extent of his inebriation, and so on. Taylor added that profound causes, by explaining everything, explain nothing. This is not a bad analogy, together with its caveat, to bear in mind when looking into the causes of the invasion of Kuwait.

Without taking Taylor's analogy too literally, there would seem to be four causes for the invasion of Kuwait at the "profound" end of Taylor's spectrum. *First* is the failure of the Arab political order, as it has evolved since the end of World War II both in the Mashriq and Maghrib, to approximate in any of its constituent sovereign states to minimal levels of genuine power sharing or accountability in government, much less to self-sustaining parliamentary institutions operating within democratic norms and constraints. To be sure, democratic regimes have, in the last century or so, waged wars of aggression, but a case can still be made that regimes, where a monopoly of power is exercised by the chief executive

Walid Khalidi is a research fellow at Harvard University. This article originally appeared as the first section of "The Gulf Crisis: Origins and Consequences," an occasional paper published in early January 1991 by the Institute for Palestine Studies. The second section of his essay may be found on pages 161–171 of this book.

through the physical elimination of rivals and the mobilization, through terror, of mass obedience around a personality cult, are more prone to military adventurism and external aggression. In Iraq's case, it is not only that in every sense *l'État, c'est Saddam,* but that the mesmerizing predominance of his personality, *because* of his treatment of all rivals, whether individual or collective, creates what can only be described as a Castration Syndrome. Such a syndrome, of course, exists all over the world in smaller or larger measure in many government cabinets (Margaret Thatcher, it is rumored, was no fanatical practitioner of the primus-inter-pares concept), corporations, and other decision-making bodies. But the syndrome in Saddam's Iraq seems to have reached such archetypal dimensions that the survival imperative left him totally isolated from reality by paralyzing any countervailing advice from presidential aides and counsellors.

Second is the cumulative effect—corrosive, destabilizing, and disruptive—on the Arab political system of the contemporary Arab version of England's fifteenth-century War of the Roses—the undeclared intra-Baath civil war that has raged since the mid-1960s between Baghdad and Damascus. This has centered on the Himalayan egos of Hafez al-Assad and Saddam Hussein, fueling and deepening Arab disarray and constituting in the last decades the single most formidable obstacle to inter-Arab cooperation in the countries east of Suez. An index of the animus that has locked the two leaders in its mortal embrace can be glimpsed from Assad's interruption of oil supplies to Iraq at the height of Iraq's vulnerability to Iranian invasion during the Iran-Iraq war, and from Saddam's tit for Assad's tat in his prompt support of *both* Maronite militia leaders Samir Geagea and General Michel Aoun as soon as the cease-fire with Iran was in place in August 1988. It is no coincidence that Abu Abbas (of *Achille Lauro* fame) became a protégé of Saddam's—wasn't Ahmed Jibril (of Lockerbie fame) a protégé of Assad's? Nor is it a coincidence that Saddam Hussein's conditions for withdrawal from Kuwait included Syria's withdrawal from Lebanon. After all, if Assad was entitled to invade Lebanon, how could Saddam Hussein be denied the equal right of invading Kuwait?

Third is the absence since the mid-1970s of a moral center of gravity in the Arab world which could exert its healing influence at times of internecine crisis (for example, Nasser's intervention in the civil war in Jordan in 1970). For, despite early obituaries of pan-Arabism, and notwithstanding ubiquitous Arab disarray and the consolidation of *raison d'État* (state sovereignty) over *raison de la nation* (the pan-Arab concept of a single Arab nation), the Arab world still paradoxically constitutes a single area of psychological, emotional, and intellectual resonance transcending state frontiers, a phenomenon that even the most defiant *étatiste* incumbent cannot permanently ignore—witness Mubarak's eagerness to return the Arab League to Cairo. Cairo had constituted such a moral center of gravity under Nasser, which after Nasser's death shifted to Riyadh under King Faisal until the latter's assassination in 1975. But Cairo has still not recovered its earlier role. This is not so much because of Sadat's peace with Israel per se, but rather because of the pervasive Arab perception that Egypt, captain of the ship, had abandoned deck by concluding a *separate* peace with Israel, giving the latter the opportunity, the incentive, the excuse, and the power (because of the military disengagement of Egypt) to consolidate its colonization of the occupied territories, to annex Jerusalem (1980) and the Golan (1981), to lash out against Iraq (1981) and Tunisia (1985), and to devastate Lebanon. To be sure, many Arab governments, including Iraq, Syria, and the PLO, have assiduously wooed Mubarak's Egypt since then, but this was patently for tactical considerations without being conducive to the restoration to Egypt of its former moral stature. This is partly exemplified by Mubarak's pre-crisis failure to mediate successfully between Iraq and Kuwait or subsequently to rally a larger majority of Arab countries against Iraq. This loss of moral stature could be largely adduced to a perception by Arab mass opinion and the intelligentsia that Egypt, since Camp David, has evolved into the nonautonomous fulcrum of specifically American policies in the region.

Fourth is the emergence of Iraq in the wake of the Iran-Iraq war as a regional power second only to Israel. Immense military imbalance between countries, the relations of which are characterized by tensions deriving from irredentist claims, frontier disputes, and regional competition, is inherently unstable because the paramount power's preponderance of strength in relation to its neighbors acts as an incentive to aggression. This is almost an ineluctable law of political physics, examples of the applicability of which abound throughout history and have certainly not been lacking in the Middle East, being especially evident in Israel's relations with its neighbors since 1948. The immense disparity of power between Iraq and Kuwait, with the background of Iraq's inventory of grievances against Kuwait, is yet another reminder of this law.

B U T T O return (not too literally) to Taylor's analogy of the car accident, focusing this time on the *particular* causes at the other end of the spectrum: the driver's conduct and more specifically at Saddam Hussein himself. What was Saddam Hussein's "mood" during the period between the cease-fire with Iran in August 1988 and the invasion of Kuwait on 2 August 1990? Rereading his speeches at the Arab summit in Baghdad at the end of May 1990, and his diplomatic correspondence with the Arab League and Arab leaders in the intervening weeks before 2 August, it is possible to encapsulate this mood in a number of recurrent themes which, however contrived, nevertheless yield insights into Saddam's self-image and motivational drives. The main themes seem to be the following:

- At horrendous cost in Iraqi lives (Saddam's favorite phrase in Arabic is *anhar al-damm*, "rivers of blood") and material assets, he, Saddam, blocked *al-bawwabah al-sharqiyyah*, "the Eastern Gateway" to the Arab world in the face of Khomeini's hordes. It is this that saved the other Arab Gulf states, notably Kuwait, from certain ruin.
- This superhuman achievement, against overwhelming odds, has vindicated Baghdad's historic role (heir as it is to the ancient glories of the Abbasids) as *the* regional metropolis, confirming Iraq's paramount ranking in the hierarchy of the Gulf states.
- The salvation of the other Gulf states, thanks to Iraq's sacrifices, imposes on these states a moral and material indebtedness to Iraq commensurate with the scale of Iraq's sacrifices under Saddam's leadership.
- The outcome of the Iran-Iraq war (in stemming the Khomeini tide) propelled Iraq—*not* Syria, *not* Egypt—to the leadership of the Arab world in the post–Cold War era.
- This outcome imposes upon Iraq the duty of the deterrence of Israel (which other Arab states have shirked), which Iraq alone is capable and willing to undertake because of the expansion during the war of its industrial-technological infrastructure.
- Because of Iraq's assumption of new deterrent responsibilities vis-à-vis Israel, the leading Western countries, principally the United States and Britain, have *since* the cease-fire with Iran had a secret agenda to negate and counterbalance Iraq's post–cease-fire preeminence.
- To counter these Western machinations and to maintain its deterrent capacity against both Iranian revanchism and Israeli adventurism, Iraq urgently needs to reconstruct its economy and expand its industrial-technological infrastructure.
- This can only be achieved if Iraq increases its oil revenues through higher oil prices, if its war debts to the Gulf states are cancelled, and

if it is the beneficiary of an Arab "Marshall Plan" put together by these states, the very survival of which is owed to Iraq and Saddam.

Unfortunately, God has not seen fit to allow us to observe the future through the prism of hindsight. But that these were the ingredients of Saddam's post–cease-fire mood is there for us to see, not interlinearly, not through inference, but in the very words he used, particularly in the speech he delivered at a closed session of the Baghdad summit at the end of May in the presence of all his Arab peers. In retrospect, it is astounding how the explosive potential of Saddam's post–cease-fire mood was missed by all who were present at this session, despite recurrent cues thrown out by Saddam at the time and a lengthening inventory of ostensible grievances against Kuwait elaborated by his foreign minister in the following weeks.

What did this inventory consist of? We may divide these grievances (while reserving judgment on their merits or cogency) by the phases during which they were articulated, into three groups.

First, the grievances that surfaced *before* the Iran-Iraq war. These were mainly three:

(1) The historical claim that Kuwait had been an administrative subdistrict of the Iraqi province of Basra in Ottoman times and was therefore an integral part of modern Iraq. This claim was first articulated under the Iraqi monarchy in the late 1930s (before Kuwait became oil rich or independent) by the flamboyantly nationalist King Ghazi (1935–1939). It was revived by the "revolutionary" Iraqi president Abdul Karim Qassim (1958–1963) soon after the abrogation of the British protectorate over Kuwait and the declaration of Kuwaiti independence in June 1961. It was only the landing of British troops in Kuwait, and to a lesser extent the Arab League's opposition to Qassim, that deterred him from invading Kuwait at the time. Iraq boycotted the Arab League from 1961 until the downfall of Qassim in 1963 in protest against the League's stance. The return of Iraq to the Arab League was accompanied by Iraq's recognition of Kuwaiti independence in the autumn of that year and Kuwaiti membership in the United Nations. Iraq's historical claim to Kuwait remained in virtual abeyance until 2 August 1990. Meanwhile, in February 1980, Saddam Hussein proclaimed his National Covenant, one of the principal pillars of which was "the renunciation of the use of force by any Arab country against another and the resolution of all inter-Arab disputes by peaceful means."

(2) The delineation of the international frontiers between Iraq and Kuwait. In 1973 a contingent of Iraqi troops crossed the frontier and

occupied a Kuwaiti military post. They subsequently withdrew from the post but the incident signalled the persistence of the issue of frontier delineation.

(3) The issue of access to the Gulf. Iraq is a country of some 170,000 square miles but is virtually landlocked, with a coastline on the Gulf of only fifteen miles. Its main port, Basra, just below the confluence of the Tigris and Euphrates rivers, is linked to the Gulf by a single stretch of river (the Shatt al-Arab) which also constitutes a border between Iraq and Iran. West of the Shatt al-Arab and starting at the extreme northeast corner of Kuwait on the border with Iraq is a Gulf estuary that points in the direction of Basra but falls short of it by some ten miles. Immediately facing the entrance to this estuary on the Gulf are two islands belonging to Kuwait, Warba and Bubiyan. The frontier between Iraq and Kuwait lies *between* Warba and the entrance to this estuary, and at certain points is less than one mile off the Iraqi coastline.

A major bone of contention between Iraq and Iran had been the delineation of the frontier between them on the Shatt al-Arab. Under the Algiers Agreement in 1975, Iraq accepted the *thalweg* —the midpoint between the two banks—as the frontier. It was this agreement that Iraq repudiated when it invaded Iran, only to return to it after invading Kuwait.

Already before the Algiers Agreement and as early as 1973, the Baathist regime in Iraq had pressed Kuwait to lease to it the uninhabited islands of Warba and Bubiyan. The acceptance of the *thalweg* in 1975, and the building of a naval port in the meantime at Umm al-Qasr at the entrance of the western estuary opposite Warba, increased Iraq's interest in this island and in its neighbor Bubiyan. Iraqi planning envisaged the widening and extension of this western estuary to link up northwards with Basra and thus provide Iraq with an alternative access to the Gulf other than the Shatt al-Arab.

Second, the grievances that grew *during* the Iran-Iraq war.

Although the grievances just mentioned remained in practical abeyance because of Iraq's preoccupation with Iran, they were, nevertheless, simultaneously being exacerbated below the surface. The issue of access to the Gulf became more acute because of the then still-uncertain outcome of hostilities and the blocking of the Shatt al-Arab with the debris of war and accumulated silt. By the same token, Iraqi interest grew in a post-war alternative to the Shatt al-Arab, and therefore in Warba and Bubiyan. At the same time, all Kuwaiti activity along the border (for example, building of new frontier posts and oil installations) during Iraq's war with Iran was perceived by Iraq as a unilateral attempt by

Kuwait to strengthen its case on the issue of the delineation of the frontier. In addition, a new burgeoning grievance began to emerge, based on the Iraqi perception or claim that during the hostilities with Iran, Kuwait was drawing more than its share from the common north-south Rumaila oil field, whose southern tip straddled the border inland from the Gulf.

Third, the grievances that were articulated in the period *between* the cease-fire with Iran in August 1988 and the Jidda conference just prior to the invasion on 2 August. There were seven main grievances, and all were new:

(1) Overproduction of OPEC quotas. In the closed session of the heads of state already referred to on the last day of the Baghdad summit on 30 May 1990, Saddam claimed that some Gulf countries had begun early in 1990 to produce beyond their OPEC quotas to such an extent that the price in certain instances had plummeted to $7 per barrel, although the agreed-upon price was $18 per barrel. He claimed that every one-dollar drop in the price per barrel meant a loss of $1 billion per annum for Iraq. He explicitly stated that in Iraq's present economic state this overproduction was an "act of war": war, he said, could be waged by military means by "sending armies across frontiers, by acts of sabotage, by killing people and by supporting coups d'état, but war can also be waged by economic means . . . and what is happening is war against Iraq." He said he hoped the situation could be rectified, and hinted that the price of oil could be raised to $25 per barrel. This was the only grievance that Saddam aired at this session before his peers, including the emir of Kuwait. He did not mention any Arab country by name. But he made it clear that he had reached the end of his tether. "I must frankly tell you that we have reached a stage where we can no longer take any more pressure." He did, however, seem to leave the door open for an amicable settlement by expressing the hope that future summits would produce agreement. Some six weeks later, his foreign minister, Tariq Aziz, in a thirty-seven-page memorandum dated 15 July to the secretary-general of the Arab League, explicitly named Kuwait and the United Arab Emirates (UAE) as the two "culprits" in overproduction. Aziz also articulated in this same memorandum the six other new grievances;

(2) The Iraqi debt to Kuwait. Aziz did not give a figure for this debt, but stated that this "assistance" from Kuwait to Iraq during its war with Iran should not be considered a "debt" and should be cancelled;

(3) The oil allegedly taken from the Rumaila field. Aziz claimed that

from 1980 to 1990 Kuwait pumped $2.4 billion worth of oil belonging to Iraq from this field; he said that Kuwait owed Iraq this amount;

(4) Kuwait's "war" on Iraq. Aziz claimed that Kuwait's pumping of "Iraqi" oil from Rumaila was "tantamount to an act of war," while its attempt "to effect the economic collapse" of Iraq (through overproduction) was "not less than an act of war." This was a variation on the theme propounded by Saddam on 30 May;

(5) Kuwait's alleged complicity with foreign powers. Aziz claimed that the overproduction of Kuwait and the UAE was synchronized with efforts of foreign powers to denigrate Iraq because of its increasing championship of the Palestinian cause and its role as a deterrent to Israel;

(6) An Arab "Marshall Plan" for Iraq. Iraq claimed it was entitled to expect the Gulf countries to launch a "Marshall Plan" to support its recovery from the war, just as the United States had done in Europe after World War II;

(7) Kuwait's alleged reluctance to negotiate with Iraq. Aziz claimed that in June 1988, even before the cease-fire with Iran and soon after the Iraqi victory at Fao, Iraq informed Kuwait of its readiness to settle all outstanding issues amicably but that Kuwait had temporized. There was no mention of Saudi Arabia in this memorandum. Aziz also did not raise the issues either of Iraq's historical claims to Kuwait or of access to the Gulf and to the two islands. He did, however, refer to "the issue of frontier delineation that remained unresolved in spite of all attempts at a settlement during the sixties and seventies." Like his boss, Aziz seemed to leave the door open for reconciliation. He expressed the hope that the coming summit in Cairo would address the dispute.

To list this inventory of Iraqi grievances against Kuwait is not to endorse them. Iraq was duty bound by its membership in the Arab League (and the U.N.) and by its own recognition of Kuwaiti independence in 1963 to respect this independence. It was bound by the norms of pan-Arabism which it purported to uphold no less than by the 1980 National Covenant of its own president to refrain from acts of violence against an Arab country. Kuwait could hardly be expected to commit suicide by accepting its own disappearance from the political map. It was fully entitled to defend its territorial integrity and its economic, oil, and financial policies against all attempts at coercion. But the list of Iraqi grievances does indicate the existence of a three-decades long background of tension in Iraqi-Kuwaiti relations constituting an extended prologue to the invasion of 2 August. It also serves to indicate a new escalation in the tension between the two countries following the cease-fire with Iran some *two years* before the invasion of Kuwait.

To revert to the particular causes in Taylor's analogy, it is too early to assess the significance of the different steps taken by the different parties in the slide towards 2 August in the aftermath of the cease-fire with Iran. No matter what the outcome of the Gulf crisis, writers will dispute for generations to come this or that advanced chain of causation, just as they dispute to this day the significance of events preceding and following Sarajevo in 1914. When did Saddam decide to go to war against Kuwait? Before the May 1990 Baghdad summit or at its conclusion? Before or after his meeting with Mubarak on 24 July? Before or after his meeting with U.S. ambassador April Glaspie on 25 July? Before or after the Jidda Conference at the end of July? What actually happened at Jidda? Was Saddam bent from the beginning on staying in Kuwait? Did he intend to invade Saudi Arabia? Whose version of the events of 2–7 August should we believe: King Hussein's or Mubarak's? What chances of a reconciliation would there have been if Mubarak had not publicly condemned Iraq's action on 3 August, just ahead of the meeting of the Arab League Council of Arab Foreign Ministers? How to apportion the blame for acts of omission or commission by *Iraqi* actors, *non-Iraqi Arab* actors, and *non-Arab* actors? Was human folly the exclusive monopoly of Saddam Hussein?

Two things are certain: the Arab countries failed to detect the highly explosive potential in the juxtaposition of Iraq's inventory of grievances and Saddam's post-1988 cease-fire "mood," and if they did detect it, they failed (because of the "profound" causes alluded to) effectively to defuse the rapidly deteriorating crisis. One "particular" cause stands out: the willfulness of the "driver," Saddam, a willfulness that gathered speed in the prudence vacuum in which he had cocooned himself, and for which he alone is to blame.

THE RISE OF SADDAM HUSSEIN

Judith Miller and Laurie Mylroie

SADDAM HUSSEIN loves *The Godfather*. It is his favorite movie, one he has seen many times. He is especially fascinated by Don Corleone, a poor boy made good, whose respect for family is exceeded only by his passion for power. The iron-willed character of the Don may perhaps be the most telling model for the enigmatic figure that rules Iraq. Both come from dirt-poor peasant villages; both sustain their authority by violence; and for both, family is key, the key to power. Family is every-thing, or "almost" everything, because Saddam, like the Godfather, ultimately trusts no one, not even his next of kin. For both, calculation and discipline, loyalty, and ruthlessness are the measure of a man's character.

There is, however, a difference. Where the Don was a private man, obsessed with secrecy, seeking always to conceal his crimes behind a veil of anonymity, Saddam is a public figure who usurped political power and seizes every opportunity to advertise his might in order to impress upon his countrymen that there is no alternative to his rule. To visit Iraq is to enter the land of Big Brother. Enormous portraits of Saddam Hussein, black-haired and mustachioed, full of power and a strange serenity, stare down all over Baghdad. His photograph is everywhere—even on the dials of gold wristwatches. In the land where the Sumerians invented writing, discourse has been degraded to a single ubiquitous image.

But perhaps this difference matters not at all. For both the Don and

Judith Miller, a special correspondent covering the Persian Gulf for *The New York Times,* and Laurie Mylroie, Bradley Foundation Fellow at Harvard University's Center for Middle East-ern Studies, are co-authors of the best-selling *Saddam Hussein and the Crisis in the Gulf.* This excerpt is adapted from chapters 3 and 4 of their book.

Saddam relish power and seek respect, the more so because each knows what it means to have none. Neither ever forgot any insult, however trivial or imagined, both secure in the knowledge that, as Mario Puzo observed of his fictional character, "in this world there comes a time when the most humble of men, if he keeps his eyes open, can take his revenge on the most powerful." And in this likeness there perhaps lies the key to understanding Saddam Hussein's ambition.

Saddam Hussein was born fifty-three years ago on April 28, 1937, to a miserably poor, landless peasant family in the village of al-Auja, near the town of Takrit, on the Tigris River, a hundred miles north of Baghdad. (Although Muslims do not generally share the Western custom of celebrating birthdays, Saddam has made his a national holiday in Iraq.) The Arab town of Takrit lies in the heart of the Sunni Muslim part of Iraq. But in Iraq, the Sunnis are a minority. More than half the country is Shiite, the Sunnis' historical and theological rivals. Takrit had prospered in the nineteenth century, renowned for the manufacture of *kalaks,* round rafts made of inflated animal skins. But as the raft industry declined, so did the fortunes of the town. By the time Saddam was born, it had little to offer its inhabitants.

Communication with the outside world was difficult. While the Baghdad–Mosul railway ran through Takrit, the town had but one paved road. Saddam's nearby village was even worse off. It had only dirt roads. Its people, including Saddam and his family, lived in huts made of mud and reeds and burned cow dung for fuel. No one—either in Takrit or in al-Auja—had electricity or running water. The central government in Baghdad seemed far away, its authority limited to the presence of some local policemen.

Iraq was then a seething political cauldron, governed by a people who knew little of government. The Ottoman Turks had ruled Iraq for 500 years, before a brief decade of British rule. Britain's mandate over Iraq ended in 1932, only five years before Saddam was born. Within four years of Iraq's independence, hundreds of Assyrians, an ancient Christian people, would perish at the hands of the Iraqi army. Five years later, similar atrocities would be committed in Baghdad's ancient Jewish quarter. Between independence and Saddam's first breath of life, the Iraqi army had doubled in size. It saw itself as the embodiment of the new Iraqi state, "the profession of death" that would forge a nation out of the competing religious, tribal, and ethnic factions tearing at one another's throat. It was into this volatile world that Saddam Hussein was born.

Accounts of Saddam's early years are murky. Official hagiographies shed little light. The unsavory aspects of Saddam's harsh and brutal childhood are not something he wants known. It is usually said that Saddam's father, Hussein al-Majid, died either before Saddam's birth or when he was a few months old. But a private secretary of Saddam's, who later broke with him, has suggested that Saddam's father abandoned his wife and young children. Whatever the truth, after her husband was gone, Saddam's mother, Subha, was on her own until she met Ibrahim Hassan, a married man. Eventually she convinced him to get rid of his wife, and to marry her instead. By Muslim law, Ibrahim was permitted four wives, but Subha insisted on being the only one.

Saddam's stepfather was a crude and illiterate peasant who disliked his stepson and treated him abusively. Years later, Saddam would bitterly recall how his stepfather would drag him out of bed at dawn, barking, "Get up, you son of a whore, and look after the sheep." Ibrahim often fought with Subha over Saddam, complaining, "He is a son of a dog. I don't want him." Still, Ibrahim found some use for the boy, often sending Saddam to steal chickens and sheep, which he then resold. When Saddam's cousin, Adnan Khayrallah, who would become Iraq's defense minister, started to go to school, Saddam wanted to do the same. But Ibrahim saw no need to educate the boy. He wanted Saddam to stay home and take care of the sheep. Saddam finally won out. In 1947, at the age of ten, he began school.

He went to live with Adnan's father, Khayrallah Tulfah, his mother's brother, a schoolteacher in Baghdad. Several years before, Khayrallah had been cashiered from the Iraqi army for supporting a pro-Nazi coup in 1941, which the British suppressed, instilling in Khayrallah a deep and lasting hatred for Britain and for "imperialism." Whether Saddam's stepfather kicked him out of the house or whether he left at his own initiative for his uncle's home in Baghdad is unclear. What is certain is that Khayrallah Tulfah—who would later become mayor of Baghdad—would come to wield considerable influence over Saddam.

Having started elementary school when he went to live with Khayrallah, Saddam was sixteen when he finished intermediary school, roughly the equivalent of an American junior high school. Like his uncle, he wanted to become an army officer, but his poor grades kept him out of the prestigious Baghdad Military Academy. Of the generation of Arab leaders who took power in the military coups of the 1950s and 1960s, only Saddam Hussein had no army experience, though his official biography notes his love of guns starting at the age of ten. In 1976, he would correct the deficiency by getting himself appointed lieutenant general, a rank equal to chief of staff. When Saddam became president in 1979 he would promote himself to field marshal and would insist on personally directing the war against Iran.

Baghdad was utterly different from the world he had left behind in al-Auja. Yet Saddam still lived with Takritis. Khayrallah's home was on the western bank of the Tigris, in the predominantly lower-class Takriti district of al-Karkh. As in most Middle Eastern cities, peasants from the same region tended to cluster in certain neighborhoods when they moved to the city, giving each other support and maintaining their rural clan connections.

Times were unusually turbulent when Saddam was a student in Baghdad. In 1952, Lieutenant Colonel Gamal Abdel Nasser led a coup that toppled Egypt's monarchy. Though there had been considerable sympathy in the United States for the Egyptian officers, Nasser and the West were soon at odds. Nasser's purchase in 1955 of huge amounts of Soviet arms and his nationalization of the Suez Canal in 1956 led France, Britain, and Israel to attack Egypt that year. Most Egyptians—indeed, most Arabs—believed that Arab nationalism, through Nasser, won a tremendous victory when the invasion was halted, Israel forced to withdraw from the Sinai, and the canal returned to Egyptian control. That the United States was almost single-handedly responsible for that outcome did not reduce the tremendous popular enthusiasm for Nasser among the Arabs.

Saddam soon found himself swept up in a world of political intrigue whose seductions were far more compelling than the tedium of schoolwork. In 1956, Saddam participated in an abortive coup against the Baghdad monarchy. The next year, at the age of twenty, he joined the Baath party, one of several radical nationalist organizations that had spread throughout the Arab world. But the Baath in Iraq were a tiny and relatively powerless band of about 300 members in those days.

In 1958, a non-Baathist group of nationalist army officers, led by General Abdul Karim Qassim, succeeded in overthrowing King Faisal II. The fall of the monarchy intensified plotting among Iraq's rival dissident factions. A year after Qassim's coup, the Baath tried to seize power by machine-gunning Qassim's car in broad daylight. Saddam (whose name translates as "the one who confronts") was a member of the hit team. He had already proven his mettle, or in the jargon of the American underworld had "made his bones," by murdering a Communist supporter of Qassim in Takrit. The Communists were the Baath's fierce rivals—in fact, the man Saddam killed was his brother-in-law. There had been a dispute in the family over politics, and his uncle Khayrallah had incited Saddam to murder him. Although Saddam and Khayrallah were arrested, they were soon released. In the anarchic confusion of Baghdad after the monarchy's fall, political crimes were common and often unpunished.

Iraqi propaganda embellishes Saddam's role in the attempt on Qassim's life, portraying him as a bold and heroic figure. He is said to have been seriously wounded in the attack. Bleeding profusely, he orders a comrade to dig a bullet out of his leg with a razor blade, an operation so painful it causes him to faint. He then disguises himself as a Bedouin tribesman, swims across the Tigris River, steals a donkey, and flees to safety across the desert to Syria.

The truth is less glamorous. Iraqi sources present at the time insist that Saddam's role in the failed assassination attempt was minor, that he was only lightly wounded, and that the wound was inadvertently inflicted by his own comrades. A sympathetic doctor treated Saddam and several others much more seriously hurt at a party safe house. Saddam would later have the opportunity to reward him for his help. When the Baath party finally succeeded in taking power in 1968, the doctor was made dean of the Medical College of Baghdad University, a post he held until he broke with Saddam in 1979.

From Syria, Saddam went to Cairo, where he would spend the next four years. The stay in Egypt was to be his only extended experience in another country. Supported by an Egyptian government stipend, he resumed his political activities, finally finishing high school at the age of twenty-four. In Cairo he was arrested twice, and both times quickly released. The first arrest occurred after he threatened to kill a fellow Iraqi over political differences. He was arrested again when he chased a fellow Baathist student through the streets of Cairo with a knife. The student was later to serve as Jordan's information minister.

Saddam entered Cairo University's Faculty of Law in 1961. He eventually received his law degree not in Cairo, but in Baghdad in 1970, after he became the number two man in the regime. It was an honorary degree.

While in Cairo, Saddam married his uncle Khayrallah's daughter, Sajida, in 1963. His studies in Egypt ended abruptly in February when Baathist army officers and a group of Arab nationalist officers together succeeded in ousting and killing General Qassim, a figure of considerable popularity, particularly among the poor of Iraq. Of Qassim, Hanna Batatu, the author of an authoritative history of Iraq, has written: "The people had more genuine affection for him than for any other ruler in the modern history of Iraq."

Many people refused to believe that Qassim was dead. It was rumored that he had gone into hiding and would soon surface. The Baathists found a macabre way to demonstrate Qassim's mortality. They displayed his bullet-riddled body on television, night after night. As Samir al-Khalil, in his excellent book *Republic of Fear,* tells it: "The body was propped upon a chair in the studio. A soldier sauntered around, handling its parts. The camera would cut to scenes of devastation at the Ministry of Defense where Qassim had made his last stand. There, on location, it lingered on the mutilated corpses of Qassim's entourage (al-Mahdawi, Wasfi Taher, and others). Back to the studio and close-ups now of the entry and exit points of each bullet hole. The whole macabre sequence closes with a scene that must forever remain etched on the memory of all those who saw it: the soldier grabbed the lolling head by the hair, came right up close, and spat full face into it."

Saddam was elated. He hurried back to Baghdad to assume his part in the revolution. He was twenty-six years old.

Saddam quickly found his place in the new regime. He became an interrogator and torturer in the Qasr-al-Nihayyah, or "Palace of the End," so called because it was where King Faisal and his family were gunned down in 1958. Under the Baath the palace was used as a torture chamber.

Few in the West are aware of Saddam's activities there. But an Iraqi arrested and accused of plotting against the Baath has told of his own torture at the palace by Saddam himself: "My arms and legs were bound by rope. I was hung on the rope to a hook on the ceiling and I was repeatedly beaten with rubber hoses filled with stones." He managed to survive his ordeal; others were not so lucky. When the Baath, riven by internal splits, was ousted nine months later in November 1963 by the army, a grisly discovery was made. "In the cellars of al-Nihayyah Palace," according to Hanna Batatu, whose account is based on official government sources, "were found all sorts of loathsome instruments of torture, including electric wires with pincers, pointed iron stakes on which prisoners were made to sit, and a machine which still bore traces of chopped-off fingers. Small heaps of blooded clothing were scattered about, and there were pools on the floor and stains over the walls."

During the party split in 1963, Saddam had supported Michel Aflaq, a French-educated Syrian, the party's leading ideologue and co-founder of the party. Saddam was rewarded the next year when Aflaq sponsored him for a position in the Baath regional command, the party's highest decision-making body in Iraq. With this appointment, Saddam began his rapid ascent within the party.

His growing prominence was also due to the support of his older cousin, General Ahmad Hassan al-Bakr, the party's most respected military figure and a member of the party from its earliest days. It is said that Saddam's wife helped to cement Saddam's relations with Bakr by persuading Bakr's son to marry her sister, and by promoting the marriage of two of Bakr's daughters to two of her brothers. The party's affairs were rapidly becoming a family business. In 1965, Bakr became secretary-general of the party. The next year, Saddam was made deputy secretary-general.

During the period of his initial rise in the party, Saddam spent a brief interlude in prison, from October 1964 to his escape from jail sometime in 1966. There, as Saddam later recounted, in the idleness of prison life he reflected on the mistakes that had led to the party's split and its fall from power. He became convinced that the "Revolution of 1963" was stolen by a "rightist military aristocracy" in alliance with renegade elements of the Baath party. Divisions within the party, which had less than 1,000 full members at that time, had to end. Unity was essential for power, even if it had to be purchased by purge and blood. He determined to build a security force within the party, to create cells of loyalty which answered to no one but himself, to ensure that victory once won would be kept.

Upon his escape from prison, Saddam quickly set about building the party's internal security apparatus, the Jihaz Haneen, or "instrument of yearning." Those deemed "enemies of the party" were to be killed; unfriendly factions intimidated. Saddam's reputation as an architect of terror grew.

Two years later, on July 30, 1968, Saddam and his Baathist comrades succeeded in seizing and holding state power. Bakr became president and commander in chief in addition to his duties as secretary-general of the Baath party and the chairman of its Revolutionary Command Council. Saddam was made deputy chairman of the council, in charge of internal security. He quickly moved to strengthen control and expand his base within the party. The security services graduated hundreds of Saddam's men from their secret training schools, among them his half brothers, Barzan, Sabawi, and Wathban; another graduate, his cousin Ali Hassan al-Majid, would earn notoriety years later for his genocidal suppression of the Kurds during the Iran-Iraq war and his leading role in the invasion of Kuwait; another graduate was Arshad Yassin, his cousin and brother-in-law, whom the world would come to know as the bodyguard who repeatedly stroked the head of Stuart Lockwood, the young British "guest," as Saddam tried to get him to talk about milk and cornflakes.

Saddam was thirty-one. His penchant for asserting his authority by title—today he holds six—was evident even then. He insisted on being called "Mr. Deputy." No one else in Iraq was Mr. Deputy. It was Saddam's title, his alone. Although he would remain Mr. Deputy for a decade, he was increasingly regarded as the regime's real strongman.

The hallmarks of the new regime soon became apparent. Barely three months after the coup, the regime announced on October 9, 1968, that it had smashed a major Zionist spy ring. Fifth columnists were denounced before crowds of tens of thousands. On January 5, 1969, seventeen "spies" went on trial. Fourteen were hung, eleven of whom were Jewish, their bodies left to dangle before crowds of hundreds of thousands in Baghdad's Liberation Square. Even the Egyptian newspaper *al-Ahram* condemned the spectacle: "The hanging of fourteen people in the public square is certainly not a heartwarming sight, nor is it the occasion for organizing a festival." Baghdad radio scoffed at the international condemnation, of which there was shockingly little, by declaring, "We hanged spies, but the Jews crucified Christ." Over the next year and a half, a tapestry of alleged treason was unraveled, providing a steady spectacle of denunciation and execution. The victims were no longer primarily Jews. Very soon they were mostly Muslims. The Jews had been but a stepping-stone to the regime's real target, its political rivals. The Baath began their rule with an inauguration of blood.

Saad al-Din Ibrahim, a respected Egyptian scholar, was later to call such regimes "new monarchies in republican garb." Disillusioned with what he regarded as the failure of the new breed of "revolutionary leaders" to deliver on the radical promises they had made for transforming Arab society when they seized power, Ibrahim concluded: "Despite the presence of a political party, popular committees, and the president's claim that he is one of the people . . . the ruler in his heart of hearts does not trust to any of this nor to his fellow strugglers of all those years. The only people he can trust are first, the members of his family; second, the tribe; third, the sect, and so we have arrived at the neo-monarchies in the Arab nation.

"The matter is not restricted to the appointment of relatives in key positions, but to how those relatives commit all sorts of transgressions, legal, financial, and moral without accounting, as if the country were a private estate to do what they like."

From the beginning Saddam's base was the security services. Through them he controlled the party. Saddam established the financial autonomy of his power base early on, in an innovative way. Although Islam forbids gambling, horse racing had been a popular sport under the monarchy. Qassim had banned horse races; Saddam reintroduced them.

He used the funds that betting generated to provide an unfettered, independent source of revenue. After 1973, when the price of oil quadrupled, Saddam's resources rose accordingly. He began to stash away considerable sums for the party and security services, often in accounts outside the country, which are today frozen because of international sanctions imposed in response to the invasion of Kuwait.

If Bakr continued to live modestly after 1968, Saddam and his associates were bent on reversing a lifetime of personal indignities, real and imagined. He used his new political power to acquire the social and economic standing he had long coveted. Years of struggle and deprivation filled him with a measure of greed far greater than those whom he had usurped. It made him far more ruthless in his determination to hold on to power and to break all who stood in his way or who might one day challenge his rule.

NO EPISODE better reveals the essence of Saddam's regime than the baptism of blood that accompanied his ascension to absolute power in July 1979. For eleven years Saddam had waited, working in apparent harmony with his older cousin, head of the Baath party, and president of the republic, Ahmad Hassan al-Bakr. For years Saddam had worked to build a loyal and ruthless secret police apparatus. On the surface, all was well. Behind the scenes, trouble was brewing for Saddam.

The triumph of the Ayatollah Ruhollah Khomeini over the shah of Iran in January 1979 had aroused Iraq's Shiites, politically powerless, although they comprised fifty-five percent of the population. Deadly riots had erupted in a huge Shiite slum in east Baghdad, after the government had arrested the Shiites' foremost religious leader. The Baath party organization had collapsed in that sector of the city. The disturbances were so serious that Bakr concluded that it would be unwise to defy Shiite opinion within the party. But Saddam opposed any concessions. The party's Shiites, he felt, had failed to control their co-religionists. He suspected them of leniency toward the rioters, and he felt they must be purged and punished. Shiites within the party, who had been associated with Saddam, began to gather around Bakr. They were joined by some non-Shiites and army officers. They began to cast about for a way to check Saddam.

Ironically, Saddam himself had provided them a way. In the fall of 1978, Iraq and Syria, ruled by murderously rival Baath parties, suddenly announced that they would unite. Saddam was the architect of that policy. He wanted the Arab states to break their ties with Egypt, ostensibly to punish Cairo for the peace treaty it was about to sign with Israel. If he could force the Arabs to ostracize Egypt, the most important and populous Arab state, he could open the way for Iraq's dominance of the Arab world. Saddam succeeded, at least in his first step. At the November 1978 Arab summit in Baghdad, Saddam threatened to attack Kuwait, while Syrian president Hafez al-Assad warned the Saudis, "I will transfer the battle to your bedrooms." The Arab states agreed to break all ties with Egypt.

Unity with Syria, however, threatened to undermine Saddam within Iraq. It soon became apparent that Bakr could become president of a Syrian-Iraqi federation, Assad could be vice president, and Saddam would be number three. His rivals urged unity with Syria as a way of blunting his ambitions, while Saddam became increasingly apprehensive that they might succeed.

While Saddam saw the danger to himself in the proposed union, the Takritis saw their monopoly of power threatened, along with their immense privileges. Saddam decided to press the sixty-four-year-old Bakr to resign so that he could become president and leaned heavily on the family to support him. According to Iraqi sources, Khayrallah Tulfah, backed by his son Adnan, urged Bakr to step down for the good of the clan. Reluctantly, Bakr came to agree, although not before sending Assad a secret request to hasten union negotiations because "there is a current here which is anxious to kill the union in the bud before it bears fruit," according to British journalist Patrick Seale.

On July 16, 1979, President Bakr's resignation was announced, officially for reasons of health. Saddam Hussein was named president, as well as secretary-general of the Iraqi Baath party, commander in chief, head of the government, and chairman of the Revolutionary Command Council.

Saddam had succeeded in carrying out his putsch. On July 22 he staged an astonishing spectacle to inaugurate his presidency when he convened a top-level party meeting of some 1,000 party cadres. This meeting was recorded and the videotape distributed to the party. A few minutes of that tape have appeared on American television and it has been briefly described elsewhere, but no full account of that extraordinary meeting has been published before. The following account is based on an audiotape made available to the authors and the testimony of an individual who has seen the video.

The meeting begins with Muhyi Abdul Hussein al-Mashhadi, secretary of the Revolutionary Command Council and a Shiite party member for over twenty years, reading a fabricated confession detailing his participation in a supposed Syrian-backed conspiracy. Muhyi reads hurriedly, with the eager tone of a man who believes that his cooperation will win him a reprieve. (It did not.) Then Saddam, after a long, rambling statement about traitors and party loyalty, announces: "The people whose names I am going to read out should repeat the slogan of the party and leave the hall." He begins to read, stopping occasionally to light and relight his cigar. At one point he pronounces a first name, "Ghanim," but then changes his mind and goes on to the next name.

After Saddam finishes reading the list of the condemned, the remaining members of the audience begin to shout, "Long live Saddam," and "Let me die! Long live the father of Uday [Saddam's eldest son]." The cries are prolonged and hysterical. When the shouting dies down, Saddam begins to speak, but stops suddenly to retrieve a handkerchief. Tears stream down his face. As he dabs his eyes with the handkerchief, the assembly breaks into loud sobbing.

Recovering himself, Saddam speaks: "I'm sure many of our comrades have things to say, so let us discuss them." Party members call for a wider purge. One man rises, and says, "Saddam Hussein is too lenient. There has been a problem in the party for a long time. . . . There is a line between doubt and terror, and unbalanced democracy. The problem of too much leniency needs to be addressed by the party." Then Saddam's cousin, Ali Hassan al-Majid, declares: "Everything that you did in the past was good and everything that you will do in the future is good. I say this from my faith in the party and your leadership." After more appeals from the party faithful to search out traitors, Saddam brings the discussion to a close. More than twenty men, some of the most prominent in Iraq, have been taken from the hall. Saddam concludes, "We don't need Stalinist methods to deal with traitors here. We need Baathist methods." The audience erupts into tumultuous applause.

In the days following, Saddam obliges senior party members and government ministers to join him in personally executing the most senior of their former comrades. The murdered include Mohammed Mahjoub, a member of the ruling Revolutionary Command Council; Mohammed Ayesh, head of the labor unions, and Biden Fadhel, his deputy; Ghanim Abdul Jalil, a Shiite member of the council and once a close associate of Saddam's; and Talib al-Suweleh, a Jordanian. Saddam's two most powerful opponents were dispatched before the July 22 meeting took place: General Walid Mahmoud Sirat, a senior army officer and the core of the opposition to Saddam, was tortured and his body mutilated; Adnan Hamdani, deputy prime minister, who had been in Syria on government business, was taken from the airport on his return and promptly murdered. Some sources believe that as many as 500 people may have been executed secretly in Saddam's night of the long knives. The true figure may never be known.

The savagery of Saddam's victory was meant to make him seem invincible. His rivals had been smashed; his primacy as absolute leader secured. He had replaced the state with the party, and now the party with himself, the giver of life and death. The terror that was his to dispense would make people fearful, but it would also inspire awe, and in a few, the appearance of mercy would even evoke gratitude. Saddam had made good his promise of 1971 when he had declared that "with our party methods, there is no chance for anyone who disagrees with us to jump on a couple of tanks and overthrow the government." From 1920 until 1979, Iraq had experienced thirteen coups d'état. Saddam was determined that his would be the last.

The key to understanding Saddam's rule, in the opinion of Samir al-Khalil, author of *Republic of Fear*, lies in the sophisticated way the regime has implicated ordinary people in the violence of the party by absorbing them into the repressive organs of the state. As Khalil writes: "Success is achieved by the degree to which society is prepared to police itself. Who is an informer? In Baathist Iraq the answer is anybody." A European diplomat stationed in Baghdad once told a reporter from *The New York Times* that "there is a feeling that at least three million Iraqis are watching the eleven million others."

His assessment may not be exaggerated. The Ministry of Interior is the largest of twenty-three government ministries. Khalil estimates that "the combined numbers of police and militia . . . greatly exceed the size of the standing army, and [are] in absolute terms twice as large as anything experienced in Iran under the shah." And this in a nation whose population is just under one-third the size of Iran's.

In 1984, about 25,000 people were full members of the Baath party; another 1.5 million Iraqis were sympathizers or supporters. The former are generally prepared to embrace the party line; the latter are often in the party for some peripheral reason. Party membership may be a requirement for their jobs. However lukewarm their attachment to the party, and it is for many of these, they are still part of the system, obliged to attend the weekly party meetings. If one multiplies each member by four or five dependents, the Baath can be said to have implicated slightly under half the entire population. About thirty percent of the eligible population is employed by the government. If one includes the army and militia, the figure jumps to fifty percent of the urban work force—this in a society in which sixty-five percent of its citizens now live in urban areas. For all practical purposes, state and party are synonymous.

· · ·

THE INQUISITION Saddam has loosed on his people is perhaps difficult to understand. After all, with Iraq's immense oil wealth, why squander the nation's youth, its resources, and its future in a self-inflicted bloodletting extreme even by the standards of the Middle East? There is something elemental in Saddam's behavior. Robert Conquest, the author of *The Great Terror,* the classic work on Stalin's Gulag, has perhaps described one part of the answer: "One does not establish a dictatorship in order to safeguard a revolution; one makes the revolution in order to establish the dictatorship. The object of persecution is persecution. The object of torture is torture. The object of power is power."

THE IRAQ LOBBY:
KISSINGER, THE BUSINESS FORUM & CO.

Joe Conason

N O   A D V O C A T E   O F   military force in the Persian Gulf has been more widely quoted in recent weeks than Henry A. Kissinger. In op-ed articles and television appearances, he has offered his antiseptic-sounding prescription of "surgical and progressive" air strikes against Iraqi targets and has urged the destruction of the Iraqi regime. These views have been cited repeatedly by hawkish editorialists and were treated as front-page news by *The New York Times*. None of this is startling —until one considers that the former secretary of state's consulting firm, Kissinger Associates, under the auspices of a pro-Iraq interest group, was not so long ago offering economic advice to Saddam Hussein.

Of course, Henry Kissinger isn't the only American businessman who has abruptly changed his view of Iraq. Before the current crisis erupted, dozens of major U.S. and multinational corporations—nearly all of them members of a little-known trade association called the U.S.-Iraq Business Forum—eagerly supplied the Hussein regime with everything from rice to computers to helicopters, and anticipated that Hussein would spend billions more. But because Kissinger and his associates straddle the worlds of business and diplomacy, they offer a particularly striking example of how U.S. policy elites virtually ignored the threat to regional (and global) security and to human rights posed by Iraq until the invasion of Kuwait made that threat too obvious to overlook.

Though Kissinger now says that Hussein should be deposed because he "used poison gas against his own dissident population," that did not prevent his consulting firm—or other corporate powers—from continu-

Joe Conason is editor-at-large of *Details* magazine. This article was published in the October 1, 1990, issue of *The New Republic*.

ing to do business in Baghdad for years after Iraq's chemical warfare capability had been unleashed against Iraqi minorities (and Iranian soldiers).* If anything, Hussein was coddled by government officialdom at the urging of his U.S. business partners. The companies seeking Iraq's petrodollars arranged for U.S. taxpayers to assume the risk of doing business with Hussein through commodity credits and loan guarantees underwritten by the federal government.

Keeping these subsidies in place wasn't easy, given the nature of the Iraqi regime. Safeguarding them from congressional sanctions and the federal bureaucracy was, from 1982 until August 1990, the raison d'être of the U.S.-Iraq Business Forum. Based in Washington, where it worked closely with the Iraqi Embassy, over the past few years the Forum and its powerful members have quietly kept the U.S. credits and loans pouring into Baghdad. By June 1989 these efforts raised the Forum in Hussein's estimation so high that he invited a number of the group's leading members—accompanied by a representative of the legendary Dr. Kissinger—to Baghdad for a four-day program of meetings and banquets with cabinet officials and other top members of his government, and he himself granted them a highly unusual two-hour audience.

The Forum's membership, currently more than fifty firms, has expanded as rapidly as the growth in trade between the United States and Iraq. (Annual sales grew from about $400 million in 1985 to $1.5 billion in 1989, and had been expected to double again this year.) Its board of directors includes officials of Amoco, Mobil, Westinghouse, Caterpillar, and the First City Bancorporation of Texas (whose chairman and CEO, A. Robert Abboud, also chairs the Forum). Its daily affairs in Washington are overseen by Forum president Marshall W. Wiley, a lawyer at the huge lobbying law firm of Sidley & Austin and a former U.S. ambassador to Oman. (He also ran the U.S. interests section in Baghdad before full diplomatic relations resumed in 1984.) The bland, reassuring Wiley is assisted by executive director Mary E. King, a pioneering civil rights activist who served as associate director of ACTION, the umbrella agency for the Peace Corps and its domestic offshoots, during the Carter administration.

Neither the Forum nor any of its officers or members is registered with the Justice Department as an agent for Iraq, although they have spent

---

* Editors' note: The fact that Iran and Iraq used chemical weapons against each other during their eight-year war is beyond dispute. But some U.S. intelligence officials have come to believe that the infamous gassing of Iraqi Kurds in the town of Halabja in March of 1988 may have been the result of an *Iranian*, not Iraqi, attack. There is little doubt, however, that after the cease-fire with Iran in August Baghdad unleashed chemical attacks against the Kurds.

much of the past five years seeking to promote that nation's interests in Washington. "We're not putting out propaganda about Iraq to the general public," Wiley told me in an interview last May, while admitting that his mission of advocating more trade "does have a public relations aspect to it." He draws a fine line, arguing that the Forum doesn't lobby, leaving that task to its constituents. "We keep our members informed," he explained, "so they can then pursue their own interests as they see them."

But in fact the Forum has insistently put out a soft line on Iraq that goes well beyond Wiley's occasional appearances on TV programs like *This Week with David Brinkley,* or his letters opposing sanctions that appear in *The Washington Post* and *The Washington Times.* In May 1988, while Hussein was wiping out thousands of Kurdish civilians, the Forum sponsored a Washington symposium on Iraq that was wholly dominated by apologists for the regime. The keynote speakers were Nizar Hamdoon, then Iraq's ambassador to the United States, and Abdul Rahim al-Chalabi, Iraq's oil minister, and much of the discussion was given over to their country's rapid growth and the enormous market it would create for imported capital and consumer goods. A. Peter Burleigh, deputy assistant secretary of state for Near Eastern affairs, closed his remarks by cheerfully noting that the administration looked "to those in the U.S.-Iraq Business Forum to help preserve—and expand—the overall U.S.-Iraqi relationship through its commercial side, as only the private sector can do."

Several months later Wiley prevailed upon his friends in the Reagan administration to oppose economic sanctions, which were under consideration after Hussein's use of poison gas against the Kurds was revealed. In an October 1988 letter to President Reagan on Forum stationery— which lists such corporate affiliates as Mobil, Amoco, and GM—Wiley wrote, "We fully understand and agree with your desire to limit the use of chemical weapons," but he insisted that imposing sanctions on Iraq "would have the opposite effect." Sanctions were never imposed, and have been consistently opposed, until now, by the Reagan and Bush administrations. It is worth considering the possibility that had sanctions been imposed two years ago, the present crisis might never have begun.

The Forum's pro-Iraq activities in Washington have been financed by dues of member companies, not by the Iraqi treasury. But as early as May 1985, before the Forum even opened its doors, Ambassador Hamdoon gave Wiley a letter on embassy letterhead. It bluntly advised "any United States company interested in doing business with Iraq" that it "would do well to join the Forum." Several months later the Hussein regime announced publicly that for companies wishing to do business in Iraq membership in the Forum was practically mandatory. Flanked by Foreign Minister Tariq Aziz, Hamdoon told a Washington audience: "Our people in Baghdad will give priority—when there is competition between two companies—to the one that is a member of the Forum." A directory of Forum members was later issued to officials of every ministry in Baghdad, with instructions to use it when awarding contracts or procuring supplies.

By directing contributions to Iraq's friend in Washington, Iraq's foreign ministry took advantage of what many regard as a loophole in the Foreign Agents Registration Act, which mandates a detailed report of agent activities every six months. Because it was not registered as an official agent of the Iraqi regime, the Forum was able to operate far more freely in Washington and maintained credibility as an advocate of American interests, rather than a mouthpiece for a discredited tyranny.

The ultimate sign of appreciation for services rendered came in the spring of 1989, when the Iraqi government invited the Forum's "blue ribbon" trade delegation to Baghdad. Present in addition to Abboud, Wiley, and King were CEOs or senior executives of Amoco, Mobil, Occidental Petroleum, Westinghouse, General Motors, Xerox, Bell Helicopter Textron, and several other Fortune 500 companies. Invitations were extended only to member companies with annual sales in excess of $500 million, but an exception was made for Alan Stoga, an economist specializing in international finance and oil markets who is Kissinger's senior associate.

True to the secrecy that is his boss's obsession, Stoga has refused to discuss his visit to Baghdad, or any interests the Kissinger firm and its clients may have in Iraq. According to Wiley, Stoga "was asked to accompany us, although Kissinger Associates is not officially part of the Forum, because of his general knowledge of international finance and banking problems." At the time, as the Forum's newsletter pointed out, Iraq's massive debt was "the principal constraint" on U.S. trade, and Stoga's job was to explain how Hussein could restructure his debt and obtain loans from U.S. commercial banks and other lenders.

Private financing would have meant bigger profits, not only for financial institutions like Chase Manhattan that have long retained Kissinger, but for other Kissinger clients doing deals in Iraq. Although Kissinger Associates closely guards the identities of its clientele, the list of acknowledged clients includes several firms that have won large contracts from the Hussein regime in the past few years: Volvo, whose chairman, Pehr Gyllenhammar, sits on Kissinger's own board; Hunt Oil, which also sent an executive on the Baghdad trip; Fiat, whose subsidiary has been implicated in weapons sales to Iraq; Coca-Cola; and the Yugoslav construction giant Energoprojekt. At least one other Kissinger client, Britain's Midland Bank, is one of a small group of commercial houses already holding large amounts of Iraqi paper, so it too would have benefited from fresh loans by other lenders.

The nature and substance of the Kissinger firm's advice to its clients is another closely guarded secret. But given Kissinger's own Middle East expertise and that of many of his employees and ex-employees (notably Lawrence Eagleburger, now deputy secretary of state, and national security adviser Brent Scowcroft, a prominent pre-Kuwait advocate of cooperation with Saddam Hussein), it is reasonable to assume that the firm's advice on Iraq was sought and given.

The former secretary of state's business interests in the Middle East (and around the world) pose an ethical problem for journalists when they seek him out as the nation's most prominent foreign policy expert. When Kissinger appears in the media to comment upon the Gulf crisis, reporters and editors have refrained from questioning him about his interests in Iraq (or Saudi Arabia and Kuwait, for that matter). They made the same omission last year when he took to the airwaves to discuss China, a country where he has substantial commercial interests. In the China case the omission was more egregious, since Kissinger was defending the Chinese government and arguing that the United States should "not do any sanctions" in response to the Tiananmen Square massacre. But even though Kissinger's post-Kuwait message on Iraq was very different, it might have been worth asking him if he thought his firm's previous activities had in any way contributed to the Iraqi arrogance that produced the crisis.

Kissinger too has declined all requests to be interviewed about the June 1989 trade delegation. Explaining its activities has been left to Wiley. "Iraq plays an important role now in bringing about stability in the Gulf region as an offset to Iran," Wiley told me after the Baghdad visit. "This balance of power is important to us because of our interest further down the Gulf in the countries that are friendly to us and where we have substantial energy reserves that must be protected. So Iraq plays an important political and geopolitical role in addition to being an important trading partner for us, and we can't push all these considerations to the side and shut our eyes to them because of some perceived human rights violations." Wiley added piously: "We should work with the Iraqi government to try to improve their human rights behavior, in whatever ways we can. [But] we will not achieve that if we cut off our ties with Iraq."

That view prevailed in the State Department until Hussein invaded Kuwait, although other Mideast experts disagreed. In a 200-page report on Iraq issued in February 1990, the human rights group Middle East Watch exhaustively documented Iraq's record of brutality. It recommended that the United States terminate all credits and loans to Baghdad—effectively ending most trade—"until such time as the Iraqi government dramatically curbs abuses." Many of the same media outlets now decrying Hussein's atrocities and repression ignored the Middle East Watch report when it was published.

And almost no one noticed the report's footnote about the June 1989 trade delegation, which mentioned Kissinger Associates. There was a touch of morbid irony in the fact that Stoga arrived in Baghdad on June 4 —the day Kissinger's old friends in Beijing sent the tanks into Tiananmen Square. Meanwhile, the U.S.-Iraq Business Forum is effectively out of business. But when the crisis recedes, no matter what tyrant rules in Baghdad, it seems safe to predict that Marshall Wiley and his corporate allies will be back, insisting that it is in our interest to help them make money.

WHAT WASHINGTON GAVE SADDAM
FOR CHRISTMAS

Murray Waas

T H E R E A G A N administration, in apparent violation of federal law, engaged in a massive effort to supply arms and military supplies to the regime of Saddam Hussein during the Iran-Iraq war. Some of these efforts to supply arms to Iraq appear not only to have violated federal law but, in addition, a U.S. arms embargo then in effect against Iraq. The arms shipments were also clearly at odds with the Reagan administration's stated policy of maintaining strict U.S. neutrality in the Iran-Iraq war. And, in the light of the current conflict, they were certainly wrong-headed. Some of these American weapons were made available to Iraq through third countries that, with secret U.S. approval, would simply transfer the arms to then-embargoed Iraq, according to classified documents and sources close to the program.

There is no evidence that President George Bush—then serving as vice president—knew of the covert efforts to arm Saddam Hussein. But several sources, including senior White House officials, say Bush was a key behind-the-scenes proponent in the Reagan administration of a broader policy that urged tilting toward Iraq during the war. Bush and other White House insiders feared a military victory by the Ayatollah Khomeini, and they came to see Saddam as a bulwark against the fundamentalist Islamic fervor Khomeini was spreading throughout the Mideast. After he was elected president, Bush pursued this policy even further, attempting to develop closer business, diplomatic, and intelligence ties between Iraq and the United States.

Murray Waas is a veteran free-lance writer whose work has appeared in *The Village Voice*, *Harper's*, and *The Nation*. This article originally appeared, in slightly longer form, in the December 18, 1990, issue of *The Village Voice*.

The secret history of U.S. government approval of potentially illegal arms sales to Saddam Hussein is the story of how the Reagan and Bush administrations aided and abetted the Iraqi regime, allowing Saddam Hussein to build up the fourth-largest military arsenal in the world. It is the story of how two American presidencies assisted Saddam in obtaining chemical and biological weapons and the means of delivering them, threatening entire cities.

And it is the story of how, as the Reagan and Bush administrations carried out their ill-conceived policy of tilting toward Iraq, there was no lack of American citizens willing to profit from it. Major U.S.-based corporations such as AT&T, United Technologies, General Motors, and Philip Morris were only too glad to explore expanded trade with Saddam Hussein—as long as he paid his bills on time.

AMERICA'S EFFORTS to secretly arm Saddam Hussein began in the early years of the first term of the Reagan administration. In March of 1982, reports began filtering back to the State Department from the U.S. embassy in Amman that Jordan's King Hussein was pressing for the U.S. to militarily assist Iraq. Iraq was suffering serious reverses in its war with Iran: The Ayatollah's forces had leveled many of Iraq's major oil facilities and were laying siege to Basra, Iraq's second-largest city and only port. King Hussein urged that the U.S. find some way to help arm Iraq in order to prevent a total victory by Iran.

Shortly thereafter William Eagleton, then the U.S. chargé d'affaires in Baghdad and the senior U.S. diplomat in Iraq, recommended to his superiors that the Reagan administration reverse its policy and allow shipments of U.S. arms to Iraq through third countries. Officials throughout the Reagan administration favoring the Iraqi tilt supported the recommendation.

To carry out Eagleton's plan, the U.S. would have to lift its arms embargo against Iraq, something Congress, outraged by Saddam's record on human rights and terrorism, certainly would never allow. A more likely option was to arm Iraq secretly, without lifting the embargo —but this, too, had its drawbacks, chief among them the Arms Export Control Act, which makes it illegal to transfer U.S. arms through third countries to regimes officially prohibited from receiving them. Countries that import arms from the U.S. pledge before any sale is made that they will not transfer the arms to another country without official, written approval from the U.S. government. The law also makes it a crime for U.S. citizens—including government officials—to arrange arms sales to a third country for the purpose of transferring them to a prohibited country.

Still, Eagleton pressed his case, stopping short of advocating deliberately breaking the law. In October 1983, Eagleton cabled his superiors, recommending: "We can selectively lift restrictions on third party transfers of U.S. licensed military equipment to Iraq." Later, in the same highly classified cable, he made the suggestion that "We go ahead and we do it through Egypt."

High-level U.S. intelligence sources say that the Reagan administration shortly thereafter adapted the Eagleton scenario, sending arms through third party countries, despite the fact that some of the transactions appear on their face to violate the Arms Export Control Act.

These sources say that U.S. arms shipments were made regularly to Jordan, Egypt, and Kuwait—with advance White House knowledge and approval of their transshipment to Iraq. Like the arms-for-hostages deal with Iran engineered by the Reagan administration, these third country shipments while a congressional arms embargo was in effect were apparently against the law. Among the weapons made available to Saddam, with White House approval, were top-of-the-line HAWK anti-aircraft missiles, originally sent to Jordan's King Hussein and quietly passed along to Iraq.

SADDAM'S MILITARY machine is partly a creation of the Western powers. Margaret Thatcher, perhaps the most bellicose Western leader, allowed British arms concerns to sell billions of dollars worth of tanks, missile parts, and artillery to Iraq. The French have sold Saddam Mirage fighter jets and Exocet missiles (like the one that took the lives of thirty-seven sailors aboard the U.S.S. *Stark* during the Iran-Iraq war). The West Germans have been the chief supplier to six Iraqi plants producing nerve and mustard gases.

The U.S. had an arms embargo against Iraq all during this time, making direct American sales illegal. But after the Reagan administration decided to tilt toward Iraq, the arms embargo had little effect. Besides making their own sales via Jordan, Kuwait, and Egypt, the Americans simply encouraged other nations to send arms to Saddam in their place.

"The billions upon billions of dollars of shipments from Europe would not have been possible without the approval and acquiescence of the Reagan administration," recalls a former high-level intelligence official.

One good example of the sort of arms transfer encouraged by the

Americans was a $1.4 billion sale—brokered by Miami-based arms-dealer Sarkis Soghanalian, and perhaps the largest legal deal of his career—of howitzers to Iraq by the French government. U.S. intelligence sources say the Iraqis first approached the Reagan administration about purchasing long-range 175 mm artillery from the U.S. directly. But because of the arms embargo, the White House instead encouraged the Iraqis to ask private arms traffickers—like Sarkis Soghanalian—to make the deal happen.

Soghanalian was put in charge of obtaining the artillery by the Iraqis in 1981, and he approached several European governments before French President François Mitterrand agreed to sell 155 mm howitzers to Iraq. The Reagan administration, through a diplomatic back channel, encouraged the French to finalize the sale. The French agreed to supply the howitzers, Soghanalian said in a sworn deposition, only if they could keep their role secret. The Iranian government was holding several French hostages, and France didn't want to antagonize the Ayatollah. Soghanalian agreed to mask the real source of the arms through a series of complicated transactions known to those involved by the codeword "Vulcan."

Two reliable law enforcement officials who have been able to review highly classified U.S. intelligence files on the French howitzer sale—including documents from the CIA, the National Security Agency, the Pentagon, and the State Department—say those files show that the U.S. intelligence agencies had extensive prior knowledge of and monitored the massive howitzer sale to Iraq. It is also clear from those same files that the Reagan administration did nothing to discourage the sales.

The French-made howitzers—the most expensive, powerful, and sophisticated in the world—have since been photographed by U.S. spy satellites on the Iraq-Saudi border, aimed at allied troop positions.

WHILE THE Reagan administration was busy encouraging its European allies to ship arms to Iraq, it was simultaneously engaging in a high-level campaign to stop those same countries from arming its opponent, Iran. The effort was codenamed "Operation Staunch." Some officials associated with Operation Staunch say that, without it, Iran might have prevailed in the Iran-Iraq war.

The U.S. government official in charge of the operation was Richard Fairbanks. A longtime diplomat who served as assistant secretary of state before being named President Reagan's special envoy to the Middle East in 1982, Fairbanks had played key roles in attempts to resolve the civil war in Lebanon and build on the Camp David accords.

Fairbanks quietly made several trips to European capitals, with letters of introduction from Reagan himself, appealing to high-level officials to stop selling arms to the Khomeini regime. He had some major successes: South Korea, Italy, Portugal, Spain, and Argentina all canceled plans to sell arms to Iran after talking with Fairbanks.

When Fairbanks left the State Department in the fall of 1985, he called Operation Staunch a success: "It might not have been a 100 percent success," he told an interviewer, "but we definitely managed to stop most major weapons systems from reaching Iran from U.S. allies. By the time I returned to private law practice in September 1985, Iran's major suppliers were almost all Soviet bloc countries."

Within months of formulating and executing the U.S. tilt to Iraq as a senior State Department official, Fairbanks went to work as a paid lobbyist and adviser to the Iraqi government. Fairbanks's new employer was the Washington law firm of Paul, Hastings, Janofsky, and Walker.

According to the firm's registration form as a foreign agent, it had been retained by the Iraqi government "to provide counseling and analysis relevant to the United States' policies of interest to the government of Iraq and . . . to assist in arranging and preparing for meetings with United States elected officials." The registration statement does not list who those elected officials might have been—although the law clearly states all such contacts must be publicly disclosed.

The Justice Department record does disclose, however, that the regime of Saddam Hussein paid Fairbanks and his firm some $334,885 between early 1986 and March 1990. The records do not indicate further activities after that date. Among other things, Fairbanks provided Saddam with public relations advice free of charge in June 1987, after the Iraqis accidentally hit the U.S.S. *Stark* with a French-made Exocet missile, killing thirty-seven American sailors.

Assisting Fairbanks with the Iraqi account at the law firm was another former State Department official, James Plack. While Plack was former deputy assistant secretary of state for Near Eastern affairs, he had been an architect of the policy to tilt toward Iraq.

At the same time that Fairbanks was on the Iraqi payroll, he also served as a key foreign policy adviser to the presidential campaign of George Bush. Throughout 1988, Fairbanks was co-chairman of a group of Middle East experts who advised Bush during the campaign.

One member of the advisory group, who requested that his name not be used, said he recalls Fairbanks arguing during one panel discussion that, should Bush be elected president, "he should stay the course of the

Reagan administration and work to develop stronger relations with Iraq." The panel member says he was unaware that Fairbanks was a paid lobbyist for the Iraqi government at the time. "I don't think anyone else on the panel was any more aware than I was."

After the election, Bush rewarded Fairbanks—then still on the Iraqi payroll—with an appointment as a member of the U.S. Trade Representative's Investment Policy Advisory Committee Group. At first glance, that is only a part-time position on a panel of private citizens who advise the president on trade policy; but members of the panel are routinely provided access to highly classified intelligence information, and are required to have security clearances.

MEANWHILE, THE Iraqis were also able to receive hundreds of millions of dollars of military equipment from the U.S. directly, using a loophole in the arms embargo. Between 1985 and 1990, the Iraqis purchased from the U.S. some $782 million in "dual use" goods— matériel, ostensibly intended for civilian uses, that has military applications as well. Many of the sales were allowed by the Reagan and Bush administrations over the objections of the Pentagon, which argued they would inevitably be used for military purposes.

Commerce Department records indicate that the agency approved 273 transfer licenses for "dual use" matériel sent to Iraq between 1985 and 1990. In 1982, for example, Iraq purchased sixty Hughes Helicopters—a civilian version of the familiar, dragonfly-like chopper widely used in Vietnam by the U.S. Army—that the Iraqi government promised would only be used for civilian transport. However, an eyewitness account appearing in *Aviation Week and Space Technology* reported that at least thirty of the helicopters were being used to train military pilots. The Reagan administration did not even mount a diplomatic protest.

Sources in the defense industry familiar with the sale say that Soghanalian brokered the deal for Hughes—and received a large commission.

Despite the broken pledge of two years earlier, in 1984 the State Department approved an additional sale of forty-five Bell 214 helicopters to the Hussein regime. The Bell 214 can be converted to military purposes at a minimal cost. Iraq pledged that the helicopters would only be used for "recreation"; Soghanalian again served as the broker.

"It is beyond belief that Iraq . . . would purchase forty-five helicopters at $5 million apiece simply to transport civilian VIPs," Representative Howard Berman wrote then secretary of state George Shultz in

November 1984. "The helicopter which Iraq wishes to purchase, the 214ST, was originally designed for military purposes."

The State Department wrote back, arguing, "We believe that increased American penetration of the extremely competitive civilian aircraft market would serve the United States' interests by improving our balance of trade and lessening unemployment in the aircraft industry."

Sure enough, evidence surfaced that the helicopters were being used for military purposes. In October 1988, a *Washington Post* reporter given a tour by Iraqi authorities of the Iranian front witnessed Iraqi military pilots flying the Bell 214s. He also observed other Bells lined up at three Iraqi military air bases alongside Soviet MIGs.

The Reagan administration once again did not muster a word of protest with the Iraqi government. Privately, State Department officials defended the Iraqis, claiming the planes were only being used to transport military officials to the front. Only if they had been used in combat, the Iraqis said, would it be a violation.

Things did not improve once George Bush took office—in fact, the matériel with potential military applications sold to Iraq actually shifted into a far more alarming area—the prerequisites of weapons of mass destruction. According to confidential Pentagon documents, between 1985 and 1990 the Commerce Department ignored explicit Pentagon objections and approved more than a dozen exports to Iraq—including precursor chemicals necessary for the manufacture of nerve gas—that would be used by Saddam Hussein to enhance his ability to make chemical and nuclear war.

Stephen Bryen, who as the Pentagon's under secretary of defense for trade security policy from 1985 to 1988 oversaw the exports for the Defense Department, said: "It was routine for our recommendations to be ignored. They disregarded five years of thorough technical and intelligence evaluations by Defense and CIA. The key to all this I believe is who the businessmen and corporations were who were making huge profits from all this."

Once you've made a mass-death weapon, you need some means of delivering it to your target. On February 23, 1990, the Commerce Department allowed Internal Imaging Systems, a California company, to ship computer and related equipment to Iraq that is designed for infrared imaging enhancement. The export license was allowed despite the fact that three years earlier, CIA technical evaluations determined that the imaging system could be used for near real-time tracking of missiles.

Then the Pentagon attempted to halve the size of a shipment by Electronic Associates, a New Jersey firm that wanted to send $449,000 worth of hybrid analog computer systems used in missile wind-tunnel experiments. Indeed, the Pentagon uses the same type of system at its White Sands missile range in New Mexico.

A White House meeting was scheduled to discuss the matter. But unknown to these Pentagon officials, the hardware had already been sent to Iraq seven months earlier—with Commerce Department approval.

Only two days before the Iraqi invasion of Kuwait, a Pennsylvania firm, Homestead Engineering, obtained a Commerce Department license to export forges and computer equipment that can be used in the manufacture of 16-inch gun barrels. Such guns could deliver huge payloads to targets hundreds of miles away.

If the Iran-Iraq war served as the pretext for the U.S. tilt toward Iraq, its end did not lead the Reagan and Bush administrations to rethink the policy. The U.S. backing of Saddam, including the covert arms sales, did not moderate the dictator's behavior; it only seemed to encourage more brutality.

On August 20, 1988, the day the Iran-Iraq cease-fire went into effect, Saddam Hussein did not see a need to end the terror. Now he could mass his military forces against the troublesome Kurdish population in northern Iraq. Only five days later, Iraqi warplanes and helicopters dropped chemical weapons on villages throughout Iraqi Kurdistan.

"As described by the villagers, the bombs that fell on the morning of August 25 did not produce a large explosion," a report by the Senate Foreign Relations Committee would later relate. "Only a weak sound could be heard and then a yellowish cloud spread out from the center of the explosion and became a thin mist. The air became filled with a mixture of smells—'bad garlic,' 'rotten onions,' and 'bad apples.'

"Those who were very close to the bombs died almost instantly. Those who did not die instantly found it difficult to breathe and began to vomit. The gas stung their eyes, skin and lungs . . . Many suffered temporary blindness. Those who could not run from the growing smell, mostly the very old, the very young, died.

"The survivors who saw the dead reported that blood could be seen trickling out of the mouths of some of the bodies. A yellowish fluid could also be seen oozing out the noses and mouths of some of the dead." Ahmad Mohammed, a Kurd, recalled that day. "My mother and father were burnt; they just died and turned black."

Bashir Shemessidin testified: "In our village, 200 to 300 people died. All the animals and birds died. All the trees dried up. It smelled like something burned. The whole world turned yellow."

In the first week of September, Iraqi Minister of State Saadoun Hammadi, a member of Saddam Hussein's inner circle, came to Washington to meet with Secretary of State Shultz. The State Department, uncharacteristically, condemned the use of gas. "The Secretary today conveyed to Iraqi Minister of State Hammadi our view that Iraqi's use of chemical weapons . . . is unjustifiable and abhorrent." Such violence, the statement went on to say, was "unacceptable to the civilized world." It was one of the few public condemnations of Iraq by the Reagan administration.

But the administration did not match its rhetoric with action. The very next day, the U.S. Senate passed a tough trade sanctions bill against Iraq. The Reagan administration and Secretary Shultz lobbied vehemently against the sanctions, and they were never enacted.

Nor did the administration even make a symbolic gesture of its displeasure, such as recalling the newly arrived U.S. ambassador in Baghdad. Only a few days later, the U.S. ambassador to Bulgaria was recalled after that country's ethnic Turkish minority was mistreated—but the first use of nerve gas in history to slaughter innocent civilians merited no such rebuke.

George Bush took office a short time later. Not only did Bush fail to speak out against Iraqi human rights abuses, his policy favored Saddam's regime even more than Reagan's. Through 1988, Iraq had been provided $2.8 billion in U.S. agricultural products under the Commodity Credit Corporation (CCC) credit-guarantee program. In his first days in office, Bush *doubled* the amount of the guarantees, to about $1 billion a year.

Soon thereafter, the United Nations Human Rights Commission passed a resolution calling on Iraq to account for its use of chemical weapons against the Kurds. Twelve European nations, including Ireland, Britain, and France, were among those who sponsored the resolution for the appointment of a special rapporteur to "make a thorough study of the human rights situation in Iraq." Not only did the Bush administration not join in sponsoring the resolution; it even worked against its passage.

THE UNITED States and Iraq had an almost nonexistent relationship before Ronald Reagan became president. The Baath rule of terror required foreign enemies—and America was a popular one. As late as 1980, Saddam vowed that Americans "were the enemies of the Arab nation and the enemies of Iraq," swearing that someday he would destroy them.

Soon the Reagan administration was providing Iraq billions of dollars in U.S. credit guarantees for the purchase of agricultural and industrial goods. In 1983, the president moved to ease Iraq's ever-burgeoning war debt by providing loans through the Commodity Credit Corporation credit guarantee program, allowing Saddam's regime to purchase American grain and farm products. Through 1988, Reagan's last year in office, Saddam was awarded $2.8 billion in agricultural credits.

Next, the administration started to pressure the Export-Import Bank, a congressionally funded bank charged with promoting foreign trade, to extend loan guarantees to the Iraqis. To become eligible for the Export-Import Bank's loan guarantees, Iraq had to first be taken off the State Department's list of countries accused of sponsoring terrorism. Iraq was removed from the list in 1982 after announcing the expulsion of Abu Nidal, an official of the Popular Front for the Liberation of Palestine.

Intelligence officials say the expulsion was merely cosmetic: Abu Nidal continued to use Iraq as a base of operations.

"All the intelligence I saw indicated that the Iraqis continued to support terrorism to much the same degree they had in the past," Noel Koch, then in charge of the Pentagon's counterterrorism program, said. "We took Iraq off the list and shouldn't have done it. We did it for political reasons. The purpose had to do with the policy to tilt toward Iraq in the Iran-Iraq war."

Koch says he personally objected to the decision, as did his counterpart at the State Department, Ambassador Robert Sayre, the coordinator of counterterrorism. But it did little good. "He told me his recommendation was overruled at a higher level," Koch said.

In 1984, formal diplomatic relations were restored between the U.S. and Iraq. The following year, the two nations exchanged ambassadors for the first time in nearly two decades.

Also in 1984, the U.S. Export-Import Bank began extending Iraq short-term loan guarantees for the purchase of U.S.-manufactured goods, reversing a previous ban.

Beyond the troubling questions about Saddam's support of terrorism, the Export-Import Bank also had reservations about lending to Iraq because of its immense war debts. The bank only restored loan guarantees to Iraq after what one official calls "immense political pressure" to do so from senior Reagan administration officials.

In 1984 and 1985, the bank made some $35 million in short-term loan guarantees to Iraq. But after Iraq borrowers failed to pay back the loans on time, the bank discontinued further dealings with Saddam. Despite this, in 1987, the Reagan administration once again pressured the bank to provide an additional $135 million in short-term credit guarantees for U.S. purchases.

LAST OCTOBER 15, during a campaign stop in Dallas, President Bush held his audience captive with tales of Iraqi atrocities in Kuwait. He told of "newborn babies thrown off incubators"* and "dialysis patients ripped from their machines." He spoke passionately of "the story of two young kids passing out leaflets: Iraqi troops rounded up their parents and made them watch while these two kids were shot to death—executed before their eyes.

"Hitler revisited. But remember, when Hitler's war ended, there were the Nuremberg trials."

The president, appearing decisive and defiant, told the crowd, "America will not stand aside."

But in April 1989—long before the invasion of Kuwait but long after George Bush had assumed the presidency—Amnesty International had found the torture of children so pervasive in Iraq that it devoted an entire report to the subject. Iraqi children were routinely subjected to "extractions of fingernails, beatings, whippings, sexual abuse, and electrical shock treatment" as well as "beatings with metal cables while naked and suspended by the wrists from the ceiling." Young girls had "been found hung upside down from the feet during menstruation" with "objects inserted into their vaginas." The report told of the summary execution of twenty-nine young children from one village. When the bodies of those children were returned to their families, "some of the victims had their eyes gouged out."

What did George Bush have to say then? Nothing; he made no public comment on the report.

Just six months later, Bush assistant secretary for Near Eastern and South Asian affairs John Kelly gave a major policy address on Iraq. He, too, did not have a single word to say about Iraq's torture of children, or even the more general topic of human rights. Rather, reflecting the policy of his president, he simply stated, "Iraq is an important state with great potential. We want to deepen and broaden our relationship."

---

* Editors' note: Doubts about the truth of this atrocity were first raised by Alexander Cockburn in his "Beat the Devil" column in the February 4, 1991, issue of *The Nation*. And as Chris Hedges reported in *The New York Times* on February 28 from liberated Kuwait, "Hospital officials said that stories circulated about the killing of 300 children were incorrect."

PRELUDE TO WAR

KUWAIT: HOW THE WEST BLUNDERED

The Economist

I N   R E T R O S P E C T , the first signal, back in February 1990, was one of the clearest. But none of the analysts at Foggy Bottom took proper notice, so the thing we are going to call "The Conception" continued to grow and prosper inside the State Department. It survived, despite four later signals, until the night of August 1st–2nd, when the leading T-72 tanks of Saddam Hussein's Republican Guard churned across the sand toward Kuwait City.

The first signal may have been overlooked because, back in February, nobody was paying much attention to Jordan. Bar some agency photographers who had flown reluctantly up from Cairo, few Western journalists were on hand to notice the arrival of Iraq's president at Amman airport. Ever fearful of assassination, he came in an unmarked executive jet, having sent ahead an airliner packed with underlings. Jordan's King Hussein swathed him in kisses and led him down a red carpet to review an honor guard from the Arab Legion. Egypt's President Hosni Mubarak had received the same welcome less than an hour earlier.

Egypt and Iraq are the strongest powers of the Arab world. Meetings between their presidents are carefully monitored. Yet the Amman meeting was expected to be dull. The occasion was the first birthday of the Arab Cooperation Council (ACC), a new regional club dear to the heart of Jordan's king but of marginal interest to Egypt, Iraq, and (the then) North Yemen, its other members. The Jordanians put on a good show: The Army closed down whole sections of Amman, and the comings and goings dominated Jordanian television. By and large nobody else seemed much interested.

This article was published, without byline, in the September 29, 1990, issue of *The Economist*.

Yet something curious happened in Amman. To King Hussein's evident distress, the meeting broke up a day early.

The official excuse was that some of the assembled dignitaries had urgent business elsewhere. The real reason was that President Mubarak took exception to a speech by President Hussein, broadcast on Jordanian television on February 24th.

Much of the speech had been the usual windy rhetoric about the achievements of the ACC and the ever-present need for pan-Arab solidarity. But one passage was different. Drawing attention to the waning power of the Soviet Union, the Iraqi president predicted that for five years the United States would enjoy unusual freedom of maneuver in the Middle East. It would, he declared, use this freedom to the detriment of the Arabs. Were not the Americans helping Soviet Jews emigrate to Israel? Had they not kept their warships on patrol in the Gulf, despite the end of the Iran-Iraq war? The reason for these things, said Mr. Hussein, was clear:

> The country that will have the greatest influence in the region, through the Arab Gulf and its oil, will maintain its superiority as a superpower without an equal to compete with it. This means that if the Gulf people, along with all Arabs, are not careful, the Arab Gulf region will be governed by the wishes of the United States. . . . [Oil] prices would be fixed in line with a special perspective benefiting American interests and ignoring the interests of others.

The answer, said Mr. Hussein, was to use the oil money that Arabs had invested in the West to enforce changes in American policy. Perhaps it should be withdrawn and re-invested in the Soviet Union and Eastern Europe. Either way, there was no place among "good" Arabs for "the faint-hearted who would argue that, as a superpower, the United States will be the decisive factor and others have no choice but to submit."

Although a whiff of anti-Americanism is expected on such occasions, the tone of this speech ought to have sounded an alarm. It visibly angered Mr. Mubarak, America's main Arab ally and the grateful recipient of nearly $2 billion a year of American aid. It called into question—or should have—the received wisdom that the ACC would become a new force for moderation in the Middle East. And it showed a side of Saddam Hussein that most Iraq-watchers had hoped was extinct: Saddam as the would-be master of the Gulf. All of this should have been noticed. But The Conception got in the way.

What Conception? Toward the end of his eight-year war against Iran,

Western Saddam-watchers had started a debate about the big change the war had wrought in him and his country. Before invading Iran in 1980, Iraq was a pro-Soviet Middle East "radical." In 1978, it had taken the lead in punishing Egypt for seeking peace with Israel. It was a sanctuary for the deadliest Palestinian terror gangs. And it made no secret of its wish to challenge both Iran and the weaker Arab states to the south for mastery of the Gulf.

By the end of the war Iraq was behaving quite differently. Its economy was tied more closely to the West than to the Soviet Union. Its arsenal now bristled with Western as well as Soviet weapons. Israel, President Hussein had begun to hint, was a marginal issue: He would endorse whatever peace deal satisfied the Palestinians. Relations with Saudi Arabia, Kuwait, and the other Gulf Arabs had never been better. Historically fearful of Iraq and Iran alike, the Gulf Arabs had at last decided to back their Arab brother. In return, Mr. Hussein seemed ready to leave them in peace.

The argument among observers was not whether these changes had happened, but how long they would last. One school of opinion considered Mr. Hussein a reformed character; the war had taught him the limits of Iraqi power and thus trimmed his youthful ambitions. Another, the artful-dodger school, argued that he was playing the moderate only to drum up Western support against Iran. After victory, the same old Saddam would emerge with all his previous ambitions intact.

Some of his postwar actions should have strengthened the artful-dodger view of the Iraqi president. He started meddling in Lebanon, suggesting a continuing taste for foreign adventures. The razing of Iraq's Kurdish villages showed he was as ruthless as ever with internal opponents. Yet by the start of 1990 the reformed-character analysis was accepted. America's State Department and Britain's Foreign Office felt that Saddam was a chastened man, aware of the limits of Iraq's power and eager to bind his country to the West.

Thanks to The Conception, Mr. Hussein's Amman speech was not interpreted as a challenge to the United States. Most Iraq experts preferred to see it as a sign of his own nervousness. His mistreatment of the Kurds—and the possibility of sanctions—had become a talking point in the American Congress. Word had come out of a meeting between the State Department and the Kurdish leader, Jalal Talabani. The Voice of America had run a broadcast criticising Iraq's secret police. No wonder the reformed character was worried. What he needed was reassurance, not retribution.

The second signal came on April 2, when Mr. Hussein proudly announced that Iraqi scientists had developed advanced chemical weapons. "By God," he added, "we will make the fire eat up half of Israel, if it tries to do anything against Iraq." This time the State Department's response was swift. A State Department spokesman called the threat "inflammatory, outrageous and irresponsible." Israel hinted that an Iraqi chemical attack could provoke an Israeli nuclear strike. The second signal had been received loud and clear. But was its meaning properly understood?

Perhaps not. In May, a group of Israeli foreign-policy experts paid a quiet visit to London and Washington. They were worried. In their view Iraq's recent behavior showed that the reformed character was really just the artful dodger after all. Between February and April, Mr. Hussein had demanded the withdrawal of the American Navy from the Gulf, called on fellow Arabs to reactivate the oil weapon, and threatened not just to attack Israel—America's main ally in the region—but to burn it with chemical weapons. Add Iraq's challenge to Syria in Lebanon, plus a relentless arms build-up, and the evidence was plain: the bad old pre-war Iraq was back again.

The Israeli visitors failed to budge The Conception. The view in the State Department and Foreign Office was that the burn-Israel threat, like the Amman speech, was mainly a sign of Iraqi nervousness. In March, Mr. Hussein had been fiercely criticised in the West for the hanging of a journalist from Britain and for trying to buy triggers that could be used in a nuclear bomb. Perhaps, said the apologists, the reformed character was being honest when he claimed to see the Western agitation as the prelude to a repeat of Israel's 1981 air strike at Iraq's nuclear facilities, and was simply warning Israel off.

The third signal, from May's Arab League summit meeting in Baghdad, was harder to detect. This time it was masked by a lot of noise. Yet, once heard, its purport should have been clear enough.

The League had convened the summit for two purposes: to denounce the influx of Soviet Jews to Israel and to support Mr. Hussein's burn-Israel speech. Just before the kings and presidents arrived in Iraq's capital, an Israeli had shot dead seven Palestinian workers near Tel Aviv, and the Americans had blocked a PLO proposal that international observers be sent to the occupied territories. Anti-American feeling ran high. President Mubarak worked hard on America's behalf, but Iraq's leader was the hero of the hour. Not since Nasser had an Arab leader uttered such chilling, and chillingly plausible, threats against Israel. Arabs everywhere were thrilled.

However, in a private session of the summit it was not Israel but his fellow Arabs that Mr. Hussein denounced. Some of the Gulf states, he said, were keeping the price of oil too low by pumping too much of it. Since every dollar off the price of a barrel cost Iraq $1 billion a year in lost revenues, this was an "economic war" on Iraq. Though none of this outburst was made public, the British and Americans quickly learnt about it. What they did not do was pay careful attention to it.

Could the world have known, in the first half of 1990, that Mr. Hussein was planning to invade Kuwait? Quite likely not: He may not even have been planning yet, let alone have decided to go ahead. But what should have been plain after the Baghdad summit was that not just American "imperialism" (signal one) and Israel (signal two) but also the Gulf Arabs (signal three) had something to fear from the supposedly re-formed character. Unfortunately, the feedback that Mr. Hussein received from his first three signals gave him a misleading impression.

When the Iraqi leader equated America with "imperialism" at the end of February, it was the first time he had done so for a decade. His call on the American Navy to leave the Gulf came when only half-a-dozen war-ships were still there, down from fifty at the height of the Gulf war—a war in which (except for the Iran-Contra aberration) America had tilted Iraq's way. By calling the Americans imperialists, bent on dominating the Middle East, Mr. Hussein was, to say the least, being ungrateful. He got no response.

April's threat to Israel drew harsh words from the State Department. Ten days later, though, five American senators, headed by the Republican leader, Mr. Robert Dole, met Mr. Hussein in the Iraqi city of Mosul. They handed over a letter denouncing his quest for nuclear and chemical weapons. But the Iraqis, who bugged the room, later released a transcript which suggested that the senators had fawned on the dictator.

Mr. Dole represents Kansas, a big exporter of grain to Iraq. He told Mr. Hussein that the Voice of America journalist responsible for criticising Iraq's secret police had been sacked. Mr. Alan Simpson, from Wyoming, said Mr. Hussein's problems were not with America's people but with its "haughty and pampered" press. A fortnight later Mr. John Kelly, the State Department's undersecretary for Middle East affairs, was on Capitol Hill, fighting congressional moves to impose economic sanctions. His argument: Events since February had indeed "raised new questions about Iraqi intentions in the region," but sanctions would impair the administration's ability to exert "a restraining influence." He was repeating this refrain until the week before Iraq's tanks rumbled into Kuwait.

If America's reply to the burn-Israel speech was a muddle, the Arab reply was as clear as a bell. Within three days of the threat, the foreign ministers of the ACC had stoutly defended his right to make it. King Hussein of Jordan agreed with Iraq that it was the victim of a Zionist plot. Even the Syrians, Iraq's arch-rivals, were impressed by the Iraqi leader's bellicosity. Poison gas plus anti-Zionist bluster had turned him into the new Saladin. No wonder he began to feel his fellow Arabs would let him get away with anything. They bear a heavy responsibility for what followed.

After the fourth signal there could be no excuse for calling the invasion of Kuwait a surprise. This signal came during Mr. Hussein's Revolution Day speech on July 17. In it he combined all his themes of the previous six months in a ferocious attack on Kuwait and the United Arab Emirates. Iraq, he said, had become the Arabs' one reliable defender. Thanks to its new weapons, the imperialists no longer dared to launch a military attack on it, so had turned to economic warfare instead. Imperialism's agents were those Gulf rulers whose policy of keeping oil prices low was "a poisoned dagger" thrust into Iraq's back.

The day before the speech, Iraq sent a more detailed tally of grievances to the secretary-general of the Arab League. They went beyond the overproduction of oil. Iraq accused Kuwait of planting military posts inside Iraq and stealing from an Iraqi oilfield. Both Kuwait and the UAE were indeed, said the note, part of "an imperialist-Zionist plot against the Arab nation." It all sounded, said *The Economist* on July 21, "alarmingly like a pretext for invasion."

On July 24, in chilling confirmation, came the fifth and final signal. Two Iraqi armoured divisions moved from their bases to positions on Kuwait's border.

On July 25 America's ambassador in Baghdad, Ms. April Glaspie, was summoned to her now-famous conversation with Mr. Hussein. The Iraqi transcript of the meeting (America has not released its own version) has her listening to a belligerent exposition of the Iraqi dictator's grievances. Her response was, well, diplomatic.

It was a privilege, she said, to meet the president himself. Americans too had confronted colonialism. They understood Iraq's desire for dearer oil to strengthen its economy. The United States took no sides in the border dispute with Kuwait. If Mr. Hussein were to spend just five minutes on American television, this "would help us to make the American people understand Iraq." But, after these and other nonsenses, Ms. Glaspie did at last ask—"in the spirit of friendship, not of confrontation" —why Iraqi troops were massing on the border.

Mr. Hussein's answer was that he had just spoken to Egypt's President

Mubarak on the telephone, and completed arrangements for "a protocol meeting" in Saudi Arabia between the Kuwaiti prime minister and a senior Iraqi official. The meeting would then transfer "for deeper discussion" to Baghdad. Mr. Mubarak, confided Mr. Hussein, had told him that the Kuwaitis were scared by the troop concentrations:

> I said to him that, regardless of what is there . . . assure the Kuwaitis and give them our word that we are not going to do anything until we meet with them. When we meet and when we see that there is hope, then nothing will happen. But if we are unable to find a solution, then it will be natural that Iraq will not accept death, even though wisdom is above everything else. There you have the good news.

Lamentably—if the Iraqi record is correct—this satisfied Ms. Glaspie. She knew that Egypt's president had visited Mr. Hussein in Baghdad the day before. Now she knew that Mr. Hussein had promised him not to invade Kuwait until talks had been given a chance. The American assumption was that the Iraqi tanks were meant to intimidate Kuwait at the negotiating table, and that they would probably succeed in doing so. Hardly good news, maybe, but—evidently—tolerable.

Yet Ms. Glaspie knew that the threat of invasion was still there. Even so, she—that is, the United States—did not warn the Iraqi president of what could happen, and has, if he put it into effect: that America would send a mighty army ready to hit back.

On August 1, Mr. Hussein kept, but only half-kept, his promise to give talks a chance. Kuwait's crown prince, Sheikh Saad al-Sabah, met the vice chairman of Iraq's Revolutionary Command Council, Mr. Izzat Ibrahim, in Jidda, the Saudi summer capital. But the "protocol" talks collapsed, and the promised second round, in Baghdad, was never allowed to happen. Early on August 2 Iraq's invasion began.

Some of the State Department's critics now say Ms. Glaspie's interview with President Hussein was the final, fatal sign of American weakness that tempted him over the brink. Maybe. He had hinted he would fight if talking failed; she had said the United States took no sides in this quarrel between Arabs. But it is too simple to pin the blame on one interview, let alone one ambassador.

For five months, from his speech in Amman in February until he marched into Kuwait in August, the assumption that Mr. Hussein was a reformed character established a pattern. He would do or say something outrageous. Western experts would warn their governments not to over-react. The underreaction was then construed in Baghdad as weakness. "In Saddam's world, when you issue a threat you expect to get a counter threat," says Professor Amatzia Baram, of Haifa University. "If you don't, it means weakness, appeasement and eventually retreat."

REALPOLITIK IN THE GULF:
A GAME GONE TILT

Christopher Hitchens

O N   T H E   M O R N I N G before Yom Kippur late this past September, I found myself standing at the western end of the White House, watching as the color guard paraded the flag of the United States (and the republic for which it stands) along with that of the Emirate of Kuwait. The young men of George Bush's palace guard made a brave showing, but their immaculate uniforms and webbing could do little but summon the discomforting contrasting image—marching across our TV screens nightly—of their hot, thirsty, encumbered brothers and sisters in the Saudi Arabian desert. I looked away and had my attention fixed by a cortege of limousines turning in at the gate. There was a quick flash of dark beard and white teeth, between burnoose and kaffiyeh, as Sheikh Jabir al-Ahmad al-Sabah, the exiled Kuwaiti emir, scuttled past a clutch of photographers and through the portals. End of photo op, but not of story.

Let us imagine a photograph of the emir of Kuwait entering the White House, and let us see it as a historian might years from now. What might such a picture disclose under analysis? How did this oleaginous monarch, whose very name was unknown just weeks before to most members of the Bush administration and the Congress, never mind most newspaper editors, reporters, and their readers, become a crucial visitor—perhaps *the* crucial visitor—on the president's autumn calendar? How did he emerge as someone on whose behalf the president was preparing to go to war?

Christopher Hitchens is the Washington editor of *Harper's* and writes the "Minority Report" column for *The Nation*. He is the author of several books, most recently, *Blood, Class and Nostalgia: Anglo-American Ironies*. This article was originally published in the January 1991 issue of *Harper's*.

We know already, as every historian will, that the president, in having the emir come by, was not concerned with dispelling any impression that he was the one who had "lost Kuwait" to Iraq in early August. The tiny kingdom had never been understood as "ours" to lose, as far as the American people and their representatives knew. Those few citizens who did know Kuwait (human-rights monitors, scholars, foreign correspondents) knew it was held together by a relatively loose yet unmistakably persistent form of feudalism. It could have been "lost" only by its sole owners, the al-Sabah family, not by the United States or by the "Free World."

What a historian might make of our imaginary photo document of this moment in diplomatic history that most citizens surely would not is that it is, in fact, less a discrete snapshot than a still from an epic movie—a dark and bloody farce, one that chronicles the past two decades of U.S. involvement in the Persian Gulf. Call the film *Rules of the Game of Nations* or *Metternich of Arabia*—you get the idea. In this particular scene, the president was meeting at the White House with the emir to send a "signal" to Iraqi President Saddam Hussein that he, Bush, "stood with" Kuwait in wanting Iraq to pull out its troops. After the meeting, Bush emerged to meet the press, not alone but with his national security adviser, Brent Scowcroft. This, of course, was a signal, too: Bush meant business, of a potentially military kind. In the game of nations, however, one does not come right out and *say* one is signaling (that would, by definition, no longer be signaling); one waits for reporters to ask about signals, one denies signaling is going on, and then one trusts that unnamed White House aides and State Department officials will provide the desired "spin" and perceptions of "tilt."

On ordinary days the trivial and empty language of Washington isn't especially awful. The drizzle of repetitive key words—"perception," "agenda," "address," "concern," "process," "bipartisan"—does its job of masking and dulling reality. But on this rather important day in an altogether unprecedented process—a lengthy and deliberate preparation for a full-scale ground and air war in a faraway region—there was not a word from George Bush—not a *word*—that matched the occasion. Instead, citizens and soldiers alike would read or hear inane questions from reporters, followed by boilerplate answers from their president and interpretations by his aides, about whether the drop-by of a feudal potentate had or had not signaled this or that intent.

There is a rank offense here to the idea of measure and proportion. Great matters of power and principle are in play, and there does in fact exist a chance to evolve a new standard for international relations rather than persist in the old follies of superpower *raisons d'état;* and still the official tongue stammers and barks. Behind all the precious, brittle, Beltway in-talk lies the only idea young Americans will die for in the desert: the idea that in matters of foreign policy, even in a democratic republic, the rule is "leave it to us." Not everybody, after all, can be fitted out with the wildly expensive stealth equipment that the political priesthood requires to relay and decipher the signal flow.

THE WORD concocted in the nineteenth century for this process—the shorthand of Palmerston and Metternich—was "realpolitik." Maxims of cynicism and realism—to the effect that great states have no permanent friends or permanent principles, but only permanent interests—became common currency in post-Napoleonic Europe. Well, there isn't a soul today in Washington who doesn't pride himself on the purity of his realpolitik. And an organization supposedly devoted to the study and promulgation of such nineteenth-century realism—the firm of Henry Kissinger Associates—has furnished the Bush administration with several of its high officers, including Brent Scowcroft and Deputy Secretary of State Lawrence Eagleburger, along with much of its expertise.

Realpolitik, with its tilts and signals, is believed by the faithful to keep nations from war, balancing the powers and interests, as they say. Is what we are witnessing in the Persian Gulf, then, the breakdown and failure of realpolitik? Well, yes and no. Yes, in the sense that American troops have been called upon to restore the balance that existed before August 2, 1990. But that regional status quo has for the past two decades known scarcely a day of peace—in the Persian Gulf, it has been a balance of terror for a long time. Realpolitik, as practiced by Washington, has played no small part in this grim situation.

To even begin to understand this, one must get beyond today's tilts and signals and attempt to grasp a bit of history—something the realpoliticians are loath for you to do. History is for those clutching values and seeking truths; realpolitik has little time for such sentiment. The world, after all, is a cold place requiring hard calculation, detachment.

LEAFING THROUGH the history of Washington's contemporary involvement in the Gulf, one might begin to imagine the cool detachment in 1972 of arch-realpolitician Henry Kissinger, then national security adviser to Richard Nixon. I have before me as I write a copy of the report of the House Select Committee on Intelligence Activities chaired by Congressman Otis Pike, completed in January 1976, partially leaked, and then censored by the White House and the CIA. The committee found that in 1972 Kissinger had met with the shah of Iran, who solicited his aid in destabilizing the Baathist regime of Ahmad Hassan al-Bakr in Baghdad. Iraq had given refuge to the then-exiled Ayatollah Khomeini and used anti-imperialist rhetoric while coveting Iran's Arabic-speaking Khuzistan region. The shah and Kissinger agreed that Iraq was upsetting the balance in the Gulf; a way to restore the balance—or, anyway, to find some new balance—was to send a signal by supporting the landless, luckless Kurds, then in revolt in northern Iraq.

Kissinger put the idea to Nixon, who loved (and loves still) the game of nations and who had already decided to tilt toward Iran and build it into his most powerful regional friend, replete with arms purchased from U.S. manufacturers—not unlike Saudi Arabia today, but more on that later. Nixon authorized a covert-action budget and sent John Connally, his former Treasury secretary, to Teheran to cement the deal. (So the practice of conducting American Middle East policy by way of the free-masonry of the shady oilmen did not originate with James Baker or George Bush. As the U.S. ambassador to Iraq, April Glaspie, confided to Saddam Hussein in her now-famous meeting last July 25, almost as though giving a thumbnail profile of her bosses: "We have many Americans who would like to see the price go above $25 because they come from oil-producing states." Much more later on *that* tête-à-tête.)

The principal finding of the Pike Commission, in its study of U.S. covert intervention in Iraq and Iran in the early 1970s, is a clue to a good deal of what has happened since. The committee members found, to their evident shock, the following:

> Documents in the Committee's possession clearly show that the President, Dr. Kissinger and the foreign head of state [the shah] hoped that our clients [the Kurds] would not prevail. They preferred instead that the insurgents simply continue a level of hostilities sufficient to sap the resources of our ally's neighboring country [Iraq].

Official prose in Washington can possess a horror and immediacy of its own, as is shown by the sentence that follows:

> This policy was not imparted to our clients, who were encouraged to continue fighting.

"Not imparted." *"Not imparted"* to the desperate Kurdish villagers to whom Kissinger's envoys came with outstretched hands and practiced grins. "Not imparted," either, to the American public or to Congress. "Imparted," though, to the shah and to Saddam Hussein (then the Baathists' number-two man), who met and signed a treaty temporarily ending their border dispute in 1975—thus restoring balance in the region. On that very day, all U.S. aid to the Kurds was terminated—a decision that, of course, "imparted" itself to Saddam. On the next day he launched a search-and-destroy operation in Kurdistan that has been going on ever since and that, in the town of Halabja in 1988, made history by marking the first use of chemical weaponry by a state against its own citizens.*

By the by, which realpolitician was it who became director of the CIA in the period—January 1976—when the Kurdish operation was being hastily interred, the Kurds themselves were being mopped up by Saddam, and the Pike Commission report was restricted? He happens to be the same man who now wants you to believe Saddam is suddenly "worse than Hitler." But forget it; everybody else has.

SOMETHING OF the same application of superpower divide-and-rule principles—no war but no peace, low-intensity violence yielding no clear victor or loser, the United States striving for a policy of Mutual Assured Destabilization—seems to turn up in Persian Gulf history once again four years later. Only now the United States has tilted away from Iran and is signaling Saddam Hussein. Iranians of all factions are convinced that the United States actively encouraged Iraq to attack their country on September 22, 1980. It remains unclear exactly what the U.S. role was in this invasion; but there is ample evidence of the presence of our old friends, wink and nod.

Recently, I raised the matter of September 1980 tilts and signals with Admiral Stansfield Turner, who was CIA director at the time, and with Gary Sick, who then had responsibility for Gulf policy at the National Security Council. Admiral Turner did not, he said, have any evidence that the Iraqis had cleared their invasion of Iran with Washington. He could say, however, that the CIA had known of an impending invasion and had advised President Jimmy Carter accordingly. Sick recalled that Iraq and the United States had broken diplomatic relations in 1967 during the Arab-Israeli Six-Day War, so that no official channels of communication were available.

Such contact as there was, Sick told me, ran through Saudi Arabia and, interestingly enough, Kuwait. This, if anything, gave greater scope to

* See note on page 80.

those who like dealing in tilts and signals. Prominent among them was realpol (by way of Trilateralism) Zbigniew Brzezinski, who was then Carter's national security adviser. As Sick put it: "After the hostages were taken in Teheran [in November 1979], there was a very strong view, especially from Brzezinski, that in effect Iran should be punished from all sides. He made public statements to the effect that he would not mind an Iraqi move against Iran." A fall 1980 story in London's *Financial Times* took things a little further, reporting that U.S. intelligence and satellite data—data purporting to show that Iranian forces would swiftly crack—had been made available to Saddam through third-party Arab governments.

All the available evidence, in other words, points in a single direction. The United States knew that Iraq was planning an assault on a neighboring country and, at the very least, took no steps to prevent it. For purposes of comparison, imagine Washington's response if Saddam Hussein had launched an attack when the shah ruled Iran. Or, to bring matters up to date, ask yourself why Iraq's 1980 assault was not a violation of international law or an act of naked aggression that "would not stand."

Sick cautioned me not to push the evidence too far because, as he said, the actual scale of the invasion came as a surprise. "We didn't think he'd take all of Khuzistan in 1980," he said of Saddam. But nobody is suggesting that anyone expected an outright Iraqi victory. By switching sides, and by supplying arms to both belligerents over the next decade, the U.S. national security establishment may have been acting consistently rather than inconsistently. A market for weaponry, the opening of avenues of influence, the creation of superpower dependency, the development of clientele among the national security forces of other nations, and a veto on the emergence of any rival power—these were the tempting prizes.

How else to explain the simultaneous cosseting of both Iran and Iraq during the 1980s? The backstairs dealing with the Ayatollah is a matter of record. The adoption of Saddam Hussein by the power worshipers and influence peddlers of Washington, D.C., is less well remembered. How many daily readers of *The New York Times* recall that paper's 1975 characterization of Iraq as "pragmatic, cooperative," with credit for this shift going to Saddam's "personal strength"? How many lobbyists and arms peddlers spent how many evenings during the eighties at the Washington dinner table of Iraq's U.S. ambassador, Nizar Hamdoon? And how often, do you imagine, was Hamdoon asked even the most delicately phrased question about his government's continued killing of the Kurds, including unarmed women and children; its jailing and routine torturing of political prisoners during the 1980s; its taste for the summary trial and swift execution?

It can be amusing to look up some of Saddam's former fans. Allow me to open for you the April 27, 1987, issue of *The New Republic,* where we find an essay engagingly entitled "Back Iraq," by Daniel Pipes and Laurie Mylroie. These two distinguished Establishment interpreters, under the unavoidable subtitle "It's time for a U.S. 'tilt,' " managed to anticipate the recent crisis by more than three years. Sadly, they got the name of the enemy wrong:

> The fall of the existing regime in Iraq would enormously enhance Iranian influence, endanger the supply of oil, threaten pro-American regimes throughout the area, and upset the Arab-Israeli balance.

But they always say that, don't they, when the think tanks start thinking tanks? I could go on, but mercy forbids—though neither mercy nor modesty has inhibited Pipes from now advocating, in stridently similar terms, the prompt obliteration of all works of man in Iraq.

EVEN AS the Iraqi ambassador in Washington was cutting lucrative swaths through "the procurement community," and our policy intellectuals were convincing one another that Saddam Hussein could be what the shah had been until he suddenly was not, other forces (nod, wink) were engaged in bribing Iran and irritating Iraq. Take the diary entry for May 15, 1986, made by Oliver North in his later-subpoenaed notebook. The childish scrawl reads:

- —Vaughan Forrest
- —Gene Wheatin w/Forrest
- —SAT flights to
- —Rob/Flacko disc. of Remington
- —Sarkis/Cunningham/Cline/Secord
- —Close to Sen. Hugh Scott
- —TF 157, Wilson, Terpil et al blew up Letier
- —Cunningham running guns to Baghdad for CIA, then weaps, to Teheran
- —Secord running guns to Iran

This tabulation contains the names of almost every senior Middle East gunrunner. The penultimate line is especially interesting, I think, because it so succinctly evokes the "two track" balancing act under way in Iran and Iraq. That tens of thousands of young Arabs and Persians were actually dying on the battlefield . . . but forget that too.

We now understand from sworn testimony that when North and Robert McFarlane, President Reagan's former national security adviser, went with cake and Bible to Teheran in May 1986, they were pressed by their Iranian hosts to secure the release of militant Shiite prisoners held in Kuwait. Their freedom had been the price demanded by those who held American hostages in Beirut. Speaking with the authority of his president, North agreed with the Iranians, explaining later that "there is a need for a non-hostile regime in Baghdad" and noting that the Iranians knew "we can bring our influence to bear with certain friendly Arab nations" to get rid of Saddam Hussein.

Bringing influence to bear, North entered into a negotiation on the hostage exchange, the disclosure of which, Reagan's Secretary of State George Shultz said later, "made me sick to my stomach." North met the Kuwaiti foreign minister and later told the Iranians that the Shiite prisoners in Kuwait would be released if Iran dropped its support for groups hostile to the emir. When Saddam learned of the deed, which took place at the height of his war with Iran, he must have been quite fascinated.

It's at about this point, I suspect, that eyes start to glaze, consciences start to coarsen, and people start to talk about "ropes and sand" and the general inpenetrability of the Muslim mind. This reaction is very convenient to those who hope to keep the waters muddy. It is quite clear that Saddam Hussein had by the late 1980s learned, or been taught, two things. The first is that the United States will intrigue against him when he is weak. The second is that it will grovel before him when he is strong. The all-important corollary is: The United States is a country that deals only in furtive signals.

IT IS AGAINST this backdrop—one of signals and nods and tilts and intrigues—and *not* against that of Bush's anger at Iraqi aggression (he is angry, but only because realpolitik has failed him) that one must read the now-famous transcript of the Glaspie-Saddam meeting last July. Keep in mind, too, that at this point, just a bit more than a week before Iraqi troops marched into Kuwait, Glaspie is speaking under instructions, and the soon-to-be "Butcher of Baghdad" is still "Mr. President."

The transcript has seventeen pages. For the first eight and a half of these, Saddam Hussein orates without interruption. He makes his needs and desires very plain in the matter of Kuwait, adding two things that haven't been noticed in the general dismay over the document. First, he borrows the method of a Coppola godfather to remind Glaspie that the United States has shown sympathy in the near past for his land and oil complaints against Kuwait:

> In 1974, I met with Idriss, the son of Mullah Mustafa Barzani [the Kurdish leader]. He sat in the same seat as you are sitting now. He came asking me to postpone implementation of autonomy in Iraqi Kurdistan, which was agreed on March 11, 1970. My reply was: We are determined to fulfill our obligation. You also have to stick to your agreement.

After carrying on in this vein, and making it clear that Kuwait may go the way of Kurdistan, Saddam closes by saying he hopes that President Bush will read the transcript himself, "and will not leave it in the hands of a gang in the State Department. I exclude the secretary of state and [Assistant Secretary of State John] Kelly, because I know him and I exchanged views with him."

Now, the very first thing that Ambassador Glaspie says, in a recorded discussion that Saddam Hussein has announced he wishes relayed directly to the White House and the non-gang elements at Foggy Bottom, is this:

> I clearly understand your message. We studied history at school. They taught us to say freedom or death. I think you know well that we as a people have our experience with the colonialists.

The confused semiotics of American diplomacy seem to have compelled Glaspie to say that she gets his "message" (or signal) rather than that she simply understands him. But the "message" she *conveys* in that last sentence is surely as intriguing as the message she receives. She is saying that she realizes (as many Americans are finally beginning to) that one large problem with the anomalous borders of the Gulf is the fact that they were drawn to an obsolete British colonial diagram. That fact has been the essence of Iraq's grudge against Kuwait at least since 1961. For Saddam Hussein, who has been agitating against "the colonialists" for most of his life, the American ambassador's invocation of Patrick Henry in this context had to be more than he hoped for.

But wait. She goes even further to assure him:

> We have no opinion on the Arab-Arab conflicts, like your border disagreement with Kuwait. I was in the American embassy in Kuwait

during the late 60s. The instruction we had during this period was that we should express no opinion on this issue, and that the issue is not associated with America. *James Baker has directed our official spokesmen to emphasize this instruction.* [Italics mine.]

I used to slightly know Ambassador Glaspie, who is exactly the type of foreign-service idealist and professional that a man like James Baker does not deserve to have in his employ. Like Saddam, Baker obviously felt more comfortable with John Kelly as head of his Middle East department. And why shouldn't he? Kelly had shown the relevant qualities of sinuous, turncoat adaptability—acting as a "privacy channel" worker for Oliver North while ostensibly U.S. ambassador to Beirut and drawing a public reprimand from George Shultz for double-crossing his department and his undertaking, to say nothing of helping to trade the American hostages in that city. Raw talent of this kind—a man to do business with—evidently does not go unnoticed in either the Bush or Saddam administration.

Baker did not have even the dignity of a Shultz when, appearing on a Sunday morning talk show shortly after the Iraqi invasion, he softly disowned Glaspie by saying that his clear instructions to her in a difficult embassy at a crucial time were among "probably 312,000 cables or so that go out under my name." Throughout, the secretary has been as gallant as he has been honest.

The significant detail in Ambassador Glaspie's much more candid post-invasion interview with *The New York Times* was the disclosure that "we never expected they would take all of Kuwait." This will, I hope, remind you that Gary Sick and his Carter-team colleagues did not think Iraq would take all of Iran's Khuzistan region. And those with a medium-term grasp of history might recall as well how General Alexander Haig was disconcerted by General Ariel Sharon's 1982 dash beyond the agreed-upon southern portion of Lebanon all the way to Beirut. In the world of realpolitik there is always the risk that those signaled will see nothing but green lights.

A revised border with Kuwait was self-evidently part of the price that Washington had agreed to pay in its long-standing effort to make a pet of Saddam Hussein. Yet ever since the fateful day when he too greedily took Washington at its word, and the emir of Kuwait and his extended family were unfeelingly translated from yacht people to boat people, Washington has been waffling about the rights of the Kuwaiti (and now, after all these years, Kurdish) victims. Let the record show, via the Glaspie transcript, that the Bush administration had a chance to consider these rights and these peoples in advance, and coldly abandoned them.

And may George Bush someday understand that a president cannot confect a principled call to war—"hostages," "Hitler," "ruthless dictator," "naked aggression"—when matters of principle have never been the issue for him and his type. On August 2, Saddam Hussein opted out of the game of nations. He'd had enough. As he told Glaspie:

> These better [U.S.-Iraqi] relations have suffered from various rifts. The worst of these was in 1986, only two years after establishing relations, with what was known as Irangate, which happened during the year that Iran occupied [Iraq's] Fao peninsula.

Saddam quit the game—he'd had it with tilt and signal—and the president got so mad he could kill and, with young American men and women as his proxies, he killed.

Today, the tilt is toward Saudi Arabia. A huge net of bases and garrisons has been thrown over the Kingdom of Saud, with a bonanza in military sales and a windfall (for some) in oil prices to accompany it. This tilt, too, has its destabilizing potential. But the tilt also has its compensations, not the least being that the realpoliticians might still get to call the global shots from Washington. Having taken the diplomatic lead, engineered the U.N. Security Council resolutions, pressured the Saudis to let in foreign troops, committed the bulk of these troops, and established itself as the only credible source of intelligence and interpretation of Iraqi plans and mood, the Bush administration publicly hailed a new multilateralism. Privately, Washington's realpols gloated: *We* were the superpower—deutsche marks and yen be damned.

GENERALLY, IT must be said that realpolitik has been better at dividing than at ruling. Take it as a whole since Kissinger called on the shah in 1972, and see what the harvest has been. The Kurds have been further dispossessed, further reduced in population, and made the targets of chemical experiments. Perhaps half a million Iraqi and Iranian lives have been expended to no purpose on and around the Fao peninsula. The Iraqis have ingested (or engulfed) Kuwait. The Syrians, aided by an anti-Iraqi subvention from Washington, have now ingested Lebanon. The Israeli millennialists are bent on ingesting the West Bank and Gaza. In every country mentioned, furthermore, the forces of secularism, democracy, and reform have been dealt appalling blows. And all of these crimes and blunders will necessitate future wars.

That is what U.S. policy has done, or helped to do, to the region. What has the same policy done to America? A review of the Pike Commission, the Iran-Contra hearings, even the Tower Report and September's perfunctory House inquiry into the Baker-Kelly-Glaspie fiasco, will disclose the damage done by official lying, by hostage trading, by covert arms sales, by the culture of secrecy, and by the habit of including foreign despots in meetings and decisions that are kept secret from American citizens. The Gulf buildup had by Election Day brought about the renewal of a moribund consensus on national security, the disappearance of the bruited "peace dividend" ("If you're looking for it," one Pentagon official told a reporter this past fall, "it just left for Saudi Arabia"), and the re-establishment of the red alert as the preferred device for communicating between Washington and the people.

The confrontation that opened on the Kuwaiti border in August 1990 was neither the first nor the last battle in a long war, but it was a battle that now directly, overtly involved and engaged the American public and American personnel. The call was to an exercise in peace through strength. But the cause was yet another move in the policy of keeping a region divided and embittered, and therefore accessible to the franchisers of weaponry and the owners of black gold.

An earlier regional player, Benjamin Disraeli, once sarcastically remarked that you could tell a weak government by its eagerness to resort to strong measures. The Bush administration uses strong measures to ensure weak government abroad and has enfeebled democratic government at home. The reasoned objection must be that this is a dangerous and dishonorable pursuit, in which the wealthy gamblers have become much too accustomed to paying their bad debts with the blood of others.

U.S. SENATORS CHAT WITH SADDAM

(April 12, 1990)

This is an excerpt from the transcript of a meeting on April 12, 1990, between Iraqi President Saddam Hussein and five U.S. senators—Robert Dole, Alan Simpson, Howard Metzenbaum, James McClure, and Frank Murkowski. U.S. Ambassador April Glaspie also attended. The American delegation met President Hussein in Mosul, Iraq, at a time when Hussein had come under criticism in the Western media for his human-rights record, his threats to attack Israel with chemical weapons, and his government's hanging of a British reporter accused of espionage. In addition, Congress was considering imposing trade sanctions against Iraq. The transcript was originally released by the Iraqi embassy in Washington.

PRESIDENT SADDAM HUSSEIN: Daily the Arabs hear scorn directed at them from the West, daily they bear insults. Why? Has the Zionist mentality taken control of you to the point that it has deprived you of your humanity? . . .

SENATOR DOLE: There are fundamental differences between our countries. We have free media in the U.S. When you say "Western," Mr. President—I don't know what you mean when you say "the West." I don't know whether or not you mean the government. There is a person who did not have the authority to say anything about . . . [your] government. He was a commentator for the VOA (the Voice of America, which represents the government only) and this person was removed from it. Please allow me to say that only 12 hours earlier President Bush had assured me that he wants better relations, and that the U.S. government wants better relations with Iraq. We believe—and we are leaders in the U.S. Congress—that the Congress also does not represent Bush or the government. I assume that President Bush will oppose sanctions, and he might veto them, unless something provocative were to happen, or something of that sort.

AMBASSADOR GLASPIE: As the ambassador of the U.S., I am certain that this is the policy of the U.S.

SENATOR DOLE: We in the Congress are also striving to do what we can in this direction. The president may differ with the Congress, and if there is a divergent viewpoint, he has the right to express it, and to exercise his authority concerning it. . . .

SENATOR SIMPSON: I enjoy meeting candid and open people. This is a trademark of those of us who live in the "Wild West." . . . One of the reasons that we telephoned President Bush yesterday evening was to tell the President that our visit to Iraq would cost us a great deal of popularity, and that many people would attack us for coming to Iraq. . . . But President Bush said, "Go there. I want you there. . . . If you are criticized because of your visit to Iraq, I will defend you and speak on your behalf." . . . Democracy is a very confusing issue. I believe that your problems lie with the Western media and not with the U.S. government. As long as you are isolated from the media, the press—and it is a haughty and pampered press; they all consider themselves political geniuses, that is, the journalists do; they are very cynical—what I advise is that you invite them to come here and see for themselves.*

HUSSEIN: They are welcome. We hope that they will come to see Iraq and, after they do, write whatever they like. . . . [But] I wonder, as you may wonder, if governments, for example, the U.S. government, were not behind such reports [negative news stories about Iraq]. How else could all of this [negative media coverage of Iraq] have occurred in such a short period of time?

SIMPSON: It's very easy. . . . They all live off one another. Everyone takes from the other. When there is a major news item on the front page of *The New York Times,* another journalist takes it and publishes it. . . .

---

* Editor's note: These sentiments did not prevent Senator Simpson from calling CNN correspondent Peter Arnett, who reported from Baghdad during the Gulf war, an Iraqi "sympathizer" with a relative who was "active in the Vietcong."

SENATOR METZENBAUM: Mr. President, perhaps you have been given some information on me beforehand. I am a Jew and a staunch supporter of Israel. I did have some reservations on whether I should come on this visit.

HUSSEIN: You certainly will not regret it afterward.

METZENBAUM: I do not regret it. Mr. President, you view the Western media in a very negative light. I am not the right person to be your public-relations man, but allow me to suggest a few things, as I am more concerned about peace than I am about any other particular factor. I do not want to talk about whether the entire West Bank should be given up, or half of Jerusalem, or any other parts [of Israel]. This issue should be left to the parties concerned. However, I have been sitting here and listening to you for about an hour, and I am now aware that you are a strong and intelligent man and that you want peace. But I am also convinced that if . . . you were to focus on the value of the peace that we greatly need to achieve in the Middle East then there would not be a leader to compare with you in the Middle East. I believe, Mr. President, that you can be a very influential force for peace in the Middle East. But, as I said, I am not your public-relations man.

THE GLASPIE TRANSCRIPT:
SADDAM MEETS THE U.S. AMBASSADOR

(July 25, 1990)

On July 25, 1990, President Saddam Hussein of Iraq summoned the United States Ambassador, April Glaspie, to his office in the last high-level contact between the two governments before the Iraqi invasion of Kuwait on August 2. Here is the complete transcript of the meeting, which also included the Iraqi Foreign Minister, Tariq Aziz, as released by Baghdad. The State Department has neither confirmed nor denied its accuracy.

PRESIDENT SADDAM HUSSEIN: I have summoned you today to hold comprehensive political discussions with you. This is a message to President Bush:

You know that we did not have relations with the U.S. until 1984 and you know the circumstances and reasons which caused them to be severed. The decision to establish relations with the U.S. were taken in 1980 during the two months prior to the war between us and Iran.

When the war started, and to avoid misinterpretation, we postponed the establishment of relations hoping that the war would end soon.

But because the war lasted for a long time, and to emphasize the fact that we are a nonaligned country, it was important to re-establish relations with the U.S. And we chose to do this in 1984.

It is natural to say that the U.S. is not like Britain, for example, with the latter's historic relations with Middle Eastern countries, including Iraq. In addition, there were no relations between Iraq and the U.S. between 1967 and 1984. One can conclude it would be difficult for the U.S. to have a full understanding of many matters in Iraq. When relations were re-established we hoped for a better understanding and for better cooperation because we too do not understand the background of many American decisions.

We dealt with each other during the war and we had dealings on various levels. The most important of those levels were with the foreign ministers.

We had hoped for a better common understanding and a better chance of cooperation to benefit both our peoples and the rest of the Arab nations.

But these better relations have suffered from various rifts. The worst of these was in 1986, only two years after establishing relations, with what was known as Irangate, which happened during the year that Iran occupied the Fao peninsula.

It was natural then to say that old relations and complexity of interests could absorb many mistakes. But when interests are limited and relations are not that old, then there isn't a deep understanding and mistakes could leave a negative effect. Sometimes the effect of an error can be larger than the error itself.

Despite all of that, we accepted the apology, via his envoy, of the American president regarding Irangate, and we wiped the slate clean. And we shouldn't unearth the past except when new events remind us that old mistakes were not just a matter of coincidence.

Our suspicions increased after we liberated the Fao peninsula. The media began to involve itself in our politics. And our suspicions began to surface anew, because we began to question whether the U.S. felt uneasy with the outcome of the war when we liberated our land.

It was clear to us that certain parties in the United States—and I don't say the president himself—but certain parties who had links with the intelligence community and with the State Department—and I don't say the secretary of state himself—I say that these parties did not like the fact that we liberated our land. Some parties began to prepare studies entitled, "Who will succeed Saddam Hussein?" They began to contact Gulf states to make them fear Iraq, to persuade them not to give Iraq economic aid. And we have evidence of these activities.

Iraq came out of the war burdened with a $40 billion debt, excluding the aid given by Arab states, some of whom consider that too to be a debt although they knew—and you knew too—that without Iraq they would not have had these sums and the future of the region would have been entirely different.

We began to face the policy of the drop in the price of oil. Then we saw the United States, which always talks of democracy but which has no time for the other point of view. Then the media campaign against Saddam Hussein was started by the official American media. The United States thought that the situation in Iraq was like Poland, Romania or Czechoslovakia. We were disturbed by this campaign but we were not disturbed too much because we had hoped that, in a few months, those who are decisionmakers in America would have a chance to find the facts and see whether this media campaign had had any effect on the lives of Iraqis. We had hoped that soon the American authorities would make the correct decision regarding their relations with Iraq. Those with good relations can sometimes afford to disagree.

But when planned and deliberate policy forces the price of oil down without good commercial reasons, then that means another war against Iraq. Because military war kills people by bleeding them, and economic war kills their humanity by depriving them of their chance to have a good standard of living. As you know, we gave rivers of blood in a war that lasted eight years, but we did not lose our humanity. Iraqis have a right to live proudly. We do not accept that anyone could injure Iraqi pride or the Iraqi right to have high standards of living.

Kuwait and the U.A.E. were at the front of this policy aimed at lowering Iraq's position and depriving its people of higher economic standards. And you know that our relations with the Emirates and Kuwait had been good. On top of all that, while we were busy at war, the state of Kuwait began to expand at the expense of our territory.

You may say this is propaganda, but I would direct you to one document, the Military Patrol Line, which is the borderline endorsed by the Arab League in 1961 for military patrols not to cross the Iraq-Kuwait border.

But go and look for yourselves. You will see the Kuwaiti border patrols, the Kuwaiti farms, the Kuwaiti oil installations—all built as closely as possible to this line to establish that land as Kuwaiti territory.

Since then, the Kuwaiti government has been stable while the Iraqi government has undergone many changes. Even after 1968 and for ten years afterwards, we were too busy with our own problems. First in the north, then the 1973 war, and other problems. Then came the war with Iran which started ten years ago.

We believe that the United States must understand that people who live in luxury and economic security can reach an understanding with the United States on what are legitimate joint interests. But the starved and the economically deprived cannot reach the same understanding.

We do not accept threats from anyone because we do not threaten anyone. But we say clearly that we hope that the U.S. will not entertain too many illusions and will seek new friends rather than increase the number of its enemies.

I have read the American statements speaking of friends in the area. Of course, it is the right of everyone to choose their friends. We can have no objections. But you know you are not the ones who protected your friends during the war with Iran. I assure you, had the Iranians overrun the region, the American troops would not have stopped them, except by the use of nuclear weapons.

I do not belittle you. But I hold this view by looking at the geography and nature of American society into account. Yours is a society which cannot accept 10,000 dead in one battle.

You know that Iran agreed to the cease-fire not because the United States had bombed one of the oil platforms after the liberation of the Fao. Is this Iraq's reward for its role in securing the stability of the region and for protecting it from an unknown flood?

So what can it mean when America says it will now protect its friends? It can only mean prejudice against Iraq. This stance plus maneuvers and statements which have been made has encouraged the U.A.E. and Kuwait to disregard Iraqi rights.

I say to you clearly that Iraq's rights, which are mentioned in the memorandum, we will take one by one. That might not happen now or after a month or after one year, but we will take it all. We are not the kind of people who will relinquish their rights. There is no historic right, or legitimacy, or need, for the U.A.E. and Kuwait to deprive us of our rights. If they are needy, we too are needy.

The United States must have a better understanding of the situation and declare who it wants to have relations with and who its enemies are. But it should not make enemies simply because others have different points of view regarding the Arab-Israeli conflict.

We clearly understand America's statement that it wants an easy flow of oil. We understand America saying that it seeks friendship with the states in the region, and to encourage their joint interests. But we cannot understand the attempt to encourage some parties to harm Iraq's interests.

The United States wants to secure the flow of oil. This is understandable and known. But it must not deploy methods which the United States says it disapproves of—flexing muscles and pressure.

If you use pressure, we will deploy pressure and force. We know that you can harm us although we do not threaten you. But we too can harm you. Everyone can cause harm according to their ability and their size. We cannot come all the way to you in the United States, but individual Arabs may reach you.

You can come to Iraq with aircraft and missiles but do not push us to the point where we cease to care. And when we feel that you want to injure our pride and take away the Iraqis' chance of a high standard of living, then we will cease to care and death will be the choice for us. Then we would not care if you fired 100 missiles for each missile we fired. Because without pride life would have no value.

It is not reasonable to ask our people to bleed rivers of blood for eight years then to tell them, "Now you have to accept aggression from Kuwait, the U.A.E. or from the U.S. or from Israel."

We do not put all these countries in the same boat. First, we are hurt and upset that such disagreement is taking place between us and Kuwait and the U.A.E. The solution must be found within an Arab framework and through direct bilateral relations. We do not place America among the enemies. We place it where we want our friends to be and we try to be friends. But repeated American statements last year made it apparent that America did not regard us as friends. Well the Americans are free.

When we seek friendship we want pride, liberty and our right to choose.

We want to deal according to our status as we deal with the others according to their status.

We consider the others' interests while we look after our own. And we expect the others to consider our interests while they are dealing with their own. What does it mean when the Zionist war minister is summoned to the United States now? What do they mean, these fiery statements coming out of Israel during the past few days and the talk of war being expected now more than at any other time?

We don't want war because we know what war means. But do not push us to consider war as the only solution to live proudly and to provide our people with a good living.

We know that the United States has nuclear weapons. But we are determined either to live as proud men, or we all die. We do not believe that there is one single honest man on earth who would not understand what I mean.

We do not ask you to solve our problems. I said that our Arab problems will be solved amongst ourselves. But do not encourage anyone to take action which is greater than their status permits.

I do not believe that anyone would lose by making friends with Iraq. In my opinion, the American president has not made mistakes regarding the Arabs, although his decision to freeze dialogue with the PLO was wrong. But it appears that this decision was made to appease the Zionist lobby or as a piece of strategy to cool the Zionist anger, before trying again. I hope that our latter conclusion is the correct one. But we will carry on saying it was the wrong decision.

You are appeasing the usurper in so many ways—economically, politically and militarily as well as in the media. When will the time come when, for every three appeasements to the usurper, you praise the Arabs just once?

When will humanity find its real chance to seek a just American solution that would balance the human rights of two hundred million human beings with the rights of three million Jews? We want friendship, but we are not running for it. We reject harm by anybody. If we are faced with harm, we will resist. This is our right, whether the harm comes from America or the U.A.E. or Kuwait or from Israel. But I do not put all these states on the same level. Israel stole the Arab land, supported by the U.S. But the U.A.E. and Kuwait do not support Israel. Anyway, they are Arabs. But when they try to weaken Iraq, then they are helping the enemy. And then Iraq has the right to defend itself.

In 1974, I met with Idriss, the son of Mullah Mustafa Barzani [the late Kurdish leader]. He sat in the same seat as you are sitting now. He came asking me to postpone implementation of autonomy in Iraqi Kurdistan, which was agreed on March 11, 1970. My reply was: we are determined to fulfil our obligation. You also have to stick to your agreement. When I sensed that Barzani had evil intention, I said to him: give my regards to your father and tell him that Saddam Hussein says the following. I explained to him the balance of power with figures exactly the way I explained to the Iranians in my open letters to them during the war. I finished this conversation with the result summarized in one sentence: if we fight, we shall win. Do you know why? I explained all the reasons to him, plus one political reason—you [the Kurds in 1974] depended on our disagreement with the shah of Iran [Kurds were financed by Iran]. The root of the Iranian conflict is their claim of half of the Shatt al-Arab waterway. If we could keep the whole of Iraq with Shatt al-Arab, we will make no concessions. But if forced to choose between half of Shatt al-Arab or the whole of Iraq, then we will give the Shatt al-Arab away, to keep the whole of Iraq in the shape we wish it to be.

We hope that you are not going to push events to make us bear this wisdom in mind in our relations with Iran. After that [meeting with Barzani's son], we gave half of Shatt al-Arab away [1975 Algeria agreement]. And Barzani died and was buried outside Iraq and he lost his war.

[At this point, Saddam Hussein ends his message to Bush, and turns to Ambassador Glaspie]

We hope we are not pushed into this. All that lies between relations with Iran is Shatt al-Arab. When we are faced with a choice between Iraq living proudly and Shatt al-Arab then we will negotiate using the wisdom we spoke of in 1975. In the way Barzani lost his historic chance, others will lose their chance too.

With regards to President Bush, I hope the president will read this himself and will not leave it in the hands of a gang in the State Department. I exclude the secretary of state and Kelly because I know him and I exchanged views with him.

AMBASSADOR GLASPIE: I thank you, Mr. President, and it is a great pleasure for a diplomat to meet and talk directly with the president. I clearly understand your message. We studied history at school. They taught us to say freedom or death. I think you know well that we as a people have our experience with the colonialists.

Mr. President, you mentioned many things during this meeting which I cannot comment on on behalf of my Government. But with your permission, I will comment on two points. You spoke of friendship and I believe it was clear from the letters sent by our president to you on the occasion of your national day that he emphasizes—

HUSSEIN: He was kind and his expressions met with our regard and respect.

GLASPIE: As you know, he directed the United States administration to reject the suggestion of implementing trade sanctions.

HUSSEIN (smiling): There is nothing left for us to buy from America. Only wheat. Because every time we want to buy something, they say it is forbidden. I am afraid that one day you will say, "You are going to make gunpowder out of wheat."

GLASPIE: I have a direct instruction from the president to seek better relations with Iraq.

HUSSEIN: But how? We too have this desire. But matters are running contrary to this desire.

GLASPIE: This is less likely to happen the more we talk. For example, you mentioned the issue of the article published by the American Information Agency and that was sad. And a formal apology was presented.

HUSSEIN: Your stance is generous. We are Arabs. It is enough for us that someone says, "I am sorry, I made a mistake." Then we carry on. But the media campaign continued. And it is full of stories. If the stories were true, no one would get upset. But we understand from its continuation that there is a determination [to harm relations].

GLASPIE: I saw the Diane Sawyer program on ABC. And what happened in that program was cheap and unjust. And this is a real picture of what happens in the American media—even to American politicians themselves. These are the methods the Western media employs. I am pleased that you add your voice to the diplomats who stand up to the media. Because your appearance in the media, even for five minutes, would help us to make the American people understand Iraq. This would increase mutual understanding. If the American president had control of the media, his job would be much easier.

Mr. President, not only do I want to say that President Bush wanted better and deeper relations with Iraq, but he also wants an Iraqi contribution to peace and prosperity in the Middle East. President Bush is an intelligent man. He is not going to declare an economic war against Iraq.

You are right. It is true what you say that we do not want higher prices for oil. But I would ask you to examine the possibility of not charging too high a price for oil.

HUSSEIN: We do not want too high prices for oil. And I remind you that in 1974 I gave Tariq Aziz the idea for an article he wrote which criticized the policy of keeping oil prices high. It was the first Arab article which expressed this view.

TARIQ AZIZ: Our policy in OPEC opposes sudden jumps in oil prices.

HUSSEIN: Twenty-five dollars a barrel is not a high price.

GLASPIE: We have many Americans who would like to see the price go above $25 because they come from oil-producing states.

HUSSEIN: The price at one stage had dropped to $12 a barrel and a reduction in the modest Iraqi budget of $6 billion to $7 billion is a disaster.

GLASPIE: I think I understand this. I have lived here for years. I admire your extraordinary efforts to rebuild your country. I know you need funds. We understand that and our opinion is that you should have the opportunity to rebuild your country. But we have no opinion on the Arab-Arab conflicts, like your border disagreement with Kuwait.

I was in the American embassy in Kuwait during the late '60s. The instruction we had during this period was that we should express no opinion on this issue and that the issue is not associated with America. James Baker has directed our official spokesmen to emphasize this instruction. We hope you can solve this problem using any suitable methods via Klibi or via President Mubarak. All that we hope is that these issues are solved quickly. With regard to all of this, can I ask you to see how the issue appears to us?

My assessment after twenty-five years' service in this area is that your objective must have strong backing from your Arab brothers. I now speak of oil. But you, Mr. President, have fought through a horrific and painful war. Frankly, we can only see that you have deployed massive troops in the south. Normally that would not be any of our business. But when this happens in the context of what you said on your national day, then when we read the details in the two letters of the foreign minister, then when we see the Iraqi point of view that the measures taken by the U.A.E. and Kuwait is, in the final analysis, parallel to military aggression against Iraq, then it would be reasonable for me to be concerned. And for this reason, I received an instruction to ask you, in the spirit of friendship—not in the spirit of confrontation—regarding your intentions.

I simply describe the concern of my government. And I do not mean that the situation is a simple situation. But our concern is a simple one.

HUSSEIN: We do not ask people not to be concerned when peace is at issue. This is a noble human feeling which we all feel. It is natural for you as a superpower to be concerned. But what we ask is not to express your concern in a way that would make an aggressor believe that he is getting support for his aggression.

We want to find a just solution which will give us our rights but not deprive others of their rights. But at the same time, we want the others to know that our patience is running out regarding their action, which is harming even the milk our children drink, and the pensions of the widow who lost her husband during the war, and the pensions of the orphans who lost their parents.

As a country, we have the right to prosper. We lost so many opportunities, and the others should value the Iraqi role in their protection. Even this Iraqi [the president points to the interpreter] feels bitter like all other Iraqis. We are not aggressors but we do not accept aggression either. We sent them envoys and handwritten letters. We tried everything. We asked the Servant of the Two Shrines—King Fahd—to hold a four-member summit, but he suggested a meeting between the oil ministers. We agreed. And as you know, the meeting took place in Jidda. They reached an agreement which did not express what we wanted, but we agreed.

Only two days after the meeting, the Kuwaiti oil minister made a statement that contradicted the agreement. We also discussed the issue during the Baghdad summit. I told the Arab kings and presidents that some brothers are fighting an economic war against us. And that not all wars use weapons and we regard this kind of war as a military action against us. Because if the capability of our army is lowered then, if Iran renewed the war, it could achieve goals which it could not achieve before. And if we lowered the standard of our defenses, then this could encourage Israel to attack us. I said that before the Arab kings and presidents. Only I did not mention Kuwait and U.A.E. by name, because they were my guests.

Before this, I had sent them envoys reminding them that our war had included their defense. Therefore the aid they gave us should not be regarded as a debt. We did no more than the United States would have done against someone who attacked its interests.

I talked about the same thing with a number of other Arab states. I explained the situation to brother King Fahd a few times, by sending envoys and on the telephone. I talked with brother King Hussein and with Sheikh Zaid after the conclusion of the summit. I walked with the sheikh to the plane when he was leaving Mosul. He told me, "Just wait until I get home." But after he had reached his destination, the statements that came from there were very bad—not from him, but from his minister of oil.

Also after the Jidda agreement, we received some intelligence that they were talking of sticking to the agreement for two months only. Then they would change their policy. Now tell us, if the American president found himself in this situation, what would he do? I said it was very difficult for me to talk about these issues in public. But we must tell the Iraqi people who face economic difficulties who was responsible for that. . .

GLASPIE: I spent four beautiful years in Egypt.

HUSSEIN: The Egyptian people are kind and good and ancient. The oil people are supposed to help the Egyptian people, but they are mean beyond belief. It is painful to admit it, but some of them are disliked by Arabs because of their greed.

GLASPIE: Mr. President, it would be helpful if you could give us an assessment of the effort made by your Arab brothers and whether they have achieved anything.

HUSSEIN: On this subject, we agreed with President Mubarak that the prime minister of Kuwait would meet with the deputy chairman of the Revolution Command Council in Saudi Arabia, because the Saudis initiated contact with us, aided by President Mubarak's efforts. He just telephoned me a short while ago to say the Kuwaitis have agreed to that suggestion.

GLASPIE: Congratulations.

HUSSEIN: A protocol meeting will be held in Saudi Arabia. Then the meeting will be transferred to Baghdad for deeper discussion directly between Kuwait and Iraq. We hope we will reach some result. We hope that the long-term view and the real interests will overcome Kuwaiti greed.

GLASPIE: May I ask you when you expect Sheikh Saad to come to Baghdad?

HUSSEIN: I suppose it would be on Saturday or Monday at the latest. I told brother Mubarak that the agreement should be in Baghdad Saturday or Sunday. You know that brother Mubarak's visits have always been a good omen.

GLASPIE: This is good news. Congratulations.

HUSSEIN: Brother President Mubarak told me they were scared. They said troops were only twenty kilometers north of the Arab League line. I said to him that regardless of what is there, whether they are police, border guards or army, and regardless of how many are there, and what they are doing, assure the Kuwaitis and give them our word that we are not going to do anything until we meet with them. When we meet and when we see that there is hope, then nothing will happen. But if we are unable to find a solution, then it will be natural that Iraq will not accept death, even though wisdom is above everything else. There you have good news.

AZIZ: This is a journalistic exclusive.

GLASPIE: I am planning to go to the United States next Monday. I hope I will meet with President Bush in Washington next week. I thought to postpone my trip because of the difficulties we are facing. But now I will fly on Monday.

NIGHTMARE FROM THE THIRTIES

Charles Krauthammer

"I'll see to it that prices remain stable. That's what I
have my storm troopers for."

—*Hitler, on inflation*

HITLER ANALOGIES are not to be used lightly. To be compared
to Hitler is too high a compliment in evil to pay to most tyrants. The
time has come, however, to bestow the compliment on a tyrant who is
truly a nightmare out of the 1930s: Saddam Hussein, president (soon for
life) of Iraq.

Hussein has a million-man army left over from the war he started with
Iran, and he is itching to do something useful with it. So last week he
threatened to attack a defenseless Arab neighbor, Kuwait, over a dispute
he concocted about cash.

Kuwait, together with other Arab Gulf states, sustained Hussein
through his eight-year Iranian war with tens of billions of dollars in
loans. Gratitude is not one of Hussein's strong points. He now accuses
Kuwait of stealing Iraqi oil, and, together with another local pygmy (the
United Arab Emirates), of destroying his economy by overproducing oil,
thus driving down prices. His tiny neighbors are to return the stolen oil,
unilaterally cut oil production and forgive all war debts (estimated at
between $30 billion and $60 billion). Otherwise, he promises that
"Iraqis will not forget the saying that cutting necks is better than cutting
[one's] means of living."

Charles Krauthammer is a contributing editor of *The New Republic* and a nationally syndicated
columnist. This column was published in *The Washington Post* on July 27, 1990, six days before
the Iraqi invasion of Kuwait.

What raises Hussein to the Hitlerian level is not just his unconventional technique—violence—for regulating prices. Nor is it merely his penchant for domestic brutality—the wholesale murder of political opponents, the poison gas attacks on his own Kurdish minority, the *Republic of Fear* (as a now anonymous expatriate calls his book on Hussein's Iraq) that he has constructed.

What makes him truly Hitlerian is his way of dealing with neighboring states. In a chilling echo of the '30s, Iraq, a regional superpower, accuses a powerless neighbor of a "deliberate policy of aggression against Iraq," precisely the kind of absurd accusation Hitler lodged against helpless Czechoslovakia and Poland as a prelude to their dismemberment.

The diplomacy practiced by the fascist powers of the '30s was to accumulate massive military power for translation into immediate gain—territorial, economic, political—through extortion and, if still necessary, war. Hussein has mastered the technique. As one Iraqi expert says, "Hussein has never met a weapon he didn't use."

Whether Hussein will in fact use his weapons against Kuwait will depend purely on whether or not he feels that he needs to occupy Kuwait in order to turn it into a vassal state. The threat alone might make it submit. But Kuwait is not Hussein's ultimate objective. Saudi Arabia is. The Saudis have a long history of acquiescing to regional bullies. If Hussein can successfully bully Kuwait and the Emirates, the Saudis will follow.

Saudi production decisions alone can make oil prices rise or fall dramatically. If Hussein could dictate not just Iraqi production but Saudi, Kuwaiti, Emirate and the rest of Arab Gulf production, he would realize his fondest ambition. He would become not just King of the Gulf but King Oil.

Why should Americans care about this? Because King Oil's hostility to America is today unmatched in the world, except possibly for that of Iran, from whom the United States helped save Hussein during the Iran-Iraq war. (The gratitude problem again.) Hussein's declared objective is to raise oil prices to at least $25 a barrel. Last week oil was $14 a barrel. Such an oil shock, not seen since the '70s, would be ruinous for Western economies, and in particular the U.S. economy, which now imports half its oil.

Last week's thuggery finally jolted the Bush administration out of its policy of craven appeasement of Iraq. It had been resisting congressional efforts to punish Iraq by stopping subsidies for American-Iraqi trade. Perhaps now it will consider supporting Senator Daniel Inouye's (D-Hawaii) bill denying all assistance and banning all trade with Iraq.

Hussein is roughly $80 billion in debt, and banks are not lending to him because he doesn't feel he has to pay loans back. It is because Iraq is hurting economically that Hussein has decided to solve his problem with storm troopers. A quarantine would kick him while he's (financially) down, which is the best time to kick a bully. Once he gains control of world oil prices, he will be much harder to stop.

Even if a quarantine does not stop him, however, there is an important lesson to be learned from Hussein's emergence as a world disturber. With the collapse of communism, it has become fashionable to believe that the use of force as a means to achieve political objectives has become obsolete. Force may indeed be obsolete in some places (Western Europe, for example). The Persian Gulf, however, is not such a place. And while Iraq begins its thrust into the Gulf by sending 30,000 troops and tanks to the Kuwaiti border, Congress debates how much to cut the U.S. carrier fleet, our best deterrent against such regional thugs.

"The day of the dictator is over," declared President Bush in his Inaugural Address. In many places, yes. But it is precisely because in some places dictators remain, massively armed and practiced in Hitler's formula for turning arms into power, that this heady time is no time for disarmament.

Hussein will undoubtedly be appeased this time. But there will be a next. Like all bullies, he will in the end be deterred only by superior force. We had better make sure we have it.

THE U.N. RESOLUTIONS:
THE COMPLETE TEXT

RESOLUTION 660
2 August 1990

The Security Council,

Alarmed by the invasion of Kuwait on 2 August 1990 by the military forces of Iraq,

Determining that there exists a breach of international peace and security as regards the Iraqi invasion of Kuwait,

Acting under Articles 39 and 40 of the Charter of the United Nations,

1. *Condemns* the Iraqi invasion of Kuwait;

2. *Demands* that Iraq withdraw immediately and unconditionally all its forces to the positions in which they were located on 1 August 1990;

3. *Calls upon* Iraq and Kuwait to begin immediately intensive negotiations for the resolution of their differences and supports all efforts in this regard, and especially those of the League of Arab States;

4. *Decides* to meet again as necessary to consider further steps to ensure compliance with the present resolution.

RESOLUTION 661
6 August 1990

The Security Council,

Reaffirming its resolution 660 (1990) of 2 August 1990,

Deeply concerned that that resolution has not been implemented and that the invasion by Iraq of Kuwait continues with further loss of human life and material destruction,

Determined to bring the invasion and occupation of Kuwait by Iraq to an end and to restore the sovereignty, independence and territorial integrity of Kuwait,

Noting that the legitimate Government of Kuwait has expressed its readiness to comply with resolution 660 (1990),

Mindful of its responsibilities under the Charter of the United Nations for the maintenance of international peace and security,

Affirming the inherent right of individual or collective self-defence, in response to the armed attack by Iraq against Kuwait, in accordance with Article 51 of the Charter,

Acting under Chapter VII of the Charter of the United Nations,

1. Determines that Iraq so far has failed to comply with paragraph 2 of resolution 660 (1990) and has usurped the authority of the legitimate Government of Kuwait;

2. Decides, as a consequence, to take the following measures to secure compliance of Iraq with paragraph 2 of resolution 660 (1990) and to restore the authority of the legitimate Government of Kuwait;

3. Decides that all States shall prevent:
(a) The import into their territories of all commodities and products originating in Iraq or Kuwait exported therefrom after the date of the present resolution;

(b) Any activities by their nationals or in their territories which would promote or are calculated to promote the export or transshipment of any commodities or products from Iraq or Kuwait; and any dealings by their nationals or their flag vessels or in their territories in any commodities or products originating in Iraq or Kuwait and exported therefrom after the date of the present resolution, including in particular any transfer of funds to Iraq or Kuwait for the purposes of such activities or dealings;

(c) The sale or supply by their nationals or from their territories or using their flag vessels of any commodities or products, including weapons or any other military equipment, whether or not originating in their territories but not including supplies intended strictly for medical purposes, and, in humanitarian circumstances, foodstuffs, to any person or body in Iraq or Kuwait or to any person or body for the purposes of any business carried on in or operated from Iraq or Kuwait, and any activities by their nationals or in their territories which promote or are calculated to promote such sale or supply of such commodities or products;

4. Decides that all States shall not make available to the Government of Iraq or to any commercial, industrial or public utility undertaking in Iraq or Kuwait, any funds or any other financial or economic resources and shall prevent their nationals and any persons within their territories from removing from their territories or otherwise making available to that Government or to any such undertaking any such funds or resources and from remitting any other funds to persons or bodies within Iraq or Kuwait, except payments exclusively for strictly medical or humanitarian purposes and, in humanitarian circumstances, foodstuffs;

5. Calls upon all States, including States nonmembers of the United Nations, to act strictly in accordance with the provisions of the present resolution notwithstanding any contract entered into or licence granted before the date of the present resolution;

6. Decides to establish, in accordance with rule 28 of the provisional rules of procedure of the Security Council, a Committee of the Security Council consisting of all the members of the Council, to undertake the following tasks and to report on its work to the Council with its observations and recommendations:

(a) To examine the reports on the progress of the implementation of the present resolution which will be submitted by the Secretary-General; *(b)* To seek from all States further information regarding the action taken by them concerning the effective implementation of the provisions laid down in the present resolution;

7. *Calls upon* all States to co-operate fully with the Committee in the fulfilment of its task, including supplying such information as may be sought by the Committee in pursuance of the present resolution;

8. *Requests* the Secretary-General to provide all necessary assistance to the Committee and to make the necessary arrangements in the Secretariat for the purpose;

9. *Decides* that, notwithstanding paragraphs 4 through 8 above, nothing in the present resolution shall prohibit assistance to the legitimate Government of Kuwait, and calls upon all States: *(a)* To take appropriate measures to protect assets of the legitimate Government of Kuwait and its agencies; *(b)* Not to recognize any regime set up by the occupying Power;

10. *Requests* the Secretary-General to report to the Council on the progress of the implementation of the present resolution, the first report to be submitted within thirty days;

11. *Decides* to keep this item on its agenda and to continue its efforts to put an early end to the invasion by Iraq.

RESOLUTION 662
9 August 1990

The Security Council,

Recalling its resolutions 660 (1990) and 661 (1990),

Gravely alarmed by the declaration by Iraq of a "comprehensive and eternal merger" with Kuwait,

Demanding, once again, that Iraq withdraw immediately and unconditionally all its forces to the positions in which they were located on 1 August 1990,

Determined to bring the occupation of Kuwait by Iraq to an end and to restore the sovereignty, independence and territorial integrity of Kuwait,

Determined also to restore the authority of the legitimate Government of Kuwait,

1. *Decides* that annexation of Kuwait by Iraq under any form and whatever pretext has no legal validity, and is considered null and void;

2. *Calls upon* all States, international organizations and specialized agencies not to recognize that annexation, and to refrain from any action or dealing that might be interpreted as an indirect recognition of the annexation;

3. *Further demands* that Iraq rescind its actions purporting to annex Kuwait;

4. *Decides* to keep this item on its agenda and to continue its efforts to put an early end to the occupation.

RESOLUTION 664
18 August 1990

The Security Council,

Recalling the Iraqi invasion and purported annexation of Kuwait and resolutions 660, 661 and 662,

Deeply concerned for the safety and well-being of third state nationals in Iraq and Kuwait,

Recalling the obligations of Iraq in this regard under international law,

Welcoming the efforts of the Secretary-General to pursue urgent consultations with the Government of Iraq following the concern and anxiety expressed by the members of the Council on 17 August 1990,

Acting under Chapter VII of the United Nations Charter,

1. Demands that Iraq permit and facilitate the immediate departure from Kuwait and Iraq of the nationals of third countries and grant immediate and continuing access of consular officials to such nationals;

2. Further demands that Iraq take no action to jeopardize the safety, security or health of such nationals;

3. Reaffirms its decision in resolution 662 (1990) that annexation of Kuwait by Iraq is null and void, and therefore demands that the government of Iraq rescind its orders for the closure of diplomatic and consular missions in Kuwait and the withdrawal of the immunity of their personnel, and refrain from any such actions in the future;

4. Requests the Secretary-General to report to the Council on compliance with this resolution at the earliest possible time.

RESOLUTION 665
25 August 1990

The Security Council,

Recalling its resolutions 660 (1990), 661 (1990), 662 (1990) and 664 (1990) and demanding their full and immediate implementation,

Having decided in resolution 661 (1990) to impose economic sanctions under Chapter VII of the Charter of the United Nations,

Determined to bring an end to the occupation of Kuwait by Iraq which imperils the existence of a Member State and to restore the legitimate authority, and the sovereignty, independence and territorial integrity of Kuwait which requires the speedy implementation of the above resolutions,

Deploring the loss of innocent life stemming from the Iraqi invasion of Kuwait and determined to prevent further such losses,

Gravely alarmed that Iraq continues to refuse to comply with resolutions 660 (1990), 661 (1990), 662 (1990) and 664 (1990) and in particular at the conduct of the Government of Iraq in using Iraqi flag vessels to export oil,

1. *Calls upon* those Member States cooperating with the Government of Kuwait which are deploying maritime forces to the area to use such measures commensurate to the specific circumstances as may be necessary under the authority of the Security Council to halt all inward and outward maritime shipping in order to inspect and verify their cargoes and destinations and to ensure strict implementation of the provisions related to such shipping laid down in resolution 661 (1990);

2. *Invites* Member States accordingly to co-operate as may be necessary to ensure compliance with the provisions of resolution 661 (1990) with maximum use of political and diplomatic measures, in accordance with paragraph 1 above;

3. *Requests* all States to provide in accordance with the Charter such assistance as may be required by the States referred to in paragraph 1 of this resolution;

4. *Further requests* the States concerned to coordinate their actions in pursuit of the above paragraphs of this resolution using as appropriate mechanisms of the Military Staff Committee and after consultation with the Secretary-General to submit reports to the Security Council and its Committee established under resolution 661 (1990) to facilitate the monitoring of the implementation of this resolution;

5. *Decides* to remain actively seized of the matter.

RESOLUTION 666
13 September 1990

The Security Council,

Recalling its resolution 661 (1990), paragraphs 3 (c) and 4 of which apply, except in humanitarian circumstances, to foodstuffs,

Recognizing that circumstances may arise in which it will be necessary for foodstuffs to be supplied to the civilian population in Iraq or Kuwait in order to relieve human suffering,

Noting that in this respect the Committee established under paragraph 6 of that resolution has received communications from several Member States,

Emphasizing that it is for the Security Council, alone or acting through the Committee, to determine whether humanitarian circumstances have arisen,

Deeply concerned that Iraq has failed to comply with its obligations under Security Council resolution 664 (1990) in respect of the safety and well-being of third State nationals, and reaffirming that Iraq retains full responsibility in this regard under international humanitarian law including, where applicable, the Fourth Geneva Convention,

Acting under Chapter VII of the Charter of the United Nations,

1. *Decides* that in order to make the necessary determination whether or not for the purposes of paragraph 3 (c) and paragraph 4 of resolution 661 (1990) humanitarian circumstances have arisen, the Committee shall keep the situation regarding foodstuffs in Iraq and Kuwait under constant review;

2. *Expects* Iraq to comply with its obligations under Security Council resolution 664 (1990) in respect of third State nationals and reaffirms that Iraq remains fully responsible for their safety and well-being in accordance with international humanitarian law including, where applicable, the Fourth Geneva Convention;

3. *Requests,* for the purposes of paragraphs 1 and 2 of this resolution, that the Secretary-General seek urgently, and on a continuing basis, information from relevant United Nations and other appropriate humanitarian agencies and all other sources on the availability of food in Iraq and Kuwait, such information to be communicated by the Secretary-General to the Committee regularly;

4. *Requests further* that in seeking and supplying such information particular attention will be paid to such categories of persons who might suffer

specially, such as children under 15 years of age, expectant mothers, maternity cases, the sick and the elderly;

5. *Decides* that if the Committee, after receiving the reports from the Secretary-General, determines that circumstances have arisen in which there is an urgent humanitarian need to supply foodstuffs to Iraq or Kuwait in order to relieve human suffering, it will report promptly to the Council its decision as to how such need should be met;

6. *Directs* the Committee that in formulating its decisions it should bear in mind that foodstuffs should be provided through the United Nations in co-operation with the International Committee of the Red Cross or other appropriate humanitarian agencies and distributed by them or under their supervision in order to ensure that they reach the intended beneficiaries;

7. *Requests* the Secretary-General to use his good offices to facilitate the delivery and distribution of foodstuffs to Kuwait and Iraq in accordance with the provisions of this and other relevant resolutions;

8. *Recalls* that resolution 661 (1990) does not apply to supplies intended strictly for medical purposes, but in this connection recommends that medical supplies should be exported under the strict supervision of the Government of the exporting State or by appropriate humanitarian agencies.

RESOLUTION 667
16 September 1990

The Security Council,

Reaffirming its resolutions 660 (1990), 661 (1990), 662 (1990), 664 (1990), 665 (1990) and 666 (1990),

Recalling the Vienna Conventions of 18 April 1961 on diplomatic relations and of 24 April 1963 on consular relations, to both of which Iraq is a party,

Considering that the decision of Iraq to order the closure of diplomatic and consular missions in Kuwait and to withdraw the immunity and privileges of these missions and their personnel is contrary to the decisions of the Security Council, the international Conventions mentioned above and international law,

Deeply concerned that Iraq, notwithstanding the decisions of the Security Council and the provisions of the Conventions mentioned above, has committed acts of violence against diplomatic missions and their personnel in Kuwait,

Outraged at recent violations by Iraq of diplomatic premises in Kuwait and at the abduction of personnel enjoying diplomatic immunity and foreign nationals who were present in these premises,

Considering that the above actions by Iraq constitute aggressive acts and a flagrant violation of its international obligations which strike at the root of the conduct of international relations in accordance with the Charter of the United Nations,

Recalling that Iraq is fully responsible for any use of violence against foreign nationals or against any diplomatic or consular mission in Kuwait or its personnel,

Determined to ensure respect for its decisions and for Article 25 of the Charter of the United Nations,

Further considering that the grave nature of Iraq's actions, which constitute a new escalation of its violations of international law, obliges the Council not only to express its immediate reaction but also to consult urgently to take further concrete measures to ensure Iraq's compliance with the Council's resolutions,

Acting under Chapter VII of the Charter of the United Nations,

1. *Strongly condemns* aggressive acts perpetrated by Iraq against diplomatic premises and personnel in Kuwait, including the abduction of foreign nationals who were present in those premises;

2. *Demands* the immediate release of those foreign nationals as well as all nationals mentioned in resolution 664 (1990);

3. Further demands that Iraq immediately and fully comply with its international obligations under resolutions 660 (1990), 662 (1990) and 664 (1990) of the Security Council, the Vienna Conventions on diplomatic and consular relations and international law;

4. Further demands that Iraq immediately protect the safety and well-being of diplomatic and consular personnel and premises in Kuwait and in Iraq and take no action to hinder the diplomatic and consular missions in the performance of their functions, including access to their nationals and the protection of their person and interests;

5. Reminds all States that they are obliged to observe strictly resolutions 661 (1990), 662 (1990), 664 (1990), 665 (1990) and 666 (1990);

6. Decides to consult urgently to take further concrete measures as soon as possible, under Chapter VII of the Charter, in response to Iraq's continued violation of the Charter, of resolutions of the Council and of international law.

RESOLUTION 669
24 September 1990

The Security Council,

Recalling its resolution 661 (1990) of 6 August 1990,

Recalling also Article 50 of the Charter of the United Nations,

Conscious of the fact that an increasing number of requests for assistance have been received under the provisions of Article 50 of the Charter of the United Nations,

Entrusts the Committee established under resolution 661 (1990) concerning the situation between Iraq and Kuwait with the task of examining requests for assistance under the provisions of Article 50 of the Charter of the United Nations and making recommendations to the President of the Security Council for appropriate action.

RESOLUTION 670
25 September 1990

The Security Council,

Reaffirming its resolutions 660 (1990), 661 (1990), 662 (1990), 664 (1990), 665 (1990), 666 (1990), and 667 (1990),

Condemning Iraq's continued occupation of Kuwait, its failure to rescind its actions and end its purported annexation and its holding of third State nationals against their will, in flagrant violation of resolutions 660 (1990), 662 (1990), 664 (1990) and 667 (1990) and of international humanitarian law,

Condemning further the treatment by Iraqi forces of Kuwaiti nationals, including measures to force them to leave their own country and mistreatment of persons and property in Kuwait in violation of international law,

Noting with grave concern the persistent attempts to evade the measures laid down in resolution 661 (1990),

Further noting that a number of States have limited the number of Iraqi diplomatic and consular officials in their countries and that others are planning to do so,

Determined to ensure by all necessary means the strict and complete application of the measures laid down in resolution 661 (1990),

Determined to ensure respect for its decisions and the provisions of Articles 25 and 48 of the Charter of the United Nations,

Affirming that any acts of the Government of Iraq which are contrary to the abovementioned resolutions or to Articles 25 or 48 of the Charter of the United Nations, such as Decree No. 377 of the Revolution Command Council of Iraq of 16 September 1990, are null and void,

Reaffirming its determination to ensure compliance with Security Council resolutions by maximum use of political and diplomatic means,

Welcoming the Secretary-General's use of his good offices to advance a peaceful solution based on the relevant Security Council resolutions and noting with appreciation his continuing efforts to this end,

Underlining to the Government of Iraq that its continued failure to comply with the terms of resolutions 660 (1990), 661 (1990), 662 (1990), 664 (1990), 666 (1990) and 667 (1990) could lead to further serious action by the Council under the Charter of the United Nations, including under Chapter VII,

Recalling the provisions of Article 103 of the Charter of the United Nations,

Acting under Chapter VII of the Charter of the United Nations,

1. Calls upon all States to carry out their obligations to ensure strict and complete compliance with resolution 661 (1990) and in particular paragraphs 3, 4 and 5 thereof;

2. Confirms that resolution 661 (1990) applies to all means of transport, including aircraft;

3. Decides that all States, notwithstanding the existence of any rights or obligations conferred or imposed by any international agreement or any contract entered into or any licence or permit granted before the date of the present resolution, shall deny permission to any aircraft to take off from their territory if the aircraft would carry any cargo to or from Iraq or Kuwait other than food in humanitarian circumstances, subject to authorization by the Council or the Committee established by resolution 661 (1990) and in accordance with resolution 666 (1990) or supplies intended strictly for medical purposes or solely for UNIIMOG [The United Nations Iran-Iraq Military Observer Group];

4. Decides further that all States shall deny permission to any aircraft destined to land in Iraq or Kuwait, whatever its State of registration, to overfly its territory unless:
(*a*) The aircraft lands at an airfield designated by that State outside Iraq or Kuwait in order to permit its inspection to ensure that there is no cargo on board in violation of resolution 661 (1990) or the present resolution, and for this purpose the aircraft may be detained for as long as necessary; or

(b) the particular flight has been approved by the Committee established by resolution 661 (1990); or
(c) The flight is certified by the United Nations as solely for the purposes of UNIIMOG;

5. Decides that each State shall take all necessary measures to ensure that any aircraft registered in its territory or operated by an operator who has his principal place of business or permanent residence in its territory complies with the provisions of resolution 661 (1990) and the present resolution;

6. Decides further that all States shall notify in a timely fashion the Committee established by resolution 661 (1990) of any flight between its territory and Iraq or Kuwait to which the requirement to land in paragraph 4 above does not apply, and the purpose for such a flight;

7. Calls upon all States to co-operate in taking such measures as may be necessary, consistent with international law, including the Chicago Convention, to ensure the effective implementation of the provisions of resolution 661 (1990) or the present resolution;

8. Calls upon all States to detain any ships of Iraqi registry which enter their ports and which are being or have been used in violation of resolution 661 (1990), or to deny such ships entrance to their ports except in circumstances recognized under international law as necessary to safeguard human life;

9. Reminds all States of their obligations under resolution 661 (1990) with regard to the freezing of Iraqi assets, and the protection of the assets of the legitimate Government of Kuwait and its agencies, located within their territory and to report to the Committee established under resolution 661 (1990) regarding those assets;

10. Calls upon all States to provide to the Committee established by resolution 661 (1990) information regarding the action taken by them to implement the provisions laid down in the present resolution;

11. Affirms that the United Nations Organization, the specialized agencies and other international organizations in the United Nations system are required to take such measures as may be necessary to give effect to the terms of resolution 661 (1990) and this resolution;

12. Decides to consider, in the event of evasion of the provisions of resolution 661 (1990) or of the present resolution by a State or its nationals or through its territory, measures directed at the State in question to prevent such evasion;

13. Reaffirms that the Fourth Geneva Convention applies to Kuwait and that as a High Contracting Party to the Convention Iraq is bound to comply fully with all its terms and in particular is liable under the Convention in respect of the grave breaches committed by it, as are individuals who commit or order the commission of grave breaches.

RESOLUTION 674
29 October 1990

The Security Council,

Recalling its resolutions 660 (1990), 661 (1990), 662 (1990), 664 (1990), 665 (1990), 666 (1990), 667 (1990) and 670 (1990),

Stressing the urgent need for the immediate and unconditional withdrawal of all Iraqi forces from Kuwait, for the restoration of Kuwait's sovereignty, independence and territorial integrity and of the authority of its legitimate government,

Condemning the actions by the Iraqi authorities and occupying forces to take third-State nationals hostage and to mistreat and oppress Kuwaiti and third-State nationals, and the other actions reported to the Security Council, such as the destruction of Kuwaiti demographic records, the forced departure of Kuwaitis, the relocation of population in Kuwait and the unlawful destruction and seizure of public and private property in Kuwait, including hospital supplies and equipment, in violation of the decisions of the Council, the Charter of the United Nations, the Fourth Geneva Convention, the Vienna Conventions on Diplomatic and Consular Relations and international law,

Expressing grave alarm over the situation of nationals of third States in Kuwait and Iraq, including the personnel of the diplomatic and consular missions of such States,

Reaffirming that the Fourth Geneva Convention applies to Kuwait and that as a High Contracting Party to the Convention Iraq is bound to comply fully with all its terms and in particular is liable under the Convention in respect of the grave breaches committed by it, as are individuals who commit or order the commission of grave breaches,

Recalling the efforts of the Secretary-General concerning the safety and well-being of third-State nationals in Iraq and Kuwait,

Deeply concerned at the economic cost and at the loss and suffering caused to individuals in Kuwait and Iraq as a result of the invasion and occupation of Kuwait by Iraq,

Acting under Chapter VII of the Charter of the United Nations,

Reaffirming the goal of the international community of maintaining international peace and security by seeking to resolve international disputes and conflicts through peaceful means,

Recalling the important role that the United Nations and its Secretary-General have played in the peaceful solution of disputes and conflicts in conformity with the provisions of the Charter,

Alarmed by the dangers of the present crisis caused by the Iraqi invasion and occupation of Kuwait, which directly threaten international peace and security, and seeking to avoid any further worsening of the situation,

Calling upon Iraq to comply with the relevant resolutions of the Security Council, in particular its resolutions 660 (1990), 662 (1990) and 664 (1990),

Reaffirming its determination to ensure compliance by Iraq with the Security Council resolutions by maximum use of political and diplomatic means,

1. *Demands* that the Iraqi authorities and occupying forces immediately cease and desist from taking third-State nationals hostage, mistreating

and oppressing Kuwaiti and third-State nationals and any other actions, such as those reported to the Security Council and described above, that violate the decisions of this Council, the Charter of the United Nations, the Fourth Geneva Convention, the Vienna Conventions on Diplomatic and Consular Relations and international law;

2. *Invites* States to collate substantiated information in their possession or submitted to them on the grave breaches by Iraq as per paragraph 1 above and to make this information available to the Security Council;

3. *Reaffirms* its demand that Iraq immediately fulfil its obligations to third-State nationals in Kuwait and Iraq, including the personnel of diplomatic and consular missions, under the Charter, the Fourth Geneva Convention, the Vienna Conventions on Diplomatic and Consular Relations, general principles of international law and the relevant resolutions of the Council;

4. *Also reaffirms* its demand that Iraq permit and facilitate the immediate departure from Kuwait and Iraq of those third-State nationals, including diplomatic and consular personnel, who wish to leave;

5. *Demands* that Iraq ensure the immediate access to food, water and basic services necessary to the protection and well-being of Kuwaiti nationals and of nationals of third States in Kuwait and Iraq, including the personnel of diplomatic and consular missions in Kuwait;

6. *Reaffirms* its demand that Iraq immediately protect the safety and well-being of diplomatic and consular personnel and premises in Kuwait and in Iraq, take no action to hinder these diplomatic and consular missions in the performance of their functions, including access to their nationals and the protection of their person and interests and rescind its orders for the closure of diplomatic and consular missions in Kuwait and the withdrawal of the immunity of their personnel;

7. *Requests* the Secretary-General, in the context of the continued exercise of his good offices concerning the safety and well-being of third-State nationals in Iraq and Kuwait, to seek to achieve the objectives of paragraphs 4, 5 and 6 above and in particular the provision of food, water and basic services to Kuwaiti nationals and to the diplomatic and consular missions in Kuwait and the evacuation of third-State nationals;

8. *Reminds* Iraq that under international law it is liable for any loss, damage or injury arising in regard to Kuwait and third States, and their nationals and corporations, as a result of the invasion and illegal occupation of Kuwait by Iraq;

9. *Invites* States to collect relevant information regarding their claims, and those of their nationals and corporations, for restitution or financial compensation by Iraq with a view to such arrangements as may be established in accordance with international law;

10. *Requires* that Iraq comply with the provisions of the present resolution and its previous resolutions, failing which the Security Council will need to take further measures under the Charter;

11. *Decides* to remain actively and permanently seized of the matter until Kuwait has regained its independence and peace has been restored in conformity with the relevant resolutions of the Security Council.

12. *Reposes* its trust in the Secretary-General to make available his good offices and, as he considers appropriate, to pursue them and to undertake diplomatic efforts in order to reach a peaceful solution to the crisis caused by the Iraqi invasion and occupation of Kuwait on the basis of Security Council resolutions 660 (1990), 662 (1990) and 664 (1990), and calls upon all States, both those in the region and others, to pursue on this basis their efforts to this end, in conformity with the Charter, in order to improve the situation and restore peace, security and stability;

13. *Requests* the Secretary-General to report to the Security Council on the results of his good offices and diplomatic efforts.

RESOLUTION 677
28 November 1990

The Security Council,

Recalling its resolutions 660 (1990) of 2 August 1990, 662 (1990) of 9 August 1990 and 674 (1990) of 29 October 1990,

Reiterating its concern for the suffering caused to individuals in Kuwait as a result of the invasion and occupation of Kuwait by Iraq,

Gravely concerned at the ongoing attempt by Iraq to alter the demographic composition of the population of Kuwait and to destroy the civil records maintained by the legitimate Government of Kuwait,

Acting under Chapter VII of the Charter of the United Nations,

1. *Condemns* the attempts by Iraq to alter the demographic composition of the population of Kuwait and to destroy the civil records maintained by the legitimate Government of Kuwait;

2. *Mandates* the Secretary-General to take custody of a copy of the population register of Kuwait, the authenticity of which has been certified by the legitimate Government of Kuwait and which covers the registration of the population up to 1 August 1990;

3. *Requests* the Secretary-General to establish, in co-operation with the legitimate Government of Kuwait, an Order of Rules and Regulations governing access to and use of the said copy of the population register.

RESOLUTION 678
29 November 1990

The Security Council,

Recalling and reaffirming its resolutions 660 (1990) of 2 August 1990, 661 (1990) of 6 August 1990, 662 (1990) of 9 August 1990, 664 (1990) of 18 August 1990, 665 (1990) of 25 August 1990, 666 (1990) of 13 September 1990, 667 (1990) of 16 September 1990, 669 (1990) of 24 September 1990, 670 (1990) of 25 September 1990, 674 (1990) of 29 October 1990 and 677 (1990) of 28 November 1990,

Noting that, despite all efforts by the United Nations, Iraq refuses to comply with its obligation to implement resolution 660 (1990) and the above-mentioned subsequent relevant resolutions, in flagrant contempt of the Security Council,

Mindful of its duties and responsibilities under the Charter of the United Nations for the maintenance and preservation of international peace and security,

Determined to secure full compliance with its decisions,

Acting under Chapter VII of the Charter,

1. Demands that Iraq comply fully with resolution 660 (1990) and all subsequent relevant resolutions, and decides, while maintaining all its decisions, to allow Iraq one final opportunity, as a pause of goodwill, to do so;

2. Authorizes Member States co-operating with the Government of Kuwait, unless Iraq on or before 15 January 1991 fully implements, as set forth in paragraph 1 above, the foregoing resolutions, to use all necessary means to uphold and implement resolution 660 (1990) and all subsequent relevant resolutions and to restore international peace and security in the area;

3. Requests all States to provide appropriate support for the actions undertaken in pursuance of paragraph 2 of the present resolution;

4. Requests the States concerned to keep the Security Council regularly informed on the progress of actions undertaken pursuant to paragraphs 2 and 3 of the present resolution;

5. Decides to remain seized of the matter.

IRAQ'S OCCUPATION OF KUWAIT:
EXCERPTS FROM
AMNESTY INTERNATIONAL'S REPORT
(December 19, 1990)

WIDESPREAD ABUSES of human rights have been perpetrated by Iraqi forces following the invasion of Kuwait on 2 August. These include the arbitrary arrest and detention without trial of thousands of civilians and military personnel; the widespread torture of such persons in custody; the imposition of the death penalty and the extrajudicial execution of hundreds of unarmed civilians, including children. In addition, hundreds of people in Kuwait remain unaccounted for, having effectively "disappeared" in detention, and many of them are feared dead. To date, an estimated 300,000 Kuwaitis have fled their country, as well as several hundred thousand foreign nationals working in Kuwait. Their accounts of the abuses they have either witnessed or experienced have received worldwide media coverage. This document details some of these abuses, confining itself to those violations which fall within Amnesty International's mandate.

Amnesty International takes no position on the conflict in the Gulf, and does not condone killings and other acts of violence perpetrated by the parties to the conflict. What concerns the organization are human rights violations taking place in that context. Those violations which have been reported since 2 August are entirely consistent with abuses known to have been committed in Iraq over many years, and which have been documented by Amnesty International in its numerous reports. Iraq's policy of the brutal suppression of all forms of internal dissent continues to be implemented, and the people of Iraq remain its victims. Amnesty International has repeatedly placed such information on the public record, and regrets that until the invasion of Kuwait, the international community did not see fit to apply serious pressure in an attempt to put an end to these abuses.

Immediately after the invasion, Iraq announced that a nine-man "Provisional Free Kuwait government" had been set up. It was headed by Colonel Ala Hussein Ali, said to be a Kuwaiti national. However, less than a week later, on 8 August, the transitional government was dismissed and Iraq announced the annexation of Kuwait. By 28 August, Kuwait was declared to be Iraq's 19th province, while the border area with Iraq was incorporated as an extension of the province of Basra. Ali Hassan al-Majid, Iraq's Minister of Local Government and a cousin of President Saddam Hussein, was appointed as its governor. In 1987–1988, he had held responsibility for law and order in the northern Kurdish provinces of Iraq. . . .

To date, Iraq has not implemented any of the Security Council resolutions, although it announced on 6 December that all detained Western nationals would be released. Aside from the perpetration of those human rights violations documented in this report, widespread destruction and looting of public and private property was carried out. Most critical of these has been the looting of medicines, medical equipment and food supplies. The massive scale of destruction and looting which has been reported suggests that such incidents were neither arbitrary nor isolated, but rather reflected a policy adopted by the government of Iraq. According to information received, this policy caused embarrassment on the part of some Iraqi soldiers who were called upon to implement it. A number of people who had fled Kuwait told Amnesty International that Iraqi soldiers had apologized to them for the destruction of their country, stating that they were led to believe that they had been deployed in order to thwart an external attack on Kuwait. A Kuwaiti doctor specialising in occupational medicine described to Amnesty International the looting and destruction of al-Shuaib Industrial Centre where he had worked. On the fourth day after the invasion, members of Iraq's Republican Guards had apparently destroyed medical equipment, thrown files on the floor and torn down photographs of the emir of Kuwait. The doctor said: "I went into the dental clinic, which was also completely destroyed. I noticed that on one of the walls of the clinic the following words were written in large letters: 'Dear Kuwaiti doctors—we are sorry but we are under orders.' "

Since occupying Kuwait, Iraqi forces are reported to have meted out collective punishments against the local population in retaliation for armed attacks against them. Several incidents were reported involving the burning or blowing up of homes in districts where Iraqi soldiers had been killed. A night curfew was imposed in Kuwait City at the start of the invasion and remained in force until 23 November. Filming and photography are prohibited, and the offices of all newspapers and magazines have been closed down. The Iraqi authorities took over the printing presses of *al-Qabas,* one of Kuwait's daily newspapers, to issue their own newspaper, *al-Nida.* At least three *al-Qabas* employees, two Lebanese nationals and one Egyptian, were arrested on 25 August reportedly for refusing to cooperate with the Iraqi authorities. In September and October the Iraqi government issued a series of regulations aimed at completing the "Iraqization" of Kuwait. These regulations required Kuwaitis to take up Iraqi identity papers in lieu of existing Kuwaiti documents; to replace Kuwaiti car number plates with Iraqi ones; to change the clock to correspond to Iraqi time (previously there was an hour's difference between the two countries); and to use Iraqi rather than Kuwaiti currency (initially parity of the Iraqi dinar with the Kuwaiti dinar was enforced, the harder Kuwaiti currency being worth 20 Iraqi dinars before the invasion. Subsequently, Iraq declared that only its own currency was legal tender). A number of districts, streets and public buildings were renamed, particularly those which carried the names of members of Kuwait's al-Sabah family.

Since 2 August, Iraq has denied the media access to Kuwait. More importantly, it has denied access to the International Committee of the Red Cross (ICRC). In the first week of September, ICRC President Cornelio Sommaruga visited Baghdad and held three meetings with Iraqi Foreign Minister Tariq Aziz. The terms of a possible agreement defining the ICRC's operating procedures were discussed. In keeping with the ICRC's mandate to act in the event of international armed conflict on the basis of the 1949 Geneva Conventions, one of the organization's main objectives was to provide protection and assistance, in both Iraq and Kuwait, to the various categories of civilians affected by the events. The ICRC did not succeed in obtaining the Iraqi government's authorization to launch an operation in Iraq and Kuwait for the victims of the crisis. The government has given no reason for its refusal to grant ICRC access.

Similarly, Iraq has failed to respond to appeals on behalf of victims of human rights violations in both Iraq and Kuwait launched by various non-governmental organizations, including Amnesty International. On 3 August, the organization appealed publicly to the Iraqi government on behalf of Iraqi exiles living in Kuwait who were reported to have been arrested immediately following the invasion. There are grave fears for their lives as they risk torture and execution in Iraq. On 23 August, Amnesty International expressed its concerns to the Iraqi government about a wide range of human rights violations, including continuing arbitrary arrests, rape, summary executions and extrajudicial killings. The organization stressed that the arrest and continued detention of Western nationals was contrary to fundamental internationally recognized standards of human rights, and urged the immediate and unconditional release of all such detainees. It requested that their names and whereabouts be made known, and that they be granted immediate and regular access to consular officials. Amnesty International called upon the Iraqi government to take immediate steps to prevent incidents of rape by Iraqi forces, to investigate such incidents and to bring those responsible to justice. The organization also expressed its concern about the extension of the scope of the death penalty to include looting and the hoarding of food. In response to the execution in the third week of August of several people said to have been found guilty of looting, Amnesty International urged the government to refrain from carrying out any further executions. It also asked under what laws the executions had been carried out and for details of any legal proceedings followed in their cases. Finally, the organization expressed grave concern about the extrajudicial killings of unarmed civilians, including children, by Iraqi forces. It urged the Iraqi government to take urgent steps to prevent further such killings, to investigate those incidents which had occurred and to bring those responsible to justice.

On 29 August, Amnesty International sent urgent appeals to the government on behalf of six Kuwaiti men, all Shiite Muslims aged between 18 and 26. They had been arrested on 3 August after taking part in a demonstration in the al-Sulaibikhat district of Kuwait City. Reports received by Amnesty International indicated that the six detainees had been transferred to Baghdad for detention. On 3 October, Amnesty International once more expressed its concerns in a public statement about the widespread abuses being perpetrated by Iraqi forces in Kuwait, including mass arrests, torture under interrogation, summary executions and mass extrajudicial killings.

The Iraqi government failed to respond to any of Amnesty International's appeals. However, on 3 October Iraq's embassy in London issued a public statement commenting on Amnesty International's own statement issued the same day. The embassy did not deny that human rights abuses had taken place, but dismissed Amnesty International's statement as "an embarrassment to the practice of reporting."

WHY SOME ARABS SUPPORT SADDAM

Walid Khalidi

G IVEN THE brutality of Iraq's invasion of Kuwait, it could appear surprising that Saddam has elicited a not inconsiderable measure of Arab support. This has come not only from incumbents, but also from the intelligentsia and the masses, and this despite the condemnation of most of these supporters of the actual acts of aggression against Kuwait.

To probe into this question is not an exercise in mitigation, justification, or rationalization. For, whatever the reasons the Iraqi authorities give for their action, and whatever the motivations of the major Western powers in their reactions to it, the Iraqi invasion of Kuwait in concept and in execution, constitutes a violation of the central humane values of the Islamic Arab heritage and of the accepted norms of international behavior.

No one can condone the aggression that Kuwait has suffered at the hands of an Arab neighbor. The invasion of Kuwait wrests the right of self-determination of Kuwait from those to whom it naturally belongs—the people of Kuwait. It sanctions the seizure by one country of the territory, the properties, and the assets of another. It visits upon the weak the anguish of occupation and displacement. It proclaims the primacy of might over right.

The invasion of Kuwait is fraught with disastrous consequences. It adds to the disruption of the Arab social fabric and exacerbates its centrifugal and polarizing tendencies. It retards the prospects for the progress and advancement of the Arab world. It gives heart to its ene-

Walid Khalidi is a research fellow at Harvard University. This article originally appeared as the second section of "The Gulf Crisis: Origins and Consequences," an occasional paper published in early January 1991 by the Institute for Palestine Studies.

mies and besmirches its image abroad. It squanders the patrimony of the Arab world and diverts attention from the real challenges facing it regionally and internationally in the post–Cold War era. To all this must be added the toll in human suffering that has already come to pass and the catastrophic losses in civilian lives attendant on any major military confrontation.

Nevertheless, to probe into the question of the support Saddam has elicited is a legitimate and necessary exercise in the comprehension of powerful psychopolitical perceptions and emotions that reverberate across the frontiers of the Arab countries. It is legitimate and necessary, because these perceptions and emotions are part of the reality. It is easy for Arab Naipauls or aspirants to such a status to mock and debunk this reality and to vie in establishing its irrational roots, as if even irrationality were not inherent in human nature, whether Arab or non-Arab. Such patronizing attitudes will not make this reality disappear nor will they facilitate the tremendous task of its containment.

Certain aspects of the support for Saddam are noteworthy. A roll call at the level of governments would reveal an almost fifty-fifty split. The countries of the Gulf Cooperation Council are solidly and understandably anti-Saddam. They include Saudi Arabia, Kuwait, Bahrain, Qatar, the United Arab Emirates, and Oman. The non-Gulf Arab countries in the anti-Saddam coalition are Egypt, Syria, Morocco, Lebanon, Djibouti, and Somalia. It strains the imagination to assume that Syria's support is disinterested or rooted in addiction to the highest norms of international morality, or that Lebanon, Djibouti, and Somalia have the leeway to decide for themselves. In spite of his dispatch of two battalions (about 2,200 men) to Saudi Arabia, King Hassan of Morocco has lamented the failure of the Arab League to resolve the conflict and is strongly in favor of an Arab diplomatic solution. Such moral significance as might have attached to Egypt's strong anti-Saddam stand (if only by virtue of its being the most populous Arab country) is vitiated in the eyes of many Arabs by the perception of its being the beneficiary of Camp David at the expense of the other occupied territories and of its heavy dependence on American aid.

Those outside the anti-Saddam coalition include Jordan, the PLO, Yemen, the Sudan, Libya, Tunisia, Algeria, and Mauritania. With the exception of Libya, all these countries are desperately short of foreign exchange and do not obviously gain from staying outside the anti-Saddam coalition or from antagonizing the United States. In spite of the punitive measures already taken against these countries, they continue to stay outside the anti-Saddam coalition, though they have endorsed the U.N. sanctions. It is striking that in the cases of Jordan, Tunisia, and Algeria, the democratization of political life (particularly in Jordan) has gone farther than in the rest of the Arab world. Moreover, these countries have been particularly friendly to the United States in the past.

The attitude of the countries that did not join the anti-Saddam coalition could be examined with reference to the resolutions taken at the two Arab League meetings held in Cairo in the week after 2 August: the Council of Foreign Ministers' meeting on 3 August, and the summit of Arab heads of state on 10 August. The former meeting strongly condemned the invasion and called for the immediate and unconditional withdrawal of Iraqi forces and for the holding of an Arab summit to work out a negotiated settlement. More significantly, it expressed outright opposition to *foreign* intervention. Nevertheless, seven of the twenty-one members of the Arab League failed to endorse these resolutions. Of these seven, five (Yemen, Mauritania, the PLO, Sudan, and Jordan) expressed reservations; Libya absented itself from the voting session, while Iraq opposed. The voting of these countries, other than Iraq, reflected in varying degrees their pre-invasion relations with Iraq and the Gulf countries (particularly Kuwait), their public opinions at home, their leaders' perceptions of the merits of the Iraqi and Kuwaiti "cases," and these leaders' assessment of the productivity of the 3 August resolutions in defusing the crisis. Publicly, at least, it was this last consideration that seemed uppermost in the dissenters' minds. Their main argument was that formal collective condemnation of Iraq preempted the chances of success of an inter-Arab settlement at the envisaged summit by negating the summit's potential mediatory role.

Between the 3 August meeting and the 10 August summit, Saudi Arabia and other Gulf countries asked for U.S. help, and U.S. forces began to arrive in the region. Already on 2 August, the Security Council had condemned Iraq's invasion and called for its "complete, immediate and unconditional withdrawal" (resolution 660). On 6 and 9 August the Security Council imposed sanctions on Iraq and declared the annexation of Kuwait null and void in resolutions 661 and 662 respectively. The summit meeting on 10 August endorsed the resolutions of the Council of Foreign Ministers of 3 August condemning Iraq and endorsed the three Security Council resolutions. It called for the restoration of the legitimate government of Kuwait and, most significantly, supported the measures taken by Saudi Arabia and the Gulf countries in "self-defense" (that is, the request for foreign forces). It also agreed to the dispatch of Arab forces to help the Gulf countries "repel outside aggression."

This time the countries endorsing these resolutions dropped from fourteen to twelve out of the twenty-one, with the ranks of the original seven dissenters (of 3 August) augmented by Algeria and Tunisia. Of these nine, Jordan, Mauritania, and Sudan expressed serious reservations; Algeria and Yemen formally abstained; the PLO, Libya, and Iraq voted against; and Tunisia absented itself. The dissenters' posture was motivated by the original considerations referred to above, in addition to mounting alarm at the arrival in the Gulf of foreign troops, particularly those of the United States and Britain. Already before the arrival of foreign troops, popular pro-Saddam demonstrations had broken out in some of the dissenting countries (notably Jordan) but by 10 August these demonstrations of support had spread to all of them.

It was not only the pressure of their publics that dictated their voting on 10 August, however; they were all genuinely concerned at the danger of a military confrontation between the U.S.-led coalition and Iraq and fearful of its consequences for themselves and for the region as a whole. Nor did any of the dissenting countries at the government level condone the invasion of Kuwait or the violation of the moral and legal principles it entailed. All of them denounced the invasion in face-to-face meetings with Saddam and in repeated unilateral public statements. What they balked at was formal, collective denunciation. This condemnation of the invasion combined with misgivings about the foreign presence was also evident at the populist religious level. Sheikh Abbasi Madani, for example, leader of the Algerian Islamic Front, the views of which contributed to the vote of the Algerian government at the 10 August summit, had no qualms about denouncing the invasion, describing it in a technical Koranic term as *"baghi"* (that is, an outrage, an injustice, a wrong), but nevertheless expressed fears that the West would exploit the crisis for its own purposes.

The moral and political dilemma posed by the invasion of Kuwait was perhaps most poignant for Jordan and the PLO. King Hussein had for decades been the principal exponent, at the expense of his popularity and standing at home, of a peaceful resolution of the Arab-Israeli conflict. Simultaneously, he was the staunchest and most outspoken Arab supporter, in the face of mounting Syrian hostility, of Iraq in its war against Khomeini. He had carried his championship of the anti-Khomeini cause to the point where, as in the Amman summit of 1987, he was perceived by most Palestinians and the outside world to have relegated the fate of the occupied territories to oblivion, thus inadvertently contributing to the explosion of the *intifada*. The economic and logistical links forged between Jordan and Iraq during the eight years of war with

Iran had both drawn him closer to Saddam Hussein personally and rendered Jordan increasingly dependent on Iraq economically. Meanwhile, all his peaceful overtures towards Israel had proved sterile and had been rewarded in Israel by Shamir's talk of "Jordan equals Palestine," and in the United States by congressional opposition to military and economic aid to Jordan. At the same time King Hussein had labored indefatigably to "return" Egypt to the Arab fold, but his close relationship with Iraq had, already in the pre-crisis period, greatly strained his relations with the Gulf countries.

The PLO was in an even less enviable position. The principles violated by Saddam in his invasion of Kuwait were the very principles from which the Palestinian cause drew its moral strength. The "terrorist" image that Arafat was so desperate to shed was only reconfirmed by a close association with Saddam after the latter's invasion of Kuwait. In theory, a U.N. stand led by the United States against the aggression of an occupier was precisely the phenomenon that the PLO should itself be assiduously seeking.

Even before the crisis, Arafat had allowed his movement to draw closer to Iraq than its long-term interest dictated. After the cease-fire with Iran in August 1988, Saddam wooed Arafat with all the ardor of an enamored suitor: facilities, logistics, financial support, and bravado pronouncements on the deterrence of Israel, not to mention the joint bliss for Saddam and Arafat of the illusion of scoring points against their inveterate enemy Hafez al-Assad—all this apparently proved irresistible. What Arafat, for all his proverbial tactical adroitness, had lost sight of was the paltry distinction between Assad's frying pan and Saddam's fire. That Arafat succumbed to all these temptations could prove to be his greatest strategic blunder since the foundation of Fatah.

To be sure, there are reasons to explain Arafat's conduct. Like the leaders of the other dissenting countries, he had to cope with the populist feelings aroused by the Gulf crisis. And in the years prior to the crisis, he had strained to the limit his relations with the Palestinian radicals and Syria by probing the outermost circumference of concessions to Israel in the hopes of having a dialogue with the United States. No sooner had this last begun than it became clear that the new Bush administration, despite Secretary Shultz's assurances that the dialogue would be "substantive," was bent on treating Arafat like a criminal on probation, denying him a visa to attend the U.N., hounding the PLO out of U.N. bodies, and for some eight months talking past him via Egypt about Shamir's elections plan in order to appease Tel Aviv. Meanwhile, Arafat had succeeded in preventing the *intifada* leaders from resorting to arms despite the escalating brutalities of the Israeli army and the growing menace of massive Soviet immigration, only to see all his moderation culminate in the suspension of Washington's dialogue because of the raid organized by Abu Abbas (no protégé of his) against Israel.

Nevertheless, PLO policy since the invasion of Kuwait leaves much to be desired. It is understandable that Arafat, like other Arab leaders, felt unable to endorse the Arab League resolutions of 3 August and 10 August. It is less understandable that he did not try to distance himself from Saddam after the invasion of Kuwait, both as a matter of principle and in the long-term interests of his movement and his cause.

The argument adduced by the other Arab countries for not joining in formal collective condemnation—namely, the need to retain a mediatory role—is less cogent for the PLO than for the others. The support for the Palestinian cause in the Arab world depends on the maintenance by the PLO of friendly relations with *all* the Arab countries. Even if moral considerations were not at issue—and they are—antagonizing more than half the Arab states, particularly those that have enabled the PLO to operate for the last quarter of a century, is hardly in Palestinian interests. Arafat has clearly let slip from his memory a cardinal tenet of Fatah since its creation—that the Palestine cause is best served by keeping the PLO *away* from inter-Arab disputes. Nor has the mediatory role of the PLO been preserved or enhanced, as is evidenced by the rejection of the PLO's mediation by the Gulf countries. The PLO's failure to come out publicly, repeatedly, and forcefully against the invasion of Kuwait and in favor of Iraqi withdrawal in accordance with the U.N. resolutions has gravely damaged its political credibility and international standing.

As for the support at the popular level, it should first be made clear that Saddam is not seen as another Nasser. Whereas the emotions evoked by Nasser were, overwhelmingly, love and admiration, the counterpart sentiment evoked by Saddam, even among his Arab supporters, is fear. Whereas the prospect of the union of Syria and Egypt under Nasser in 1958 was greeted with joy by the Arab intelligentsia and masses, who saw it not only as an end in itself but also as the nucleus of an expanding Arab political entity, one would be hard pressed today to find many Arab volunteers for citizenship under Saddam. Nor is Saddam seen as a Bismarck. There could be very few Arabs who believe, in this day and age, that the path to Arab unity is via the aggression visited upon Kuwait, or who still have any remnant of faith in the viability of the Baath *hizb al-tali'ah* (vanguard party), which Saddam leads in Iraq, as an instrument of inter-Arab coordination and harmony. The fact that despite these considerations Arab support of Saddam still stands is an index of the abysmal depth of disillusionment with the Arab status quo—political, social, and economic—as well as with the regional policies of the United States. If this support spans, as it were, a spectrum, the poles of which are cerebral-analytical and despairing-nihilistic, the least common denominator between these poles is the yearning for change, even if the process is initiated by the brutality of Saddam's assault upon this status quo.

More specifically, there would seem to be five main reasons for the extent of support elicited by Saddam.

First is the alacrity, the scale, and the declared justifications advanced by the United States in its reaction to the invasion and in leading and forging such a coalition against Iraq. It is a sad pointer to the depth of the alienation between so much of the Arab world and the U.S. that this American reaction had the effect of submerging any negative attitudes generated by Saddam's *causative* act of aggression. That this should have been so is the harvest of many decades of steady erosion of U.S. moral credibility in Arab eyes, largely because of its policies on the Palestine problem and the Arab-Israeli conflict since 1948.

Fair-mindedness, even-handedness, impartiality, and non-partisanship; championship of the occupied against the occupier, the weak against the strong; espousal of the principle of self-determination, of the sacrosanctity of Security Council resolutions, and of the right of return of refugees to their homes; dedicated pursuit of justice; resistance to the violation of international frontiers and territorial annexation, to the seizure of the lands of others and their colonization, to the forcible displacement and replacement of peoples, to disregard for human rights in the form of collective punishment, deportations and the carpet bombing of civilian targets—these and other germane principles are rightly or wrongly *not* associated in Arab consciousness (not even in that of the peoples or rulers of the Gulf countries themselves) with the practice of the American administration and Congress in the Arab world.

Thus when all these principles suddenly and concurrently are invoked by the United States with such uncharacteristic zeal and vigor, the reaction is not only one of deep skepticism and defiant and reflexive anger at such moral selectivity, but of an equally deep fear and suspicion of ulterior motives, despite the obvious merits of the Kuwaiti case.

Second, it is not that Saddam is seen as Robin Hood. When he disposed of vast resources before his war with Iran he was not noted for his largesse toward his have-not brethren. Nor, conversely, was the lifestyle of the Kuwaiti ruling family and political elite profligate by Gulf standards. Moreover, and despite the suspension of Parliament in 1986, political life in Kuwait was freer than in most other Arab countries while its press was privately owned and more outspoken in its coverage and editorial comments than that of any other Arab country with the possible exception of Lebanon. The quality of some of its public institutions—for example, the Kuwait Institute for Scientific Research (KISR)—was outstanding. Hundreds of thousands of Arab professionals over the years found rewarding employment in the public and private sectors of Kuwait. Nor was Kuwait unforthcoming in its aid to less fortunate countries. The Kuwait Fund for Arab Economic Development (founded in 1961) extended loans at concessionary terms (low interest rates, comfortable grace periods, long maturities) with no-strings attached to Arab and Third World countries in equal amounts. The total for these loans between 1962 and 1989 was about $5.47 billion. This was above and beyond government-to-government assistance which totalled $12.6 billion over the 1974–1987 period, averaging $900 million annually. This concessional assistance exceeded seven percent of the GNP in certain years, and remained well above the target seven-tenths percent of GNP set by the U.N. or the aid/GNP ratio achieved by any donor among the industrialized countries.

Notwithstanding, the main feature of the Arab socioeconomic status quo was the incongruence between the geography of wealth and that of population distribution. To be sure, the Gulf countries opened wide their gates to immigrant Arab (and non-Arab) labor, skilled and unskilled, generating considerable remittances for the countries of origin. This, however, left unchanged the fact that eight percent of the 200 million Arabs who lived in the oil countries owned more than fifty percent of the aggregate gross national product of the Arab world and that the per capita income of the native populations of the oil countries ranged between $15,000 and $20,000 while that of the vast majority of the 200 million Arabs was below $1,000—for example, Egypt's 53 million ($690), Morocco's 25 million ($750), Sudan's 24 million ($310), Yemen's 9 million ($545).

Irrespective of its record, Kuwait represented this status quo and Saddam's action was seen as delivering a belated electric shock to it which, given the bankruptcy of inter-Arab institutions, might goad the system toward greater distributive justice. The "vote" was here not so much pro-Saddam or anti-Kuwait as anti the socioeconomic status quo, despite the merits of the Kuwaiti case.

At the same time, if the incongruence between the geographic distribution of wealth and demography could be said to be God-made and hence immune to critical assault, no such reprieve could be won for the man-made Western orientation of the investment strategies of the oil-rich countries. And even if it is conceded that the insecurity of investment conditions in the Arab countries, no less than rational investment calculus, dictate an investment strategy oriented toward the highly industrialized Western countries, the counter argument points to the lack of proportionality between the investments *inside* and those *outside* the Arab world and to the perpetuation, at least partly by this lack, of the continued underdevelopment of the non–oil-rich Arab countries.

Yet another layer of antipathy to the socioeconomic status quo derives from the perceived failure of the investor countries to elicit a reasonable *political* quid pro quo, particularly from the United States, for "services" rendered whether in the form of keeping oil prices down, underwriting the American national deficit, supporting the American dollar, or contributing to the vitality of the U.S. public and private sectors.

Not only has no morsel of a political quid pro quo been perceived, but the investor countries have seemed to acquiesce in an unseemly threshold of humiliation on issues of vital concern to the Arab world at the hands of successive U.S. administrations and Congresses—witness, for example, the no less than thirty-three vetoes cast between 1972 and 1990 by the United States against Security Council resolutions critical of Israeli actions in the occupied territories and in Lebanon.

Hence the fears that the U.S. reaction to the invasion of Kuwait is fundamentally motivated by a determination to maintain a status quo favorable to it—fears which, however exaggerated, do not necessarily require the invocation of an atavistic paranoia embedded in the Arab or Muslim heritage. Hence again, a vote, not pro-Saddam nor anti-Kuwait, but anti this socioeconomic status quo with all its ramifications, despite the merits of the Kuwaiti case.

Third, it is not that Saddam is seen as a Saladin. Saladin was a paragon of chivalry, noblesse oblige, and compassion—attributes of which no one can accuse Saddam. Nor will there be a repeat of Saladin's victorious march to Jerusalem. There is no military solution to the Palestine problem. There are no Saladins in the nuclear age. There is no Saladin against a heavily nuclear Israel endowed, according to the London International Institute of Strategic Studies, with at least 100 nuclear bombs.

But all Arabs, including the Arabs of the Gulf countries, had become sick and tired of the pusillanimity of Arab leaders everywhere in the face of the sabre-rattling of the Begins, the Shamirs, the Eytans, and the Sharons of Israel. Nor are there many people who think that Israel would come to the negotiating table unless it perceived some degree of mutual deterrence between itself and the Arab world. The quest for such a deterrence has eluded the Arab world since 1948, particularly in the face of the American commitment to maintain Israel's strategic preponderance over any combination of Arab countries.

The quest for such a deterrence has become more compelling in the last few years because of the sacrifices and tribulations of the *intifada*, the consolidation of the maximalist trend in Israel, the banishment from political discourse of the peace-for-land formula, the rejection of Palestinian self-determination, the rehabilitation of the Sharons, the continuing colonization of the occupied territories, the mounting salience of the proposition of the mass expulsion of the Palestinian population ("Transfer"), and of the "Jordan is Palestine" equation. The quest for such a deterrence has drawn strength from the permissiveness of Washington concerning Shamir's own elections plan, the breaking off by Washington of its dialogue with the PLO, and above all, from the convergence (however inadvertent) between Washington and Israel in capping the Jewish refugee quotas to the United States and in diverting this human flood of Soviet Jewish refugees toward the shores of the eastern Mediterranean. This last development, taken against the background of Shamir's motto of a "Big Israel to accommodate a Big Population" and Arab memories of the not-so-distant past, have generated a well founded fear that this vast new *aliya* will bring in its wake what earlier *aliyas* have brought and constitute a prelude to an even greater Israeli hegemony in the region.

Hence to many Arabs, if it takes a brutal Saddam to pose an element of deterrence to Israel, so be it. Hence the not altogether farfetched suspicion that talk about destroying the technological-industrial infrastructure of Iraq is in fact designed to circumvent such an outcome and perpetuate Israel's nuclear monopoly and superpower status in the Middle East.

Fourth is that many Arabs believe that Iraq's case against Kuwait is not devoid of all merit. This did not, to be sure, justify Iraq's invasion and looting of Kuwait and rubbing it off the political map—but it did warrant serious attention from the Gulf countries before the invasion and today.

Fifth, Saddam's 12 August "peace plan" based on the concept of linkage: that is, simultaneous withdrawals of occupying forces whether Iraqi (from Kuwait and Iran), Syrian (from Lebanon) or Israeli (from the Palestinian occupied territories, southern Lebanon and the Golan), makes sense to many people both inside and outside the Arab world. However, in the precise form presented by Saddam, postulating the acceptance of the *simultaneity* of the other withdrawals with Iraqi withdrawal from Kuwait, it is clearly a non-starter. But in a modified form, incorporating the concept of *sequential* withdrawals on the other fronts *after* his own withdrawal from Kuwait, it has a considerable creative potential for defusing the Gulf crisis itself and for inaugurating the so-called "new order" in the post-crisis Arab world. The mere presentation of his plan has made a deep and favorable impression on Arab public opinion (apart from the Gulf countries) because, whatever his tactical motivations, it has put these other regional conflicts, particularly the Palestine problem and Arab-Israeli conflict, on the world agenda from which they have for too long been banished. Already, not only the Soviet Union and France are explicitly talking about sequential linkage, but even the United States and Britain have hinted at it.

Of course the denial by some in absolute terms of any linkage between the Gulf crisis and the Arab-Israeli conflict has been an exercise in fatuity. Even before Saddam had announced his plan, the reaction of the United States to the Gulf crisis had of itself automatically generated an emotional, moral, and analytical linkage that was reflected in Arab support for him. But by making the concept of the linkage an integral part of his plan, Saddam insured that the concept also became part of the political and diplomatic discourse about the resolution of the crisis. At the same time, the strategic alliance between the United States and Israel ineluctably created a linkage between the Gulf crisis and the Arab-Israeli conflict, whether Israel's profile was high or low. Israel's opposition to the post-crisis arms deal with Saudi Arabia, the U.S. grant of $700 million in military aid to Israel to counterbalance its arms deal to Saudi Arabia, the concerted campaign by the United States, Britain, and Israel against Iraq's nuclear capabilities, the sharing with Israel by the United States of satellite intelligence regarding Iraqi military dispositions, the recent visits by the U.S. Secretary of the Air Force to Israel, the reference by the deposed U.S. Air Force Chief of Staff General Michael Dugan to the transfer by Israel to the United States of Israeli-built *Have Nap* "stand-off" missiles with one-ton warheads for use against Iraq by B-52 bombers—all are manifestations and confirmations of this linkage. Whether Israel's profile is high or low, the United States and Israel are in Bush's words "on a good wavelength" on Iraq. Indeed, to some observers, the ostensible low profile of Israel is the sculptured stillness of the crouching predator before the pounce—witness the talk in senior Israeli military circles of an Israeli first strike against Iraq, a scenario which the United States might not, in certain circumstances, consider altogether undesirable.

THE GENEVA MEETING

(Remarks of January 9, 1991)

James A. Baker 3d, Tariq Aziz, George Bush

The following is a transcript of Secretary of State James A. Baker 3d's statement after his January 9 meeting with Iraqi Foreign Minister Tariq Aziz.

I HAVE JUST given President Bush a full report of our meeting today. I told him that Minister Aziz and I had completed a serious and extended diplomatic conversation in an effort to find a political solution to the crisis in the Gulf. I met with Minister Aziz today not to negotiate, as we had made clear we would not do, that is, negotiate backwards from United Nations Security Council resolutions, but I met with him today to communicate. And "communicate" means listening as well as talking. And we did that, both of us.

The message that I conveyed from President Bush and our coalition partners was that Iraq must either comply with the will of the international community and withdraw peacefully from Kuwait or be expelled by force.

Regrettably, in over six hours of talks, I heard nothing today that suggested to me any Iraqi flexibility whatsoever on complying with the United Nations Security Council resolutions.

There have been too many Iraqi miscalculations. The Iraqi government miscalculated the international response to the invasion of Kuwait, expecting the world community to stand idly by while Iraqi forces systematically pillaged a peaceful neighbor. It miscalculated the response, I think, to the barbaric policy of holding thousands of foreign hostages, thinking that somehow cynically doling them out a few at a time would somehow win political advantage, and it miscalculated that it could divide the international community and gain something thereby from its aggression.

So let us hope that Iraq does not miscalculate again. The Iraqi leadership must have no doubt that the twenty-eight nations which have deployed forces to the Gulf in support of the United Nations have both the power and the will to evict Iraq from Kuwait.

The choice is Iraq's. If it should choose to continue its brutal occupation of Kuwait, Iraq will be choosing a military confrontation which it cannot win, and which will have devastating consequences for Iraq.

I made these points with Minister Aziz not to threaten but to inform, and I did so with no sense of satisfaction. For we genuinely desire a peaceful outcome, and as both President Bush and I have said on many occasions, the people of the United States have no quarrel with the people of Iraq.

I simply wanted to leave as little room as possible for yet another tragic miscalculation by the Iraqi leadership. And I would suggest to you, ladies and gentlemen, that this is still a confrontation that Iraq can avoid.

The path of peace remains open, and that path is laid out very clearly in twelve United Nations Security Council resolutions adopted over a period of over five months. But now the choice lies with the Iraqi leadership. The choice really is theirs to make. And let us all hope that that leadership will have the wisdom to choose the path of peace.

The following are excerpts from the statement made by the Iraqi Foreign Minister, Tariq Aziz, after his meeting with Secretary of State James A. Baker 3d.

If we had an earlier opportunity, several months ago, I told the secretary that we might have been able to remove a lot of misunderstandings between us—there was a chance, or there is a chance, for that. Because he spoke at length about his government's assumptions of miscalculations by Iraq—and when I came to that point, I made it clear to him that we have not made miscalculations. We are very well aware of the situation. We have been very well aware of the situation from the very beginning.

And I told him that we have heard a lot of talk on his side and on the side of President Bush that the Iraqis have not got the message, they don't know what's going [on] around them. . . . I told him if we had met several months ago, I would have told you that we do know everything. We know what the deployment of your forces in the region means; we know what the resolutions you imposed on the Security Council mean; and we know all the facts about the situation—the political facts, the military facts, and the other facts. So talking about miscalculation is incorrect.

I hear Secretary Baker describing our meeting in form and I say also that from the professional point of view, it was a serious meeting. We both listened to each other very carefully. We both gave each other enough time to explain the views we wanted to explain—to convey the information we wanted to convey. From this aspect, about this aspect of the talks, I am satisfied.

But we had grave, or big differences about the issues we addressed. Mr. Baker reiterated the very well-known American position. He is interested in one question only; that's the situation in the Gulf, and the Security Council resolutions about that situation. I told him very clearly, and I repeated my idea and explained it at length, that what is at stake in our region is peace, security, and stability. What's at stake is the fate of the whole region . . . which has been suffering from wars, instabilities, hardships, for several decades.

If you are ready to bring about peace to the region—comprehensive, lasting, just peace to the whole region of the Middle East—we are ready to cooperate. I told him I have no problem with the international legality. I have no problem with the principles of justice and fairness.

Concerning the new world order, or the international world order, I said I have no problem with that order. And we would love to be partners in that order. But that order has to be implemented justly, and in all cases, not using that order in a single manner, in a selective manner, impose it on a certain case . . . and neglect the other issues and not show sincerity and seriousness about implementing it on other issues.

He said that he does not believe that what happened on the 2d of August and later was for the cause of the Palestinian question, or to help the Palestinians. I explained to him the history of Iraq's interest in the Palestinian question. I explained to him that the Palestinian question is a matter of national security to Iraq. If the Palestinian question is not resolved, we do not feel secure in our country. . . .

And I told him that the United States actually implemented embargo on Iraq before the 2d of August. We had dealings with the United States in the field of foodstuffs; we used to buy more than a billion dollars of American products. And we were faithful and accurate in our dealing with the American relevant institutions. Early in 1990, the American administration suspended that deal, which was profitable to both sides. And we were denied food from the United States.

Then the United States government decided to deny Iraq the purchase of a very large list of items. That was done also by the British government and other Western governments. So the boycott was there before the 2d of August. The threat to the security of Iraq was there before the 2d of August. The threat to the Palestinians was there before that date. The threat to the security of Jordan was there before that date.

If the matter is the implementation or the respect of . . . Security Council resolutions, we have a number of resolutions about the Palestinian question. They have been neglected for decades. The last two important resolutions, 242 and 338: The first was adopted in 1967, the other in 1973, and they are not yet implemented. And the United States and members of the coalition . . . have not sent troops to impose the implementation of those resolutions. They have not taken measures against Israel . . .

On the contrary, the United States government has covered the Israeli position, protected it politically at the Security Council and that's very well known to everybody. And the United States government still supplies Israel with military and financial means to stick to its intransigence. So if the matter is respect of international law, Security Council resolutions, we would like you to show the same attention to all Security Council resolutions. And if you do that, a lot of differences between us will be removed.

Concerning the threats—or no threats, which the Secretary referred to and has addressed to you—the tone of his language was diplomatic and polite. I reciprocated. But the substance was full of threats. And I told him, also in substance, that we will not yield to threats. We would like to have genuine constructive dialogue . . . in order to make peace in the region and between our two nations . . .

You hear that I declined to receive the letter from President Bush to my president. At the beginning of the meeting, Secretary Baker told me that he carries a letter from his president to my president, and he handed over a copy to me. I told him I want to read this letter first. And I read it . . . carefully and slowly, and I knew what it was about. I told him I am sorry, I cannot receive this letter.

And the reason is that the language in this letter is not compatible with the language that should be used in correspondence between heads of state. I have no objection that Mr. Bush would state his position very clearly. . . . But when a head of state writes to another head of state a letter, and if he really intends to make peace with that head of state or reach genuine understanding, he should use a polite language. . . . Therefore, because the language of that letter was contrary to the traditions of correspondence between heads of state, I declined to receive it.

The following is an excerpt from President Bush's White House press conference immediately following the Baker-Aziz meeting in Geneva.

I have spoken with the Secretary of State, Jim Baker, who reported to me on his nearly seven hours of conversation with the Iraqi Foreign Minister, Tariq Aziz. Secretary Baker made it clear that he discerned no evidence whatsoever that Iraq was willing to comply with the international community's demand to withdraw from Kuwait and comply with the United Nations resolutions.

Secretary Baker also reported to me that the Iraqi foreign minister rejected my letter to Saddam Hussein, refused to carry this letter and give it to the president of Iraq. The Iraqi ambassador here in Washington did the same thing.

This is but one more example that the Iraqi government is not interested in direct communications, designed to settle the Persian Gulf situation. The record shows that whether the diplomacy is initiated by the United States, the United Nations, the Arab League, or the European Community, the results are the same, unfortunately. The conclusion is clear: Saddam Hussein continues to reject a diplomatic solution.

I sent Secretary Jim Baker to Geneva, not to negotiate, but to communicate, and I wanted Iraqi leaders to know just how determined we are that the Iraqi forces leave Kuwait without condition or further delay.

Secretary Baker made clear that by its full compliance with the twelve relevant United Nations Security Council resolutions, Iraq would gain the opportunity to rejoin the international community. And he also made clear—he also made clear how much Iraq stands to lose if it does not comply.

Let me emphasize that I have not given up on a peaceful outcome. It's not too late. I've just been on the phone subsequent to the Baker press conference with King Fahd, with President Mitterrand, to whom I've talked twice today, Prime Minister Mulroney, and others are contacting other coalition partners to keep the matter under lively discussion. It isn't too late.

But now, as before, as it's been before, the choice of peace or war is really Saddam Hussein's to make.

QUESTIONS AND ANSWERS

Q. You said in an interview last month that you believed in your gut that Saddam Hussein would withdraw from Kuwait by January 15. After the failure of this meeting today, what does your gut tell you about that, and in your gut, do you believe that there is going to be war or peace?

A. I can't misrepresent this to the American people. I am discouraged. I watched much of the Aziz press conference and there was no discussion of withdrawal from Kuwait. The United Nations resolutions are about the aggression against Kuwait. They're about the invasion of Kuwait, about the liquidation of a lot of the people in Kuwait. It's about the restoration of the legitimate government to Kuwait. And here we were listening to a forty-five–minute press conference after the secretary stated—secretary of state of the United States had a six-hour—six hours worth of meetings over there and there was not one single sentence relating to their willingness to get out of Kuwait.

And so, Terry, I have to say I certainly am not encouraged by that, but I'm not going to give up, and I told this to our coalition partners, and I'll be talking to more of them when I finish here. We've got to keep trying. But this was—this was a total stiff-arm, this was a total rebuff.

THE LETTER TO SADDAM

(January 9, 1991)

George Bush

The following is the text of the letter that President Bush wrote to Iraqi President Saddam Hussein and that Iraqi Foreign Minister Tariq Aziz refused to deliver.

MR. PRESIDENT:

We stand today at the brink of war between Iraq and the world. This is a war that began with your invasion of Kuwait; this is a war that can be ended only by Iraq's full and unconditional compliance with U.N. Security Council resolution 678.

I am writing you now, directly, because what is at stake demands that no opportunity be lost to avoid what would be a certain calamity for the people of Iraq. I am writing, as well, because it is said by some that you do not understand just how isolated Iraq is and what Iraq faces as a result.

I am not in a position to judge whether this impression is correct; what I can do, though, is try in this letter to reinforce what Secretary of State [James A.] Baker [3d] told your foreign minister and eliminate any uncertainty or ambiguity that might exist in your mind about where we stand and what we are prepared to do.

The international community is united in its call for Iraq to leave all of Kuwait without condition and without further delay. This is not simply the policy of the United States; it is the position of the world community as expressed in no less than twelve Security Council resolutions.

We prefer a peaceful outcome. However, anything less than full compliance with U.N. Security Council resolution 678 and its predecessors is unacceptable.

There can be no reward for aggression. Nor will there be any negotiation. Principle cannot be compromised. However, by its full compliance, Iraq will gain the opportunity to rejoin the international community.

More immediately, the Iraqi military establishment will escape destruction. But unless you withdraw from Kuwait completely and without condition, you will lose more than Kuwait.

What is at issue here is not the future of Kuwait—it will be free, its government will be restored—but rather the future of Iraq. This choice is yours to make.

The United States will not be separated from its coalition partners. Twelve Security Council resolutions, twenty-eight countries providing military units to enforce them, more than one hundred governments complying with sanctions—all highlight the fact that it is not Iraq against the United States, but Iraq against the world.

That most Arab and Muslim countries are arrayed against you as well should reinforce what I am saying. Iraq cannot and will not be able to hold on to Kuwait or exact a price for leaving.

You may be tempted to find solace in the diversity of opinion that is American democracy. You should resist any such temptation. Diversity ought not to be confused with division. Nor should you underestimate, as others have before you, America's will.

Iraq is already feeling the effects of the sanctions mandated by the United Nations. Should war come, it will be a far greater tragedy for you and your country.

Let me state, too, that the United States will not tolerate the use of chemical or biological weapons or the destruction of Kuwait's oil fields and installations. Further, you will be held directly responsible for terrorist actions against any member of the coalition.

The American people would demand the strongest possible response. You and your country will pay a terrible price if you order unconscionable acts of this sort.

I write this letter not to threaten, but to inform. I do so with no sense of satisfaction, for the people of the United States have no quarrel with the people of Iraq.

Mr. President, U.N. Security Council resolution 678 establishes the period before January 15 of this year as a "pause of good will" so that this crisis may end without further violence.

Whether this pause is used as intended, or merely becomes a prelude to further violence, is in your hands, and yours alone. I hope you weigh your choice carefully and choose wisely, for much will depend upon it.

George Bush

WASHINGTON PREPARES FOR WAR

Elizabeth Drew

L ONG AFTER the war with Iraq is over, long into the future, people will be going over and over the story, trying to figure out how we got into this war, and whether it was necessary. The extent to which the latter question will be studied will depend on things that can't be known now—not only on how actually successful the war is but also whether it is a political success. There have been wars that a lot of people opposed at the time, and also thought were botched and not worth the cost in lives lost, but that have gone down in myth as political successes. Grenada is a fairly recent example. As people positioned themselves on the Iraqi war —before it broke out—they knew that when it was over they would be politically called to judgment. They also knew that the war would be of a scale we haven't seen since Vietnam and in an area that held all sorts of near-term and long-term dangers.

A lot of people here had seen this war coming for a long time—whether or not they supported it—but as it drew nearer many of those who didn't want it to happen went through a process of denial. Some were still grasping at straws, thinking there still could be some deal, an hour before the bombs started falling. But the possibility of war had been clear ever since Bush said, on August 5, that the aggression against Kuwait "will not stand." It was evident from conversations with adminis-tration officials from very early on that some of them believed it would come to war—and that some thought that just as well. Once the presi-dent committed the nation to the liberation of Kuwait, the policy of

Elizabeth Drew is the Washington correspondent of *The New Yorker,* and the author of six books, including *Politics and Money: The New Road to Corruption.* This article is an excerpt from her "Letter from Washington" in the February 4, 1991, issue of *The New Yorker.*

starting with sanctions and of at least appearing to pursue the diplomatic course while the troops and equipment were dispatched to the Gulf region had its own logic, whether the outcome was to be a peaceful solution or war. It was clear from very early on that some officials saw sanctions and diplomacy as the necessary political precursors of war— that each would be, as one official put it, "a box to check." In the early days, an official said to me that by the time we went to war the president would be able to say that he had tried sanctions and tried diplomacy. They were also the necessary logistical precursors of war: The military needed time to build up its forces in the Gulf region.

It isn't the case, as so many people believe, that the administration gave no thought to the long-range implications of such a war, or its downsides. From almost the beginning, I heard people who seemed to accept the idea of a war acknowledge its possible negative consequences. They were as aware as outside people of the dangers of creating a power vacuum that Syria or Iran might fill and of encouraging fundamentalist Muslim extremism. But, for these officials, smashing Saddam Hussein's military machine—and, if possible, his regime—had priority. It was a case of first things first. Some thought has been given to post-crisis security arrangements, and some papers have been written—even if far more thought has been given to ridding the region of the threat posed by Saddam Hussein, and more time was devoted to that end. The same policymakers had to think near term (what the president should say today; how to respond to peace initiatives by others) and long term. It is out of awareness of some of the long-term dangers that the war has so far been conducted with the aim of not destroying Iraq itself but destroying Iraq's most dangerous military wherewithal. The idea, as a senior administration official put it recently, is "just to substantially reduce Iraq's ability to threaten its neighbors." He went on, "But we realize there's a place for an Iraq with some military capability once this is over. It will always be a major player, by virtue of its location and population. We don't want to alienate the Iraqi people—just deal with their leader, who has taken them down this dangerous path."

Of course, the president's issue with Saddam Hussein has never been simply about Kuwait. Over the months, Bush has told us that it's also about oil, about Iraq's possession of chemical weapons and effort to achieve a nuclear weapon, about the threat Hussein poses to his other neighbors, and about the need to establish a "new world order" in the wake of (what seemed to be) the end of the Cold War. Trying to read Bush's mind and to understand his impulses on Iraq has been a major pastime here—an exercise that takes people into geopolitics and amateur psychoanalysis. Some people who know Bush maintain that for him the rape of Kuwait was an issue of principle. Over the months, in meeting with congressional leaders, Bush spoke with evident feeling about Iraq's brutal treatment of Kuwait. Not long ago, a White House aide said to me that on Iraq Bush "is unlike he is on any other issue." The aide went on to explain, "Usually, he sees the complexities, and doesn't care all that much. He didn't care all that much about capital gains. But this touches some deep inner core. He was deeply offended by the aggression against Kuwait. Later, the atrocities also upset him deeply." Not long after that conversation, Bush said in a letter to college students, "There is much in the modern world that is . . . washed in shades of gray. But not the brutal aggression of Saddam Hussein. . . . It's black and white."

The theory that Bush had been influenced by Henry Stimson—William Howard Taft's secretary of war, Herbert Hoover's secretary of state, and then Franklin Roosevelt's secretary of war—recently enjoyed a certain vogue here. A biography of Stimson, by the British writer Godfrey Hodgson, was published last fall, and Bush was said to be reading it. Like Bush, Stimson was a New England blue blood, a member of the Yankee establishment—even a Yalie who belonged to Skull and Bones—and, Hodgson points out, Stimson gave the commencement address when young George Bush was graduating from Andover. (Bush mentions this in his autobiography.) Stimson was one of the founding fathers of the Eastern foreign-policy establishment, and stood for collective security and resistance to aggression. There is also a theory that Bush's resolve was strengthened by Margaret Thatcher when the two met in Aspen on August 2, that Mrs. Thatcher saw the invasion of Kuwait as a matter of principle.

But there is another view of what was going on with Bush—which he reinforced by his own rhetoric—before the war began. In this view, Bush was proving something to himself and the world—showing what a tough guy he is. When he personalized the issue as one between him and Saddam Hussein, when he swaggered and did his Clint Eastwood routine, when he said that Hussein is "going to get his ass kicked," he gave credence to the idea that he was proving something. This is a speculation that members of Congress—even ones who don't much admire Bush—are reluctant to talk about openly. A senator said to me recently, reluctantly, "We all know instinctively this is not a strong man. It's greatly disturbing. I try not to think about it. I don't know anyone who's honest with himself who doesn't think this." One important member of Congress said to me not long ago that before the war began "a good many people" in Congress were concerned about Bush's behavior—about what this person called Bush's "obsession" with Iraq, his "fixation" on it, "to the exclusion of everything else. A lot of people who met with him did get concerned." The answer is probably some blend of both theories. Last fall, an important member of Congress who had met with Bush several times said, unhappily, "I don't know whether he's convinced Saddam Hussein, but he's sure convinced me." It seems most likely that some very important principles are involved for Bush—ones he might not apply in a less strategically situated place, or an area without oil, or one that didn't pose a threat to governments headed by friends of his— and that he is proving something. Unfortunately, his rhetoric and manner at times compromised the seriousness of his purpose.

There is also reason to conclude that Bush was spoiling for a fight with Saddam Hussein for some time. Hussein's obduracy raises the question of whether a political settlement was ever possible, but—deliberately or not—Bush left little room for one. It was clear for some time that some of Bush's top advisers thought that in the long run it would be better to take Saddam Hussein on now, before he was in a position to cause more trouble. (It became known here not long ago that John Sununu, the president's chief of staff, was telling people that a short, successful war would be pure political gold for the president—would guarantee his reelection. It's also believed by some here that among the reasons for the President's deciding to bring things to a head in January, getting the United Nations to set a deadline, were both economic and political ones; according to this line of thought, the president didn't want to risk a protracted war in an election year.)

In fact, at the first National Security Council meeting the president held in August, after the invasion of Kuwait, it was understood that the question had to do with stopping Hussein from menacing other Arab states and from eventually going after Israel with chemical or nuclear weapons. Once other important Arab nations—primarily Saudi Arabia and Egypt—signed on to this rationale, the United States was committed to reducing Iraq's military strength irrespective of Kuwait. (The Saudis are said to be more concerned about reducing Iraq's million-man army than about its possible weapons—or about Kuwait.) From the beginning, one of Bush's stated goals was "stability in the Persian Gulf region," which could mean a lot of things. This is why it eventually became the administration's explicit position that even if Iraq withdrew from Kuwait a return to the status quo ante wouldn't suffice—that, one way or another, Iraq's weaponry had to be reduced. This goal wasn't explicitly part of the United Nations resolutions, but the last one adopted, which

184 · THE GULF WAR READER

authorized the use of force, also said a goal was "to restore . . . security in the area." Some officials believed all along that the only way to achieve it was by military means. When Brent Scowcroft, the national security adviser, was asked on *Meet the Press* on the Sunday before the invasion whether Hussein's chemical weapons and nuclear potential could as effectively be eliminated by other than military means, he answered quickly and flatly, "No." A couple of months earlier, Scowcroft had asked a strategically placed member of Congress if he didn't feel that war was the more effective way of getting rid of these weapons. Scowcroft, whose mild demeanor masks a very tough inner core, has been believed to be, next to Bush, the most "hawkish" of the policymakers. Scowcroft is a kind man, and a thoughtful one, but also a very tough infighter; he prevailed in some important instances even over Secretary of State James Baker. However, by various accounts, the president needed no pushing toward a showdown with Saddam Hussein.

Two things made the dealing with this particular policy issue unusual. The first is that very few people were in on the policymaking. The secretive president held the decisions very tightly; out of the entire government, no more than a dozen—and probably fewer than ten—were actually in on them. (Only three people had been in on the decision, later overturned, to send Baker to Baghdad.) A lot more people kibitzed, worked on pieces of the policy, were willing to talk about the policy, but only a tiny group was in on the decisions. Such an arrangement isn't conducive to fully airing opinions. From the time the first commitments were made, there appears to have been no great internal debate; there were differences in degree, but this war had no George Ball. Baker had been reluctant to get involved militarily, fearing the political effect of body bags, but he appears to have let no great distance develop between himself and the president. It is worth remembering that the biggest decision was taken early and hastily: that, one way or another, Iraq would be completely forced out of Kuwait. The line was absolute. The second thing that made this issue unusual was the amount of dissembling that went on. Publicly and even in most private conversations, no one, of course, was for war—even though some saw it as the preferred solution. Everyone was for a "peaceful resolution." But those words don't mean much; the real issue was how "peaceful resolution" was defined. Candor came in short blips. On this more than any other issue, one had to try to figure out why someone was saying what he was saying.

In early December, a senior official referred to what he called the "messy solution": Saddam Hussein withdraws from less than all of Kuwait and remains in power with his weapons intact. But any removal of weapons would be temporary; the only way to be sure that the Iraqi regime doesn't menace its neighbors with terrible weapons for some time to come is to remove the Iraqi regime *and* its weapons. War, of course, provides its own messy solutions. This was, in fact, a major factor in the thinking of many of those—congressmen, former officials—who preferred to stay with sanctions longer or actually (whether they said so or not) opposed a war.

Just as officials all said they preferred a peaceful solution, they said—virtually up to the point where Marlin Fitzwater, the president's spokesman, announced a week ago Wednesday evening, "The liberation of Kuwait has begun"—that the president hadn't made a decision to go to war, even though it seemed that the president had long since decided on war. Toward the end of November, shortly before the United Nations deadline of January 15 was set, a senior official indicated that, for credibility, we wouldn't be able to wait long after the deadline had passed. We could never be quite sure, as we passed the markers on the way to war, exactly what the president was thinking or how many of the "diplomatic" paths were real. It was noticeable that administration officials described any partial withdrawal from Kuwait—one that left the disputed islands and oil field in the hands of Iraq—as "the nightmare scenario." The "nightmare" may have been less Hussein's acquisition of territory than his remaining well armed and in power. It was also noticeable that as the deadline drew near some officials spoke with obvious anxiety about the possibility that Hussein might make enough of a move toward withdrawal that it would become politically impossible for us to go to war. There will always be some mystery about this story. The memoirs won't necessarily tell us the truth; historians will draw various conclusions. There is little question that American policy toward Iraq before August 2 will be looked upon with disfavor, but though the subject is in the air people in Washington feel now is no time to argue about that. The real measurement of the "success" of this war can't be made for years—until we have seen its aftereffects.

IT SEEMS CLEAR that some of the president's advisers were more interested in a negotiated outcome than others. One has to be careful about this, because of the self-servingness of officials and their aides, but there is real evidence that Baker and his closest advisers believed longer than others did that there could and should be a political settlement. A lot of people think that the president, by his terms for a settlement and by his rhetoric, pushed Hussein—as well as himself—into a corner. A former Pentagon official says, "You don't talk to Arabs like they're dogs in the street; you don't say you're going to kick their ass. This is not to say he would have backed down, but that level of discourse isn't conducive to a diplomatic solution." A key senator says that the threat of war "stirred Saddam's Arab macho." Scowcroft didn't like the idea of Baker going to Baghdad: He was concerned that something that the president had done, as an official puts it, "for domestic reasons," would raise questions in our Arab allies' eyes about our resolve, and signal weakness to Saddam Hussein. It was for these reasons—and because of suspicions that Baker might be too interested in negotiating—that the president refused to bargain on dates for the Baghdad meeting. In the end, the president scuttled the trip, blaming the Iraqis for refusing to set a date for the meeting before January 12. And no sooner was the possible trip to Baghdad announced than the president defined its terms in a manner that made it difficult for Hussein to accept—saying "There can be no face-saving," "I'm not in a negotiating mood," "They must withdraw without condition," "There will be no give" on a Middle East peace conference. When I asked a senior administration official in early January why Saddam Hussein had stuck on a meeting on the twelfth, not offering an earlier date, he said, "Initially, the Iraqis were interested in the offer of meetings, but when they realized we wouldn't play the game with dates, and wouldn't negotiate, they backed off."

The State Department did in fact appear more interested in trying to make a deal with Hussein than the White House was, and, after it was announced that Baker would meet Iraqi Foreign Minister Tariq Aziz in Geneva on January 9, an official confirmed to me that the president and Scowcroft had reined Baker in by moving the meeting to Geneva, and having it held with Aziz rather than Hussein. Though Baker partisans have taken care during this crisis to portray him as more the man of peace than the president and Scowcroft, and one must be chary of the Baker people's efforts, of which there have been many, to paint Baker as the good guy, it is apparently the case that Baker, who is congenitally more of a dealmaker than other officials, was more inclined than others to try to work something out. Bush and Baker are very close, and Baker has a great deal of influence with the president, but it appears that in this instance the president's (and Scowcroft's) will prevailed. As soon as the Geneva meeting was announced, there arose the question of whether Baker might go on to Baghdad if invited by Aziz. The president, in one of his Friday-afternoon pre–helicopter-boarding press availabilities on the South Lawn of the White House, said, in answer to this question, flatly, "No." It was noticeable that Baker, on a television interview program over that weekend, and even in his press conference in Geneva, was careful to say that "the president" had decided that he couldn't go on to Baghdad. (On the interview program, he added, "I'll leave it right there.") Publicly, administration officials said that the Baghdad meeting —on the twelfth or any time after the Geneva meeting—had been nixed because it would give Saddam Hussein an opportunity to drag us into negotiations past the deadline, and, while that was true enough, it wasn't the whole truth. Baker was sent to Geneva with very little maneuvering room, but, as it happened, so was Tariq Aziz. A trip to Baghdad might not have made any difference, but State Department officials, perhaps in an attempt to cover themselves, concede privately that Baker's not going to Baghdad omitted a step from "going the extra mile" (as the president pledged) for a peaceful settlement.

The rationale for our no-concessions, no-compromise policy was that anything that made Saddam Hussein appear to have gained anything from his attack on Kuwait would make him a hero in the eyes of the Arab world, and a future menace. But not everyone in the Arab world, including some of our allies there, saw it that way—nor did everyone here. Some people here thought that Hussein would never withdraw from Kuwait voluntarily—that in order to stay in power he didn't dare. Some people's claiming now to have thought that all along may be retroactive wisdom, but as the crisis played out there were people in both camps— that he would, and that he wouldn't—but more people, including some experts in the Arab world, who thought that he would. After the war broke out, one well-placed official told me—honestly, I think (even though he hadn't mentioned it before)—that he had never thought Saddam Hussein would withdraw from Kuwait, as a matter of survival, particularly after he had given up his gains from his long war with Iran. This person said, "Saddam didn't think he'd be challenged over his invasion of Kuwait, and, once challenged, Arab pride was involved. He couldn't have two losses in a row."

Historians—in the middle distance and far into the future—will pore over the question of whether there were missed opportunities. The question will arise—it is already with us—as to whether the administration foreclosed efforts by other countries to make a settlement. Not long ago, word circulated in Washington that an Algerian initiative, in mid-December, had the concurrence of the Saudis as well as the Iraqis but was scotched by Washington. Officials deny that. There will remain questions about whether, by insisting that there be no "linkage" between a possible Middle East peace conference to deal with the Israeli-Palestinian issue—not even "the appearance" of linkage—the administration closed off an exit. The administration was correct when it argued that Saddam Hussein hadn't invaded Kuwait to help the Palestinian cause—that his call for a peace conference was a diversion—and at the end he failed to respond positively even to a French proposal, openly opposed by us, that came as close as anything to linking a withdrawal by Iraq to a peace conference. (The French actually worded the proposal to take care of some of our concerns about a peace conference.) On the Saturday before the war began, Bush, speaking about United Nations Secretary-General Javier Pérez de Cuéllar's trip to Baghdad, then under way, said that it was acceptable for the secretary-general to talk to Hussein about a peace conference, but "it depends on how it's put forward," which seemed to raise the possibility that we might go to war over semantics.

Another influence on Bush, it seems, has been his friends who head moderate Arab regimes—President Hosni Mubarak, of Egypt, and King Fahd, of Saudi Arabia. Bush prides himself on developing personal relationships with foreign leaders, and his friendships with these particular leaders had been a source of concern to people deeply committed to the interests of Israel. Now these people find Bush's being pals with these Arab leaders just fine, because of the coincidence of Egypt's and Saudi Arabia's and Israel's interests in ridding the Middle East of the menace of Saddam Hussein. Throughout the crisis, we were told that the Saudi and the Egyptian leaders were most eager to see the end of the dangerous Iraqi regime. One of the more interesting and colorful figures in this whole story is the Saudi Ambassador to the United States, Prince Bandar bin Sultan—a dashing forty-one-year-old former fighter pilot, who has a very friendly relationship with Bush as well as with a lot of other people around town and has been in and out of American policy (including the Iran-Contra affair) for years. Bandar, who is King Fahd's nephew, is described by people who know the situation well as being more hawkish than the king (or than his father, the Saudi defense minister) and also, as the king's protégé, as having been an influence on him of late. Bandar made well known here his unhappiness with the original announcement of the Baker mission to Baghdad—both because he hadn't been told about it ahead of time and because he thought it gave Saddam Hussein a trophy. Bandar was also upset that Bush had proposed that our allies would sit in on the discussions, because that made them look all the more like our patsies—and that proposal, one of a few that hadn't been thought through when the trip was first announced, was quickly dropped, for various reasons.

• • •

THE CONGRESSIONAL debate over authorizing the president to use force to drive Iraq from Kuwait was, as described, serious, and even sombre, but for the great majority of the members it was not as difficult a decision as has been suggested. As one congressional aide explained it to me afterward, "it was the most difficult *vote* any of them had ever cast; it wasn't the most difficult decision." What he meant was that by far most of the members of Congress decided without difficulty where their vote would come out, but few savored actually casting it. The aide said, "The vote was a potential career-killer—either way." The members of Congress knew that they could be caught on the wrong side of history—but when they voted there was no telling which side that would be. This is one reason so many people wanted to speak on the issue, forcing both the House and the Senate to meet in overnight sessions on Friday, January 11. Most of those who voted to authorize the president to use force understood that they were committing young Americans to war. A Republican congressman, who supported the use-of-force resolution, said to me afterward, "Last year, I went to a memorial for a serviceman who died in Panama. Twenty-three of our military people died there. That number doesn't sound so big until you look the family in the eye."

The vote was more partisan than the issue is—in Washington as well as in the rest of the country. Not all Republicans, and certainly not all people who have supported the military or military action in the past, were behind the idea of going to war over Kuwait—or of going to war at all. However, the president had got himself, and the country's prestige, so committed to the deadline set by the United Nations (at our behest) that by the time the debate began, on Thursday, January 10, there was no question as to the outcome of the vote. Similarly, there is a natural tendency, especially strong among Republicans, to rally around the president—but the vote was a close call for a few Republicans. Two Republican senators and three Republican representatives opposed the use-of-force resolution. And not all of those in what has come to be termed the war party care a fig about Kuwait. Still, they do think that the menace of Saddam Hussein has to be put an end to. There is also a significant group of people—many but not all of whom have former ties to the military—who have been "hawkish" in the past but don't think that the invasion of Kuwait should have been defined as threatening our vital interests. (Some point out that there is no oil shortage now.)

Some of the ten Democrats in the Senate and the eighty-six Democrats in the House who supported the use-of-force resolution did so in large part because of their overriding concern for the fate of Israel, which wanted to be rid of the danger posed by Saddam Hussein. Not all the

Democrats who backed the use of force did it because of Israel, and those who did gave other reasons as well, but everyone knew it was an important factor. And not all Democrats close to Israel supported the use-of-force resolution; in fact, according to the American Israel Public Affairs Committee (AIPAC), Jewish members in both chambers were divided roughly fifty-fifty. Before the voting, on Saturday, January 12, the White House, working closely with AIPAC, lobbied Jewish members of Congress and other Democrats who had close ties to Israel. Some of this lobbying wasn't very subtle: on the Friday morning before the vote, over a hundred members of Congress, a large proportion of them Jewish, were invited to a breakfast meeting with Bush; a few of those invited were very liberal members who had never voted a dime for defense and were most unlikely to vote for the war (and didn't).

The White House had also been instrumental in the setting up last December of the Committee for Peace and Security in the Gulf, headed by Richard Perle, a defense conservative who had served in the Reagan administration; Ann Lewis, a liberal Democratic activist; and Representative Stephen Solarz, of New York, a senior Democrat on the Foreign Affairs Committee. Solarz co-sponsored the resolution authorizing the president to use force, in the process angering several of his Democratic colleagues. (There was less anger directed at him than at Les Aspin, the chairman of the House Armed Services Committee, who had started out questioning the wisdom of going beyond the policy of deterring an attack on Saudi Arabia and ended up a champion of the administration's position.) But the anger wasn't as bitter as that over aiding the Contras; many people on each side thought that the other side might have a point; people seemed to want to avoid bitterness. The issue was too big, and the political outcome too uncertain. Defense contractors also lobbied for the president's position. AIPAC turned loose its nationwide network of contributors, prominent businessmen, and social friends of members. It is impossible to get inside a politician's head and know what combination of factors—merits, presidential calculations or other long-term ambitions, friendships—motivated him. The politician himself may not know.

There is good reason to suspect that some members of Congress voted to continue sanctions in the comfortable knowledge that their position wouldn't prevail—and they wouldn't have to live with the consequences. Not all those who voted for the resolution to keep sanctions in place longer, with the use of force as an eventual option, actually thought that the option should be used. Some Democrats reasoned that, either way, this would be Bush's war—if it was politically successful, he would get the credit, and if it wasn't he would get the blame—so there was more percentage in voting against it. For some Democrats, arguing that sanctions should be stayed with longer was a way of extending the horizon, buying time and hoping something would happen. Senate Armed Services Committee Chairman Sam Nunn's support for the sanctions approach was a major factor in making the vote closer in the Senate (where the sanctions approach was defeated by a vote of 46–53) than it was in the House (where staying with sanctions was defeated 183–250). Nunn, who had been a strong supporter of the military (thus sometimes putting himself at odds with his fellow Democrats), gave other Senate Democrats "cover" for voting against the use of force.

Nunn, who had said that the use of force is "justified" but not necessarily "wise" or "in our national interest," was a co-sponsor of the sanctions resolution. That he played such a prominent role was a surprise to the White House, which had expected him to go with what was becoming the prevailing wind in Washington—and to not confront the president on such an issue. Nunn was (and remains) convinced that sanctions were wrecking Iraq's economy and weakening its ability to maintain its military machine, and that, over time, this might have ended with an uprising against Hussein (we have seen successful uprisings against brutal dictators in the past year), if not a withdrawal from Kuwait. Even if it hadn't, Nunn's thinking went, the Iraqi military machine would be all the weaker the longer sanctions remained in place. Nunn was also concerned about the long-term effects of the war.

Because the vote was so close in the Senate, some Democrats there were angry with Majority Leader George Mitchell (whom they generally admire) for not having called them into session in early December, shortly after Nunn held his hearings that bolstered the sanctions cause, when the momentum on Capitol Hill seemed to be going their way. They argue that if the vote had been taken then they could have stopped the war. But it is quite likely that even if there had been such a Senate vote Bush would have found a way to go to war. House Speaker Thomas Foley argues that in December some people who opposed going to war would have voted its authorization—following upon the United Nations vote—on the ground that this gave the president another means of diplomatically pressuring Saddam Hussein to withdraw. Since Bush was publicly arguing then that he needed the threat of force in order to reach a peaceful resolution of the matter, many Democrats were painfully aware that if they voted to deny him that authority they would be accused of undermining the president's diplomatic efforts. Also, at the time the White House didn't want a vote (there had been a fierce internal argument over this), because Foley had warned the president it would be a contentious and close one. When the Democratic leadership held off the vote in December, it was aware that the president's position would gain strength with the passage of time if diplomatic efforts failed and Hussein didn't withdraw.

Shortly after the New Year, the White House, discerning that it had the votes in both the House and the Senate, decided that it was preferable to have a close vote rather than no vote at all—and that this would remove the argument that the president was going to war without regard for Congress's opinion. Many members—even supporters of the president's policy—were insisting upon Congress's constitutional prerogative of being the institution that can declare war. In the end, the constitutional issue wasn't so much settled as detoured. At the same time that the White House was changing its mind on having a vote, many Democrats, including the congressional leadership, were concluding that to continue to forestall a vote on the issue was untenable. Besides, liberals were clamoring for a vote before a war began. They wanted to go on record. They got their vote. The Democratic leadership quietly asked the president for his assurance that he wouldn't start the war before they had a chance to vote, sometime around or just after January 15, and the president replied that he could make no such guarantees.

The resolution that was adopted by both chambers on January 12 didn't declare war, but everyone knew—or should have known—that that was its effect. To the end, some of its supporters were arguing that it was simply a diplomatic maneuver. As Foley warned the House in his speech on Saturday, just before the vote, "Do not do it"—authorize the president to use force—"under the notion that you merely hand him another diplomatic tool. . . . The president has signalled no doubt about this. He has said again and again that if given the power he may well use it, perhaps sooner than we realize." (At the breakfast the day before, Defense Secretary Dick Cheney had quietly told some congressmen, in effect, "Don't vote for this if you think we're not going.") Many members of Congress were angry at being put in such a position: they had been presented with a fait accompli, and vowed, "Never again." A president had found a new way to take the country to war. In an irony of historic proportions, several Democrats were hoist: over the years, they had argued against the United States' taking unilateral action in foreign crises. But George Bush, by working multilaterally through the United Nations (and unilaterally making troop commitments), had rendered Congress irrelevant.

In the days immediately following the vote, as the deadline approached, Washington became increasingly sombre. Even many of those who wanted a war became solemn. For those who had hoped that such an outcome could be averted, there was a feeling of helplessness. As the last hopes for a diplomatic settlement evaporated—Pérez de Cuéllar's mission to Baghdad failed, the French proposal failed, a last-minute appeal on the night of the fifteenth by Pérez de Cuéllar went unanswered—an almost surreal atmosphere settled over the capital. The administration was set against anything that might enable Saddam Hussein to postpone the deadline—the only thing it would have accepted, officials said, was the sudden and unmistakable movement of masses of Iraqi soldiers north, out of Kuwait. It had also decided not to attack immediately after the deadline, because we would look too eager, but to attack soon, so as to make the deadline real. (Actually, there had been some confusion as to exactly when the deadline expired, and it was finally decided that that would occur at midnight, Eastern Standard Time.) An early attack would also preempt any efforts to delay by Saddam Hussein. People outside the administration spent a lot of time speculating as to when the attack might come—some continuing to disbelieve it might happen. (The Pentagon leaked dates that turned out to be later than the attack.) Worry and anxiety ran deep. On Capitol Hill, members felt it inappropriate to introduce bills, or go about their business as if nothing else were going on. One senator quietly instructed his staff not to schedule political events in February—he would probably need the time, he said, to attend funerals. A senator said to me on the afternoon of the sixteenth, "It seems like everything has stopped." Another senator said that he had gone to the senators' private dining room expecting his colleagues to talk about the impending war, but "they were talking about what's going on in the Ethics Committee—nobody wanted to talk about the war."

Two days before the war began, the president was described to me, by someone who had seen him recently, as convinced we could have a short war, and prepared to wage it—as "very composed." Around the same time, a very senior administration official said that the policymakers took as their model previous short Middle East wars—the Six-Day War, in 1967, and the 1973 Yom Kippur War, which lasted eighteen days. The open terrain in the Middle East, he said, is conducive to short wars, and to an air war. On the sixteenth, members of Congress and their staffs received briefings on potential terrorist acts on Capitol Hill and elsewhere, and came away shaken. The sixteenth was a gray, cold, rainy day—almost eerily still. People had run out of things to say to each other, and seemed to clasp the silence to them, knowing it wouldn't last.

INTERVENTION AND ESCALATION: THE DEBATE

IN DEFENSE OF SAUDI ARABIA

(*Speech of August 8, 1990*)

George Bush

The following are excerpts from President Bush's address from the Oval Office on August 8, announcing the deployment of troops to Saudi Arabia.

IN THE life of a nation, we're called upon to define who we are and what we believe. Sometimes the choices are not easy. As today's president, I ask for your support in the decision I've made to stand up for what's right and condemn what's wrong all in the cause of peace.

At my direction, elements of the 82d Airborne Division as well as key units of the United States Air Force are arriving today to take up defensive positions in Saudi Arabia. I took this action to assist the Saudi Arabian government in the defense of its homeland. No one commits America's armed forces to a dangerous mission lightly. But after perhaps unparalleled international consultation and exhausting every alternative, it became necessary to take this action.

Let me tell you why. Less than a week ago in the early morning hours of August 2, Iraqi armed forces, without provocation or warning, invaded a peaceful Kuwait. Facing negligible resistance from its much smaller neighbor, Iraq's tanks stormed in blitzkrieg fashion through Kuwait in a few short hours.

With more than 100,000 troops along with tanks, artillery and surface-to-surface missiles, Iraq now occupies Kuwait.

This aggression came just hours after Saddam Hussein specifically assured numerous countries in the area that there would be no invasion. There is no justification whatsoever for this outrageous and brutal act of aggression.

A puppet regime imposed from the outside is unacceptable. The acquisition of territory by force is unacceptable. No one, friend or foe, should doubt our desire for peace and no one should underestimate our determination to confront aggression.

Four simple principles guide our policy.

First, we seek the immediate unconditional and complete withdrawal of all Iraqi forces from Kuwait. Second, Kuwait's legitimate government must be restored to replace the puppet regime. And third, my administration, as has been the case with every president from President Roosevelt to President Reagan, is committed to the security and stability of the Persian Gulf. And fourth, I am determined to protect the lives of American citizens abroad.

Immediately after the Iraqi invasion, I ordered an embargo of all trade with Iraq, and together with many other nations announced sanctions that both froze all Iraqi assets in this country and protected Kuwait's assets.

The stakes are high. Iraq is already a rich and powerful country. It possesses the world's second-largest reserves of oil and over a million men under arms. It's the fourth-largest military in the world.

Our country now imports nearly half the oil it consumes and could face a major threat to its economic independence. Much of the world is even more dependent upon imported oil and is even more vulnerable to Iraqi threats. We succeeded in the struggle for freedom in Europe because we and our allies remained stalwart. Keeping the peace in the Middle East will require no less.

But we must recognize that Iraq may not stop using force to advance its ambitions. Iraq has amassed an enormous war machine on the Saudi border capable of initiating hostilities with little or no additional preparations. Given the Iraqi government's history of aggression against its own citizens as well as its neighbors, to assume Iraq will not attack again would be unwise and unrealistic. And therefore, after consulting with King Fahd, I sent Secretary of Defense Dick Cheney to discuss cooperative measures we could take.

Following those meetings, the Saudi government requested our help. And I responded to that request by ordering U.S. air and ground forces to deploy to the Kingdom of Saudi Arabia.

Let me be clear, the sovereign independence of Saudi Arabia is of vital interest to the United States. This decision, which I shared with the Congressional leadership, grows out of the longstanding friendship and security relationship between the United States and Saudi Arabia.

U.S. forces will work together with those of Saudi Arabia and other nations to preserve the integrity of Saudi Arabia and to deter further Iraqi aggression. Through their presence, as as well through training and exercises, these multinational forces will enhance the overall capability of Saudi armed forces to defend the kingdom.

I want to be clear about what we are doing and why.

America does not seek conflict. Nor do we seek to chart the destiny of other nations. But America will stand by her friends. The mission of our troops is wholly defensive. Hopefully, they'll not be needed long. They will not initiate hostilities but they will defend themselves, the Kingdom of Saudi Arabia and other friends in the Persian Gulf.

And one more thing. I'm asking the oil companies to do their fair share. They should exercise restraint and not abuse today's uncertainties to raise prices.

QUESTIONS AND ANSWERS

Q. How long will you keep American forces in Saudi Arabia, and why not use them to drive the Iraqi troops out of Kuwait?

A. Well, as you know from what I said, they're there in a defensive mode right now. And therefore, that is not the mission, to drive the Iraqis out of Kuwait. We have economic sanctions that I hope will be effective to that end, and I don't know how long they'll be there. They just got there—are just getting there.

Q. Is this an open-ended commitment? I mean, could this drag on for years?

A. Nothing is open ended. But I'm not worrying about that there at all. I'm worrying about getting them there and doing what I indicated in our speech in there is necessary—the defense of the Saudis and the trying, through concerted international means, to reverse out this aggression.

Q. Mr. President, you said in your speech this morning that the puppet regime in Kuwait was unacceptable, and so was the acquisition of territory. At the same time, though, you said that the—that the deployments are wholly defensive. The question is, how do you actually expect to force Hussein to withdraw from Kuwait?

A. Economic sanctions in this instance, if fully enforced, can be very, very effective. It is a rich country in terms of oil resources. They're a poor country, in a sense, because he squandered much of the resource on military might, and there are some indications that he's already beginning to feel the pinch. And nobody can stand up forever to total economic deprivation.

SADDAM'S NEXT TARGET

A. M. Rosenthal

W IN O R lose in the gamble for control of the world's oil, Saddam
Hussein's next major target will be Israel.

If he wins, he will turn to the attack against Israel. He will lead the final
Holy War as the one, true Muslim conqueror, crying destruction to the
Jews and death to all Arabs who question his vision, course, and glory.

Even if he sees himself in danger of defeat and disgrace in the Gulf,
thanks to President Bush's courage, war with Israel will remain just as
important to him. He will back off in the Gulf and then try to rally the
Arab world to war against Israel as his only hope for political redemption.

The Israelis are not Saudis. They do not demand the support of the
entire world as a precondition to stand and fight.

But the risk of combat with Israel may seem better to Saddam Hussein
than the alternative he will face if he simply accepts defeat in the Gulf.
The alternative will be removal from power. In the Middle East, that
usually coincides with execution.

We can all see now that the only puzzle about Saddam Hussein's
conquest of Kuwait is why the world refused to see it coming.

Even that is no vast mystery. The West and the Soviet Union helped
create this man of evil dreams. They simply refused to believe he would
turn against them, not after they had supplied him with weapons and
loans and all.

But Saddam Hussein's dream of dominating the Arab Middle East was

A. M. Rosenthal is the former executive editor of *The New York Times,* and is now a columnist
for the paper. This piece appeared in *The Times* on August 9, 1990.

never separate from his vision of ultimate duty and destiny—the elimination of the state of Israel.

In the crisis over Kuwait and oil, much of the world forgets that neither are the full goal of Saddam Hussein—not as long as Israel stands.

But high on the list of those who do not forget are Yasir Arafat and other leaders of the Palestine Liberation Organization.

They are not alone. For all other Arabs who long for Israel's extinction, Saddam Hussein's passion against the Jews is what counts, not the fate of the oil-fat ruling families of the Gulf states.

In Jerusalem members of the Israeli government have not forgotten either. There is satisfaction that the U.S. finally awoke to the danger of the Iraqi killer and that President Bush has taken courageous, clear action to try to stop him in the Gulf.

And Israel has the pleasure of seeing cherished Western myths vanish, puff, like soap bubbles. One was that Arab "moderates" like President Mubarak of Egypt were valuable for their "influence" on hard customers like Saddam Hussein.

Another was that, say what you want about Arab leaders, they are men of honor.

Saddam Hussein lied to every Arab brother he could put his arm around. The Emir of Kuwait fled his country so fast the helicopter was still warming up. And King Hussein of Jordan, enriched with American aid and guaranteed as a Plucky Little King, ran to the invader of Kuwait as fast as his royal little feet could take him.

But Israelis who have spent their lives studying Arab dictators know Saddam's danger to them will not vanish if the international movement organized by Mr. Bush prevents Iraq from controlling Saudi Arabian oil.

King Hussein is on Dictator Hussein's side now. Given the king's past record of picking losers, that may not be good for either of them.

But the King might not find Saddam quite as easy to desert.

The Iraqi may not attack Israel directly—that can wait. Instead he will suggest that the P.L.K. invite some Iraqi brigades to enter Jordan, which borders Israel, to join the Iraqi military advisers already there.

Wouldn't that mean Israeli reprisal? In other words, can't we go on expecting the Israelis to fight off attacks as they have for over forty years?

Yes, we can. But even Israelis prefer to live rather than die for their country, given any choice.

In Washington Congress is talking about how the U.S. could prevent an Iraqi move against Israel.

Mr. Bush might be able to do it—by saying beforehand that Iraqi troops easing into Jordan, even with the king's approval, would violate vital U.S. interests and invite American retaliation.

That kind of presidential warning has so far prevented an Iraqi attack against Saudi Arabia. Not every Iraqi is an evil dreamer of death. Those who are not may decide after another presidential threat that Saddam has to be retired, however these things are arranged in Baghdad.

By taking his stand now, Mr. Bush could not only save some Israeli blood but might prevent more American soldiers from dying facing the unholy killers of the Middle East.

WASHINGTON'S "VITAL INTERESTS"

Thomas L. Friedman

I N H I S statement to the nation on Wednesday explaining the decision to send American troops to the Arabian Peninsula, President Bush said that the defense of Saudi Arabia was of "vital interest" to the United States. But Mr. Bush and his top aides have not clearly defined just how the Iraqi invasion and annexation of Kuwait touches the lives of Americans or affects their future.

For many Americans, the connection is not clear. Beyond the quick jump in gasoline prices, many people seem to share the view of Katie Safier of Miami, who mused in an interview, "Why should we be involved? We could get oil from Mexico."

One reason Bush administration officials have not clearly articulated what is at stake is that the real political and economic interests involved are not quite so lofty as some of the broad principles used by the president to explain the operation.

The United States has not sent troops to the Saudi desert to preserve democratic principles. The Saudi monarchy is a feudal regime that does not even allow women to drive cars. Surely it is not American policy to make the world safe for feudalism. This is about money, about protecting governments loyal to America and punishing those that are not and about who will set the price of oil.

The failure to spell out the American stakes and justify them is also

Thomas L. Friedman is chief diplomatic correspondent for *The New York Times* and author of the best-selling *From Beirut to Jerusalem*. This article was published on the front page in the August 12, 1990, issue of *The New York Times* under the headline "Confrontation in the Gulf: U.S. Gulf Policy—Vague 'Vital Interest.'"

due to the inarticulate way the president and his advisers try to explain foreign policy to the American people.

In addition, President Bush, Secretary of State James A. Baker 3d and other top officials live in a rarefied world of foreign policy discussions with a set of assumptions about the pivotal importance of the Persian Gulf—to such a degree that it does not always occur to officials to spell out what is at stake.

As Mr. Baker told his NATO allies on Friday, without much elaboration, "Since 1949, every American president has said that the Gulf is a vital U.S. and Western interest."

Why? To listen to American officials speaking privately, these interests can be divided into three broad categories, each of which is worthy of scrutiny.

One is the price of oil. Another is who controls the oil. The third is the need to uphold the integrity of national boundaries so that predatory regional powers will not simply begin devouring their neighbors.

The oil price argument goes as follows: If Iraq is able to get away with annexing Kuwait, it will control twenty percent of the world's oil reserves. If, in turn, it could also intimidate Saudi Arabia, the Iraqis would have influence over forty-five percent of the world's oil reserves.

This would be bad for the United States, so the argument goes, because President Saddam Hussein would then be able to dominate pricing by the Organization of Petroleum Exporting Countries.

But the United States did not threaten Saudi Arabia in the early 1970s when Riyadh totally dominated OPEC oil pricing and even used an oil boycott to try to force Washington to change its policies toward Israel.

Why is the United States' reaction different when Iraq is doing the dominating?

The answer, officials say, is that President Saddam Hussein of Iraq wants oil prices to rise more quickly than Saudi Arabia does.

At the OPEC meeting last month, before the Iraqi invasion of Kuwait, President Hussein was pressing his OPEC colleagues to increase prices from around $15 a barrel to $25.

The other OPEC producers, including Saudi Arabia, shared his desire for a higher price, but they wanted a price of only $21 a barrel so as not to stimulate alternative energy production by the West. The difference for Americans between $21 a barrel and $25 a barrel is about 5 cents a gallon at the gasoline station pump.

In other words, by the price argument, one reason that the Bush administration is sending 100,000 soldiers to Saudi Arabia is for the sake of 5 cents a gallon less. Some people say that in some ways it would actually be in the American interest to have higher oil prices, to rekindle research and development of alternative energy sources.

Such research was on its way to making the United States more independent of foreign oil before the Reagan and Bush administrations abandoned support for the projects.

But officials argue that there is a lot more at stake than a 5 cent increase at the pump. President Hussein, they say, was only asking for $25 a barrel because he did not then dominate OPEC enough to seek more.

Oil is the single most important commodity in the industrial world, and its assured supply at reasonable prices is considered essential for economic growth—not just in the United States but also in Western Europe, Japan and the world at large.

If the Iraqi leader could, directly or indirectly, control forty percent of the world's oil reserves, they go on, who knows what price he would demand. $40 a barrel? Maybe $50 a barrel?

Such an increase would almost surely tip all Western economies into recession. But it is not at all clear that Mr. Hussein would have any more interest in raising oil prices to $50 a barrel than Saudi Arabia did when it dominated OPEC.

The Iraqis understand the world oil market as well as the Saudis. That means understanding that if prices are pushed too high too fast, the West will find alternative energy sources, which will sooner or later drive the price of oil way down.

The second category is control of the oil. It is in the American interest, so the argument goes, that control of oil be divided among many states. But to the extent that it is not, Washington would like control to be in Saudi hands.

The reason is that, unlike Iraq, Saudi Arabia's leaders have historically been more responsive to American interests and staunchly anti-Soviet. President Bush cannot say that out loud, though, because it would embarrass the Saudi monarchy.

The United States is not sending troops to the Gulf simply to help Saudi Arabia resist aggression. It is sending troops to support the OPEC country that is more likely to cater to Washington's interests.

In the past, when the United States was confronting the Soviet Union and competing for influence with Moscow in the Middle East, the stake in whose allies controlled what oil reserves had a military and strategic dimension. But today, with the Soviet Union cooperating in this crisis, that argument has lost much of its urgency.

The third and final vital interest at stake, administration officials say, is the stability of the post-Cold War world. If President Hussein gets away with taking over Kuwait by force, then other regional powers might be tempted to use similar means to advance their interests in their corners of the world.

That, officials say, means that it is essential for future world stability that the United States and Soviet Union stand together and give a clear signal that such action will not be tolerated. The sovereignty of nations must be upheld.

As Secretary of State Baker said in a speech to NATO this week, "If might is to make right, then the world will be plunged into a new dark age."

Yet, the administration has not always acted on that credo in other areas of the world. During its first eighteen months in office it supported a policy in Cambodia that would eventually have involved bringing the Khmer Rouge guerrillas back into the ruling coalition.

The Khmer Rouge are held responsible for the deaths of more than a million Cambodians during their reign of terror in the 1970s. Although American policy has not been altered, might-makes-right was considered acceptable for Cambodia because it served the American strategic interest of countering the influence of the pro-Soviet Vietnamese government.

In other words, both the might-makes-right arguments and those of national sovereignty are really, at best, more palatable ways of saying that the United States interest in preserving the status quo and stability in the Persian Gulf is primarily economic.

At root, then, the vital interests to which President Bush referred are both genuine and significant, given America's current dependence on foreign oil. Laid bare, American policy in the Gulf comes down to this: Troops have been sent to retain control of oil in the hands of a pro-American Saudi Arabia, so prices will remain low.

As an editorial cartoon in *The Boston Globe* suggested, the interest at stake may be, in short, to make the world safe for gas guzzlers. The cartoon shows President Bush in the Oval Office addressing the American people. He says: "Fellow Americans, I have sent our troops to the Middle East. . . . They are there to defend the security . . . the value . . . the principle we hold dear—18 miles per gallon."

IF MY MARINE SON IS KILLED . . .

Alex Molnar

DEAR PRESIDENT BUSH:

I kissed my son goodbye today. He is a twenty-one-year-old marine. You have ordered him to Saudi Arabia.

The letter telling us he was going arrived at our vacation cottage in northern Wisconsin by Express Mail on August 13. We left immediately for North Carolina to be with him. Our vacation was over.

Some commentators say you are continuing your own vacation to avoid appearing trapped in the White House, as President Carter was during the Iran hostage crisis. Perhaps that is your reason. However, as I sat in my motel room watching you on television, looking through my son's hastily written last will and testament and listening to military equipment rumble past, you seemed to me to be both callous and ridiculous chasing golf balls and zipping around in your boat in Kennebunkport.

While visiting my son I had a chance to see him pack his chemical weapons suit and try on his body armor. I don't know if you've ever had this experience, Mr. President. I hope you never will.

I also met many of my son's fellow soldiers. They are fine young men. A number told me that they were from poor families. They joined the Marines as a way of earning enough money to go to college.

None of the young men I met are likely to be invited to serve on the board of directors of a savings and loan association, as your son Neil was. And none of them have parents well enough connected to call or write a

Alex Molnar, professor of education at the University of Wisconsin in Milwaukee, is a founder of the Military Families Support Network. This piece appeared on *The New York Times* op-ed page on August 23, 1990.

general to insure that their child stays out of harm's way, as Vice President Quayle's parents did for him during the Vietnam War.

I read in today's *Raleigh News and Observer* that, like you, Vice President Quayle and Secretary of State Baker are on vacation. Meanwhile, Defense Secretary Cheney is in the Persian Gulf. I think this symbolizes a government that no longer has a non-military foreign policy vision, one that uses the military to conceal the fraud that American diplomacy has become.

Yes, you have proved a relatively adept tactician in the last three weeks. But if American diplomacy hadn't been on vacation for the better part of a decade, we wouldn't be in the spot we are today.

Where were you, Mr. President, when Iraq was killing its own people with poison gas? Why, until the recent crisis, was it business as usual with Saddam Hussein, the man you now call a Hitler?

You were elected vice president in 1980 on the strength of the promise of a better life for Americans, in a world where the U.S. would once again "stand tall." The Reagan-Bush administration rolled into Washington talking about the magic of a "free market" in oil. You diluted gas mileage requirements for cars and dismantled federal energy policy. And now you have ordered my son to the Middle East. For what? Cheap gas?

Is the American "way of life" that you say my son is risking his life for the continued "right" of Americans to consume twenty-five to thirty percent of the world's oil? The "free market" to which you are so fervently devoted has a very high price tag, at least for parents like me and young men and women like my son.

Now that we face the prospect of war I intend to support my son and his fellow soldiers by doing everything I can to oppose any offensive American military action in the Persian Gulf. The troops I met deserve far better than the politicians and policies that hold them hostage.

As my wife and I sat in a little cafe outside our son's base last week, trying to eat, fighting back tears, a young marine struck up a conversation with us. As we parted he wished us well and said, "May God forgive us for what we are about to do."

President Bush, the policies you have advocated for the last decade have set the stage for military conflict in the Middle East. Your response to the Iraqi conquest of Kuwait has set in motion events that increasingly will pressure you to use our troops not to defend Saudi Arabia but to attack Iraq. And I'm afraid that, as that pressure mounts, you will wager my son's life in a gamble to save your political future.

In the past you have demonstrated no enduring commitment to any principle other than the advancement of your political career. This makes me doubt that you have either the courage or the character to meet the challenge of finding a diplomatic solution to this crisis. If, as I expect, you eventually order American soldiers to attack Iraq, then it is God who will have to forgive you. I will not.

THE HITLER ANALOGY

William Safire

THE MOST excruciating choice faced by ethical people is called *triage*. When a field hospital is overwhelmed with casualties, someone has to decide which of the wounded can be saved before allocating scarce medicine and treatment—denying it to those with little chance of survival.

If anyone wondered whether the analogy of Saddam Hussein to a predecessor aggressor and mass murderer, Adolf Hitler, might be an exaggeration, all doubt was removed yesterday when the Iraqi dictator forced the world to triage.

He assembled a roomful of English-speaking women and children he held prisoner. Television cameras recorded the fear of the parents and teachers and the uncomprehending boredom of the children as the smiling "Butcher of Baghdad" dangled them before the world as the first to be sacrificed when the civilized world launched its counterattack.

One of the dictator's uniformed goons caressed the head of a little boy, turning it toward the camera for a close-up. Only a few weeks ago, we saw film of Saddam's nerve-gas attack on the undefended Kurdish village of Halabja, and viewers could recall a heartbroken Kurd coming up to the camera to display the body of his poisoned child.*

The children displayed yesterday are among those Saddam plans to place at nuclear facilities and poison-gas plants first to be taken out when the world acts to cut out its cancer.

Triage is inescapable: If we negotiate with the kidnapper, we would

William Safire is a columnist for *The New York Times*. This column was published in *The New York Times* on August 24, 1990.
* See editors' note, page 80.

save the lives of these children—at the cost of tens of thousands, perhaps millions, of other children sure to be incinerated when Saddam acquires nuclear bombs. President Bush's choice is Hobson's choice—that is, no choice at all.

However, by moving quickly we can reduce the capacity of this generation's Hitler to put innocent lives at risk. Nearly 10,000 Western civilians, mostly British and American, are holed up in captured Kuwait City. If Saddam gets his hands on them, as he intends to, they are to be designated human targets and doomed.

Every day's delay increases the danger to them and strengthens Saddam's political hand. A hundred hostage deaths is a horror; ten thousand deaths is a hundred times horror. In coming weeks he hopes to mobilize the families of hostages on American TV, paralyzing the president by eroding support at home.

That's why he sends his English-speaking foreign minister, a Christian, forward to interviewers to call for "dialogue" to avert war, as if war had not already begun. Saddam may have bought off the Iranians; he is now offering all the money he stole in Kuwait to Syria to get his old rival, Hafez al-Assad, to swing his way. (Hafez would, if he believed Saddam, but he must suspect a double cross.)

Delay works for Iraq militarily, too. An assault on the allied forces in Saudi Arabia would be unwise, but he can accomplish the same mission with terrorist teams; several are probably on their way to take out the landing docks in Dhahran and oil fields throughout the Gulf.

Mr. Bush, hobbled in multilateral action by the Soviet Union—which wants oil prices high and is playing a double game—feels he needs some suitable provocation. He may get it this week if Saddam errs and besieges foreign embassies in Kuwait, the last lifelines to threatened foreigners.

Our declared-war strategy should be to (1) suppress Iraqi air defenses; (2) take out war production at the twenty-six key targets; (3) launch a three-front land war at the Turkish, Syrian and Kuwaiti borders, coincident with an internal uprising to establish an independent Kurdistan, and (4) increase the blockade and air attacks to stimulate riots and a coup. If we cannot win we should disband our armed forces and rely on Star Wars.

Saddam will probably attack Israel to shift the focus of the war, but what that gains psychologically it loses militarily.

Saddam's first miscalculation was to believe Yasir Arafat's assurance that Palestinians who ran Kuwait's banks would transfer hundreds of billions to Iraq before the West woke up. But we froze those assets within four hours and he only picked up $10 billion or so in small change.

Our purpose is to remove Saddam and Iraq's nuclear potential; our great danger is delay. Dialogue will lead to the death of more hostages or to appeasement and nuclear blackmail. The world's goal is the secure peace that follows victory.

Then we will remember triage. If hostages are used as human shields, the allies will hold war-criminal trials, and the goon we saw yesterday caressing that little boy's head will dangle from the gallows next to Saddam Hussein.

HAVE THE NEOCONS THOUGHT
THIS THROUGH?

Patrick Buchanan

T HE GULF crisis has brought to the surface of our politics a deep fissure on the Right. On one side: the Old Right, the traditionalists who seized the GOP from the Rockefeller-Eastern Establishment for Barry Goldwater in 1964, and went on to nominate Ronald Reagan in 1980. On the other, the neoconservatives, ex-liberal Democrats who got their baptismal certificates at the Reagan transition office.

For the neocons, America is already at war.

New York Times columnist Abe Rosenthal says our duty to our soon-to-be war dead is to castrate Iraq, and kill Saddam's regime. Richard Perle wants a preemptive strike on his nuclear plants. Columnist Charles Krauthammer is virtually drafting a Morgenthau Plan for pastoralization of Iraq. *The Wall Street Journal* says the relevant question is not "whether" we go to war, but "when and how." *The New Republic* urges us to find a pretext—and attack.

Henry Kissinger is point man: "A sharp and short crisis is far more in the interest of all concerned with moderation than a long siege," he writes; the "surgical and progressive destruction of Iraq's military assets" is the way to proceed.

Perhaps, the neocons will get their war. For the Israelis, who have been goading us to attack, are confidently predicting war will break out before this column appears.

Meanwhile, those of us who do not want war are being derided by our old comrades as "chicken hawks" and "isolationists."

Patrick Buchanan is co-host of CNN's *Crossfire* and a syndicated columnist. This column was published under the title "How the Gulf Crisis is Rupturing the Right," in several national newspapers on August 25, 1990.

It is time we put our cards on the table. The war for which the neocons pant has quagmire written all over it. Should the Iraqis attack, writes General John Odom, ex-head of the National Security Agency, the small U.S. force in Saudi Arabia would have a hellish time. Battles would be lost; U.S. casualties would be heavy. To stop an Iraqi invasion at the Saudi border could require six U.S. divisions. To dig armored Iraqi troops out of Kuwait could require twelve to eighteen divisions, i.e. the entire U.S. Army. America could find herself in a Korea-style meat grinder. "It is difficult to understand," Odom writes, "the reckless enthusiam . . . some pundits have for an early attack on Iraq."

Assume U.S. air power destroys the chemical plants of Saddam Hussein. What guarantee have we that such an attack will bring him down? But of one thing we may be sure: A pre-emptive strike will put the U.S. in the midst of a war producing thousands of casualties.

For what? President Bush notwithstanding, it is not our "way of life" that is threatened, but our style of life. Saddam Hussein is not a madman; he is no Adolf Hitler; while a ruthless menace to his neighbors, he is no threat to us.

Mr. Rosenthal talks of Saddam's "power to threaten the world with mass destruction." This is hyperbolic nonsense. All Mr. Bush need do is tell Saddam: "Use poison gas on my troops, and I will use atomic bombs on yours."

Have the neocons thought this through?

Could the shiekhs, sultans, emirs, and kings, whose thrones we defend, survive the violent upheavals that would follow a U.S. air strike igniting an American-Arab war? What would we do, if the King of Jordan were overthrown, and his successors opened a "second front?" Invade Jordan? We have been told that Israel is our "strategic asset" in the Middle East. But, when the crisis came, the asset suddenly became a huge liability, use of which would result in the total collapse of our Arab coalition. Is the counsel of people who sold us that bill of goods to be followed into war?

Given U.S. air and naval power, and the might of U.S. ground forces eventually, the U.S. could smash Iraq, force withdrawal from Kuwait, declaw Saddam Hussein, if not bring him down. But, who would rise from the ruins? Who would fill the power vacuum?

Are we prepared for a NATO-style treaty commitment and a huge troop presence, not only in Saudi Arabia, but Kuwait? That is what it will require to keep Iraq out. And, how would 50 million Shiites in Iran react to 50,000 American troops next door?

The West needs a stable supply of oil at predictable prices, we are told.

Indeed, we do. But, war would cost, by one estimate, $1 billion a day, the equivalent, at $40 a barrel, of 25 million barrels of oil a day, or three times what we daily import, only a fraction of which comes from the Gulf.

It is not Saddam Hussein who drove the price of oil above $30 a barrel, but our embargo. The Thief of Baghdad stole Kuwait's oil, not to sit on it, but to sell it. He is desperate for cash. If we lifted the embargo tomorrow, the price of oil would fall like a stone.

What is at stake, writes Brother Krauthammer, is a "new world order." Excuse me, but that sounds like the Wilsonian gobbledygook we followed into the trenches of World War I—when, all the time, the hidden agenda was to pull Britain's chestnuts out of the fire.

Before we send thousands of American soldiers to their deaths, let's make damn sure America's vital interests are threatened. That is not 1930s isolationism; it is 1990s Americanism.

President Bush should keep his powder dry. Starting wars is not our tradition. Tell Saddam an attack on Saudi Arabia will not only be stopped; it will bring ruin on his country. Tell him we hold him accountable for the interned Americans. Then, let the embargo choke his economy, until he withdraws from Kuwait. If it works, it works; if it fails, it fails. Kuwait is not worth the loss of the 82nd and the 101st Airborne and that's pretty much the asking price.

ENGULFED

Andrew Kopkind

WAR WILL come to the Persian Gulf—pointless, bloody, ruinous war—and the only question now is how soon it will start and how long it will last. Each day President Bush ratchets up the Rambo rhetoric and closes more alleys of diplomatic escape. Even if Saddam Hussein wanted a peaceful solution, he would be hard put to find a negotiating partner in the administration. For the fact is that Bush has now included the demilitarization of Iraq and, probably, the liquidation of Saddam as essential elements of the American mission in the Middle East. To that end Bush is willing to send thousands of Arabs and Americans to their death, throw the most volatile region of the world into chaos and commit his country to the occupation of Saudi Arabia, at the very least, well into the twenty-first century.

The blitzkrieg scenario advised by Israel and articulated recently by Henry Kissinger and columnist William Safire would have the United States begin bombing Iraqi military and industrial targets within a matter of days. Kissinger argues that time is on Saddam's side. Not only will the placement of hostages at the target sites strain the U.S. Air Force's surgical finesse but any delay will favor the formation of opposition within the Arab world, among the Western allies and inside America. Recent U.S. polls are ambiguous. They show overwhelming support for Bush's "handling" of the crisis but surprising resistance to long-term military operations where American lives are at risk. Bush may believe that his Panama putsch last December finished off the post-Vietnam syndrome hobbling U.S. military-imperial policy, but it seems that the

Andrew Kopkind is an associate editor of *The Nation* magazine, in whose September 10, 1990, issue this piece was published as an editorial.

crucial element in that operation was its brevity. Like many of Hollywood's disappointing summer blockbusters that started out big but shriveled after a few weeks, Bush's new war may not have legs.

The Pentagon, which always wants to have all its ducks in a row and its war toys in abundance before an offensive is begun, is worried that it will not be able to win a land war in Kuwait and Iraq for several more months. According to its scenario it will take that much time to amass five tank groups and the attendant men, women and matériel required to invade, take and hold Saddam's territory. There's no doubt in the military's mind that once the guns and troops are in place, the United States can make short work of the war. Air and seaborne landings, the quick destruction of Iraq's airplanes and anti-aircraft capabilities, plus carpet bombing of Arab troops with the usual complement of napalm, cluster bombs, and other "antipersonnel" weapons of mass murder—all tasteful items in the civilized leader's arsenal, as opposed to the Butcher of Baghdad's poison gas—could bring the Iraqi military to its knees in a week. Saddam would have to be dispatched, but he is already so completely demonized that no one in the West, at least, will mourn his loss. Then, perhaps with the aid of the KGB, which has long had its hand in Iraqi military affairs, new pro-Western marionettes can be inserted into the palaces of Baghdad and the Iraqi nuclear genie can be stuffed back into its bottle, leaving the Likud government of Israel as the sole regional nuclear power. What a relief!

Either war scenario may be militarily feasible, but neither of them takes the immensely complicated contradictions and dire consequences of American aggression against the "Arab nation" into the slightest account. Bush wants to restore the "legitimate" government of Kuwait to its throne, but even many previously privileged Kuwaitis are already saying that the al-Sabah dynasty is finished, and Arabs resident in the other feudal fiefdoms of the Gulf are sure that the American presence will hasten, rather than permanently postpone, the fall of the desert monarchies. Republicanism (which is not necessarily democracy) is a historically powerful force in the Middle East. From King Farouk in Egypt to the shah of Iran, dynasts have been toppled, usually by militarist/populist *caudillos* like Gamal Abdel Nasser.

The United States and the former imperial powers of Europe hate the nationalists because they cannot be counted on to serve the West's interests. The emirates and monarchies, on the other hand, have consistently broken OPEC production limitations and, perhaps more important, put their surplus petrodollars into American and Western European banks, land and industries. Kuwait, for example, has thrown about $100 billion into the Western economy—much to the chagrin of other Arabs, who want to keep the money in local banks, industries and infrastructure development. When President Bush says that our boys in Saudi Arabia are defending "our way of life," he's not so far off base: Cheap oil and abundant capital have contributed significantly to American prosperity in past decades. Saddam needs to sell his oil, and at a reasonable price, but he is not obliged or even likely to prop up the structurally flawed U.S. economy with the proceeds.

The elimination of Saddam will not permanently change the historical and geopolitical forces aswirl in the Middle East. Naked imperial intervention, which the Americans are now in the process of undertaking (far above the multilateral sanctions approved by the U.N. Security Council), is an excuse to ignore the realities of resource distribution and North-South politics. It eliminates the need for discussion of energy politics, environmental crises (Bush is, in effect, making a war that will advance global warming), economic restructuring and democratic empowerment. All Bush is doing is asserting America's post-Cold War role as the unopposable, nuclear-tipped world cop, enforcing rules of its own making for its own narrow, short-term interests.

Kissinger may worry that if the "stalemate" in the desert drags on too long a sizable opposition will develop in the United States, but the evidence of any anti-imperial leadership (as opposed to native anti-interventionist sentiment) is almost impossible to find. Some Quakers have demonstrated against the war. But even the few recognized personalities of the progressive movement, such as Jesse Jackson, have caved in when it really counted and supported U.S. military action. Congress is, it now goes without saying, hopeless (whatever happened to that deadest of letters, the vaunted War Powers Act?). Vietnam doves, such as House Armed Services Committee Chair Les Aspin, are among the most unrestrained hawks. With very few exceptions, journalism has enlisted in the war and is presenting pure propaganda as news. Something truly terrible will have to happen before the war fever breaks. And it will.

THE MYTH OF IRAQ'S OIL
STRANGLEHOLD

Doug Bandow

ONE OF the major justifications for America's intervention in the Persian Gulf is oil, both its price and its strategic value. Iraq, Kuwait and Saudi Arabia collectively possess half the world's proven petroleum reserves, the argument goes. How could we allow Saddam Hussein to control half the world's oil resources?

There are numerous flaws in this argument. First, the reserve figure vastly overstates the importance of Middle Eastern oil to the Western economy. Although Saudi Arabia possesses the largest share of the world's proven petroleum reserves, it is not the largest producer. The Soviet Union is, followed by the United States.

Could Iraq gain a stranglehold on the world's oil supplies? Before the current crisis, Iraq, Kuwait, and Saudi Arabia together accounted for about 15.7 percent of global production. Assuming Mr. Hussein controlled that production and the output of the various Gulf sheikhdoms, his share of global output would rise to about 21.5 percent.

Now, if Mr. Hussein were to conquer the Gulf and hold all its oil off the market, he could undoubtedly trigger large price increases. But this would defeat the purpose of his conquests: to produce more oil revenue. For, if he stopped his production, the beneficiaries would be the other oil producers.

As the top producer in the world, he would maximize his revenues by marginally reducing production and trying to persuade other suppliers

Doug Bandow is a senior fellow at the Cato Institute and a former special assistant to President Reagan. This piece was published on *The New York Times* op-ed page on September 17, 1990.

to follow suit. The result would be a higher oil bill for the U.S., but nothing like the cost of today's military operation.

Iraqi hegemony in the Persian Gulf would, of course, leave President Hussein in control of half the world's "reserves." But this number is highly misleading. Total proven crude reserves in 1985 were 700 billion barrels. Five years and roughly 100 billion barrels of production later, proven reserves had expanded to one trillion barrels.

What happened? A combination of new discoveries, price increases, and technological advances increased by 400 billion barrels the oil considered to be economically recoverable.

America's outer continental shelf alone is thought to contain roughly 32 billion barrels of oil—more than our current proven reserves. But since barely six percent of the area has been leased for exploration, the existence of that oil has not been proved. Just 15,000 acres of the 1.5-million-acre Arctic National Wildlife Refuge are thought to contain nine billion barrels of oil; we won't know until Congress allows drilling.

Further, some 300 billion barrels of unrecovered oil, 10 times our proven reserves and more than proven Saudi reserves, lie in beds of shale under the United States. They are not counted, however, because they are not currently worth pumping. But as prices rise and new, cost-effective technologies are developed, they may become economically recoverable.

Moreover, estimates of as yet undiscovered potential recoverable oil range from one trillion to six trillion barrels. And even these figures are based on existing prices and technology. As current reserves run down prices will rise, creating an incentive for additional exploration and development of enhanced recovery techniques. Higher prices will also stimulate production of alternative fuels and conservation, reducing oil consumption.

Thus, even if Saddam Hussein conquered the Gulf and hung onto his empire into the next century, he would never have the sort of control over oil that the widely cited fifty percent figure implies. While he is a dangerous man, the case for confronting him is not the threat to our oil supply.

TAKING INTERNATIONAL LAW SERIOUSLY

Michael Kinsley

"America and the world must support the rule of
law. And we will."

—*President Bush to a joint session
of Congress, September 11, 1990*

KUWAIT, EMBARRASSINGLY, was not a democracy or a "free"
country, as the term is commonly understood, before August 2, and
still won't be one when and if the emir is restored. Saudi Arabia suffers
the same unfortunate defect. So to justify American actions in the Persian Gulf, President Bush cannot call upon the usual rhetoric about
democracy and freedom. Instead, the reigning concept is "order." Saddam Hussein, he says, has assaulted "the very essence of international
order and civilized ideals."

The notion of "order" as a supreme value in the affairs of nations is
not universally accepted. In fact, it is at the heart of international law, an
area of thought the U.S. government has not had much time for during
the past decade. "Order," and the related concept of "sovereignty,"
assert that the status quo has its own legitimate claims, simply because it
is the status quo and disturbing it risks "chaos"—war, misery, death—as
Bush now says.

The Reagan Doctrine was a specific rejection of international law as
the illogical elevation of sovereignty over more important values such as
democracy and freedom. Why should the forces for good sign a charter

Michael Kinsley is a senior editor of *The New Republic* and co-host of CNN's *Crossfire*. This piece
was published in the October 1, 1990, issue of *The New Republic* under the title "Law and
Order."

of self-abnegation? Legal rules are fine for fishing treaties, but not for more important matters. In Grenada, in Nicaragua, as recently as nine months ago in Panama, the Reagan and Bush administrations gave scant attention to the claims of sovereignty, or of various treaties we have signed promising to eschew force against fellow signatories.

International law can be ambiguous. And even under international law, sovereignty doesn't trump everything. State Department lawyers usually have been able to cobble together some legal rationalization for various American adventures over the decade. But the efforts became more and more halfhearted. By the end, the contradiction could no longer be contained in any gray area. Our assertion of America's right to promote American values by violent means was incompatible with even the least ambitious claims of international law to protect sovereignty and limit the use of force. Conservative thinkers circled in for the kill. As Daniel Patrick Moynihan writes, with endearing overstatement, in his new book, *On the Law of Nations* (Harvard University Press): "In the annals of forgetfulness there is nothing quite to compare with the fading from the American mind of the idea of the law of nations."

Yet suddenly, in the Gulf crisis, Bush cannot cite international law often enough. "The occupation of Kuwait is illegal under international law." Iraq is "an outrageous violator of international law." "And so my message [to Iraq] is . . . : Adhere to international law." The economic sanctions: "international law . . . must be enforced." The hostages: "contrary to international law." Negotiate with Hussein? He "has been so resistant to complying with international law" that there is no point.

International law—it's not just for wussies, anymore. Why the unac-knowledged change of heart? International law serves two vital purposes for the United States in this crisis. First, with democracy unavailable, it is a high-minded value we can legitimately claim to be protecting, thereby avoiding undue emphasis on oil and other unromantic and narrowly strategic concerns. Oh sure, a police state like Iraq is worse than a feudal kingdom like Kuwait. But you cannot ask Americans to die for that kind of comparative awfulocracy. Something nobler is required.

Second, the principles and procedures of international law have been essential to gaining the support of the rest of the world. And everyone agrees that gaining the world's support is Bush's greatest triumph.

Robert Bork has written, "The major difficulty with international law is that it converts what are essentially problems of international morality . . . into arguments about law that are largely drained of morality." In fact, this is actually an advantage of all law, not just international law. Even without an automatic enforcement mechanism (international law's obvious defect), it is easier to get people to agree to apply a preexisting set of rules than to agree ad hoc on the moral merits of a particular policy. And even if we disagree on the morality of a specific case, we still share a vested interest in the rule of law generally, which inclines us to follow the rules even when a particular application doesn't suit us.

Furthermore, as Moynihan presciently points out in his book, "Allied and non-aligned nations . . . can far more readily support (or at least accept) American policies if our conduct is seen to be based on law that binds us as well as them." *The New York Times* reports as if revealing something, that the Bush administration's early resort to the United Nations was a pragmatic decision, "rather than flowing from a set of lofty principles." That's the point. International law is valuable—useful— even to superpower America.

To take one small example within the large one; there are already disputes about what constitutes "humanitarian" food supplies under the U.N. embargo of Iraq. To what extent you bend the embargo to alleviate the suffering of innocents is a tough moral question on which reasonable people can surely differ. It is extremely useful for the United States to be able to say: You may not decide this for yourself. Under the law, exceptions are up to the Security Council. That is far easier than stopping each ship for a moral argument.

Writing in *Newsweek*, George Will deplores Bush's rediscovery of international law. "President Bush will regret this recourse if he decides his policy requires removal of Saddam Hussein." True: International law makes resort to war harder. But all of Bush's hope to end this crisis short of war depends on other nations taking him seriously about international law.

Should he be taken seriously? Is international law more than just a rhetorical convenience? Having sneered at it for a decade, then having found it necessary, will the United States abandon it once again when it ceases to be convenient? This is not merely a hoity-toity question of not wishing one's country to appear hypocritical. Obviously, even the rhetorical usefulness of international law depends on others believing that this time we really mean it.

Really meaning it means giving up our own freedom of action on occasion, and allowing our own case-by-case moral assessments to be constrained by rules that will sometimes strike us as wrong. It means respecting the sovereignty of governments we rightly don't like. It means allowing the judgment of other nations to stay our hand sometimes, even when we think that judgment is mistaken. Law that need not be obeyed if you disagree with it is not law. If we want meaningful international law to be available when we find it useful, we must respect it even when we don't.

THE NEED TO NEGOTIATE

Jimmy Carter

HARDENING POSITIONS make a peaceful resolution of the Persian Gulf crisis ever less likely. How can we make the best of this situation and heal the fractured region when the crisis is over?

Despite bold and concerted action of the U.N. Security Council, a remarkable demonstration of leadership by the U.S. in marshaling forces to defend Saudi Arabia, world condemnation and economic sanctions, there are no indications that Saddam Hussein is considering a withdrawal from Kuwait or the return of the emir's family. With oil-price increases disturbing the world economy and with patience wearing thin, the world will inevitably turn to other issues, making it difficult to increase or even sustain the present level of economic pressure. If Saddam does not yield, the forced ejection of Iraqi troops by military action is the only remaining option. Some also advocate the destruction of Iraq's warmaking capability, speaking of almost bloodless "surgical" air strikes, the incompetence or disloyalty of Iraqi troops, sustained worldwide support if the U.S. invades without U.N. sanction, and a more stable Middle East after Iraq is destroyed. These assumptions are doubtful. Military forces of America and its allies can surely prevail, but there will be serious human, economic, and political costs.

It is incongruous to exalt Iraq's military threat while disparaging the competence of the Iraqis to defend their own land. The inability of either side to prevail in eight years of seesaw battles across the Iraqi-Iranian border supports the claim of military strategists that a three-to-one

This piece by former President Jimmy Carter was published in the October 22, 1990, issue of *Time*.

225

advantage is necessary for invaders. Martyrdom among devout Muslims must also be considered.

There is little doubt that an attack on Iraq without further provocation from Saddam will erode U.S. support in the Middle East. The Arab League is already split down the middle, with at least nine of its members, including some that offer lip service to the U.N. resolutions, giving overt backing to Iraq. Iran is, at best, equivocal. Saddam tries to build on this support with appeals based on brotherhood, religion, and the Palestinian cause. It is interesting to note that he has never criticized his Syrian brothers for sending forces to Saudi Arabia, nor has he built up troops along their common border. Most Muslim believers are uncomfortable with Western troops in their holy lands. Iraq's propagandists also remind poor Arabs, both individuals and nations, that oil-rich royal families have invested almost a trillion dollars in the Western world. They publicized the recent loss by a Saudi prince of $130 million at a European roulette wheel in one night. Armed conflict can exacerbate all these concerns and may unleash a violent grass-roots reaction.

Another sobering fact is that international support is not solid. Beginning with the Helsinki summit, the Soviets have indicated that they will support only a U.N. military action (which is subject to a Chinese veto). Also, they continue to connect Iraq-Kuwait and Israel-Palestinian issues.

So far, the Bush administration has not acknowledged the need for negotiations or exploratory talks, which might imply weakness or a willingness to reverse adamant public statements. Initiating peace talks is always difficult, as we remember from Korea and Vietnam. Only unconditional surrender following a total military victory can remove the need for negotiated settlements.

No matter what happens in the next few months, including total capitulation of Iraq, we should be preparing for a time when negotiations will be required. There are a few intermediaries who might expedite this process: U.N. officials; French, Soviet or other allies of ours; or leaders among the Arab nations. Any of these would be suitable, but my own preference is the Arab community. Soon after Iraq invaded Kuwait, an Arab plan was offered in Paris, Moscow, and other places. It called for Iraqis to be replaced by other Arab troops in Kuwait, a U.N. or Arab force to relieve Western forces in Saudi Arabia, and then a referendum to be held under international supervision to let Kuwaitis decide their own future. These initial ideas are unacceptable by either side, but later modifications may lead to peace.

Among Arab leaders, King Hussein of Jordan can play a key role. He is an honorable and peace-loving man who does not deserve the harsh treatment he is receiving. He has supported the U.N. resolutions that demand foreign troop withdrawal from Kuwait, the return of the emir and his family, and the imposition of economic sanctions. The king made these decisions even though Jordan shares a vulnerable border with Iraq and many of his countrymen support Saddam Hussein. Now the Jordanian monarch faces the loss of financial assistance from Saudi Arabia and others. The very survival of his nation is endangered. It would be a tragedy to permit the further destruction of Jordan. Even if other intermediaries serve, a stable Jordan will be needed in the future. A much better alternative would be for King Hussein to be recognized in the U.S., as he has been in other countries, as a key leader who, at an early stage, might help bring about a peaceful settlement of the Gulf crisis—when and if it is understood that this is the only alternative to war.

THE NEED FOR AN OFFENSIVE
MILITARY OPTION

(*Speech of November 8, 1990*)

George Bush

The following are excerpts from President Bush's news conference at the White House on November 8, 1990, when he announced the shift to an "offensive military option."

O N   A U G U S T   6 , in response to the unprovoked Iraqi invasion of Kuwait, I ordered the deployment of U.S. military forces to Saudi Arabia and the Persian Gulf to deter further Iraqi aggression and to protect our interests in the region. What we've done is right, and I'm happy to say that most members of Congress and the majority of Americans agree.

From the very beginning, we and our coalition partners have shared common political goals—the immediate, complete and unconditional withdrawal of Iraqi forces from Kuwait, restoration of Kuwait's legitimate government, protection of the lives of citizens held hostage by Iraq, both in Kuwait and Iraq, and restoration of security and stability in the Persian Gulf region. To achieve these goals, we and our allies have forged a strong diplomatic, economic and military strategy to force Iraq to comply with these objectives. The framework of this strategy is laid out in ten United Nations resolutions overwhelmingly supported by the United Nations Security Council.

In three months, the U.S. troop contribution to the multinational force in Saudi Arabia has gone from 10,000 to 230,000, as part of Operation Desert Shield. General Schwarzkopf reports that our forces in conjunction with other coalition forces now have the capability to defend successfully against any further Iraqi aggression.

After consultation with King Fahd and our other allies, I have today directed the secretary of defense to increase the size of U.S. forces committed to Desert Shield to insure that the coalition has an adequate offensive military option should that be necessary to achieve our common goals. Toward this end, we will continue to discuss the possibility of both additional allied force contributions and appropriate United Nations actions. Iraq's brutality, aggression and violations of international law cannot be allowed to succeed. . . .

[R]ight now Kuwait is struggling for survival. And along with many other nations, we've been called upon to help. The consequences of our not doing so would be incalculable, because Iraq's aggression is not just a challenge to the security of Kuwait and other Gulf nations, but to the better world that we all have hoped to build in the wake of the Cold War. And therefore, we and our allies cannot and will not shirk our responsibilities. The state of Kuwait must be restored, or no nation will be safe, and the promising future we anticipate will indeed be jeopardized.

QUESTIONS AND ANSWERS

Q. Mr. President, it sounds like you're going to war. You have moved from a defensive position to an offensive position and you have not said how many more troops you are sending or really why.

A. Well, I said why right now, and I hope that it's been very clear to the American people.

Q. Well is there—are there new reasons that have moved this posture?

A. No, I'm just continuing to do what we feel is necessary to complete our objectives, to fulfill our objectives that have been clearly stated.

Q. Well, are you going to war?

A. I'm not—we—I would love to see a peaceful resolution to this question. And that's what I want.

ON THE GULF AND MIDDLE EAST CRISIS

National Council of Churches of Christ

WE STAND AT a unique moment in human history, when all around us seemingly impregnable walls are being broken down and deep historical enmities are being healed. And yet, ironically, at such a moment, our own nation seems to be poised at the brink of war in the Middle East. "What then are we to say about these things?" (Romans 8:31) . . .

Two months ago, on September 14, 1990, the Executive Coordinating Committee of the National Council of the Churches of Christ in the USA addressed a message to its member communions on the Gulf crisis. That message condemned Iraq's invasion and occupation of Kuwait, raised serious questions about the decision of the U.S. government to send troops to the Gulf region and about the growing magnitude of U.S. presence, noting that the extent of the commitment of U.S. forces and weaponry was the largest since the Vietnam war. Since then, the U.S. has more than doubled the number of troops sent to the region to a number approaching a half million persons.

The message also questioned the apparent open-ended nature of the U.S. military involvement in the Middle East and the failure on the part of the administration clearly to state its goals. President Bush and administration officials have done little to clarify either of these points. Indeed the rationales offered for the steady expansion of U.S. presence have often been misleading and sometimes even contradictory. Early statements that U.S. forces had been deployed for the defense of Saudi Arabia or the enforcement of U.N. sanctions have been supplanted by

This excerpt is drawn from a longer message released by the National Council of Churches of Christ on November 14-15, 1990.

suggestions of broader goals, including expulsion of Iraqi forces from Kuwait by military means, or even offensive action against Iraq itself. The nation still has not been told in clear and certain terms what would be required for the withdrawal of U.S. troops.

The initial response of the NCCC/USA was carefully measured, recognizing the magnitude of the injustice inflicted by Iraq against Kuwait, and the unprecedented reliance by the U.S. on the mechanisms of the U.N. In contrast, the U.S. administration increasingly prepares for war, a war that could lead to the loss of tens of thousands of lives and the devastation of the region. Such talk has given rise to widespread speculation in our country, in the Middle East and elsewhere that the United States will initiate war.

In the face of such reckless rhetoric and imprudent behavior, as representatives of churches in the United States we feel that we have a moral responsibility publicly and unequivocally to oppose actions that could have such dire consequences.

Our earlier message also pointed out that the active U.S. effort to implement United Nations Security Council resolutions relating to the occupation of Kuwait by Iraq stand in marked contrast to U.S. negligence regarding the implementation of Security Council resolutions 242 and 338. These call for the withdrawal of Israeli troops from the territories occupied in the 1967 war and the convening of an international conference to resolve the Israeli-Palestinian issue. There has also been negligence regarding the implementation of Security Council resolutions 359, 360 and 361 which call for the withdrawal "without delay" of Turkish troops from Cyprus and solving the problems of the island through negotiations.

During the intervening weeks the situation in the Israeli occupied territories has, in fact, worsened. The U.S. government's condemnation of the massacre on the Haram al-Sharif/Temple Mount and its endorsement of a U.N. mission to the occupied territories was a welcome departure from past policies. The failure of the U.S. government to take any substantive measures to oppose the Israeli occupation, however, weakens the effect of its appropriate outrage over Iraqi aggression against Kuwait. The region cries out for a U.S. policy that seeks to redress all cases of injustice, including those of Israel and Palestine, Lebanon and Cyprus.

The presence of U.S. troops in the Middle East has led to an expansion of the military capacity of an already grossly overmilitarized region. The proposed billions of dollars of arms sales to Saudi Arabia, the forgiveness of military debts to Egypt and Israel and the supplying of both with new and more sophisticated weaponry, combined with a seeming lack of initiative to resolve the region's unsettled disputes, can only be seen as morally irresponsible.

The price of war and the preparation for further conflict is already being paid in human terms. Hundreds of thousands of foreign workers and their families have been compelled to leave Kuwait and Iraq, creating enormous strains on the Kingdom of Jordan and the Republic of Egypt and, ultimately on the societies to which they are returning.

The cost of the current U.S. military presence in the Gulf is estimated at $1 billion per month. This "extra-budgetary expenditure" is once again likely to reduce further the nation's capacity to address human needs in our own society. Thus, among the early victims of this tragic engagement will certainly be the growing number of the poor, homeless, sick and elderly. The corrosive effects on our own nation will be felt especially by racial/ethnic communities who make up a disproportionate number both of the poor and those who are on the front lines of military confrontation.

We are appalled by the past and present behavior of the regime in Iraq, one which has previously enjoyed U.S. support. But the demonization of the Iraqi people and their leader has led to an increased incidence of defamation of or discrimination against persons of Arab descent or appearance.

We stand on the threshold of a "new world order." Indeed, the near unanimous condemnation by the nations of the world of Iraq's illegal occupation of its neighbor, Kuwait, shows the promise of a new approach to the vocation of peacemaking for which the United Nations was created forty-five years ago. There are present in this moment seeds either of a new era of international cooperation under the rule of international law or of rule based upon superior power, which holds the prospect of continuing dehumanizing chaos.

Our churches have long sought to nurture and bring to fruition the seeds of hope. The power we would invoke is not the power of the gun, nor is it the power of wealth and affluence; we would invoke the power of the cross and the resurrection, symbols for us of love and hope. As Christians in the U.S. we must witness against weak resignation to our belief in the capacity of human beings and human societies to seek and achieve reconciliation.

The General Board of the NCCC/USA commends this message to the churches, all Christians, and persons of other faiths, inviting them to join with us in continuing prayer and urgent action to avert war in the Persian/Arabian Gulf region, and to join in the quest for a just and durable peace in the Middle East.

Resolution on the Gulf and Middle East Crisis: The General Board of the National Council of Churches, meeting in Portland, Oregon, November 14–15, 1990, recognizing its solidarity with the Christians of the Middle East and with the Middle East Council of Churches:

Urges the government of Iraq to release immediately all those citizens of other nations being held against their will in Kuwait or Iraq and to withdraw immediately its troops and occupation forces from Kuwait.

Calls for the continued rigorous application of the sanctions against Iraq authorized by the United Nations Security Council until such time as it withdraws its forces from Kuwait.

Reiterates its opposition to the withholding of food and medicine as a weapon against civilian populations.

Encourages the secretary-general of the United Nations to exercise fully his own good offices in pursuit of a rapid negotiated resolution of the present conflict in the Gulf.

Calls upon the president and U.S. Congress to pursue every means for a negotiated political solution to the crisis in the Gulf, including direct negotiations with Iraq.

Reiterates support for the convening under U.N. auspices of an international conference for a comprehensive peace in the Middle East, as a means of implementing United Nations Security Council resolutions on Israel and Palestine, Lebanon and Cyprus, recognizing that the present crisis cannot be isolated from the unresolved issues of the region as a whole.

Calls for an immediate halt to the buildup and the withdrawal of U.S. troops from the Gulf region except those which might be required and explicitly recommended by the Security Council of the United Nations in accordance with the relevant provisions of the United Nations charter.

Calls upon the U.S. government to give leadership to the institution of an immediate and complete embargo under U.N. auspices on arms transfers to the Middle East. . . .

GIVE SANCTIONS A CHANCE

(Testimony Before the Senate Armed Services Committee,
November 28, 1990)

Admiral William J. Crowe, Jr.

WAR IS always a grave decision and one which deserves both deep thought and wide public discussion. . . .

If Saddam Hussein initiates an attack on Saudi Arabia or U.S. forces, we have no choice but to react vigorously and to use force to bring Iraq to heel. It is imperative once we engage that we bring it to a successful conclusion no matter what it requires. It would be disastrous to do otherwise. I believe such a response would be defensible and acceptable to all constituencies, domestic and international.

For that reason alone, it is unlikely that Saddam Hussein will initiate further military action. Certainly everything we see to date suggests he is hunkering down for the long haul. If that prediction proves correct, President Bush will be confronted with some very painful choices.

If deposing Saddam Hussein would sort out the Middle East and permit the United States to turn its attention elsewhere and to concentrate on our very pressing domestic problems, the case for initiating offensive action immediately would be considerably strengthened. The Middle East, however, is not that simple. I witnessed it firsthand. I lived in the Middle East for a year.

Put bluntly, Saddam's departure or any other single act I am afraid will not make everything wonderful. In fact, a close look at the Middle East is rather depressing. While we may wish it otherwise, the fact is that the region has been, is, and will be for the foreseeable future plagued with a host of problems, tensions, enmities, and disagreements.

For instance, the Arab-Israeli dispute is alive and well. To say the least,

Admiral William J. Crowe, Jr., USN (retired) was chairman of the Joint Chiefs of Staff from 1985–1989.

the Palestinians have been irrevocably alienated by the Israeli government's policies. There will never be true stability in the area until this dispute is sorted out ultimately. As Henry Schuler phrased it, "Neither the feudal monarchies nor the oppressive dictatorships enjoy the stability of an institutionalized popular mandate of political participation." This suggests that political maturity and, in turn, stability is still a long way off.

Income differences on both national and individual levels are a constant source of tensions and envy throughout the region, and I witnessed this friction at close hand when I lived in Bahrain.

Muslim fundamentalism is spreading, and the process highlights the cultural, religious, and ethnic differences that abound in the area as well as the widespread distrust of the West.

Boundary disputes are legion and have been a part of the region for many years: Qatar versus Bahrain; Abu Dhabi versus Oman and Saudi Arabia; Yemen versus Saudi Arabia; Kuwait versus Iraq; and many of the Emirates versus Iran.

United States links to Israel and the dominant position of American oil companies have turned large segments of the Arab world against the U.S. in particular. The American public is well aware of this, of course.

The current crisis has divided the "moderate" Arab states for the first time. For example, Saudi Arabia has now split with its traditional friends, Jordan and Yemen. Incidentally, Yemen is now the most populous state on the peninsula—some 10 million plus. This does not bode well for the causes of stability or pluralism, both of which are also U.S. interests.

These frictions, singly or collectively, have resulted in a succession of explosions, assassinations, global terrorism, coups, revolutions, embargoes, and full-scale war on occasion. Secretary Schlesinger summed it up when he said, "The noncombat costs of recourse to war will be substantial."

Like it or not, the process of bringing stability to the Middle East will be painful and protracted with or without Saddam Hussein. Moreover, the United States, both as a leader of the free world and as the world's number one consumer of crude oil, will be integrally involved in the region politically and economically for the foreseeable future, just as we have been for the past forty years.

That conclusion may not make us comfortable, but frankly I see no way we can avoid this burden. It comes with our affluence and global reach. This reality suggests that anything we do in that part of the world should be consistent with our past policies and our future role as an international leader.

Put another way, today's problem is a great deal more complex than merely defeating Saddam Hussein. In my view, the critical foreign policy questions we must ask are not whether Saddam Hussein is a brutal, deceitful, or as Barbara Bush would put it, a dreadful man—he is all of those things. Whether initiating conflict against Iraq will moderate the larger difficulties in the Gulf region and will put Washington in a better position to work with the Arab world in the future, is in my estimation, the more important question.

I would submit that posturing ourselves to promote stability for the long term is our primary national interest in the Middle East. May I repeat it: that posturing ourselves to promote stability for the long term is our primary national interest in the Middle East. It is not obvious to me that we are currently looking at the crisis in this light. Our dislike for Hussein seems to have crowded out many other considerations.

In working through the problems myself, I am persuaded that the U.S. initiating hostilities could well exacerbate many of the tensions I have cited and perhaps further polarize the Arab world. Certainly, many Arabs would deeply resent a campaign which would necessarily kill large numbers of their Muslim brothers and force them to choose sides between Arab nations and the West.

From the Arab perspective, this fight is not simply a matter between bad and good. It is a great deal more complex than that and includes political and social perspectives deeply rooted in their history. The aftermath of such a contest will very likely multiply many-fold the anti-American resentment which we already see in the Middle East. In essence, we may be in a certain sense on the horns of a no-win dilemma. Even if we win, we lose ground in the Arab world and generally injure our ability to deal in the future with the labyrinth of the Middle East.

I firmly believe that Saddam Hussein must be pushed out of Kuwait. He must leave Kuwait. At the same time, given the larger context, I judge it highly desirable to achieve this goal in a peaceful fashion, if that is possible. In other words, I would argue that we should give sanctions a fair chance before we discard them. I personally believe they will bring him to his knees ultimately, but I would be the first to admit that is a speculative judgment.

If, in fact, the sanctions will work in twelve to eighteen months instead of six months, a tradeoff of avoiding war, with its attendant sacrifices and uncertainties, would in my estimation be more than worth it. . . .

In closing, I would make a few observations that perhaps we should keep in mind as we approach this process. Using economic pressure may prove protracted, but if it could avoid hostilities or casualties, those also are highly desirable ends. As a matter of fact, I consider them also national interests. I seldom hear them referred to in that fashion.

It is curious that just as our patience in Western Europe has paid off and furnished us the most graphic example in our history of how staunchness is sometimes the better course in dealing with thorny international problems, a few armchair strategists are counseling a near-term attack on Iraq. It is worth remembering that in the 1950s and 1960s, individuals were similarly advising an attack on the U.S.S.R. Would not that have been great?. . . .

It would be a sad commentary if Saddam Hussein, a two-bit tyrant who sits on seventeen million people and possesses a gross national product of $40 billion, proved to be more patient than the United States, the world's most affluent and powerful nation.

HOW TO CUT IRAQ DOWN TO SIZE

(*Testimony Before the Senate Armed Services Committee,*
November 28, 1990)

Henry A. Kissinger

A MERICAN OBJECTIVES have included fulfillment of stated
U.N. goals of restoration of the status quo ante in Kuwait as well as
the unconditional release of all hostages. But to contribute to President
Bush's objective of stability in the Gulf, any solution to the crisis must
also provide for a reduction of Iraq's offensive capability which now
overshadows its neighbors. Without addressing this fundamental imbalance, a solution will only postpone, and probably exacerbate, an eventual resolution of Gulf instability.

Were Saddam suddenly to accept the U.N. terms, he would in fact
preserve the essence of his power, although it would represent a huge
loss of prestige for him. Iraq would still retain its chemical and nuclear
capabilities. Its large standing army would still preserve the capacity to
overwhelm the area. Many nations in the Middle East might adjust to the
perception that the mobilization of forces from all over the world cannot
be repeated every few years.

Reducing Iraq's military potential is especially important if U.S. forces
are to be substantially withdrawn from the Gulf as I believe they should
be. At the same time, it would be undesirable to reduce Iraq's armed
forces below what is needed for equilibrium with its neighbors, especially in light of their past records, which attest to a low threshold of
resistance to the temptations of a military vacuum.

The United States had three choices in dealing with the crisis of the
Iraqi invasion of Kuwait: It could passively endorse whatever consensus
emerged in the United Nations; it could support whatever the industrial
democracies—all of which are more dependent on Mideast oil than the

Henry A. Kissinger was secretary of state in the Nixon and Ford administrations.

United States is—were prepared to do in concert; or it could take the lead in opposing Saddam Hussein and try to organize international support for an effort in which the United States would bear the principal burden.

The administration concluded that anything other than a leadership role for the United States would have ended with making Iraqi domination of Kuwait permanent and would lead to the collapse of the moderate governments in the region including Egypt. Having committed the United States to a leadership role, President Bush made another crucial decision. The American military role could have been confined to interdiction at sea and a token force on the ground to make clear that an attack on Saudi oil fields would lead to war with the United States. President Bush and his advisers opted for a massive deployment. They concluded that once they committed military forces, the best hope of ending the crisis quickly was to assemble an overwhelming force to overawe such a threat and to be able to go further if necessary.

In short, early in America's involvement there was some argument as to whether American vital interests justified a massive deployment in the Gulf. That debate has since been overtaken by the scale of our deployment and the number of countries that have followed America's leadership in the Gulf.

The perception of American failure would shake international stability. Every moderate country in the Middle East would be gravely weakened by a debâcle. Several Gulf states could not survive it. Egypt, Morocco, and even Turkey would face a tide of radicalism and fundamentalism.

The United States is approaching the point in the Middle East crisis where a choice must be made between a course relying on sanctions or, as a last resort, on a military course.

The two approaches have been presented as if they were successive phases of the same policy. In fact, they will prove mutually exclusive because by the time it is evident that sanctions alone cannot succeed, a credible military option will probably no longer exist.

To achieve the proclaimed objectives by sanctions, at least five hurdles must be overcome:

- The sanctions must bite.
- They must be maintained throughout any negotiations.
- Once the U.N. terms are achieved, arms control objectives must be addressed.

- The military option must remain intact psychologically, technically, and diplomatically during the entire course of the negotiations.
- There must be no other upheavals to deflect the United States or to rend allied cohesion.

To state these hurdles is to set forth the practical obstacles to clearing them.

For one thing, upheavals in the Middle East are a way of life. In one recent week, the second highest ranking official in Egypt was assassinated, Syria battled Christian forces in Beirut, and twenty-one Palestinians died in Jerusalem.

If the sanctions do bite within a time frame relevant to political processes, Iraq is more likely to offer to negotiate than to yield.

In that case, pressures to ease the sanctions will be difficult to resist. Which democracy will want to be responsible for starvation in Iraq and Kuwait once negotiations are under way?

The fundamental dilemma is that the U.N. terms leave no real room for negotiation—except perhaps the staging of the Iraqi withdrawal. Thus all so-called diplomatic solutions effectively dilute the U.N. objectives while maintaining Iraq's war-making potential and thus confirming Iraq as the supreme military power of the Middle East.

For example, even if Saddam accepts the principle of withdrawal from Kuwait, he has already hinted—and Soviet presidential aide Yevgeny M. Primakov has confirmed—that he would define Kuwait as excluding a strip of land containing a major oil field as well as two islands controlling access to the Shatt al-Arab. And President Mitterrand has stated that only agreement in principle to withdrawal is needed to bring about a negotiation.

Saddam's Arab neighbors will surely note that none of the proposals in the public discussion would reduce Iraq's military preeminence or restore Kuwait completely.

If they conclude that they will be condemned to live with a dominant Iraq, they will begin their own negotiations. Recent remarks by Saudi Defense Minister Sultan suggest that the haggling may already have begun.

But will the psychological basis for a military option still exist after months of such inconclusive maneuvering? And without a realistic military threat, how can the U.S.-U.N. objectives be achieved?

And having faced down the combined might of U.N. forces and of the United States, Iraq would have little incentive to make concessions to the fears of its neighbors in any subsequent arms control negotiation.

Many who opt for sanctions-induced negotiations recognize that sanctions will not be able to achieve a balance of power in the Gulf. They propose to protect a settlement by a new regional security system based on a significant American military presence in Saudi Arabia.

I consider this a dangerous mirage. If, after the adamant pronouncements from Washington and the deployment of a large expeditionary force, a regional balance of power could not be reached, no Gulf state would easily entrust its fate to a long-term American presence.

The often-heard argument that America proved its staying power in Korea and Europe misses the point. The issue in Arabia is not American staying power but the host country's domestic stability.

Conditions in the Gulf are not even remotely comparable to Europe or Northeast Asia. There, American forces contributed to domestic stability; in Saudi Arabia they would threaten it.

A substantial American ground establishment would soon become the target of radical and nationalist agitation. Once Iraq has faced down U.S. and U.N. terms, such a force would sooner or later become hostage to revolutionary Iraq, fundamentalist Iran, and events substantially out of our control.

Nor can the restoration of this military balance in the Gulf be left to subsequent arms control negotiations. For having faced down the combined might of U.N. forces and of the United States, Iraq would have little incentive to make concessions to the fears of its neighbors in any subsequent arms control negotiation.

In short, the route of sanctions and the military option can be pursued up to a certain point simultaneously. At some point, however, trying to pursue both courses will turn into an evasion incompatible with reaching what should be our objectives. At that point the U.S. must choose a strategy appropriate to its objectives or else choose objectives achievable by whatever policy we are willing to implement.

If war proved unavoidable it is to be hoped that military strategy remains related to realistic political objectives.

Outsiders should not play field marshal. But America has no national interest in weakening Iraq to a point where it becomes a tempting target for covetous neighbors.

If war does prove unavoidable, our objective should be not to destroy Iraq, but rather to raise the cost of occupying Kuwait to unacceptable levels while reducing Iraq's capacity to threaten its neighbors.

The destruction of the Iraqi military complex, especially its chemical and nuclear facilities as well as its air and missile forces, would improve the military balance in the Gulf and would speed up the effect of sanctions.

Such a strategy would rely on air and naval power and use ground forces primarily to overawe a response. As the government of Iraq, which is after all a military dictatorship, sees its principal source of power erode, a negotiation more compatible with stated U.S. objectives could result.

Even if one of the compromises sketched above came eventually to be adopted—a contingency I would regret—the setback would be eased by the reduction in the Iraqi military threat. I am extremely skeptical about a full-scale ground assault.

In the process of overcoming the current crisis, the United States must not emerge as the permanent defender of every status quo. But the path to peace and progress resides in success in the Gulf.

Afterwards the United States, together with its Arab partners, can demonstrate the benefits of cooperative action in promoting the well-being of the Arab peoples.

Too, the United States should then seek energetically to make progress toward a settlement of the Arab-Israeli conflict, especially now that looming disaster might have brought all sides second thoughts about both the nature of a peace and suitable participants in peace negotiations. But such a move cannot be linked to the resolution of the current crisis for to do so would turn Saddam into a hero in the Arab world.

It is to be hoped that a united America can find a way that avoids both a military strategy of total destructiveness and a diplomatic strategy committed to amassing U.N. resolutions—the progressive disregard of which will at some point demonstrate the U.N.'s impotence rather than an international consensus.

But whatever our destination, we must arrive at it by design rather than as captives of circumstances.

HOW CLOSE IS IRAQ TO THE BOMB?

(Testimony Before the Senate Armed Services Committee,
November 30, 1990)

Gary Milhollin

D URING THE past week, President Bush and his top military advisers have said that Iraq might produce a nuclear weapon within six
months to a year, and that we may have to go to war to prevent this from
happening. The president told U.S. troops in Saudi Arabia on Thanks-
giving that, "Every day that passes brings Saddam Hussein one step
closer to realizing his goal of a nuclear weapons arsenal—and that's
another reason, frankly, why our mission is marked by a real sense of
urgency." Last Sunday, National Security Adviser Brent Scowcroft said
that letting the international embargo against Iraq run its course, "raises
the possibility that we could face an Iraq armed with nuclear weapons."
Defense Secretary Cheney was more direct, saying that, "It's only a
matter of time until he acquires nuclear weapons and the capability to
deliver them."

These statements apparently were based on a recent Special National
Intelligence Estimate in which top U.S. officials reportedly predicted
that Iraq could develop a crude nuclear device in as little as six months to
a year in a crash program. Previously, experts inside and outside of the
government had estimated that it would take Iraq five to ten years to
develop any kind of reliable nuclear weapon. Given that President Bush
has been under pressure to clarify the objectives of Operation Desert
Shield and justify this massive commitment of force, I think it is important to ask why his administration revised its assessment of Iraq's nuclear
program in the way that it did and at the time that it did.

There are two methods by which Iraq conceivably could fulfill the
Bush administration's most pessimistic forecast and develop a crude

Gary Milhollin is director of the Wisconsin Project on Nuclear Arms Control.

nuclear weapon within a year. In either case, since Iraq has no known ability to make nuclear explosive material, it would have to use such material imported from outside sources.

The first alternative would be to divert safeguarded uranium from international inspection to make a weapon. Iraq currently possesses about 12.4 kilograms of French-supplied uranium enriched to ninety-three percent U-235, the fissile isotope used to detonate nuclear weapons. France supplied this material to run the Osirak reactor that Israel destroyed in 1981.

The French uranium is in the form of fabricated plates 1.27 millimeters thick made of an aluminum and uranium alloy. The uranium alloy is sandwiched between two aluminum cladding plates. The plates are contained in thirty-three standard fuel assemblies, plus six control elements, plus some spares. The total quantity of weapon-grade uranium weighs 12.4 kilograms, or 27 pounds.

The alloy would have to be chemically broken down in order to get pure uranium. Also, the fuel has been lightly irradiated, which is an additional barrier. It means that the processing would have to be carried out behind shielding, or by a series of workers who would each get a small dose of radioactivity.

Iraq also has about ten kilograms of eighty percent enriched uranium supplied by the Soviet Union as fuel for small research reactors. Uranium enriched to this level can be used for nuclear weapons. However, even if the two fuels could be blended, twenty kilograms of enriched uranium is not enough to make a simple gun-type nuclear bomb of the type that destroyed Hiroshima. To make a bomb with its safeguarded uranium, Iraq would have to make an implosion weapon, which is a more complex design. There is no clear evidence that Iraq has mastered such a design.

Also, the French and Soviet uranium in Iraq is safeguarded by the International Atomic Energy Agency, which inspects the material regularly to insure that it is not being diverted for weapons use. The IAEA inspected this uranium last week and a spokesman said on Tuesday that it "was where it should be, and none had been diverted."

If Iraq were to divert the French uranium to make a crude weapon, it would alert the world to its intentions, and would provoke preemptive action by the United States and its allies to prevent the construction of even one bomb. The six-month estimate has been generally interpreted to be predicated on Saddam taking this route. Secretary Cheney implied this on *Face the Nation* last Sunday when he said, "If he were to take that material [the French uranium], he could produce a crude device with it . . . in a year or less. . . .''

There is also a second possible explanation for how Iraq could make a quick bomb, which the administration has only hinted at thus far. Last Tuesday, Deputy Secretary of State Lawrence Eagleburger, who was traveling with the president in Mexico, said that, "The statements of the secretary of state and the president are based on information that there is substantial, unsafeguarded nuclear activity going on in Iraq." It is not clear whether this comment referred to Iraq's attempts to enrich its own uranium, which I will discuss shortly, or was meant to suggest that Iraq has obtained enough nuclear weapon material from an unspecified outside source to make a simple bomb without touching its safeguarded uranium.

If the administration is suggesting an outside source, it would be an extremely serious development for several reasons apart from the confrontation with Iraq. It would mean that somewhere in the world there is a clandestine source for nuclear weapon material that we do not know about. If the Bush administration does have evidence that Iraq has imported nuclear weapon material from a secret source, it should make this evidence public immediately and stop making vague insinuations about what Iraq might or might not do in the next six months. If Iraq has acquired enriched uranium from a foreign source, the problem is much bigger than keeping the peace in the Middle East. If the administration does *not* have such evidence, it should not make statements with such grave implications.

If, by one or the other of these alternatives, Iraq should produce a crude nuclear weapon in the next six months, there is another major problem with citing this threat as a cause for war. How could Saddam even be sure that this device would work, since there would be no opportunity to test it? It would surely be a reckless, desperate act for Iraq to threaten the United States, Britain, France and Israel—all of which could flatten Baghdad with nuclear weapons—with one untested bomb. Saddam Hussein is a gambler who overreached himself when he invaded Iran and Kuwait, but there is no evidence that he is likely to commit nuclear suicide.

L E T M E turn now to Iraq's long-term prospects for acquiring nuclear weapons. This is where the real Iraqi threat lies.

According to U.S. intelligence reports, Iraq seems to have acquired enough technology to be able to produce a critical mass of enriched uranium within five to ten years, even if the current trade embargo is maintained indefinitely. To do so, Iraq will have to make about a thousand machines called centrifuges, which spin uranium gas at high speed and separate the unstable U-235 atoms from the stable U-238 atoms that make up over ninety-nine percent of natural uranium. There is no question that Iraq is trying to do this, relying on imported technology.

Iraq has imported a stockpile of natural uranium from several countries around the world and has acquired key equipment for manufacturing centrifuges from German and Swiss suppliers. Saddam has brought in engineers from Germany to install and run the centrifuge-making machines, and has imported from German firms the materials to make centrifuge parts. Congressman Les Aspin recently released a "Persian Gulf Crisis Report Card," in which he gave Germany a "C" with the comment, "could contribute more," but in the nuclear area Germany has already contributed more than enough.

There are two key questions to be answered regarding Iraq's uranium enrichment potential: How quickly can Iraq manufacture more centrifuges, and how soon can it run them efficiently? Iraq already has a handful of centrifuges running experimentally, and the blueprints it needs to make more. But it takes about a thousand centrifuges to produce a bomb's worth of enriched uranium annually. There is a huge technological chasm between possessing blueprints and actually building and operating that many complex machines, which would fill a space roughly the size of a football field.

Exports have been absolutely central to the realization of Iraq's nuclear ambitions, and a review of how Saddam has gotten where he is today tells us what is wrong with our nonproliferation policy—and why going to war will not stop the bomb from spreading.

Baghdad's greatest nuclear shopping success has been in West Germany. In 1987, the German firm H & H Metalform sold Iraq at least three "flow-turn" machines—devices specially capable of making high-speed gas centrifuges. The flow-turn machine produces the rotor—the thin-walled portion of the centrifuge that rotates, one of the most difficult parts to manufacture. According to H & H, the deals were licensed by the German government. Two German dealers actually ran the H & H machines at Tuwaitha to produce centrifuges. West German officials also suspect that these dealers sold Iraq the designs for the centrifuges.

In early 1990, another German firm, Export-Union, sent Iraq fifty metric tons of "maraging" steel, a type specially developed to make centrifuge rotors. This sale was cleared by West German officials, who told Export-Union that the steel did not require an export license. From another Bonn firm, Iraq apparently bought the specially-designed "ring" magnets that hold the spinning centrifuge rotors in place.

After Germany, Iraq's next-largest supplier was Brazil. Throughout the 1980s, Brazil helped Iraq obtain uranium. According to two former Brazilian government officials, Brazil agreed to ship Iraq 100 tons of pure uranium and uranium concentrate (the form in which uranium enters the enrichment process) in the early 1980s, knowing full well that Iraq intended to make atomic bombs. Three shipments were sent in 1981, but for fear of bad publicity, Brazil stopped the deliveries before all 100 tons had gone.

Brazil also prospected for uranium in Iraq, analyzed ore samples there, supplied nuclear material and equipment for laboratory tests, and designed an underground plant to make uranium concentrate, which has not yet been built. A firm in Rio, Natron Consulting and Designing, received $5–6 million for the design. Brazil may even have taught Iraqi engineers how to operate centrifuges. Several Iraqi technical teams visited Brazil during the 1980s, at least one of which had access to the secret Aramar enrichment plant at Ipero, which also uses centrifuges—like Iraq's—based on German designs. Brazil's president, Fernando Collor, has just expressed his regret for these episodes, which he said transferred "nuclear technology" that was "potentially significant."

The Iraqi-Brazilian relationship appears to be a case of Germany's nuclear progeny playing together. Before making its flow-turn machine deal with Iraq, the German firm H & H had exported the same machines to the Brazilian Navy Committee, responsible for Brazil's uranium enrichment efforts. According to the German news magazine *Der Spiegel,* Walter Busse, an ex-employee of the West German company MAN, which makes centrifuges, established a "dense network of relations between nuclear bomb builders in Iraq and Brazil on the one hand, and German contractors on the other."

Other countries also have helped Iraq's uranium enrichment effort. In December 1989, China was reported to be helping Iraq make ring magnets for centrifuge stabilization. China is known to have supplied similar magnets to Pakistan. Also in December 1989, Western officials were reported to be monitoring exchanges of personnel between Iraq and Pakistan's centrifuge enrichment plant at Kahuta.

Switzerland entered the picture in August 1990, when it was discovered that customs officials in Frankfurt had seized end caps for centrifuges on their way to Iraq from the Swiss firm Schmiedemeccanica. End caps, specially made from high-strength steel, are needed to seal the tops and bottoms of centrifuges. Schmiedemeccanica was working under contract to Germany's H & H. As usual, in addition to the caps, Iraq was trying to get the means to make them itself. The customs agents also seized machine tools for making end caps furnished by the Swiss firm Schaeublin.

Enrichment is only the final stage of the uranium fuel cycle, which is a complex and expensive process. It begins with the acquisition of natural uranium. Iraq has several hundred tons of natural uranium, which cannot be used directly for nuclear weapons but will be needed as feedstock for an indigenous enrichment capability. It apparently imported 100 tons from Niger and 130 tons from Portugal in the early 1980s, without putting the shipments under IAEA inspection. In addition, Iraq has purchased tons of low-enriched and depleted uranium on the world market.

If Iraq ever does produce nuclear weapon material, it would like to have the other parts of the bomb—the "detonation package"—already waiting. Saddam has used his worldwide purchasing network to acquire bomb parts as well as enrichment technology, and the United States has been an important source.

We are all familiar with his attempt last March to smuggle American-made nuclear weapon triggers to Iraq. The triggers consisted of special high-performance capacitors used to detonate warheads in the U.S. arsenal. The Iraqi agents were also interested in buying krytrons, the high-speed electronic switches used in combination with the capacitors to detonate nuclear warheads.

If Iraq someday reaches the point of a nuclear test, it will have American equipment especially designed to monitor the explosion. In 1987, the American company Tektronix sold Iraq a digital oscilloscope which, according to a company official, had nuclear applications. Oscilloscopes are uniquely able to process the rapid data from nuclear weapon tests. They are also used to develop missile guidance systems and to sort the data from missile flight tests. The oscilloscope was licensed and was shipped to SAAD-16, Iraq's largest complex for chemical, missile, and nuclear weapon research.

U.S. companies have also provided equipment to Iraq that has been used directly in its ballistic missile program, and may someday help deliver an Iraqi bomb. Hewlett Packard sold Iraq $1 million worth of electronic test and measurement equipment and general-purpose computers. Wiltron provided a scalar network analyser to test and develop microwave circuits for missile-guidance radars. These sales were licensed by the U.S. Commerce Department between 1985 and 1987. If we go to war with Iraq, we may wind up bombing our own citizens, now held at Iraqi weapons sites, to destroy our own exports. And we would have to ask U.S. pilots to risk their lives to do it.

I strongly urge the Armed Services Committee to begin redressing this situation by increasing the Pentagon's role in nonproliferation policy decisions. The secretary of defense should have the power to concur in all exports of dual-use technologies and munitions, and also in re-exports by the Department of Energy. Under the current system, the export promotion agency (Commerce), the nuclear promotion agency (Energy), and the international harmony promotion agency (State) make these decisions without the help of the security promotion agency (Defense).

There are recent cases in which the Pentagon has intervened and blocked or slowed pending exports of nuclear and missile technologies, but in other cases the Department of Defense has taken scant interest in nonproliferation policy and has meekly accepted the export decisions of the Commerce and State departments. The best case is that of pending exports of supercomputers to Israel, India, and Brazil. All of these countries have secret nuclear and missile programs and are ineligible according to our own export standards to receive supercomputers, which are the most powerful tool available for nuclear weapon and missile design. However, the Pentagon—which opposed these sales under the Reagan administration—is knuckling under to other agencies that are not as well qualified to assess the security implications of these transactions, and are simply concerned with placating other governments and promoting U.S. trade.

If the Defense Department wants to be a real player in nonproliferation policy, and not simply be tapped when it is time to send in the troops as the last line of defense against Third World nuclear weapons, it should show that it is willing to devote staff and initiative to these export decisions and keep weapons technology out of proliferator countries. The Defense Technology Security Administration, which was established to control technology transfers to the Soviet bloc, needs a new job. Congress should task it with providing technical support for export licensing decisions, through the office of the secretary of defense. If we had devoted more of our military resources to controlling proliferation at the source in the past decade, we probably would not have to airlift other military resources to the Persian Gulf today.

IN SUMMARY, I would like to make three simple points. First, there is no real short-term risk of an Iraqi nuclear weapon—at least based on what the Bush administration has told us so far. The administration

250 · THE GULF WAR READER

should be ashamed of itself for misleading the public about the Iraqi bomb; there should be a reasonable limit to governmental disinformation when the stakes are so high. If the administration has hard evidence that Iraq has diverted safeguarded fissile material or acquired unrestricted fissile material from outside, the president should make it public and give Congress a real basis for exercising its constitutional power of deciding whether to commit the nation to war.

Second, I believe that Iraq is a major proliferation risk in the long term, and that the current trade embargo may not be sufficient to prevent it from acquiring nuclear weapons. However, I think our security would be better served by developing international efforts to contain Iraq's nuclear efforts as tightly as possible through nonmilitary means, with military strikes on nuclear facilities only as a last resort. We carried out a forty-year campaign to contain the Soviet Union and prevent war in Central Europe, so we should be able to organize a comprehensive system to contain Iraq, particularly since the Soviet Union is now on our side.

Third, a general war against Iraq, even to stop Hussein from making the bomb, would not solve the problem of nuclear proliferation. Iraq's pattern of arming through imports is being replicated around the world, and soldiers' blood is not a morally defensible means of export control. Reckless exports have given Israel, South Africa, India, and Pakistan the means to make nuclear weapons, and have almost done so for Argentina and Brazil. As long as there are buyers with money there will be sellers of dangerous goods. Periodic wars, randomly triggered when a nuclear aspirant invades its neighbor, are not a reliable means of containing nuclear technology.

THE DRIFT TO WAR

(Testimony Before the Senate Foreign Relations Committee,
December 5, 1990)

Zbigniew Brzezinski

Most americans, I am sure, share the hope that the president's recent and laudable decision to initiate a direct dialogue with the Iraqi government will lead to a serious and comprehensive exploration of a nonviolent solution to the ongoing crisis. Wisely, the president indicated that the purpose of such a dialogue is not to merely convey an ultimatum but to convince Iraq that its compliance with the U.N. resolution is the necessary precondition for a peaceful settlement. It is thus not an accident that those who so fervently have been advocating war have promptly denounced the president's initiative.

To be meaningful, such a dialogue has to go beyond demands for unconditional surrender but involve also some discussion of the consequences of Iraqi compliance with the U.N. resolutions. That means that Iraq, in the course of the ensuing discussions, will have to be given some preliminary indications of the likely political, territorial, and financial aftermath of its withdrawal from Kuwait.

I stress these points because those who favor only a military solution will now exercise pressure on the president to reduce the incipient dialogue essentially to a mere transmittal of an ultimatum. That, I trust, everyone recognizes would be pointless and counterproductive. It would simply accelerate the drift to war.

While it is premature to detail here the substance of a nonviolent solution to the crisis that could emerge from the proposed dialogue, it is possible to envisage a series of sequential but linked phases, all premised on Iraq having satisfied the necessary preconditions regarding Kuwait.

Zbigniew Brzezinski was assistant to the president for national security affairs in the Carter administration.

First, coercive sanctions would be maintained until Iraq implements its willingness to comply with the U.N. resolutions regarding a withdrawal from Kuwait.

Two, binding arbitration by a U.N.-sanctioned body within a specified time frame would be accepted by the governments of Iraq and Kuwait regarding territorial delimitation, conflicting financial claims, and other pertinent matters.

Three, an international conference would be convened to establish regional limitations on weapons of mass destruction, pending which a U.N.-sponsored security force would remain deployed in Kuwait and perhaps in Saudi Arabia to secure needed security.

It is important to note, Mr. Chairman, that any dialogue to the above effect would be conducted while Iraq is being subjected to severe sanctions. The United States would be therefore conceding nothing while conducting the talks. It is Iraq that is under duress, not us. It is Iraqi power that is being attritted, while ours is growing. It is Iraq that is isolated and threatened with destruction, not us.

Nor would any such outcome as the one outlined above be tantamount to rewarding aggression. Those who argue that do so because they desire only one outcome, no matter what the price to America—the destruction of Iraq. Withdrawal from Kuwait would represent a massive setback for Saddam Hussein and a victory for the international order. It would be a dramatic reversal of aggression, humiliating and painful to the aggressor.

However, it is quite possible, perhaps even probable, that the talks will initially prove unproductive. In my view, that should not be viewed as a casus belli. Instead, we should stay on course, applying the policy of punitive containment. This policy is working. Iraq has been deterred, ostracized, and punished. Sanctions, unprecedented in their international solidarity and more massive in scope than any ever adopted in peacetime against any nation—I repeat, ever adopted against any nation —are inflicting painful costs on the Iraqi economy.

"Economic sanctions," by their definition, require time to make their impact felt, but they have already established the internationally significant lesson that Iraq's aggression did not pay. By some calculations, about ninety-seven percent of Iraq's income and ninety percent of its imports have been cut off, and the shutdown of the equivalent of forty-three percent of Iraq's and Kuwait's GNP has already taken place.

This is prompting the progressive attrition of the country's economy and warmaking capabilities. Extensive rationing is a grim social reality.

Over time, all this is bound to have an unsettling effect on Saddam Hussein's power.

The administration's argument that the sanctions are not working suggests to me that in the first instance the administration had entertained extremely naive notions regarding how sanctions actually do work. They not only take time, they are by their nature an instrument for softening up the opponent, inducing in the adversary a more compliant attitude toward an eventual nonviolent resolution. Sanctions are not a blunt instrument for promptly achieving total surrender.

Worse still, the administration's actions and its rhetoric have conveyed a sense of impatience that in fact has tended to undermine the credibility of long-term sanctions. Perhaps the administration felt that this was necessary to convince Saddam Hussein that it meant business. But the consequence has been to make the administration the prisoner of its own rhetoric, with American options and timetable thereby severely constricted.

The cumulative result has been to move the United States significantly beyond the initial policy of punitive containment, with the result that the conflict of the international community with Iraq has become over-Americanized, over-personalized, and over-emotionalized. The enormous deployment of American forces, coupled with talk of no compromise, means that the United States is now pointed toward a war with Iraq that will be largely an American war, fought predominantly by Americans, in which, on our side, mostly Americans will die—and for interests that are neither equally vital nor urgent to America and which, in any case, can be and should be effectively pursued by other less dramatic and less bloody means.

Yet to justify military action the administration, echoing the advocates of war, has lately been relying on the emotionally charged argument that we confront a present danger because of the possibility that Iraq may at some point acquire a nuclear capability. In other words, not oil, not Kuwait, but Iraq's nuclear program has become the latest excuse for moving toward war.

This argument deserves careful scrutiny. But, once subjected to it, this latest case for war also does not meet the tests of vitality or urgency to the American national interest. First of all, it is relevant to note that when the United States was threatened directly by the far more powerful and dangerous Stalinist Russia or Maoist China, it refrained from engaging in preventive war. Moreover, Israel already has nuclear weapons and can thus deter Iraq, while the United States has certainly both the power to deter or to destroy Iraq.

Deterrence has worked in the past, and I fail to see why thousands of Americans should now die in order to make sure that at some point in the future—according to experts, some years from now—Iraq does not acquire a militarily significant nuclear capability.

Second, it is within our power to sustain a comprehensive embargo on Iraq to impede such an acquisition. Unlike India or Israel, Iraq does permit international inspection of its nuclear facilities. This gives us some insight into its program. Moreover, much can happen during the next several years, including Saddam's fall from power. Hence, the precipitation of war now on these grounds meets neither the criterion of urgency nor vitality.

More than that, war would be highly counterproductive to the American national interest. A war is likely to split the international consensus that currently exists. The United States is likely to become estranged from many of its European allies. And it is almost certain to become the object of widespread Arab hostility. Indeed, once started, the war may prove not all that easy to terminate, given the inflammable character of Middle Eastern politics. It could be costly in blood and financially devastating.

SANCTIONS WORK:
THE HISTORICAL RECORD

Kimberly Elliott, Gary Hufbauer, Jeffrey Schott

FIFTY-FIVE years ago, when Mussolini's troops overran Ethiopia, half-hearted sanctions by the League of Nations failed to force Italy to withdraw. Haile Selassie's futile pleas for help have haunted the world ever since.

This week, President Bush and key members of his administration including the secretaries of state and defense declared that the United Nations' far stronger sanctions against Iraq cannot be relied on to force a withdrawal from Kuwait. Only military power, they warned, is certain to get Saddam Hussein's armies out.

But sanctions can work—and under circumstances far less favorable than those present in the confrontation with Iraq. In fact, a review of 115 cases since 1914 shows that success was achieved 40 times when economic sanctions were threatened or imposed against individual countries. Moreover, the current U.N. sanctions are by far the strongest and most complete ever imposed against any country by other nations. These comparisons strongly suggest that, given time, the U.N. economic boycott can achieve by peaceful means what Bush and his advisers say can only be won by force.

A comparison with the famous case of Ethiopia, one of the 115 we have reviewed in detail, reveals important differences which apply in the current case. The embargo of Iraq is completely different from the League's halfhearted attempt to save Ethiopia (which was made even

Kimberly Elliott, Gary Hufbauer and Jeffrey Schott are the authors of *Economic Sanctions Reconsidered*, published in 1990 by the Institute for International Economics, with which they are affiliated. This article was published in the December 9, 1990, issue of *The Washington Post* under the title "The Big Squeeze: Why the Sanctions On Iraq Will Work."

weaker when the United States, a non-League member, refused to join). The current boycott covers virtually one hundred percent of Iraq's trade. This is three to four times greater coverage than the average in all previous successful sanctions cases. Beyond that, Iraq, geographically isolated and dependent on oil for ninety percent of its export revenue, is far more vulnerable to economic coercion than target nations in other sanctions actions.

Because of all these factors, it is likely that if the embargo persists, Iraqi output will shrink by about half from its 1988 total of $45 billion. This is a decline of gross national product (GNP) twenty times greater than the average impact in other successful sanction episodes. Meanwhile, the economic costs to the sanctioning countries of suspended trade with Iraq are being addressed in unusual ways and substantially mitigated. These efforts give the current sanctions a cohesion and possible longevity never seen outside the setting of global conflicts.

In addition, the administration's toughening military posture can have a welcome side effect: Such bellicosity could actually work to strengthen the resolve of the sanctioning nations to stick to their embargo as the only alternative to armed conflict.

Economic sanctions have been used in this century in pursuit of a wide variety of goals. They range from the relatively modest, such as Britain's 1933 sanctions against the Soviet Union to gain the release of some British citizens accused of spying, to the difficult, such as the U.S. sanctions against Poland from 1981 to 1987 to force the communist regime to lift martial law and loosen political restraints.

In judging whether the imposition of sanctions was a "success," we looked for evidence of two things: that the boycotters had substantially met their goals; and that sanctions had contributed at least modestly to the outcome. Successful actions include, for example, the trade embargoes and financial sanctions to weaken the enemy's fighting capability used by the Allies in World Wars I and II and by Great Britain and its allies during the Falklands conflict in 1982. On two occasions in the 1920s, the mere threat of sanctions by the League of Nations was sufficient to settle border conflicts: Yugoslavia withdrew troops from disputed territory in Albania; Greece renounced territorial claims in Bulgaria. In the postwar era, the protracted U.N. embargo of Rhodesia, much less stringently enforced than the sanctions against Iraq, helped bring about the demise of the breakaway regime of Ian Smith.

Such examples argue strongly for the likely success of the sanctions against Iraq. Secretary of Defense Richard B. Cheney himself said the embargo "clearly" has been effective "in closing off the flow of spare parts and military supplies," and the chairman of the Joint Chiefs of Staff, General Colin Powell, conceded that sanctions would have "a debilitating effect" on Iraq's military capability. Recently, CIA Director William H. Webster told the House Armed Services Committee that by next spring, "probably only energy-related and some military industries will be fully functioning."

The sanctions against Iraq are unique in the history of such economic weapons in the twentieth century. Though there is inevitably some leakage, the embargo affects virtually all of Iraq's trade and financial relations. Historically, when the sanctioning country or group accounted for fifty percent or more of the target's trade, the sanctioners had a fifty percent chance of achieving their goals. In the average successful sanctions case, the boycotters accounted for twenty-eight percent of the target's trade, far below the Iraq situation.

In addition, this embargo is backed by a multinational naval blockade and a ban on air cargo to Iraq. Except for what we consider minor smuggling through Turkey, Iran and Jordan, Iraq has been effectively isolated from the global economy. Smuggling will ebb as Saddam runs out of money, which Webster predicted would be next spring or summer.

The average cost to the target nation's economy in successful sanctions cases was 2.4 percent of GNP, about the level of lost U.S. output in the 1982 recession (the most severe since the Depression), and one-twentieth of the impact on Iraq. The cost to the target reached double digits only three other times: Nigeria vs. Biafra, 1967–70; U.S. and Britain vs. Iran, 1951–53; and the U.N. and Britain vs. Rhodesia, 1965–79. In all these cases, sanctions contributed to a positive outcome. Of eight sanctions episodes where the cost to the target was five percent of GNP or more, six resulted in at least partial success for the sanctioners.

Prior to this summer, only Ian Smith's unilateral declaration of independence in Rhodesia in 1965 had provoked mandatory, comprehensive U.N. sanctions. However, those sanctions were imposed incrementally over two years and were not universally enforced despite being mandatory. Unlike the Iraq case, the U.N. refused to impose secondary sanctions against countries violating the Rhodesian embargo.

The sanctions against Iraq were imposed so swiftly, decisively, and comprehensively that together with a credible military threat, there is a high probability they can contribute to an Iraqi withdrawal and the restoration of an independent government in Kuwait. However, our study of sanctions cases indicated that the more difficult the goals, the less effective the sanctions.

Besides the goals outlined in the U.N. resolutions, Bush and other leaders have talked of reducing Iraq's military capability, including the destruction of its nascent nuclear weapons capability. While sanctions can weaken Saddam's fighting capability because of food, fuel, and spare parts shortages and resupply problems, they cannot destroy his arms industry.

There also have been suggestions that the sanctions should be aimed at destabilizing Saddam. The United States has taken this route before—no less than ten times since World War II. In fact, the United States far exceeds all other countries in threatening or using sanctions—eighty-one attempts since 1917, of which more than seventy came after World War II. U.S. goals have varied widely—from curbing or destabilizing governments perceived to be drifting from the "Western" capitalist sphere, to forcing Britain and France in 1956 to withdraw their troops from the Suez Canal after Egypt's Gamal Nasser nationalized it. In the 1970s, the United States increased its use of sanctions, not as success-fully, to improve the observance of human rights and to inhibit the spread of nuclear weapons. In the 1980s, terrorism and drug smuggling have been major targets of U.S. sanctions.

In the ten cases of U.S. sanctions aimed at dictators, they contributed at least modestly to the downfalls of Rafael Trujillo in the Dominican Republic in the 1960s and Idi Amin in Uganda and Anastasio Somoza in Nicaragua in the 1970s. Sanctions also exacerbated the economic chaos in Nicaragua, which contributed to the electoral defeat of Daniel Ortega earlier this year.

In cases in which the goals were ambitious, sanctions took an average of nearly two years to achieve a successful outcome. This raises the question of their sustainability. Here again, the Iraq case is unique. To counter possible erosion of the boycott because the participants find the costs to their own economies too high, the United States and its allies have taken extraordinary steps, including asking Saudi Arabia and other oil exporters to boost oil production to offset lost Iraqi and Kuwaiti production. The United States also led in organizing an "economic action plan" to redirect short-term windfall profits gained by the oil producers to help developing countries. Washington also has encour-aged Japan, Germany and others to provide grants and low-cost loans to developing countries hurt by higher oil prices, lost trade and related problems.

Maintaining a cohesive alliance long enough to make the sanctions work will require continued cost-reducing measures, such as getting the Gulf oil producers to raise oil production so that prices come down and stabilize around the July OPEC target price of $21 per barrel. The United States, Germany, and Japan also should be prepared to release oil from their strategic petroleum reserves to prevent price rises when winter brings increased energy consumption. The $21 billion committed to the economic action plan also should be swiftly distributed to offset costs to the front-line coalition states and further supplemented by additional grants for as long as needed to permit the sanctions to work. The IMF and World Bank should also increase concessional loans to developing countries thrown off balance by the sudden increase in oil prices.

However, even the tightest sanctions take time to work. Evidence from previous cases suggests that it would be unfair to claim the embargo of Iraq has failed until at least a year has passed. Though there are costs to waiting, some of them can be ameliorated, as with the president's economic action plan. If after a year or two the sanctions are judged to be inadequate, the military option will still be there and Saddam's forces will be weakened by lack of supplies. The key question is whether the price of patience would be higher than the economic and human costs of going to war soon.

THE OBLIGATION TO DEBATE

(Speech of January 4, 1991)

Senator Tom Harkin

On January 3, the Senate was preparing to go into recess, with Democratic Majority Leader George Mitchell seeking unanimous consent to a resolution that would have kept the body adjourned until January 23—after the Security Council's January 15 deadline—unless he and the Republican Minority Leader Bob Michel agreed to reconvene. Senators Tom Harkin and Brock Adams objected, insisting that the president must get explicit authorization from Congress before taking offensive action against Iraq. After some discussion, Senator Mitchell reconsidered his effort to postpone the coming debate. The next day, on the Senate floor, Senator Harkin spelled out his concerns in the following speech.

THE FRAMERS of the Constitution were very, very wary of giving one person the power to declare war. Alexander Hamilton explained that certain interests are "so delicate and momentous" that to entrust them "to the sole disposal" of the president is unwise.

The framers were further concerned that the judgment to initiate war should not be lightly made. Madison spoke of war as "among the greatest of national calamities," to use his quote. Thomas Jefferson desired an "effectual check to the Dog of War." George Mason said that he was "for clogging, rather than facilitating war."

James Wilson, one of the most important participants at the Philadelphia Convention, explained the rationale for giving to Congress the power to initiate war. He said, "This system will not hurry us into war." How about that.

We keep hearing from the president that he has lost patience, that we

Tom Harkin is the Democratic senator from Iowa.

cannot have any more time, that we have a deadline. But James Wilson, one of the participants in the framing of the Constitution said:

"This system will not hurry us into war: it is calculated to guard against it. It will not be in the power of a single man, or a single body of men, to involve us in such distress, for the important power of declaring war is vested in the legislature at large and this declaration must be made with the concurrence of the House of Representatives; from this circumstance we may draw a certain conclusion that nothing but our national interest can draw us into a war."

As a congressman, Abraham Lincoln wrote that the intent of the Constitution was "that no one man should hold the power of bringing this oppression"—of war—"upon us."

Originally the framers had a clause that provided that Congress "make" war—that only Congress have the power to "make" war—but they changed it to "declare" war, in order to give the president "the power to repel certain attacks," and to clarify that it was the executive's function to "conduct" the war once Congress authorized it.

James Madison wrote that "in no part of the Constitution is more wisdom to be found than in the clause which confides the question of war or peace to the legislature and not to the executive department."

So again this unambiguous constitutional mandate was to ensure congressional debate and authorization prior to the entry into war except in the case of sudden attack.

Alexander Hamilton explained in the Federalist Papers:

"(T)he President is the commander in chief of the army and navy of the United States. In this respect his authority would be nominally the same with that of the King of Great-Britain, but in substance much inferior to it. It would amount to nothing more than the supreme command and direction of the military and naval forces, as first general and admiral of the confederacy; while that of the British king extends to the declaring of war and to the raising and regulating of fleets and armies; all which by the Constitution under consideration would appertain to the Legislature."

That is the Congress of the United States.

He made it clear they wanted to not use the word "make" but "declare" in order that the president could repel an actual and sudden invasion of the United States.

So any objective reading of the Constitution itself and the clear language of the Constitution, or any reading of the Federalist Papers, or writings of those who drafted this clear clause in the Constitution, can lead to only one clear and unambiguous conclusion: that only Congress can declare war, and the president has the power to repel attacks and invasions, which is not the situation at hand.

So again this resolution is necessary because we have been adrift in this country for some time, letting the executive branch take us from one military action to another. Whether it is Grenada, whether it is Panama, whether it is Nicaragua, wherever it might be, and now in the Mideast, Congress is not actually taking a position under the Constitution to exert its constitutional mandate.

I will be frank in admitting that there were many in this body in previous times—I will not speak of today—but in previous times who were glad to shift that responsibility to the president. You know, why take a position on it if you do not have to. Let the president get out there on the point. If he wins, they can support it; if he does not, then they can be against it. There has been a lot of talk that members of Congress want to put themselves in that kind of position. This senator believes very strongly that each person in this body and in the House must stand up and be counted on this issue. Are you for it or are you against it?

This senator believes quite clearly that the president cannot conduct offensive military operations in the Mideast unless he gets prior approval from Congress. As I said yesterday, now is the time and here is the place to debate this issue, not after the bullets start flying. After that, a different dynamic takes place. Are you going to support our young men and women who are in combat? Are you going to rally around the flag and support this country in its hour of need? Then the dynamics change. Now is the time to debate this crucial issue of the powers of the presidency.

Much has been alluded to by speakers on the floor of the Senate yesterday that no one was contacted about this resolution; that there are standard procedures that we followed in the past; that we would come in, we would swear senators in, and then we would go away and come back after the president sent down his budget and his message to Congress.

Those are normal times. But these are not normal times. We have upwards of 400,000, or soon will have 400,000, American troops in the Mideast. There is a date of January 15 set by a U.N. resolution prompted by the United States, confirmed by the Security Council, after which member nations are allowed to use force in order to get Iraqi troops out of Kuwait. All that has happened since this body last met in October.

When we left in October, many of us were under the very clear and distinct impression that the president of the United States had made a decision to continue to enforce sanctions, economic sanctions, against

Iraq, to take all diplomatic and economic means necessary to get Iraq out of Kuwait.

As I travel around my home state of Iowa, I find that people are somewhat confused about just why are we there: What is our goal? The goal has changed. One time it is to get the government of Kuwait back in power. At another time it is because of oil. Another time we are told it is because of jobs. Another time because Saddam Hussein is worse than Hitler, and we cannot allow this to happen. The reasons for us being there seem to change as the winds change.

When we left in October, on at least eight occasions, the president of the United States was quoted as saying that sanctions were working; that we should have patience. On October 19, to the National Italian American Foundation at the White House, I quote the president:

"I think the bottom line is he (Saddam) can't prevail. So, we're going to stay with this, stay the course and send a strong moral message out there, and a simple one: One big country can't bully its neighbor and take it over."

On October 1, the president was quoted as saying:

"I have heard . . . more opinions in various quarters that the sanctions are really beginning to bite hard."

On September 11, before a joint session of Congress, the president said: "Let no one doubt our staying power. . . . Together with our friends and allies, ships of the United States Navy are today patrolling Mideast waters. They've already intercepted more than 700 ships to enforce the sanctions. Three regional leaders I spoke with just yesterday told me that these sanctions are working. Iraq is feeling the heat. . . . They are cut off from world trade, unable to sell their oil. And only a tiny fraction of goods get through. . . . I cannot predict just how long it will take to convince Iraq to withdraw from Kuwait. Sanctions will take time to have their full intended effect."

Thus speaks the president of the United States.

On October 20, in San Francisco, he said:

"And I would hope that the economic sanctions . . . will convince him that he should, without conditions, get out of Kuwait."

Well, as reported in *The Washington Post* on December 7, 1990, in Latin America the president said:

"I've not been one who has been convinced that sanctions alone would bring him to his senses."

Well, no wonder the people of America are confused. Here is the president saying time and time again that we should have patience, moral leadership, economic sanctions to show a new world order for collective security with a mission that would bind together to assure that a bully like Saddam Hussein cannot succeed. Not by unleashing the dogs of war, but by isolating, sanctioning, ensuring that his economy cannot function.

There are some even today who say that Saddam has already won. Quite to the contrary, he is losing every day. Recent estimates are that Saddam Hussein and Iraq are losing somewhere in the neighborhood of $70 million a day in lost oil revenues that they cannot sell. They cannot use any of their occupied Kuwaiti ports. So he has gained nothing and he is losing every day. I think that we should have patience, as the president first said.

Or, as another one of the my distinguished colleagues said the other day, which is better: Do we want to wait a year and a half, perhaps, for sanctions to really have their effect, or to perhaps lose 20,000 American lives in a war that would take place early this year?

So all of this has happened since we adjourned in October. Immediately after the election, the president announced that we were going to double the troop strength to almost 400,000. After the election. Then the January 15 deadline was brought by the president. Secretary Baker went around the world, getting all the nations to support the vote in the U.N. Security Council.

This senator wonders, and I wonder aloud, what Secretary Baker promised all these nations to get them to vote for this resolution? I would note for the record that the day after the U.N. vote when China abstained—they could have vetoed the resolution, but China abstained—the day after, the Chinese foreign minister had a meeting with the president at the White House. After what happened in the Tiananmen Square last year, what did Secretary Baker promise China to get them to abstain the Security Council? I think that is a question that needs to be answered.

So these are not normal times. These are not the times when we can close our doors and go home. It is time for us to stand up and be counted.

WHITE SLAVES IN THE PERSIAN GULF

Arthur Schlesinger, Jr.

P R E S I D E N T   B U S H ' S gamble in the Gulf may yet pay off. Let us pray that it does—that the combination of international economic sanctions, political pressure, and military buildup will force Saddam Hussein to repent and retreat. Let us pray that the tough talk from Washington is designed primarily as psychological warfare—and that it will work.

But tough talk creates its own momentum and may seize control of policy. If the gamble fails, the president will be hard put to avoid war. Is this a war Americans really want to fight? Senator Robert Dole said the other day that Americans are not yet committed to this war, and he is surely right. And is it a war Americans are wrong in not wanting to fight?

Among our stated objectives are the defense of Saudi Arabia, the liberation of Kuwait and restoration of the royal family, and the establishment, in the president's phrase, of a "stable and secure Gulf." Presumably these generous-hearted goals should win the cooperation, respect, and gratitude of the locals. Indications are, to the contrary, that our involvement is increasing Arab contempt for the U.S.

In *The Wall Street Journal* a few days ago Geraldine Brooks and Tony Horwitz described the reluctance of the Arabs to fight in their own defense. The Gulf states have a population almost as large as Iraq's but no serious armies and limited inclination to raise them. Why should they? The *Journal* quotes a senior Gulf official: "You think I want to send

Arthur Schlesinger, Jr., is Albert Schweitzer Professor of the Humanities at the City University of New York and author of numerous books, including *The Imperial Presidency*. This piece originally appeared in the January 7, 1991, issue of *The Wall Street Journal*.

my teen-aged son to die for Kuwait?" He chuckles and adds, "We have our white slaves from America to do that."

At the recent meeting of the Gulf Cooperation Council, the Arab states congratulated themselves on their verbal condemnation of Iraqi aggression but spoke not one word of thanks to the American troops who had crossed half the world to fight for them. A Yemeni diplomat explained this curious omission to Judith Miller of *The New York Times:* "A lot of the Gulf rulers simply do not feel that they have to thank the people they've hired to do their fighting for them."

James LeMoyne reported in *The New York Times* last October in a dispatch from Saudi Arabia, "There is no mass mobilization for war in the markets and streets. The scenes of cheerful American families saying goodbye to their sons and daughters are being repeated in few Saudi homes." Mr. LeMoyne continued, "Some Saudis' attitude toward the American troops verges on treating them as a sort of contracted super-power enforcer. . . ." He quoted a Saudi teacher: "The American soldiers are a new kind of foreign worker here. We have Pakistanis driving taxis and now we have Americans defending us."

I know that the object of foreign policy is not to win gratitude. It is to produce real effects in the real world. It is conceivable that we should simply swallow the Arab insults and soldier on as their "white slaves" because vital interests of our own are involved. But, as Mr. Dole implied, the case that U.S. vital interests are at stake has simply not been made to the satisfaction of Congress and the American people.

Of course we have interests in the Gulf. But it is essential to distinguish between peripheral interests and vital interests. Vital interests exist when our national security is truly at risk. Vital interests are those you kill and die for. I write as one who has no problem about the use of force to defend our vital interests and who had no doubt that vital interests were involved in preventing the domination of Europe by Hitler and later by Stalin.

In defining our vital interests in the Gulf, the administration's trumpet gives an awfully uncertain sound. It has offered a rolling series of peripheral justifications—oil, jobs, regional stability, the menace of a nuclear Iraq, the creation of a new world order. These pretexts for war grow increasingly thin.

If oil is the issue, nothing will more certainly increase oil prices than war, with long-term interruption of supply and widespread destruction of oil fields. Every whisper of peace has brought oil prices down. And the idea of spending American lives in order to save American jobs is despicable—quite unworthy of our intelligent secretary of state.

As for the stabilization of the Middle East, this is a goal that has never been attained for long in history. Stability is not a likely prospect for a region characterized from time immemorial by artificial frontiers, tribal antagonism, religious fanaticisms and desperate inequalities. I doubt that the U.S. has the capacity or the desire to replace the Ottoman empire, and our efforts thus far have won us not the respect of the Arab rulers but their contempt.

What about nuclear weapons? The preventive-war argument is no more valid against Iraq than it was when nuts proposed it against the Soviet Union during the Cold War. In any case, Secretary of State Baker has in effect offered a no-invasion pledge if Iraq withdraws from Kuwait —a pledge that would leave Saddam Hussein in power and his nuclear facilities intact.

As for the new world order, the United Nations will be far stronger if it succeeds through resolute application of economic sanctions than if it only provides a multilateral facade for a unilateral U.S. war. Nor would we strengthen the U.N. by wreaking mass destruction that will appall the world and discredit collective security for years to come.

No one likes the loathsome Saddam Hussein. Other countries would rejoice in his overthrow—and are fully prepared to fight to the last American to bring it about. But, since the threat he poses to the U.S. is far less than the threat to the Gulf states, why are we Americans the fall guys, expected to do ninety percent of the fighting and to take ninety percent of the casualties? Only Britain, loyal as usual, has made any serious military contribution to the impending war—10,000 more troops than Egypt. If we go to war, let not the posse fade away, as befell the unfortunate marshal in *High Noon.*

And please, Mr. President, spare us the sight of Dan Quayle telling the troops that this war won't be another Vietnam. How in hell would he know?

No one ever supposed that an economic embargo would bring Iraq to its knees in a short five months. Why not give sanctions time to work? The Central Intelligence Agency already reports shortages in Iraq's military spare parts. If we must fight, why not fight a weaker rather than a stronger Iraq? What is the big rush? There is a phrase of President Eisenhower's that comes to mind: "the courage of patience."

I also recall words of President Kennedy that seem relevant during these dark days: "Don't push your opponent against a locked door." What is so terribly wrong with a negotiated settlement? Iraq must absolutely withdraw from Kuwait, but the grievances that explain, though not excuse, the invasion might well be adjudicated. As for the nuclear threat, that can be taken care of by a combination of arms embargo, international inspection throughout the Middle East and great-power deterrence. Such measures would do far more than war to strengthen collective security and build a new world order.

One has the abiding fear that the administration has not thought out the consequences of war. Fighting Iraq will not be like fighting Grenada or Panama. The war will most likely be bloody and protracted. Victory might well entangle us in Middle Eastern chaos for years—all for interests that, so far as the U.S. is concerned, are at best peripheral.

Worst of all, the Iraq sideshow is enfeebling us in areas where vital interests are truly at stake. While we concentrate energies and resources in the Middle East, Eastern Europe is in travail and the Soviet Union is falling apart. We cannot single-handedly rescue democracy in the ex-Communist states, but at least we ought to be thinking hard about ways we could help on the margin. Europe is far more essential to our national security than the Middle East.

And we confront urgent problems here at home—deepening recession, decaying infrastructure, deteriorating race relations, a shaky banking system, crime-ridden cities on the edge of bankruptcy, states in financial crisis, increasing public and private debt, low productivity, diminishing competitiveness in world markets. The crisis of our national community demands major attention and resources too. While we fiddle away in the Middle East, the American economy will continue to decline, and Japan and Germany will seize the world's commanding economic heights.

War against Iraq will be the most unnecessary war in American history, and it well may cause the gravest damage to the vital interests of the republic.

THE CASE FOR INTERVENTION

Representative Stephen J. Solarz

I R O N I E S   C A N sometimes be painful. I began my political career in 1966 as the campaign manager for one of the first anti-war congressional candidates in the country. Now, a quarter century later, I find myself supporting a policy in the Persian Gulf that might well lead to a war that many believe could become another Vietnam. Such a position is more and more anomalous, I know, in the Democratic Party. And yet I cannot accept, or be dissuaded by, the analogy with Vietnam.

In Vietnam no vital American interests were at stake. The crisis in the Gulf poses a challenge not only to fundamental American interests, but to essential American values. In Indochina the cost in blood and treasure was out of all proportion to the expected gains from a successful defense of South Vietnam. In the Gulf the potential costs of the American commitment are far outweighed by the benefits of a successful effort to implement the U.N. resolutions calling for the withdrawal of Iraq from Kuwait. The war in Vietnam dragged on for years and ended in an American defeat. A war in the Gulf, if it cannot be avoided, is likely to end with a decisive American victory in months, if not in weeks. Sometimes you are condemned to repeat the past if you *do* remember it—that is, if you draw the wrong lessons from it, and let the memory of the past distort your view of the present.

The United States clearly has a vital interest in preventing Saddam Hussein from getting away with his invasion and annexation of Kuwait.

Stephen J. Solarz, a Democratic member of the U.S. House of Representatives from New York, was a principal sponsor of the "Authorization for Use of Military Force Against Iraq Resolution." This essay was published in the January 7 and 14, 1991, issue of *The New Republic* under the title "The Stakes in the Gulf."

An aggressive Iraq bent on the absorption of its neighbors represents a serious economic threat to American interests. A hostile Iraq armed with chemical, biological, and eventually nuclear weapons represents a "clear and present danger" to American security. And a lawless Iraq represents a direct challenge to our hopes for a new and more peaceful world order. Any one of these reasons would be sufficient to justify a firm American response to this brutal and unprovoked act of aggression. Together they make a compelling case for doing whatever needs to be done, in concert with our coalition partners, to secure the withdrawal of Iraqi forces from Kuwait and to establish a more stable balance of power in one of the most volatile and strategically important parts of the world.

There is, for a start, the question of oil. If Saddam succeeds in incorporating Kuwait into Iraq, he will be in a position to control, by intimidation or invasion, the oil resources of the entire Gulf. This would enable him, and him alone, to determine not only the price, but also the production levels, of up to half the proven oil reserves in the world. This is not simply a question of the price of gas at the pump. It is a matter of the availability of the essential energy that we and our friends around the world need to heat our homes, fuel our factories, and keep our economies vigorous.

The United States needs a comprehensive energy policy that will reduce our dependence on Gulf oil. This was obvious at the time of the 1973 oil embargo, and it is obvious today. But regret at our failure to have diminished our dependence on Gulf oil, and our resolve to diminish that dependence in the future, will not solve our problem now. Even if we no longer needed to import oil, most other countries would still persist in their dependence; and to the extent that our economic well-being is linked to theirs, we cannot expect to insulate ourselves from the consequences of a cutoff in this essential source of supply.

Some have argued that Saddam's control of the oil resources of the Gulf would not pose an unacceptable threat to American interests, since he would presumably wish to sell the oil in order to raise revenues for his benign and malignant purposes. But Saddam would also be in a position to cut back dramatically on production, which would give him considerable leverage over the rest of the world, while assuring, through the inflated prices that his reduced production would command, an adequate level of revenue. It would be unthinkable for the United States to permit a rampaging dictator like Saddam to have his hands on the economic jugular of the world.

•　　•　　•

FAR MORE important than the question of oil, however, is the extent to which, in American constitutional terms, Saddam is a "clear and present danger." This is a man who twice in the last decade has led his country into war, first against Iran in 1980, and then against Kuwait in 1990. Driven by an uncontrollable appetite for power, and by the ideological imperatives of the Baath party, which is committed to unifying the Arab nation under Iraqi control, he is determined to dominate the entire Middle East. President Bush's parallels between Saddam and Hitler are wildly overdrawn. But if there are fundamental differences between Saddam and Hitler, there are also instructive similarities. Like Hitler, Saddam has an unappeasable will to power combined with a ruthless willingness to employ whatever means are necessary to achieve it.

Having stood up to the combined opposition of the superpowers, the Security Council, and the Arab League, Saddam's sense of invincibility will certainly swell—and the stage would be set for more campaigns of conquest and annexation. Moreover, if Saddam prevails in the current crisis, he might eventually pose a direct threat to the United States itself; it would be unacceptable to live in the shadow of an irrational man's nuclear arsenal, even if it is much smaller than our own. Iraq has remorselessly pursued a variety of long-range weapons programs that cannot be justified by any legitimate defensive needs. In addition to its nuclear program, Iraq is now working on an intercontinental ballistic missile system. Saddam is probably not in a position to produce a nuclear weapon within the next year, but he may well be able to do so in five to ten years. If we do not stop him now, we will almost certainly be obligated to confront him later, when he will be chillingly more formidable.

How, in the context of a political resolution of the Gulf crisis, can we deal with the threat of Iraq's destabilizing weapons of mass destruction? Ironically, they will pose less of a problem if it should come to war, since Baghdad's chemical, biological, and nuclear facilities would be high-priority targets, and its capacity to use these instruments of demonic destruction would be crippled for a long time to come. There is a real danger, however, that a peaceful resolution of the crisis would leave Saddam with his terrible arsenal intact, and his efforts to acquire nuclear weapons proceeding apace. Such an outcome would be a Pyrrhic victory. The Bush administration has so far failed to accord this problem the priority it deserves.

Some will point out that we have lived for many decades with other countries possessing such weapons and have not felt compelled to insist upon their dismantlement. Why should we be any more concerned about the acquisition of nuclear weapons by Iraq than by Pakistan, India, Brazil, Argentina, or South Africa? The answer is that although the nuclear programs of these other countries are a source of legitimate concern, none of them has already used weapons of mass destruction. Apologists for Iraq have argued further that our anxieties are misplaced, inasmuch as Iraq is a signatory to the nuclear Nonproliferation Treaty; but Baghdad used chemical weapons in spite of its signature on the treaty prohibiting their use. In the matter of treaties, Iraq is not exactly to be trusted; and an accomplished sinner like Saddam will not be overly tormented by breaking his own word.

STILL OTHERS have suggested that Iraq will not be able to develop nuclear weapons without the type of assistance that has been cut off by the sanctions. This argument fails on a number of counts. First, it assumes that the sanctions will remain in effect in perpetuity. Second, it ignores the fact that our failure to prevent Pakistan from acquiring the components for its nuclear weapons program shows that a strategy of technological denial is not likely to succeed. Third, it turns a blind eye to the chemical weapons and biological agents already in Iraq's arsenal. Fourth, there is no doubt that Iraq has already obtained sufficient fissile material from both its operable reactor and the destroyed Osirak reactor to build several nuclear weapons, even without outside assistance, in the next ten years. The Iraqi nuclear program is too far along to be stopped by an economic embargo.

Had it not been for the Israeli attack on the Osirak reactor in 1981, Iraq would in all likelihood already have nuclear weapons. Indeed, many of those who criticized the Israeli raid at the time now recognize how fortunate it was for the entire region that the Israelis acted so decisively. If Israel had heeded the advice of the timid, Iraq would likely have used nuclear weapons in its war against Iran. Put starkly, there can be no prospect for long-term stability in the Gulf unless Iraq's weapons of mass destruction are dismantled or destroyed. The only question is one of means.

It is conceivable that Saddam can be persuaded to disarm himself of these weapons, if the United States and its coalition partners make it clear that this is an essential component of a diplomatic solution to the crisis. The international community should spell out its determination to maintain the sanctions in force—even if Iraq withdraws from Kuwait and complies with the other conditions of the various U.N. resolutions—until Baghdad agrees to dismantle the weapons. Still, we must recognize that this strategy may fail—in which case the United States must retain its option to use force to eliminate both the production centers for these weapons and their long-range delivery systems. This policy will enjoy the strong support of many of our partners, including a number of Arab countries. On two recent trips to the region I was struck by the great fear of Iraq's weapons of mass destruction and the recognition of the necessity of eliminating this nonconventional threat by whatever means are required.

THE THIRD reason for thwarting Saddam's ambitions lies in our hopes for the establishment of a new world order. How we resolve the first crisis of the post-Cold War world will have profound historical consequences. Will this be a world in which relations among nations are governed by the rule of law, or will it be a Hobbesian world? Will it be a world in which the strong continue to dominate the weak, or will considerations of justice prevail over realities of force? Had the world responded with collective action when Japan invaded Manchuria, when Italy invaded Abyssinia, and when Hitler occupied the Rhineland, we might have been spared some of history's worst horrors. If we succeed in our efforts to secure the withdrawal of Iraqi forces and the restoration of the legitimate government of Kuwait through concerted international action, we will have created a powerful precedent for a much more peaceful world in the future. But if Saddam prevails, the word will have gone out to despots around the globe that the old rules still apply, that aggression still pays.

Kuwait is being devoured before our eyes. Newborn infants have been snatched out of incubators and left to die so the incubators can be carted back to hospitals in Baghdad. [See editors' note on page 95.] Thousands of Kuwaitis have been killed. Pregnant women have been bayoneted. Men have had their eyeballs burned out by cigarettes. Within a matter of months, Kuwait will have ceased to exist, the Kuwaitis having been murdered or exiled and the physical infrastructure of their country having been dismantled or destroyed. The failure of the United States and the international community to respond to previous acts of aggression is hardly a reason for not standing up to the man who is guilty of this one. The bitter fate that has befallen Kuwait should also lead the coalition of nations that has rallied to Kuwait's defense to require that Iraq pay full compensation for the havoc it has wrought. Baghdad's invasion was also the biggest bank heist in history; and if Iraq is not compelled to pay compensation, it will have been a handsome day's work for Saddam.

This crisis provides a rare opportunity, perhaps the first since the dawn of the modern age, to create a world order in which the international community upholds the sanctity of existing borders and the principle that nations should not be permitted to invade and to annex their weaker neighbors. The overwhelming votes in the U.N. Security Council demonstrate that there is, at last, an international consensus in favor of this objective. They also suggest that the dream of Franklin Roosevelt and the other founders of the United Nations, that the world organization could be used by the great powers as a mechanism for the preservation of peace, is being realized.

HOW SHALL we accomplish these essential objectives in a way that is consistent with our interests and compatible with our values? A national debate, stimulated by a series of hearings in the House and the Senate, has already begun. It would appear that there are, broadly speaking, three ways in which the withdrawal of Iraq from Kuwait, the restoration of the legitimate government in Kuwait, the payment of compensation to the victims of this aggression, and the establishment of a more stable balance of power in the region can be achieved.

The first is through the continued and perhaps protracted application of sanctions. Admiral William Crowe and General David Jones, former chairmen of the Joint Chiefs of Staff, among others, have argued that we should be willing to give sanctions a chance. If we wait another six, twelve, or eighteen months, they contend, the sanctions are likely to compel an Iraqi withdrawal from Kuwait. "What's the rush?" asks *The New York Times*. By waiting a little longer, these critics of the president's policy maintain, we can achieve our objectives without a war.

Of course it would be better to give sanctions more of a chance to work, if there is any reasonable possibility that they will bring about an Iraqi withdrawal, rather than take our troops to war. Nobody views with equanimity the loss of lives that an armed conflict would entail. And the supporters of a "go-slow" policy have rightly pointed out that the sanctions have received an unprecedented degree of support from the international community. All of Iraq's oil exports, which provided ninety percent of its foreign exchange earnings, have been cut off, and Iraq is clearly beginning to feel the economic consequences of its international isolation. Its factories are shutting down. Its productive capabilities have been impaired.

And yet it is difficult to be optimistic about the success of the sanctions. According to the detailed analysis by the International Institute for Economics of the likely impact of sanctions on Iraq, the embargo should bring about a reduction of approximately forty percent in Iraq's gross national product. This will undoubtedly be a very serious blow to the Iraqi economy. But whether it will result in a withdrawal from Kuwait is another matter. Even Crowe, whose testimony before the Senate Armed Services Committee provided political legitimacy to the "go-slow" strategy, has said that his judgment on the efficacy of sanctions is "entirely speculative."

Iraq is a fertile country, and it will be able to feed itself. The smuggling of food and other essential items is already taking place across the Iranian, Jordanian, Turkish, and Syrian borders, and Iraq will be able to adjust as the economic pinch tightens. If the analysts are correct, the per capita income of Iraq will be reduced from approximately $2,600 to $1,600 a year. Even with its forty percent reduction, however, Iraq will still have a per capita income more than twice that of Egypt, for instance, and substantially larger than that of Turkey, another of the front-line states. In any case, even if his people have to accept a less filling and nutritious diet, Saddam and his military will surely have enough to eat. This man was willing to persist in his war against Iran despite a million Iraqi casualties. It is hard to believe that he will be willing to withdraw from Kuwait simply because the Iraqi people will be forced to reduce their caloric intake or accept a diminution in their standard of living.

O N T H E military side, there is no doubt that the sanctions are having an impact. As CIA Director William Webster told Congress, the international economic boycott is likely to affect seriously the Iraqi air force within ninety days, and to degrade to a somewhat lesser extent other Iraqi forces over a period of nine to twelve months. Even so, the consensus among military experts is that even after a full year of sanctions, the capacity of the Iraqi forces in Kuwait to defend themselves will not be appreciably diminished. Most analysts believe that Saddam has written off his air force, given the vast air superiority enjoyed by the United States and its partners. The components of his military machine that constitute the core of his power—infantry, artillery, tanks, and armored vehicles already deployed in Kuwait—are precisely those that would be least affected by an extended embargo. The protracted application of sanctions will give the Iraqis time, moreover, to dig in and build up their defenses, to construct more roads and water-carrying pipelines from Iraq to Kuwait, thereby making an assault against them more costly in American lives.

Those who argue that sanctions without the use of force will be sufficient to compel an Iraqi withdrawal from Kuwait have never explained precisely how an embargo is likely to produce this result. They have failed to establish the connection between the undoubted economic impact of the sanctions and a political decision to quit Kuwait. There would appear to be only two ways in which sanctions can produce an Iraqi withdrawal from Kuwait and the other concessions necessary to end the crisis satisfactorily: either Saddam will decide to withdraw from Kuwait, or he will be overthrown by his own military and replaced by a leader (or a junta) that would make this decision.

But what are the chances, assuming the sanctions are maintained for another six to twelve months, or even longer, that Saddam will be willing to withdraw from Kuwait? He does not have to worry, after all, about running for re-election, or about a contentious Congress, or about a critical press, or about declining approval ratings in the polls. And no one can seriously believe that Saddam is more concerned about the well-being of his people than he is about the maximization of his power. This is not a sentimental man. Saddam is likely to calculate that it is a matter of time before the coalition crumbles and the sanctions erode. If all he has to worry about is the continued application of sanctions, he is much more likely to tough it out.

This leaves the possibility of an overthrow of Saddam by his military. There must be many officers in the Iraqi army who understand that Saddam is leading them down the desert dunes to disaster and would dearly like to remove him. But Saddam has managed to stifle any stirring of discontent not only in his people, but especially in his military establishment. The armed forces are riddled with informers; and Saddam has demonstrated repeatedly that he will act with extraordinary ruthlessness against anyone whom he even suspects of plotting against him. Those who run afoul of his paranoia do not live to enjoy their own.

THUS IT would appear that the prospects for the success of the sanctions are less likely than the prospects for the collapse of the coalition if we wait for the sanctions to be given more time to work. The coalition that President Bush has assembled with such skill is a fractious and fragile grouping, in which the Arab members in particular have different interests than we do. The incident on the Temple Mount in Jerusalem this fall was a clear warning about the flammability of this part of the world. The cultural repercussions of political events could easily destroy the coalition. And surely that is precisely what Saddam, a Machiavellian manipulator of men and events, will attempt to achieve.

Nor will the pressures on the coalition come only from abroad. Once it becomes clear that Bush has opted for the prolonged application of sanctions, there will be strong demands to start bringing back many of the troops that we have sent to Saudi Arabia. Four hundred thousand soldiers are not necessary, if our sole purpose is to defend Saudi Arabia. And it will be very difficult to sustain such a massive presence in Saudi Arabia indefinitely, given the logistical requirements of such a deployment. Once we begin to withdraw forces from the Gulf, our coalition partners, most of whom believe that sanctions alone cannot induce Saddam to withdraw from Kuwait, are likely to conclude that it will be only a matter of time before Saddam prevails. At that point they will begin cutting their own deals, in anticipation of emerging regional realities.

Even if the coalition were to hold together while we waited for the sanctions to work, the chances are that by the time we concluded—say, a year or two from now—that they were not sufficient to induce Saddam to withdraw, we would have lost our will to use force. While some who have urged the president to give sanctions more of a chance to work have said that they would be prepared to support the use of force if the sanctions fail, the truth is that the great majority of those who favor waiting would still oppose a war against Iraq even if the sanctions failed to achieve an Iraqi withdrawal from Kuwait. And with the sanctions eroding, and the use of force no longer a politically viable option, Saddam would be well on his way to a victory. A "go-slow" strategy, then, is more likely to play into the hands of Saddam than to deliver him into the hands of the coalition arrayed against him.

FOR THOSE who believe that there are no differences among nations that cannot be resolved diplomatically, there is always the hope of a negotiated settlement. But we must not generalize from our own fond norms. So far Saddam has not given any indication of a willingness to withdraw entirely and unconditionally from what his propaganda calls the nineteenth province of Iraq. An odd assortment of international itinerants, including Javier Pérez de Cuéllar and Kurt Waldheim, King Hussein of Jordan and Yasir Arafat, Yevgeny Primakov, Willy Brandt and Yasuhiro Nakasone, Muhammad Ali and Jesse Jackson have all beaten a path to Baghdad, only to return without anything to show for their efforts (except a handful of hostages who would have been released anyway when Saddam concluded that they were no longer valuable to him as a shield against attack). I strongly suspect that James Baker, even if he travels to Baghdad, is no more likely to come home with his pockets full of concessions.

More to the point, what exactly is there to negotiate about? Some have suggested that we offer Bubiyan and Warba, the two Kuwaiti islands that block Saddam's unfettered access to the Persian Gulf, as well as the

Rumaila oil fields, just south of the Iraqi border, in exchange for Saddam's withdrawal from the rest of Kuwait. But Kuwait, Saudi Arabia, a majority of the Arab League, the Security Council of the United Nations, and the Bush administration have all rightly rejected this idea, on the grounds that it would be a reward for aggression and set the stage for additional acts of banditry.

Saddam himself has attempted to link the question of an Iraqi withdrawal from Kuwait to an Israeli withdrawal from the West Bank and Gaza, or at least to the convening of an international conference to resolve the Palestinian problem. It should be obvious that this is simply an attempt to sow the seeds of discord among the countries arrayed against him. The two are entirely different issues. Iraq's invasion of Kuwait in 1990 was an unprovoked act of aggression, whereas Israel came into possession of the territories only after it was attacked by a coalition of Arab countries in 1967. Saddam did not invade Kuwait to help the Palestinians, but to maximize his own power. He is not moved by the plight of the Palestinians, or by anybody else's plight. He is merely exploiting it. And the Palestinians seem happy to assist in their own exploitation.

Paradoxically, if any real possibility of resolving this crisis peacefully exists, it lies not in negotiations leading to concessions that reward aggression, but in convincing Saddam that we are prepared to go to war if he does not comply with the terms of the Security Council resolutions. I suspect that it was a dawning realization that we are serious about opposing his grandiose ambitions, with force if necessary, that lay behind his recent release of the hostages. Surely it was not because he was suddenly filled with the holiday spirit.

In our joy over the reunion of the hostages with their families, however, we must not forget the threat Iraq still poses to vital American interests. Not until Saddam is finally persuaded that he has to make a choice between staying and dying or leaving and living will there be any real chance of inducing him to withdraw from Kuwait. Yet if such an ultimatum is delivered to him—and it is clearly implicit in the Security Council resolution authorizing the use of force—we have to be prepared to use force in the event he refuses to withdraw.

THIS LEADS, then, to the third way of bringing the crisis to an end. The use of force, of course, raises profound political, moral, and constitutional questions. A war will undoubtedly bring many casualties—we should not delude ourselves with notions of surgical strikes—and no one can say with certainty what would happen in the wake of such a conflict.

Force should be a last resort. But a last resort is sometimes a necessary resort. Last is not the same as never.

Some of those who oppose the use of armed force have argued that war will increase instability and anti-Americanism in the Middle East. There is a measure of truth in this analysis. Still, a peacetime victory of Saddam over the coalition would surely represent a more considerable threat to the stability of the region than a wartime victory of the coalition over Saddam. It is important to note that the Middle East countries that are supposedly most vulnerable to Arab radicalization are precisely the countries that are supporting us most strongly, because their leaders need no lessons in the consequences of allowing Saddam to go unchecked.

Of course, there will be some expressions of hostility toward the United States in the Arab world if American weapons are used against Iraqi soldiers. But those expressions will surely be offset to the extent that other Arab countries are fighting alongside us in a war against Iraq, especially if we make it clear that our intention is not to occupy Iraq but to liberate Kuwait. Recent history demonstrates that the application of American force in the Middle East does not lead to a regional recoil from America: we were warned of the possibility of massive anti-American demonstrations if we attempted to punish Qaddafi for his role in a terrorist attack against American servicemen a few years ago, but our air strike against Libya in 1986 produced little negative response in the Arab world, and even seems to have resulted in enhanced respect for the United States.

Those who are anxious about the unanticipated consequences of a war have focused attention on the casualties that would result, even from a relatively brief and decisive campaign. I yield to nobody in my concern for American lives; but we must face the hard truth that whatever the casualties we might suffer, they are likely to be far smaller than those that would be inflicted upon us if we postpone the day of reckoning until Saddam has added nuclear weapons to his current arsenal of chemical and biological weapons. Forcefully denying Saddam the instruments of a nuclear war is itself an expression of concern for American lives. And if the maintenance of a large-scale American presence in the Gulf is a source of fiscal and political anxiety, surely we will be obliged to station a much larger deterrent force in the region if we permit Saddam and his army to remain in Kuwait than if we destroy much of his military machine and his weapons of mass destruction in the process of liberating Kuwait.

· · ·

OTHERS HAVE suggested that even if we cannot force Saddam out of Kuwait, we can contain his expansionist tendencies and insulate the rest of the region from his marauding ambitions by permanently stationing American troops in the Gulf. They remind us that we contained Soviet and North Korean expansion for forty years and ask why a policy of containment cannot work in the Middle East. These critics are rather Panglossian about the realities of the Middle East. In Europe and on the Korean peninsula, the presence of American forces contributed to the stability of the countries we were trying to defend. In the Arab world, the long-term presence of many American troops would be almost certainly destabilizing.

It is doubtful, moreover, that Saudi Arabia, which is the most conservative Islamic society in the world, would permit us to maintain a sizable presence in the country for any appreciable period. The Saudis are right: if we keep our troops in the region, we may end up contributing unwittingly to the downfall of the very regimes that we set out to defend. And if we have brought 400,000 American troops to Saudi Arabia to force the Iraqis out of Kuwait, and then accept Baghdad's annexation of Kuwait as a fait accompli, the Saudis are unlikely to have much confidence in our willingness to defend them, and will be more likely to seek their security in a vassal relationship with Iraq. Just as we resisted the Finlandization of Europe, we must resist the Saddamization of the Middle East.

If the president concludes that the sanctions are not likely to work, that there is no realistic prospect for an acceptable political settlement, and that we have no alternative but to use force, it will be essential for him to go to war multilaterally rather than unilaterally. The liberation of Kuwait and the elimination of the Iraqi threat is not only an American responsibility. Our Arab and European coalition partners have just as much—indeed, some of them have more—at stake than we do. It is one thing to be the head of an international posse attempting to deprive a criminal state of the rewards of its aggression. It is quite another for the United States to arrogate to itself the role of policeman of the world. The former is a task that the American people can understand and accept. The latter is an assignment that they do not seek.

Should it come to war, however, we will not be alone. Our Arab partners in this coalition (with the possible exception of Syria) are fully prepared to go to war along with us if that should prove necessary. The British have also been stalwart in their willingness to use force—and even Neil Kinnock, the Labor leader who once supported unilateral disarmament, has spoken up in favor of force should Saddam refuse to withdraw from Kuwait. President Mitterrand has indicated that if the coalition should go to war, France will fight with it. And though it is true that the majority of the forces deployed in the Gulf are American, other countries have made sizable contributions as well. By the end of the year the British, the Egyptians, and the Syrians will have doubled their troop strength in Saudi Arabia, and the total number of foreign forces available for combat will be 225,000. The armed units from twenty-eight countries lend the coalition not only legitimacy, but a substantial increase in military power.

Would we like our coalition partners to shoulder still more of the burden? Of course. But most of those who are critical about the efforts of our European and Arab coalition partners would still be opposed to American policy even if the military contribution offered by other countries were significantly increased. At any rate, if undoing Saddam's annexation of Kuwait is in our interest, we should be prepared to do whatever is required to achieve this objective, rather than act in ways contrary to our interests simply because we have not received all the help from other nations we might have desired. A decision to use force should be based on strategic necessities, not on accounting formulas.

I F T H E president does decide on the use of force, it will be important for him to have the support not only of our coalition partners, but also of Congress. There is no more fateful decision a nation can make than that of risking the lives of its men and women by going to war. It would be a serious constitutional and political mistake on the part of the president if he were to commit our forces to combat (in the absence of an unexpected provocation, such as a preemptive Iraqi attack) without congressional authorization. And there is another reason why the president should seek the support of Congress. If we go to war and if we win a quick and decisive victory, as is quite probable, the fact that the president did not seek the prior approval of Congress may become a source of debate among historians and columnists, but is not likely to hurt the president seriously with either Congress or the American people. But war is unpredictable, and we may get bogged down in a protracted conflict. Under those circumstances, with casualties beginning to mount, the president's ability to sustain support for the war will be gravely compromised if he fails to secure the authorization of Congress before hostilities begin.

A half century ago, when Hitler invaded Poland, the British House of Commons gathered to debate what course Britain should follow. After a halting defense of government policy by Neville Chamberlain, one of the opposition MPs rose and began his remarks with the phrase, "Speaking for the Labor Party . . ." Instantly a voice thundered from the back benches: "Speak for England!" It is time to remember this advice. The crisis in the Gulf is not a Democratic issue or a Republican issue. It is an American issue.

A decision to go to war should not be made, under any circumstances, on the basis of partisan considerations. Still, the Democrats must ponder the political consequences of a reflexive refusal even to consider the use of force. The party has suffered in too many national elections from the popular perception that it is categorically and emotionally unwilling to use force under almost any circumstances other than a direct attack on the United States itself. If Democrats are not prepared to support the use of force in a situation like this, when the aggression is so unambiguous, the international community so cohesive, and the stakes so great, how can anyone ever expect the Democratic Party to support the use of force in defense of vital American interests in the far more common circumstances of confusion, ambiguity, and uncertainty?

I am not arguing that the administration's policies toward the Gulf should be immune from criticism. However skillfully the president and his subordinates have managed this crisis since August, our relationship with Iraq was handled with a comparable lack of skill prior to that date. There was no excuse for putting our policy toward Iraq on automatic pilot for two whole years after its war with Iran ended—which is exactly what the administration did, when it opposed congressional efforts to impose sanctions against Iraq, on the naive assumption that by kowtowing to Saddam we would be in a better position to influence his behavior. By declaring that we had no obligation to come to the defense of Kuwait, and by taking no position on Iraq's border dispute with Kuwait, administration spokesmen clearly contributed to a perception on Saddam's part that we would not resist his use of force in the Gulf.

There will be plenty of time later for postmortems on the genesis of this affair. Those who were responsible for creating the climate in which such an invasion could take place should bear their fair measure of responsibility.* But we must not let the discussion about the immediate

* Editors' note: According to Dilip Hiro, writing in *The Longest War* (London: Grafton, 1989), "The first overt sign of change in Iraqi-American relations came in January 1983 when Saddam Hussein published the text of his talks with U.S. Congressman Stephen Solarz during the latter's visit to Baghdad five months earlier. In it the Baathist leader declared that Iraq had never been part of the Soviet strategy in the region, and that it was in the interests of Washington to be 'present in the region when any other big or superpower is present.' At the

danger lose itself in debater's points. The challenge now is to develop a policy that will enable us to undo the consequences of Iraq's aggression.

If we succeed in blocking Saddam's ambitions and restoring Kuwait's independence, we will have preserved our continued access to a stable supply of oil. The stability of the Arab governments that have joined with us to oppose Saddam will be significantly strengthened. We will have a good chance of eliminating Saddam's weapons of mass destruction and setting back for a substantial period of time, perhaps forever, Iraq's efforts to obtain nuclear weapons. The prospects for progress in the peace process between Israel and the Arabs will be greatly enhanced. We will have reversed a monumental injustice, we will have thwarted one of the most ruthless expansionists in the world, and we will have created the basis for a new international order.

If this isn't worth fighting for, I don't know, as an American and as a Democrat, what is.

end of the meeting, Solarz, a former university professor, thanked Saddam saying 'Had you been one of my students, I would have given you an 'A' average.' "

A RETURN TO COLD WAR THINKING

(Speech of January 10, 1991)

Senator Daniel Patrick Moynihan

I WOULD LIKE to suggest that the way in which the president initially proceeded obtained the universal support of the country and the Senate. Suddenly, however, there was an institutional lurch back into the manner and mode of the Cold War.

It has been with us so long, we do not know how to act differently. We have not acquired the instincts, the institutions, the institutional memories, to do other than what we have been doing during the Cold War. We know nothing else. That is what happened on November 8—two days after the election—that suddenly lurched us into a Cold War mode.

Last November, the Committee on Foreign Relations held a series of hearings on the subject "After the Cold War." We examined changes in the American government which have taken place over the long struggle with totalitarianism which emerged, really, from the First World War. As Judith Sklar has written, "1914 is, after all, when it all began."

From 1914 to 1989, there was a seventy-five-year "war" which inevitably changed attitudes and institutions. In our hearings we were looking at the attitudes and institutions that had changed, and the ways in which they did. I chaired the hearings, so I took the opportunity to organize our inquiry around an extraordinary speech which Woodrow Wilson gave in St. Louis, Missouri on September 5, 1919. It was on that trip around the country, pleading for public support to influence the Senate to consent to the ratification of the Treaty of Versailles, which contained the League of Nations covenant, Wilson was asking for that support. He was twenty days from Pueblo, Colorado where he would collapse. It would be, in effect, the end of his presidency. . . .

Daniel Patrick Moynihan is the Democratic senator from New York.

Wilson's remarks had about them the quality of prophecy. It was the end of his life. He was trying to tell America what he would leave behind him, what would happen if we did not establish a world order where there was law, where there were procedures, where peace was enforced. And if we did not, what would come instead.

He said, "Very well, then. If we must stand apart and be the hostile rivals of the rest of the world, we must do something else. We must be physically ready for anything to come. We must have a great standing army. We must see to it that every man in America is trained in arms, and we must see to it that there are munitions and guns enough for an army. And that means a mobilized nation; that they are not only laid up in store, but that they are kept up to date; that they are ready to use tomorrow; that we are a nation in arms."

Then he said, "What would a nation in arms be? Well, you know, you have to think of the president of the United States not as the chief counselor of the nation, elected for a little while, but as the man meant constantly and every day to be commander in chief of the army and navy of the United States, ready to order it to any part of the world with a threat of war, as a menace to his own people."

Then he said, "And you can't do that under free debate; you can't do that under public counsel. Plans must be kept secret. Knowledge must be accumulated by a system which we have condemned, because we called it a spying system. The more polite call it a system of intelligence."

Then he went on a little further to say, in effect, how this world would shape itself up into one of continuing crises. And so . . . in that speech in St. Louis, which, as I say, had a prophetic quality which haunts one to this day, Woodrow Wilson said that we would see the emergence of a system of government in which the president had become commander in chief, head of the Armed Forces. That did happen. And nothing is more extraordinary evidence of it having happened than the assertions we have heard in the past month after the lurching from a defensive, deterrent position, which we responded to very well, into an offensive position on November 8. This was a decision reached in secret. It suddenly turned what had been a collective security operation with the complete support of the country and the world into an offensive, military crisis situation.

Wilson's prediction in action: the president as commander in chief, secretly moving in an atmosphere of ongoing, permanent, Orwellian crisis, asserting that this is entirely in his own hands. . . . On November 30, when asked "What do you think your responsibilities are to Congress and the people that elect them," he said, "Full consultation."

Nothing more. When asked on December 28 by David Frost, "Don't you need an authorization from Congress, in effect, for war?" he said, "We have used military force 200 times in history. I think there have been five declarations of war." In effect, he claimed that he did not need congressional support to do what, clearly, the Constitution requires of him. . . .

[It] is a kind of madness where we are living in an earlier world and acting in ways that have no relevance to the situation of the moment. We are not in an international crisis in the sense that events that took place on August 2 necessitate the confrontation of the largest set of armed forces since World War II. Nothing large happened. A nasty little country invaded a littler but just as nasty country. They have their avowed virtues, I do not doubt. There has not been much virtue on display internationally in either case. And the United States shares with the other nations of the world an interest in the resolution of the crisis, principally to establish the fact that the U.N. Charter is an international standard that will be enforced.

The world will not be particularly different after Iraq leaves Kuwait, which it will do. It will not be any better, or it will be better to the extent only that we will have established that the international community will enforce the charter. In the aftermath of the Cold War that has become possible.

So . . . all we are saying on this side of the aisle, and I hope we will hear it from the other side of the aisle, is this: Why can we not continue the president's policy of August, September, and October? That was a policy appropriate to a small disturbance in a distant part of the world where there are interests involved because that part of the world exports oil to Japan and sends oil to Europe. There is an important international interest in maintaining the standards of the charter. Fine. But not World War III. Is it not clear that we did not have World War III? It did not happen.

Suddenly our institutions are acting as if to say, "Oh, my God, we missed World War III. Maybe we can have it now here. Not there but here." That borders on the edge of the disturbed. Dr. Strangelove, where are you now that we need you?

This is so unnecessary. With what unanimity in this body the president would be supported if he simply drew back to the defensive positions of the period up to November 8 before his announcement of a secretly planned escalation to an offensive mode.

AUTHORIZATION FOR USE OF
MILITARY FORCE

(Joint Congressional Resolution of January 12, 1991)

The following is the text of the joint resolution approved by the Senate and the House of Representatives on January 12, 1991, regarding the use of force in the Persian Gulf. The vote in the Senate was 52–47; in the House it was 250–183.

To authorize the use of United States Armed Forces pursuant to United Nations Security Council Resolution 678.

WHEREAS the Government of Iraq without provocation invaded and occupied the territory of Kuwait on August 2, 1990, and

WHEREAS both the House of Representatives (in H.J. Res. 658 of the 101st Congress) and the Senate (in S. Con. Res. 147 of the 101st Congress) have condemned Iraq's invasion of Kuwait and declared their support for international action to reverse Iraq's aggression; and

WHEREAS Iraq's conventional, chemical, biological, and nuclear weapons and ballistic missile programs and its demonstrated willingness to use weapons of mass destruction pose a grave threat to world peace; and

WHEREAS the international community has demanded that Iraq withdraw unconditionally and immediately from Kuwait and that Kuwait's independence and legitimate government be restored; and

WHEREAS the U.N. Security Council repeatedly affirmed the inherent right of individual or collective self-defense in response to the armed attack by Iraq against Kuwait in accordance with Article 51 of the U.N. Charter; and

WHEREAS in the absence of full compliance by Iraq with its resolutions, the U.N. Security Council in Resolution 678 has authorized member states of the United Nations to use all necessary means, after January 15, 1991, to uphold and implement all relevant Security Council resolutions and to restore international peace and security in the area; and

WHEREAS Iraq has persisted in its illegal occupation of, and brutal aggression against Kuwait; Now, therefore, be it

Resolved by the Senate and House of Representatives of the United States of America in Congress assembled,

Section 1.
SHORT TITLE

This joint resolution may be cited as the "Authorization for Use of Military Force Against Iraq Resolution."

Section 2.
AUTHORIZATION FOR USE OF U.S. ARMED FORCES

(a) AUTHORIZATION. —The President is authorized, subject to subsection (b), to use United States Armed Forces pursuant to United Nations Security Council Resolution 678 (1990) in order to achieve implementation of Security Council Resolutions 660, 661, 662, 664, 665, 666, 667, 669, 670, 674, and 677.

(b) REQUIREMENT FOR DETERMINATION THAT USE OF MILITARY FORCE IS NECESSARY. — Before exercising the authority granted in subsection (a), the President shall make available to the Speaker of the House of Representatives and the President pro tempore of the Senate his determination that—

(1) the United States has used all appropriate diplomatic and other peaceful means to obtain compliance by Iraq with the United Nations Security Council resolutions cited in subsection (a); and (2) that those efforts have not been and would not be successful in obtaining such compliance.

(c) WAR POWERS RESOLUTION REQUIREMENTS.—

(1) SPECIFIC STATUTORY AUTHORIZATION. — Consistent with section 8(a) of the War Powers Resolution, the Congress declares that this section is intended to constitute specific statutory authorization within the meaning of section 5(b) of the War Powers Resolution.

(2) APPLICABILITY OF OTHER REQUIREMENTS. — Nothing in this resolution supersedes any requirement of the War Powers Resolution.

Section 3.
REPORTS TO CONGRESS

At least once every 60 days, the President shall submit to the Congress a summary on the status of efforts to obtain compliance by Iraq with the resolutions adopted by the United Nations Security Council in response to Iraq's aggression.

AGENCIES OF DISORDER

Edward N. Luttwak

A S I write, Iraqi troops are still in occupation of Kuwait and war is imminent. His perceived power hugely inflated by the very magnitude of the coalition assembled against him, and even more by the absurdly disproportionate war preparations made by the United States (a further *million* reservists have just been listed for possible mobilization), the sometime village ruffian, would-be murderer of dictators and dictatorial murderer Saddam Hussein is still alive, and still pretending to be both the residual legatee of the inherently secular Baath movement and a fiery Islamic activist; both the greatest exponent of an exclusively Arab nationalism and the caring father of Iraq's Kurds; both the aspiring Arab-Israeli peacemaker and the leading advocate of immediate war against Israel; both the protector of all Arab interests and the advocate of a redistribution of Arab oil revenues throughout the Third World.

It was undoubtedly Saddam Hussein alone who abruptly decided to invade Kuwait. Having pursued extortion by public threats, once the Kuwaitis failed to tremble he probably felt compelled to punish them by invasion—just as any Mafia boss must remedy by murder any failure of intimidation, lest he be murdered himself by his *sottocapi* exposed to evidence of successful defiance.

Yet Saddam Hussein's conduct also embodied the confluence of two long-established agencies of disorder; and the crisis moreover was magnified by an accident of timing. For matters could well have been resolved more quickly and more cleanly if Iraq had not collided with a

Edward N. Luttwak holds the Arleigh E. Burke Chair in Strategy at the Center for Strategic and International Studies. This article was published in the January 18, 1991, issue of the [London] *Times Literary Supplement* under the title "Saddam and the Agencies of Disorder."

United States and a president just unbalanced by complete victory in the Cold War—a victory that as always yielded its own paradoxical punishment, i.e., the obsolescence of the very attributes and instruments that allowed the outcome to be so completely successful.

The first of these agencies is the cruel joke of geology that during the present stage of the world's economic development places large and totally disposable oil revenues in the hands of grotesque tyrannies that might otherwise be prevented from projecting their foibles and misdeeds beyond municipal boundaries. It is not that oil revenues are all that vast. Austria has roughly twice the gross national product of Iraq, while the Swiss GNP is more than twice as great as Saudi Arabia's, even after the vast increase in the price of oil abruptly induced by the crisis itself. But oil revenues are different. They do not have to be extracted by taxes levied on populations whose consent is likely to be the more necessary in the degree that there is more to extract. However imperfectly earned prosperity and political participation may be correlated, great divergence is rare. Oil revenues by contrast are simply telexed into government bank accounts.

Where democratic governance is feeble or absent, as in some of the oil-exporting countries of Latin America, black Africa, and Asia but seemingly always and everywhere in the Middle East, oil monies can be spent by tyrannical rulers as they desire—and what rulers, with what desires! Saddam Hussein is uniquely evil, we are told, an Adolf Hitler *redivivus,* presumably entirely different from the other Arab oil rulers now deemed not merely respectable but actually worthy of the world's protection. But in his desires at least, Saddam Hussein is not different at all.

He has reportedly built inordinately opulent palaces for himself filled with the costliest furnishings, but so have the rulers of Saudi Arabia, Oman, Qatar, the United Arab Emirates and Kuwait itself—and Saddam Hussein can at least protest his singularity, while in Saudi Arabia alone there are some 2,000 princes who each claim their palace, with a great many having more than one. Washington's own Saudi prince, Bandar bin Sultan, a reputed intimate of President Bush and, in pre-crisis times, eloquent on the plight of the Palestinians "living in tents," averted a similar fate for himself by acquiring the largest private mansion in the capital, and also had another house built in Aspen, Colorado, whose hugeness was only granted permission after a multi-million donation to that uniquely affluent municipality, a donation that might have come in handy in, say, Gaza. Palaces aside, there have been the yachts, the villas on the Riviera, the Mayfair apartments, the jewels, whores, and assorted other fripperies of the Gulf-Arab carnival of consumption.

Other people's unearned high living easily arouses a pseudo-egalitarian indignation but is hardly criminal. Indeed luxury may be deemed virtuous in so far as it denies money to worse uses. For Saddam Hussein has also been far from exceptional in devoting enormous amounts of money to the purchase of weapons and the upkeep of military forces. For years now, not only Saudi Arabia and Libya but also small fry such as Oman have been purchasing the most elaborate and costly of all weapons of their respective categories—weapons happily and most irresponsibly sold to them by the United States and Britain as well as France and of course the Soviet Union, and indeed all others who could do so. Iraq's weapons are more dangerous to be sure, in the sense that the Iraqis can actually use them, and even maintain them in large degree. In fact when Western governments sell devastatingly powerful modern weapons to the equally lawless dictators and tribal rulers who command oil revenues, they proffer the incapacity of the recipients as their excuse, even while arguing that they have genuine defensive needs. It is the sort of thing that gives a bad name to cynicism.

That is how the U.S. government justified the sale of the very latest F-18 fighter-bombers to Kuwait last year, and the British government still justifies the sale of Tornado strike-bombers to Saudi Arabia—whose absolutist rulers constantly profess their intention of using them against Israel, and who certainly violate every species of human rights every day, having just expelled and dispossessed more innocent Yemenis than there are Kuwaitis for Iraq to expel. There may be something in the incapacity argument and perhaps a great deal in some cases, but arms too *habent fata sua.* As I write, U.S. pilots are in danger of being shot down by U.S. Hawk missiles once sold to Kuwait.

Nor is Saddam Hussein unique in using oil revenues to promote terrorism—indeed that too is almost *de rigueur* in the region. Aside from the all too notorious Qaddafi, every murderous band has been able to raise funds in the Gulf, obviously with the consent of the rulers—with Kuwait being exceptionally generous. As for Saudi Arabia, its funds are more decisive than many realize in promoting the spread of an increasingly murderous religious extremism. When half-educated youths, disappointed by their failure to cope with modern life, revert to religion, all too often they find not the old village mosque and its benign customs but a new Saudi-financed urban structure, controlled by Saudi-financed preachers of Saudi-style Islam, rigidly puritanical, rigidly intolerant of any local, usually long-established *modus vivendi* with infidels. When the

Christian Copts of Egypt, traditionalist Afghans, the Chinese and Hindus of Malaysia and Indonesia, and the animists and Christians of the Sudan come under attack, it is often the Saudi influence that is at work. Its revolting nature is more nakedly revealed at home by the arrogant denial of religious freedom, by the corporal punishment of beer drinkers on behalf of whisky-drinking princes, and by the intrusions of Saudi Arabia's "religious police," whose members now reportedly break into houses of Westerners suspected of hosting parties in which drinks are served and women are allowed to chat with men not their fathers and husbands. Such are the official practices now directly protected by more than 300,000 Americans in uniform, both male and female—as well as by the soldiers and airmen of Britain, France, and other Western countries.

It is thus not only Iraq's violence that is magnified by all too disposable oil revenues, now an agency of disorder in the Middle East simply because they allow the otherwise incapable to inflict harm far and wide—often enough with Western assistance, always with a shameful Western connivance.

True enough, Saddam Hussein's regime is nevertheless different in being responsible for overt military aggression as well, and that owes much to the second agency of disorder, which adds the worst of ideological motives to dangerous means. Instant books as up to date as last week's headlines are now offered to explain Saddam Hussein's seizure of Kuwait. . . . But the reader might gain a far deeper understanding from a brief essay first published almost two decades ago in which Saddam's name does not appear. The eponymous essay in Elie Kedourie's *Arab Political Memoirs*—a work of profound wisdom and surpassing elegance, not only in its style but also in the scientific sense of proving much with no more evidence than is needed—explains all that one needs to know of Saddam Hussein. For his mentality is that of the Baath (renaissance) movement, neither new nor original to the man—and certainly not an "Arab" mentality, that creation of Western Arabophiles (the most indulgent of friends, the worst of enemies)—which knows not ease or moderation but only strident militancy, not feasible hope but only reckless ambition, not a decent regard for self, family, neighborhood or country but only an unlimited devotion to the glory of an imaginary entity (the Arab "world") composed of all who speak any dialect philologically classified as Arabic.

Professor Kedourie recounts in the tragic voices of its disenchanted adherents how the ideology of the Baath was born as an amalgam of now wholly discredited Western ideas—the more unbalanced fragments of

Nietzsche, the racism of H. S. Chamberlain and Alfred Rosenberg, statalist socialism before its downfall, and exclusive nationalism in the rabid style of Eastern Europe. While far gentler nationalisms were sufficient to evoke the cohesion of most other Arab and non-Arab peoples seeking independence from colonial power and colonial influences, in Syria as well as Iraq with their varied ethnicities and religions, the virulent Baath prescription offered a deceptive remedy for the lack of any organic solidarity. The creation of Alawite, Christian and Muslim schoolmasters during the 1930s, it attracted the thinly educated among journalists, aspiring writers, pharmacists, dentists, doctors, and lawyers. After the Second World War it enrolled barely literate army officers and full-time party activists, who exiled, murdered or subjugated their party predecessors in both Syria and Iraq as soon as they seized power.

The Baath is a fit ideology for Saddam Hussein, as it is for Hafez al-Assad of Syria, for it rationalizes oppression as justice (justice for the Arabs only being obtainable by a very "strong" government), tyranny as freedom (freedom for the Arabs only being obtainable by the unity of autocracy), and indeed death as the most valid expression of life—given that the highest purpose of life is to advance, by death if necessary, the cause of the Baath: the renaissance of a mighty Arab power, indeed a superpower able to match the United States. Any reader of Kedourie's essay would have known that the travails of eight years of war with Iran would not suffice to induce Saddam Hussein to accord a decent interval of tranquility to the long-suffering peoples of Iraq: neither the twenty years normally required to grow a new crop of young men ready to follow NCOs in battle, nor half that span. And he would have known too that when the United States intervened, Saddam Hussein would not retreat pleading *force majeure* as enough of a face-saving excuse, for a struggle with the United States is the most appropriate of confrontations for the mighty Arab power envisaged by the Baath.

It is a pity that we have no Kedourie to instruct us in the mentality of George Bush. He too is still here, and still what he has been since Margaret Thatcher firmly instructed him in his responsibilities while both were in conference at Aspen, Colorado, on August 3, 1990—not recognizably the president of the United States (an office with a great variety of duties both foreign and domestic), but rather a very able, very hard-working and totally concentrated full-time Persian Gulf "crisis manager," with no president to report to.

A president would have avoided demeaning the office and himself by exchanging insults with Saddam Hussein; he would have avoided the wild hyperbole of the Hitler comparison—Iraq has not the capacity of the meanest province of Germany—and he would have kept matters in proportion by delegating diplomacy to the diplomats instead of doing it all himself on the telephone, for hours on end every day, for weeks on end. More substantively, a president mindful of the balance between his responsibilities would have concluded on, say, August 6, 1990, that the dominant priority was to end the crisis quickly, by bombing or by negotiations, or both—lest a prolonged crisis disturb the fragile economic equilibrium of the greatly indebted United States, precipitating a serious recession.

For by then it had been discovered that it was not only the federal government that was on the edge of insolvency but also many state governments and almost all large municipalities; not only the notoriously mismanaged savings-and-loan companies but also a great many commercial banks, including several of the very largest; not only small-time issuers of "junk bonds" but also famous airlines, celebrated department stores, most holders of commercial real property, leading industrial corporations and millions of home owners with mortgages greater than their equity.

Instead, very much in the manner of the aristocrat still disdainful of the tradesmen pleading bills at his door as he sells yet more of the family's broad acres, Bush insisted in "optimizing" the management of the crisis, careless of time and cost, only mindful of diplomatic priorities, Arab sensibilities, and the fine coordination of U.N. and bilateral proceedings. Happily leaving behind all serious concern for the economy, and even more happily content to see photographs of Saddam Hussein replacing those of Neil Bush on the front pages, George Bush threw himself into crisis management on a full-time basis with boyish enthusiasm, barely turning aside to explain, most unconvincingly, the reason for it all.

Not that there was anything much to explain about the need to stop further aggression by Iraq, or indeed to punish its aggression by the prompt use of air power. A vast majority of Americans readily agreed that "a line in the sand" had to be drawn. Any post-war president would have done that, including Jimmy Carter. But ever since 1945 such lines have always been protected in numerous crises by deterrence from afar, albeit non-nuclear, not actively defended by troops on the ground except in Europe and Korea (there was no "line" in Vietnam, nor an intervention decision as such, but only a gradual involvement). Had Bush resorted to deterrence he would have had nothing to explain. Had he then quickly proceeded to issue a withdrawal ultimatum, beginning to bomb Iraq as soon as it expired, that too would have been accepted by most Americans. Instead of deterrence and bombing, he chose defense by an expeditionary force, followed by waiting, and followed much later, from November 8, by the assembly of an army of reconquest.

Well before then, Bush was insistently pressed to explain why American "boys"—and women, and reservist fathers, and reservist mothers, had to be sent to Arabia of all places. After trying and failing to evoke support for the imperative of restoring the al-Sabah family over its enterprise of Kuwait, and keeping the al-Saud family in ownership of its own larger enterprise ("Americans do not die for princes," remarked the impeccably conservative Congressman Dornan), the Bush administration tried the "oil needs of the industrialized world" argument.

That collapsed very quickly, as two things soon became clear. First, that in what I have called the "geo-economic" era, the earlier geopolitical imperative of providing cheap energy for the Western coalition in its struggle with the Soviet Union no longer applied. On the contrary, it was possible that the United States might gain in the new geo-economic era if its chief competitors, notably Germany and Japan, were burdened by higher energy costs. After all, the United States would have to re-tool with capital and economic skills—in lieu of military power and diplomatic skills—to wage the struggle that will determine who will make the aircraft, computers, advanced materials and other high-added-value products of the next generation. Second, it soon became clear that the supposed beneficiaries of the American effort to secure their oil supplies, Germany, Japan, and the rest of them, were (correctly) persuaded that the price of oil would continue to depend on the substitution cost (roughly $25 per barrel right now), and not on who or what controlled the oil of the Persian Gulf. Hence they flatly refused to contribute seriously to the effort, offering only pennies and uselessly symbolic frigates. It was indicative that only ever-faithful Britain, not a beneficiary of cheap oil at all, was willing to join the expedition in earnest, fundamentally for reasons neither economic nor geo-economic. Operation "Tin Cup," the begging visitation of Treasury Secretary Brady to Japan last September, has so far yielded a mere fraction of the $6.6 billion Matsushita has paid to purchase the entertainment company MCA (the second law of geo-economics: if you cannot make a better product, in this case than Hollywood film and U.S. pop music, purchase the producers).

The Bush administration did finally come up with a new, fully original justification for taking on Saddam Hussein ever so slowly, with troops on the ground, under the mantle of the U.N.: the (post–Cold War) "New World Order." When public opinion reacted very negatively, foolish television pundits explained that the idea was much too abstract for the untaught masses, which could not be expected to understand. Actually the public at large understood that most un-American notion all too well. The American people have never supported any kind of "world order," old or new, but rather human rights, pluralism, and democratic expression, all often subversive of "order" in much of the world, and notably in the countries of Arabia being immediately defended. Had Americans supported world order, they could have had that commodity for the asking from the 1970s if not before, when the Soviet Union — then no mean hand at the game—offered a beautifully ordered condominium, with the noisome Chinese well isolated, and all others shared out between Washington and Moscow.

Furthermore, the particular world order being offered by the Bush administration was that of the permanent members of the U.N. Security Council, namely a disintegrating Soviet dictatorship, the world's largest non-democracy of China, conniving, declining France, unconniving but declining Britain, and the United States itself, *sans* India, or Germany, or Japan. The notion was further discredited when the associations and obligations that the "New World Order" entailed came to light. The United States in the person of George Bush had to sit on a divan if not get into bed with murderous Assad of Syria in its name and—much more important—it would have to prop up an increasingly weak, increasingly sinister Gorbachev and his crumbling U.S.S.R. edifice, against Yeltsin and the other leaders of other organic nations emerging from under the rubble. It would also have to appease and humor the grim butchers of Tiananmen, thus assisting them in preserving their oppressive monopoly of power.

Such are the dissatisfactions that moderated the support of American public opinion and of the U.S. Congress for the Bush administration, much more than any partisan sentiment in House or Senate. And such is the conditionality of its *de facto* declaration of war against Iraq that any fighting beyond the use of air-power—certainly any serious ground fighting —would certainly exceed its stringent limits. Many in Congress have noted that ground fighting would not only kill Americans but would also end with the destruction of the Iraqi army, leaving the regime of Iran free to pursue Islamic policies of expansion, in lieu of having to defend its Farsi empire, and the regime of Syria also free to do its worst. In other words, as of now the only war that the Bush administration can fight is an *inherently limited* war of air bombardment, which could have been fought as from the middle of last August, without need of all those tearfully separated reservists, or the vast deployment of army and marines as a whole, nor the agonizing prolongation of the crisis that has, as already said, hugely inflated the apparent importance, and self-importance, of Saddam Hussein.

WHO WANTS ANOTHER PANAMA?

Barbara Ehrenreich

WE DON'T want another Vietnam, everyone says, squinting into the desert sun. We want something swift and decisive, short and sweet—a Panama perhaps. For these are the two poles of our collective military memory: on the one hand, the quicksand of Vietnam; on the other, the "brilliant success" of Panama, or so it was heralded at the time —a military action so flawless, so perfectly executed that, as one of the generals responsible for carrying out the invasion boasted shortly afterward, "There were no lessons learned."

On December 20, 1989, you will recall, the U.S. Army invaded the nation of Panama and soon thereafter arrested its de facto head of state. The U.N. General Assembly swiftly denounced the invasion as a "flagrant violation of international law," but never mind—for most Americans, the lofty ends justified the brutal and lawless means. We had to stop the drug traffic. We had to restore stability and, as usual where guns and flag waving are involved, democracy.

Now, more than a year after the arrest of the loathsome dictator, it's fair to ask: What *did* we accomplish in Panama? Because if Panama is to be our standard for success and the yardstick by which any action in the Persian Gulf may be measured, we ought to know what "success" looks like—after the smoke clears, that is, and the dead have all been laid to rest.

First, there's the matter of drugs. In August 1990 *The New York Times* reported that according to Panamanian pilots and dockworkers, the cocaine traffic was back to pre-invasion levels and, if anything, "more

Barbara Ehrenreich is a columnist for *Time,* and the author of several books, including *The Worst Years of Our Lives.* This essay was published in the January 21, 1991, issue of *Time.*

open and abundant than before." American officials believe that the Panamanian banking industry still serves as a Laundromat for the hemisphere's cocaine profits, but the U.S.-installed government of Guillermo Endara is resisting a pact that would help catch drug-money depositors.

Democracy is a little harder to assess, but by all accounts most of the gains have accrued to Panama's tiny, white-skinned elite of wealth. In the wake of the invasion, labor unions have been repressed and nonwhites shut out of high-ranking government positions. With unemployment running at more than twenty-five percent, crime is rampant, and angry protest marches are once again a common sight. President Endara, who is notoriously indifferent to the nation's low-income majority, has so far refused to legitimate his apparent pre-invasion victory with new elections—a tactless omission for a man who was sworn in, with few Panamanians even present, on a U.S. military base.

Then there's the dictator. When Manuel Noriega was apprehended, some commentators wondered whether he would ever really be brought to trial, given what he might reveal about his long association with former CIA Director George Bush. They were right to wonder. With the revelation—mysteriously leaked to CNN—that the U.S. government has been eavesdropping on Noriega's conversations with his lawyers, the prosecution may have opened the door for Noriega to walk, untried, to a relaxing life in exile.

So that's the sordid aftermath of Operation Just Cause, as the invasion was called. And the human cost? Twenty-three American service members' lives—which is not bad unless one of them happened to be your husband, son, sweetheart, or father—and the lives of somewhere between 202 (the U.S. estimate) and 4,000 Panamanian civilians. That may not sound so bad either, until you recall that the number of Kuwaiti deaths in the Iraqi invasion was in the same general range: between "hundreds" (Amnesty International's estimate) and 7,000 (according to exiled Kuwaitis).

If this was "success," one shudders to think what failure might look like. And one shudders with particular horror because the same tape is now on instant replay: a cruel thug and former U.S. ally, who just happens to be sitting on a key resource (oil this time, the canal in Noriega's case), has been singled out as the president's personal nemesis and casus belli—only that the outcome, this time around, is likely to be infinitely bloodier. With all due respect to the general cited above, Panama may, after all, hold a lesson to be learned.

The first, it seems to me, has to do with the limits of official foresight. Conservative ideologues talk about a "law of unintended consequences,'' which means, roughly, that the effort to fix things sometimes worsens the damage. Of course, the ideologues apply the "law" selectively, as an argument against anti-poverty efforts, not military ventures abroad.

But if anything illustrates the pitfalls of well-intended meddling, it's Panama, not the much-maligned War on Poverty. Clearly, the aim was not to promote the cocaine trade or reduce Panama from a mere banana republic to the status of international basket case, yet that's what we seem to have accomplished. Before pulling the trigger on Saddam Hussein, shouldn't we reflect, as true conservatives surely would want us to, on the dangerous arrogance of all human schemes and designs? Shouldn't we tally up the entirely possible and thoroughly unintended consequences of a war in the Gulf? An ever deeper recession, for example, a wave of anti-American terrorism, a devastating attack on Israel?

The second lesson is that however noble the ends, the use of force always entails one tragic and, realistically speaking, *intended* consequence, and that is the loss of lives. Maybe, if President Bush ever overcomes his obsession with Saddam, he might think about how to repay the estimated $1 billion in damage caused by his invasion of Panama. But the dead, whether they number in the thousands or "only" hundreds, will not wake up to see that happy day. Nor will the tens of thousands who may die in a Gulf war—Americans, Iraqis, and others— ever stir again once the tanks have rolled away across the sand.

Before he orders another shot fired, George Bush ought to stop and count very slowly to ten because, as everyone fears, we may be wading into a Vietnam. Or what could be in the long term just about as bad— another Panama.

A JUST WAR?

Michael Walzer

WHY ARE so many people, myself among them, so confused about the confrontation in the Gulf? The confusion is particularly obvious on what might be called the near left of the political spectrum, where people were not confused at all in the Vietnam years. Editorials in *The New York Times* (more stridently in *The Nation*) urging that war be avoided, and in *The New Republic* urging that war be embraced, aim at persuading these people to take a stand. But I sense a stubborn reluctance—almost as if they believe that the right response this time is radical uncertainty. And how defensible is that, when the moment of decision draws ever nearer?

Among Americans in general there is a considerable, and more surprising, reluctance to go to war. Here the reluctance is fueled by the belief that this would be a war about oil and money, a dirty war, not worth human, or at least American, life. This seems to me a mistaken belief. The nations most in need of oil from the Gulf would rather deal than fight, confident that the market will prevail over Iraqi ambition and, if there is any such thing, Iraqi ideology. The United States, so far as its economic interests go, has little to fear from a deal that "rewards" Saddam Hussein's aggression. I sometimes admire the saving cynicism of Americans with regard to politics: It has a useful deflationary effect on the many varieties of hypocritical zeal. But it isn't admirable in this case, where all the "dirty"—that is, material—arguments point toward appeasement, not war.

Michael Walzer is a professor of social science at the Institute for Advanced Study in Princeton, and author of many books, including *Just and Unjust Wars*. This article was published in the January 28, 1991, issue of *The New Republic* under the title "Perplexed."

What makes for confusion on the near left is precisely that this would be a clean war, so obviously just that one wants to see it fought. And yet the consequences of fighting it are so uncertain that one hesitates to begin. The Vietnamese case was very different. There the war was reasonably contained and unlikely, except by our own actions, to expand beyond its territorial limits. But we were fighting *in* Vietnam and supposedly *for* Vietnam *against* what increasingly seemed to be the greater number of the Vietnamese people. That was an unjust war. Here, by contrast, we would be fighting against the Iraqi state and its leader for the sake of another country's political survival. From the standpoint of morality, it is hard to imagine a better cause or a more appropriate enemy. By contrast again, however, it isn't at all clear what the limits of this war would be. Another comparison: The American invasion of Panama was, I think, unjust, but (except for the inhabitants of a few neighborhoods in Panama City) it was not dangerous at all. An attack on Iraq would be just but dangerous.

I will consider first the justness, then the dangers. To resist aggression on one's own behalf and to come to the aid of a victim of aggression: These are the classic just causes of warfare, good reasons for deciding to fight. The aggressor, as Clausewitz wrote, is a man of peace; he wants nothing more than to march into a neighboring country unresisted. It is the victim and the victim's friends who must choose to fight. Most of us believe that aggression should be resisted and its victims rescued, whenever this is humanly possible. Of course, we have learned to accommodate overwhelming power; we don't rush to the aid of victims like the Hungarians in 1956, when fighting would raise the specter of global destruction. In general, however, it is a good thing to resist. This argument has a further consequence: It is very bad to make a deal with an aggressor at the expense of his victim. For we then make ourselves complicitous in the aggression—and in all further aggressive behavior that our action encourages, as the British and French were complicitous in the conquest of Czechoslovakia after Munich.

I have purposely used the simplest moral language ("good," "bad"), because these are fairly straightforward judgments. For some people they are made more complicated by the fact that the victim state in this case is so unattractive politically. But the feudal autocracy of Kuwait is irrelevant here. Autocracy should be overthrown, no doubt, but by the Kuwaitis, not the Iraqis. And aggression is always an attack on the status quo. When we resist, we don't endorse the status quo; we only require that it be changed by other means and by different people.

Our judgments are also complicated by the fact that the aggressor state in this case is so threatening militarily. Isn't the conquest of Kuwait merely a pretext for a preventive war against Iraq's present and future capacity for chemical, bacteriological, and nuclear attack? But U.S. leaders were not looking for pretexts before the conquest, and they seem to be saying now that a full Iraqi withdrawal would be a positive reason *not* to attack. Preventive war is never a simple issue. A country like Israel, which has been publicly threatened with gas attack and which is formally at war with Iraq, might well make a different judgment here. But the American case is clear: If we fight to liberate Kuwait, we will aim to destroy the arsenal of the aggressor. If not, we will have to deal with the arsenal by other means.

Why not deal with the aggression by other means? A number of Catholic bishops, invoking just-war theory, have insisted that the moral argument doesn't end with the fact of aggression. We must ask whether there are any means short of war for defeating the aggressor and whether the defeat can be inflicted at costs proportional to the values under attack. Unfortunately, neither just-war theory nor any other perspective in moral philosophy helps much in answering these questions. Political or military judgment is called for, and here theologians and philosophers have no special expertise.

War as a "last resort" is an endlessly receding possibility, invoked mostly by people who would prefer never to resist aggression with force. After all, there is always something else to do, another diplomatic note, another meeting. In the present case, waiting out the embargo is a permanent possibility: When does lastness come? In fact, however, politics and war commonly work on timetables, which are often interconnected. Our embargo of Iraq is not a conventional siege, which goes on and on until mass starvation forces surrender. We are committed (as we should be) to letting food and medical supplies through well before people start dying. The embargo is aimed above all at Iraq's military-industrial capacity. But Saddam can let this capacity run down indefinitely so long as he is sure that he won't be attacked. Hence the effectiveness of the embargo depends on a credible threat to fight, and (for logistical, not moral reasons) this threat can only be sustained for a time. At some point Saddam must yield or we must fight. If he doesn't yield and we don't fight, the victory will be his; there won't be a further "last resort." We can postpone that moment of decision beyond January 15; but some timetable there must be. The alternative is to make a deal now, but such is the force of the argument against aggression that even people who want to do that cannot say so out loud.

Proportionality is also an issue that moral argument reaches only in a gross way. No one would choose a war that brought millions or even hundreds of thousands of deaths or that threatened the world with nuclear destruction—merely for the sake of Kuwaiti independence. And a war cheap in human life would be welcomed by many Americans who oppose the war they think is coming. Stanley Hoffmann, in the best argument against fighting that I have read, says that "a war would be a good precedent for the future of collective security if it could be quick, easy, and lead to the kind of peace that chastises [without utterly destroying] the aggressor country. . . ." (*New York Review of Books,* January 17.) Proportionality inserts itself, as it were, between these two possibilities, vast destruction and cheap victory. But once inserted, I don't know how it is calculated. Suppose the bishops were told that the most sober estimate of casualties is 20,000 on each side. Would they insist that that figure is disproportionate to the values at stake? And if the figure is 10,000 or 5,000, would that be proportionate? How would they, or we, possibly know? Proportionality is a mathematical relation, but values like a country's independence or the defeat of aggression cannot be expressed mathematically. They will always lose out to the body count, though there are times when, if we are to preserve any decency at all, we must be prepared to count (and discount) human bodies.

All this sounds like an argument for war, and yet I feel little confidence in the argument and no readiness to join in shouting, "Let's fight." There are a lot of good reasons to be afraid of fighting. The Middle East is a terribly volatile place in which to start a war: Who can say how far the violence will extend? Modern military technology is massive and unpredictable in its effects: How many of the targets that we aim at will we manage to hit? How many homes, schools, hospitals will we hit without aiming at them? The U.S. Army and Air Force are pretty much untested: How effectively will they fight? A "quick and easy" war would be a war fought mainly through the air, but is that feasible? Would it even be tried? A ground attack that became bogged down, even for a month or two, might represent a "moral" victory for Saddam Hussein (more so than a diplomatic deal)—and with what consequences throughout the Arab world? Could Iraq carry the war to Israel, and then to the streets of Amman and Cairo?

I don't think these worries express a specifically moral anxiety. Perhaps they only express a lack of moral courage. They can each be answered, with varying degrees of probability. Given a certain set of answers, I would support an American attack. In any case, I am not prepared to join an anti-war movement modeled on that of the Vietnam years, whose protagonists claim that a war against Iraq would be unjust.

It might well be politically or militarily unwise, but that is not a matter for marching.

Once the moral and prudential arguments are worked through, as best they can be, a decision must be made. By the time this article appears, readers may be talking about that decision in the past tense. It doesn't seem likely that it will have been made democratically. Neither the people nor their representatives will have been systematically consulted. But it is another feature of the confusion of the near left, which favors democratic decision-making, that it is very difficult for us to say what form such consultations should take.

Suppose the only way to defeat aggression without actually fighting is to threaten to fight. Can a working democracy make and sustain a threat of that sort? One can't play poker by committee, certainly not if the committee holds public meetings. And if Congress is asked to approve a war once the threat has failed, what choice does it really have? We are, it seems, in the hands of our leaders; our situation is not entirely different from that of the people of Iraq, except that our leaders must stand for re-election. They will be condemned if they fail to oppose Iraqi aggression —and also if military opposition brings new catastrophes.

The real test of American democracy will come if Saddam Hussein backs down. This will represent a considerable but also an incomplete moral and political victory. The aggression will have been turned back but the military capacity of the aggressor will not have been reduced. Then we will have to find some way to force an Iraqi demobilization or at least to prevent any technological enhancement of Iraq's military strength. Such a policy will have costs, and there will be plenty of time for Congress to talk about them. Those Americans who oppose a hot war in the Gulf will have to decide whether they have the stomach for a cold war. That too would be a just war, free from our current anxieties. But it will be hard, and it will make for tense relationships with many of our allies. Whatever happens after January 15, democratic states—not ours alone—still face the difficult task of containing and disarming potential aggressors.

THE USE (AND ABUSE) OF THE
UNITED NATIONS

Noam Chomsky

I RAQ'S INVASION of Kuwait on August 2, 1990, evoked two quite different responses. The international community responded with sanctions of unprecedented severity, to be followed by diplomatic efforts to ensure withdrawal. The United States and the United Kingdom moved at once to undermine sanctions and diplomacy, and to restrict the options to the threat or use of force. What lies behind the severity of the sanctions, and the separate course followed by the United States and its British ally?

There is no shortage of answers, including impressive phrases about the sanctity of international law and the U.N. Charter, and our historic mission to punish anyone who dares violate these sacred principles by resorting to force. President Bush declared that "America stands where it always has, against aggression, against those who would use force to withhold the rule of law."

Professing high principle, Washington moved vigorously to block all efforts to resolve the crisis diplomatically, restricting its own contacts with Iraq to the delivery of an ultimatum demanding immediate and total capitulation to U.S. force—what George Bush called "going the extra mile for peace." The U.S. also sternly rejected any "linkage" with regional issues, expressing its moral revulsion at the very thought of rewarding an aggressor by considering problems of armaments, security, and others in a regional context.

Noam Chomsky is Institute Professor of Linguistics at the Massachusetts Institute of Technology and author of many books, including the forthcoming *Deterring Democracy*. This article is adapted from "Oppose the War," which was published in the February 1991 issue of *Z* magazine.

While some questioned his tactical judgment, there was widespread admiration for the president's honorable stand, and his forthright renewal of our traditional dedication to nonviolence, the rule of law, and the duty of protecting the weak and oppressed. The issue was raised to cosmic significance, with visions of a New World Order of peace and justice that lay before us if only the new Hitler could be stopped before he conquered the world—after having failed to overcome post-revolutionary Iran with its severely weakened military, even with the support of the U.S., U.S.S.R., Europe and the major Arab states. "We live in one of those rare transforming moments in history," Secretary Baker declared, "with the Cold War over and an era full of promise just ahead." Commentators marvelled at the "wondrous sea change" at the United Nations, which, to quote *The New York Times,* was "functioning as it was designed to do . . . for virtually the first time in its history" and thus offered "a bold pattern of peacekeeping" for the post–Cold War world. The standard explanation was that with the U.S. victory in the Cold War, Soviet obstructionism and the "shrill, anti-Western rhetoric" of the Third World no longer rendered the U.N. ineffective.

As a matter of logic, principles cannot be selectively upheld. As a matter of fact, the U.S. is one of the major violators of the principles now grandly proclaimed. We do not admire Saddam Hussein as a man of principle because he condemns Israel's annexation of the Syrian Golan Heights, nor do his laments over human rights abuses in the occupied territories encourage our hopes for a kinder, gentler world. The same reasoning must apply when George Bush warns of appeasing aggressors and clutches to his heart the Amnesty International report on Iraqi atrocities (after August 2), but not its reports on El Salvador, Turkey, Indonesia, the Israeli-occupied territories, and a host of others. As for the "wondrous sea change" at the United Nations, it has little to do with the end of the Cold War, or improved behavior of the Russians and Third World degenerates, whose "shrill, anti-Western rhetoric" commonly turns out to be a call for observance of international law, a weak barrier against depredations of the powerful.

The U.N. was able to respond to Iraq's aggression because—for once—the U.S. happened to be opposed to criminal acts, as distinct from the invasions of Panama, Cyprus, Lebanon, the Western Sahara, and much else. For decades, South Africa defied the U.N. and the World Court on Namibia, looting and terrorizing the occupied country and using it as a base for its terror and aggression against neighboring states, exacting an awesome toll. No one proposed bombing South Africa, or withholding food. The U.S. advocated "quiet diplomacy" and "constructive engagement," pursuing "linkage," exactly as in George Shultz's attempt to broker Israel's partial withdrawal from Lebanon—incidentally, with ample reward for the aggressor, which had also been the beneficiary of vast U.S. material aid and Security Council vetoes as it battered the defenseless country.

The answer to our question is straightforward: the response to Saddam Hussein's aggression is unprecedented because he stepped on the wrong toes. The U.S. is upholding no high principle in the Gulf; nor is any other state.

Saddam Hussein is a murderous gangster, just as he was before August 2, when he was an amiable friend and favored trading partner. His invasion of Kuwait is another crime, comparable to others, not as terrible as some; for example, the Indonesian invasion and annexation of East Timor, which reached near-genocidal levels thanks to diplomatic and material support from the U.S. and Britain, the two righteous avengers of the Gulf. The truth was revealed by U.N. Ambassador Daniel Patrick Moynihan in his memoirs, describing his success in implementing State Department directives to render the U.N. "utterly ineffective in whatever measures it undertook" in response to Indonesia's aggression, because "the United States wished things to turn out as they did, and worked to bring this about." It was stated with equal frankness by Australian Foreign Minister Gareth Evans, explaining his country's acquiescence in the forcible annexation of East Timor: "The world is a pretty unfair place, littered with examples of acquisition by force . . ." Saddam Hussein's aggression, in contrast, called forth Prime Minister Hawke's ringing declaration that "big countries cannot invade small neighbors and get away with it." If Libya were to join the Butcher of Baghdad in exploiting Kuwait's oil riches, the West's reaction would not be what it was when Australia joined the Butcher of Jakarta in the Timor Sea.

U.N. peacekeeping efforts have regularly been frustrated by the United States. The first post–Cold War U.N. session (1989–90) was typical in this regard. Three Security Council resolutions were vetoed, all by the U.S. Two condemned its murderous invasion of Panama (the U.K. abstaining in one case, and joining the U.S., along with France, in the second). The third condemned Israeli human rights abuses; the U.S. vetoed a similar resolution the following May. Alone with Israel, the U.S. voted against two General Assembly resolutions calling for observance of international law, one condemning U.S. support for the Contras, the other its economic warfare against Nicaragua, both already declared unlawful by the World Court—irrelevantly, by the standards of the U.S.

and its allies. A resolution condemning the acquisition of territory by force passed 151-3 (the U.S., Israel and Dominica voted against); this was yet another call for a political settlement of the Arab-Israel conflict, which the U.S. has blocked for twenty years.

The U.S. is far in the lead in the past twenty years in Security Council vetoes. Britain is second, France a distant third, and the U.S.S.R. fourth. The U.S. also regularly votes against General Assembly resolutions (often alone, or with a few client states) on aggression, international law, human rights abuses, disarmament, and other relevant issues. That has been the pattern since the U.N. ceased to serve as a virtual instrument of U.S. foreign policy. There is no reason to expect that the Soviet collapse will induce the U.S. and Britain to end their campaign against international law, diplomacy, and collective security—a campaign that had little to do with the Cold War, as a look at cases shows. The record offers no prospects for a bright new era.

The actual stance of the U.S. was made clear during the debate over its invasion of Panama, when U.N. Ambassador Thomas Pickering advised the Security Council that Article 51 of the Charter, which restricts the use of force to self-defense against armed attack until the Council acts, permitted the U.S. to use "armed force . . . to defend our interests." The same Article permitted the U.S. to invade Panama to prevent its "territory from being used as a base for smuggling drugs into the United States," the Justice Department added. Washington has even claimed the right of "self-defense against future attack" under Article 51 (justifying the terror bombing of Libya). In brief, like other states, the U.S. will do what it chooses, regarding law and principle as ideological weapons, to be used when serviceable, to be discarded when they are a nuisance. We do no one any favors by suppressing these truisms.

THE LIBERATION OF KUWAIT HAS BEGUN

(Speech of January 16, 1991)

George Bush

The following is a transcript of President Bush's remarks in the Oval Office two hours after White House spokesman Marlin Fitzwater announced that the "liberation of Kuwait" had begun.

JUST TWO hours ago, Allied air forces began an attack on military targets in Iraq and Kuwait. These attacks continue as I speak. Ground forces are not engaged.

This conflict started August 2, when the dictator of Iraq invaded a small and helpless neighbor. Kuwait, a member of the Arab League and a member of the United Nations, was crushed, its people brutalized. Five months ago, Saddam Hussein started this cruel war against Kuwait; tonight, the battle has been joined.

This military action, taken in accord with United Nations resolutions and with the consent of the United States Congress, follows months of constant and virtually endless diplomatic activity on the part of the United Nations, the United States and many, many other countries.

Arab leaders sought what became known as an Arab solution, only to conclude that Saddam Hussein was unwilling to leave Kuwait. Others traveled to Baghdad in a variety of efforts to restore peace and justice. Our secretary of state, James Baker, held an historic meeting in Geneva, only to be totally rebuffed.

This past weekend, in a last-ditch effort, the secretary-general of the United Nations went to the Middle East with peace in his heart—his second such mission. And he came back from Baghdad with no progress at all in getting Saddam Hussein to withdraw from Kuwait.

Now, the twenty-eight countries with forces in the Gulf area have exhausted all reasonable efforts to reach a peaceful resolution, and have no choice but to drive Saddam from Kuwait by force. We will not fail.

As I report to you, air attacks are under way against military targets in Iraq. We are determined to knock out Saddam Hussein's nuclear bomb potential. We will also destroy his chemical weapons facilities. Much of Saddam's artillery and tanks will be destroyed. Our operations are designed to best protect the lives of all the coalition forces by targeting Saddam's vast military arsenal.

Initial reports from General Schwarzkopf are that our operations are proceeding according to plan. Our objectives are clear: Saddam Hussein's forces will leave Kuwait. The legitimate government of Kuwait will be restored to its rightful place, and Kuwait will once again be free.

Iraq will eventually comply with all relevant United Nations resolutions, and then, when peace is restored, it is our hope that Iraq will live as a peaceful and cooperative member of the family of nations, thus enhancing the security and stability of the Gulf.

Some may ask, why act now? Why not wait? The answer is clear. The world could wait no longer. Sanctions, though having some effect, showed no signs of accomplishing their objective. Sanctions were tried for well over five months, and we and our allies concluded that sanctions alone would not force Saddam from Kuwait.

While the world waited, Saddam Hussein systematically raped, pillaged, and plundered a tiny nation no threat to his own. He subjected the people of Kuwait to unspeakable atrocities, and among those maimed and murdered, innocent children.

While the world waited, Saddam sought to add to the chemical weapons arsenal he now possesses, an infinitely more dangerous weapon of mass destruction—a nuclear weapon. And while the world waited, while the world talked peace and withdrawal, Saddam Hussein dug in and moved massive forces into Kuwait.

While the world waited, while Saddam stalled, more damage was being done to the fragile economies of the Third World, emerging democracies of Eastern Europe, to the entire world, including to our own economy.

The United States, together with the United Nations, exhausted every means at our disposal to bring this crisis to a peaceful end. However, Saddam clearly felt that by stalling and threatening and defying the United Nations, he could weaken the forces arrayed against him.

While the world waited, Saddam Hussein met every overture of peace with open contempt. While the world prayed for peace, Saddam prepared for war.

I had hoped that when the United States Congress, in historic debate, took its resolute action, Saddam would realize he could not prevail and would move out of Kuwait in accord with the United Nations resolutions. He did not do that. Instead, he remained intransigent, certain that time was on his side.

Saddam was warned over and over again to comply with the will of the United Nations, leave Kuwait or be driven out. Saddam has arrogantly rejected all warnings. Instead he tried to make this a dispute between Iraq and the United States of America.

Well he failed. Tonight twenty-eight nations—countries from five continents, Europe and Asia, Africa and the Arab League—have forces in the Gulf area standing shoulder to shoulder against Saddam Hussein. These countries had hoped the use of force could be avoided. Regrettably, we now believe that only force will make him leave.

Prior to ordering our forces into battle, I instructed our military commanders to take every necessary step to prevail as quickly as possible, and with the greatest degree of protection possible for American and Allied servicemen and women. I've told the American people before that this will not be another Vietnam, and I repeat this here tonight. Our troops will have the best possible support in the entire world, and they will not be asked to fight with one hand tied behind their back. I'm hopeful that this fighting will not go on for long and that casualties will be held to an absolute minimum.

This is an historic moment. We have in this past year made great progress in ending the long era of conflict and Cold War. We have before us the opportunity to forge for ourselves and for future generations a new world order, a world where the rule of law, not the law of the jungle, governs the conduct of nations.

When we are successful, and we will be, we have a real chance at this new world order, an order in which a credible United Nations can use its peacekeeping role to fulfill the promise and vision of the U.N.'s founders. We have no argument with the people of Iraq. Indeed, for the innocents caught in this conflict, I pray for their safety.

Our goal is not the conquest of Iraq. It is the liberation of Kuwait. It is my hope that somehow the Iraqi people can, even now, convince their dictator that he must lay down his arms, leave Kuwait, and let Iraq itself rejoin the family of peace-loving nations.

Thomas Paine wrote many years ago: "These are the times that try men's souls." Those well-known words are so very true today. But even as planes of the multinational forces attack Iraq, I prefer to think of peace, not war. I am convinced not only that we will prevail, but that out of the horror of combat will come the recognition that no nation can stand against a world united. No nation will be permitted to brutally assault its neighbor.

No president can easily commit our sons and daughters to war. They are the nation's finest. Ours is an all-volunteer force, magnificently trained, highly motivated. The troops know why they're there. And listen to what they say, because they've said it better than any president or prime minister ever could. Listen to Hollywood Huddleston, marine lance corporal. He says: "Let's free these people so we can go home and be free again." And he's right. The terrible crimes and tortures committed by Saddam's henchmen against the innocent people of Kuwait are an affront to mankind and a challenge to the freedom of all.

Listen to one of our great officers out there, Marine Lieutenant General Walter Boomer. He said: "There are things worth fighting for. A world in which brutality and lawlessness are allowed to go unchecked isn't the kind of world we're going to want to live in."

Listen to Master Sergeant J. P. Kendall of the 82d Airborne: "We're here for more than just the price of a gallon of gas. What we're doing is going to chart the future of the world for the next hundred years. It's better to deal with this guy now than five years from now."

And finally, we should all sit up and listen to Jackie Jones, an army lieutenant, when she says, "If we let him get away with this, who knows what's going to be next."

I've called upon Hollywood and Walter and J.P. and Jackie and all their courageous comrades-in-arms to do what must be done. Tonight, America and the world are deeply grateful to them and to their families.

And let me say to everyone listening or watching tonight: When the troops we've sent in finish their work, I'm determined to bring them home as soon as possible. Tonight, as our forces fight, they and their families are in our prayers.

May God bless each and every one of them and the coalition forces at our side in the Gulf, and may He continue to bless our nation, the United States of America.

THE MOTHER OF ALL BATTLES

(Speech of January 20, 1991)

Saddam Hussein

The following is an excerpted transcript of a speech by President Saddam Hussein, as broadcast on Baghdad Radio and translated by Reuters.

O GLORIOUS Iraqis, O holy warrior Iraqis, O Arabs, O believers wherever you are, we and our steadfastness are holding. Here is the great Iraqi people, your brothers and sons of your Arab nation and the great faithful part of the human family. We are all well. They are fighting with unparalleled heroism, unmatched except by the heroism of the believers who fight similar adversaries. And here is the infidel tyrant whose planes and missiles are falling out of the skies at the blows of the brave men. He is wondering how the Iraqis can confront his fading dreams with such determination and firmness.

After a while, he will begin to feel frustrated, and his defeat will be certain, God willing. . . . We in Iraq will be the faithful and obedient servants of God, struggling for his sake to raise the banner of truth and justice, the banner of "God is Great." Accursed be the lowly.

At that time, the valiant Iraqi men and women will not allow the army of atheism, treachery, hypocrisy and [word indistinct] to realize their stupid hope that the war would only last a few days or weeks, as they imagined and declared. In the coming period, the response of Iraq will be on a larger scale, using all the means and potential that God has given us and which we have so far only used in part. Our ground forces have not entered the battle so far, and only a small part of our air force has been used.

The army's air force has not been used, nor has the navy. The weight and effect of our ready missile force has not yet been applied in full. The fact remains that the great divine reinforcement is our source of power and effectiveness. When the war is fought in a comprehensive manner, using all resources and weapons, the scale of death and the number of dead will, God willing, rise among the ranks of atheism, injustice, and tyranny.

When they begin to die and when the message of the Iraqi soldiers reaches the farthest corner of the world, the unjust will die and the "God is Great" banner will flutter with great victory in the mother of all battles. Then the skies in the Arab homeland will appear in a new color and a sun of new hope will shine over them and over our nation and on all the good men whose bright lights will not be overcome by the darkness in the hearts of the infidels, the Zionists, and the treacherous, shameful rulers, such as the traitor Fahd.

Then the door will be wide open for the liberation of beloved Palestine, Lebanon, and the Golan. Then Jerusalem and the Dome of the Rock will be released from bondage. The Kaaba and the Tomb of the Prophet Mohammed, God's peace and blessings be upon him, will be liberated from occupation and God will bestow upon the poor and needy the things that others owed them, others who withheld from them what they owed them as God had justly ordained, which is a great deal.

Then [words indistinct], the good men, the holy warriors, and the faithful will know the truth of our promise to them that when the forces of infidelity attack the Iraqis, they will fight as they wished them to fight and perhaps in a better way, and that their promise is of faith and holy war. It remains for us to tell all Arabs, all the faithful strugglers, and all good supporters wherever they are: you have a duty to carry out holy war and struggle in order to target the assembly of evil, treason, and corruption everywhere.

You must also target their interests everywhere. It is a duty that is incumbent upon you, and that must necessarily correspond to the struggle of your brothers in Iraq. You will be part of the struggle of armed forces in your holy war and struggle, and part of the multitude of faith and the faithful. If the opposing multitude captures you, you will be prisoners in their hands, even if they refuse to admit this in their communiques and statements.

You will inevitably be released when the war ends, in accordance with international laws and agreements which will govern the release of prisoners of war. In this way you will have pleased God and honored, with your slogans and principles, the trust given to you.

God is great, God is great, God is great, and accursed be the lowly.

IS THIS ANY WAY TO WAGE PEACE?

John E. Mack and Jeffrey Z. Rubin

"THE WAR in the Gulf is not a war we wanted. We worked hard to avoid war. For more than five months we . . . tried every diplomatic avenue. . . . But time and again, Saddam Hussein flatly rejected the path of diplomacy and peace."

These were the words President Bush used in his State of the Union address, in a bid to be remembered kindly by the generations of tomorrow as a leader who pursued every avenue toward peace but was reluctantly drawn into war.

On the contrary, the actions and decisions taken by the United States after August 2, while having the appearance of diplomacy for peace, were in fact the result of deliberate choices toward a very different end. It was these choices—the president's assertions notwithstanding—that moved us inexorably along the path to war.

We demonized and dehumanized our adversary. We indulged in personal name-calling, false analogies to past wars and demonic leaders of earlier times, then deliberately provoked Hussein through threats and insults. In this way we demeaned and humiliated our opponent, while lessening his incentive to respond to the pleas that were directed to him by so many individuals and nations.

We denied our own contribution to the problem. By placing the blame entirely on the shoulders of our adversary, failing to acknowledge our own

John E. Mack and Jeffrey Z. Rubin are, respectively, president-elect and vice president-elect of the International Society of Political Psychology. Mack is a professor of psychiatry at the Harvard Medical School and founding director of the Center for Psychological Studies in the Nuclear Age. Rubin is a professor of psychology at Tufts University and executive director of the Program in Negotiation at Harvard Law School. This piece was published in the January 31, 1991, issue of the *Los Angeles Times.*

contribution (bolstering Iraq's war machine and giving permissive signals before the conflict began, for example) we put him on the defensive and further limited his ability to respond constructively.

We relied exclusively on the threatened use of force. The value of personal, quiet diplomacy, even with a leader as brutal as the Iraqi president, was disregarded and surely added to his defiance. In an interview with ABC's Peter Jennings in November, Hussein asked that a dialogue be conducted between himself and President Bush ". . . in which the eyes can meet." What he got was not dialogue but preconditions for capitulation.

Having taken the position that only military power could "solve" the Gulf crisis, we then shrouded our belligerent intent in the guise of collective will. Using the newly invigorated United Nations as a cover, we represented our determination to use force as being the result of a genuinely joint decision by the international community, rather than what it largely was: an American-engineered unilateral initiative.

We disregarded the other side's stated grievances and claims, while demanding unconditional surrender. Our original position was doomed to failure if what we sought was peace. By demanding that Iraq give up Kuwait unconditionally, while offering no negotiating incentives, we forced Hussein into a corner from which he could perceive no way out but martyrdom or fighting back.

We took no account of cultural differences. We listened to those who said that Hussein was nonreligious, and interpreted his invocations of Allah and the Koran as cynical political manipulation. We failed to consider the people's dual heritage as Iraqis and Muslims, and thus Hussein's willingness to martyr himself and to sacrifice his people in standing up to the Western "infidel."

Our policymakers relied exclusively on advisers who, following the conventional logic of power politics, predicted that Hussein would surrender Kuwait rather than permit his power to be destroyed.

We offered a response that was disproportionate to the problem. We assembled an overwhelming destructive force in the Gulf without adequately anticipating the consequences of using it as threatened. We exaggerated the original problem by arguing that international boundaries are inviolate —"sanctified," declared Representative Stephen Solarz, one of the principal proponents of the war policy. This overstatement of reality contributed a further element of ideological rigidity to justify the use of violence. In fact, Kuwait's boundaries were arbitrarily drawn in 1961 by the withdrawing British colonialists.

We overcommitted ourselves to a course of action. By developing a U.N. deadline, to which we adhered with rigid insistence, we lost room to maneuver and to explore peaceful methods of resolving the conflict. Instead, we locked ourselves into a belligerent military position and swiftly came to believe that we had invested too much in it to quit. An offer to negotiate after the January 15 deadline would have placed us in a position of unacceptable weakness, given the scope of our commitment by then.

We used public presentation of conditions in order to intimidate the other side. Our public assertions—"no negotiation, no face-saving, no linkage"— had the effect of hardening Hussein's response, not intimidating him. Withdrawal from Kuwait under the conditions we had publicly defined would have all but guaranteed his personal humiliation—something we may have wanted but that he would never have accepted.

We paid lip service to efforts at diplomatic solution. We indulged in a hypocritical pretense by announcing our "willingness to go the extra mile for peace," then refusing Hussein's demand that a meeting take place closer to January 15 than we liked. We were willing to talk only on our terms, which we knew Hussein would have to reject.

We derogated the other side's conciliatory gestures. By warning that Hussein would attempt to use concessionary behavior to pull the wool over our eyes, we made it all but impossible to give the other side the benefit of the doubt. For example, Hussein's initiative in releasing hostages was viewed not as a show of good faith, or a desire to move toward settlement, but as a cunning attempt to manipulate world opinion.

We insisted that the conflict be regarded as zero-sum. We entertained only two possibilities: Hussein could get out of Kuwait, or he could remain there and invite expulsion by force. Consistently overlooked or dismissed were all alternative approaches that could turn a win-lose exchange into one with opportunities for both sides to do well. For example, we might have expressed a willingness to address the Palestinian-Israeli conflict while officially disclaiming linkage to the Gulf crisis.

In conclusion, the Bush administration's approach to dealing with the unjustifiable Iraqi invasion of Kuwait violated the principles of political psychology, negotiating theory and the appropriate conduct of international relationships. If our purpose was to destroy Iraq as a military and political power in the Middle East, which now seems apparent, the American people were never informed of such an intention.

TOWARD A DIFFICULT PEACE MOVEMENT

Todd Gitlin

O NE WATCHES the avalanche of war sweep down upon the Middle East with the sick feeling that the consequences of pushing the first boulders were predictable. And that the damage already done to life and limb and political wisdom cannot be undone. And that it is still not too late—never too late—to try to limit the damage.

But I want to make it clear that the reason why the war is a catastrophe is not that Saddam Hussein's machinery of violence was or is innocuous. Many things are true even if George Bush says them. Saddam Hussein is a torturer of children, and a fascist tyrant. His Baath party is indeed totalitarian and expansionist, but Iraq is not Germany. It has one significant export, is no major industrial power, is virtually landlocked.

The tragedy is that there was—there remains—another way to stop and reverse Saddam Hussein's expansion: the combination of sanctions and genuinely multilateral enforcement.

This is not the place to write about Saddam Hussein's miscalculations, his hunger for Kuwait, his military machine, his appeal in the Arab world. Or about George Bush's recklessness, his monomania, and his glib assumptions about the tractability of the world. But I want to say a few words about the structure of arguments about the war. For this war is a terrible simplifier all around. On the pro-war side, one hears language corrupted to deny the terrible sufferings—"collateral damage," "KIAs." One hears cavalier assurances that sanctions would not have worked—in the face of much evidence to the contrary and without so much as a

Todd Gitlin, professor of sociology at the University of California at Berkeley, is the author of several books, including *The Sixties: Years of Hope, Days of Rage.* This article was published in the February 19, 1991, issue of *The Village Voice.*

rebuttal of that evidence. One hears automatic denials that negotiations to get Saddam Hussein out of Kuwait were possible, and no curiosity about why he sent the hostages home in December. In some quarters, especially Israel, there is we-told-you-so pleasure that the just demands of the Palestinians can once more be deferred now that many of them pathetically, infuriatingly cheer at Scud terror attacks.

The rationality of the think tank and the thrill of the video game generate fantasies of neat war and neater settlement. Like their anti-imperialist opposite numbers, pro-warriors presume that the Middle East—as if it were the Middle West!—is an inert land susceptible to the fine-tunings of American tinkering. Two sides of Wilsonian idealism: Some anti-warriors think everything the U.S. touches turns to sewage; most pro-warriors think everything the U.S. touches turns to democracy and freedom. Overthrow Mossadegh and instate the shah in 1953 to beat back the U.S.S.R.; tilt toward Iraq in the '80s to beat back Iran; now tilt toward Syria and *its* wing of the Baath party to beat back Iraq and *its* wing of the Baath party. This sort of global gamesmanship is the rationalism of fools. One of the grotesque debasements we have heard during this unfolding nightmare is that this fatal mixture of arrogance and gunslinging constitutes a "new world order."

The anti-war side has much sensible protest to be proud of—along with much effort expended to paint itself into a corner. One hears flaming anti-Semitism, harsh indifference to Israeli casualties and fright. One hears the canard that this is a "Jewish war" because the Israel lobby supported it—although the Saudi and Kuwaiti lobbies were not exactly pacific; although a majority of Jewish members of Congress opposed going to war (more than one can say for the Christians); although, as usual, Jews were overrepresented at the January 26 Washington demonstration; although not one of the inner circle who decided to go to war is a Jew.

Amid the anti-imperialist rhetoric from the speaker's stand at anti-war rallies, one hears a refusal to recognize that something is at stake in the Gulf beside the lone superpower's desire to show off its smart bombs. One hears casual dismissal of Saddam Hussein's erasure of, and atrocities in, Kuwait. One hears isolationist lack of interest in the prospect of his controlling a big bloc of world oil production, as if Iraq's military machine were a matter of indifference to global security. Given the reality of the world economy, a reality that cannot be washed away, oil is, as Arthur Waskow says, not only heroin but lifeblood—witness the dire impact of increasing oil prices on the non–oil-producing Third World. One hears the appalling sexism of the Saudis adduced as an anti-war argument—as if our ally Stalin's gulag were a reason not to have fought Hitler.

Collective security matters. Collective security must take seriously the erasure of borders. Collective security should not consist of the United States twisting Security Council arms so that they are heard cracking all over Manhattan (and distributing quids so that they can be heard falling all over Latvia and Lithuania). In this case it *should* consist of containment and the enforcement of sanctions by a genuinely multinational police. Instead, the United States, accompanied by a bodyguard of expensive clients, has hurled itself into an Arab civil war between radical nationalism (miserably latched to a fascist tyranny) and bloated emirates —a monstrous war likely now to go on, one way or another, for the rest of our lives, to the great economic, political and, I want to say, spiritual detriment of all. Against the argument that the U.S. is already hated throughout the Arab world, and can do no more damage to its standing in the region, I fear that the war has only begun, war aims are predictably stretching, and the worst is yet to come.

Antiseptic language, reinforced by Nintendo thrills, airbrushes the damage—even if the Pentagon is truly making an effort to minimize civilian deaths. Not all war is unjust, but this war was avoidable. It was not the last resort. Neither is land war now; neither is the proposed march on Baghdad. To oppose the war both tough- and tender-mindedly—not on the ground that the United States is the font of all evil, not because Israel explains Saddam Hussein, not because Saddam is the prince of noble anti-imperialism—to oppose the war in this difficult way is, on the other hand, to bear witness to another possibility: that somehow, against the odds, smart collective security and diplomacy can stop aggression with less carnage than smart bombs.

THE FORGOTTEN WAR

Robert Massa

A M I D   T H E din of news from the Gulf, a milestone passed, barely noticed. The federal Centers for Disease Control announced that the American death toll from AIDS had reached 100,000. After accidental death, the epidemic is now the leading killer of men age 25 to 44. Over the next three years, in the U.S. alone, the CDC predicts another quarter-million deaths from AIDS.

And these deaths represent only a fraction of the "casualties" in the war at home. Over the past three decades, life expectancy for African Americans has *declined,* while infant mortality is twice as high among blacks as among whites. Diseases like tuberculosis, hepatitis, measles, mumps, and whooping cough—all close to being wiped out just a few years ago—are on the rise again. The public hospital system is on the brink of collapse.

One of the few clear lessons of the war so far is the ability of America to rise to a crisis. The deployment of hundreds of thousands of soldiers and billions of dollars in equipment halfway around the world almost overnight shows that when the federal government puts its mind to something, it has awesome capabilities. Even in a time of recession and staggering deficits, our pockets are bottomless when it comes to defending what the president calls "a big idea."

Yet, the lives of Americans in need are not high on the list of priorities in Bush's New World Order. We can spend hundreds of millions—soon

Robert Massa is an associate editor of *The Village Voice,* teaches English at New York University and is currently working on a book of personal experiences in the war against AIDS. This article, in slightly different form, was published in the February 12, 1991, issue of *The Village Voice* under the title "The Other War."

to be a billion—a day to liberate oil-soaked Kuwait, but we can't provide health care to the millions at home who lack insurance. We can shelter soldiers in a hostile environment, but we can't house the homeless in our own streets.

And we can't afford to fight AIDS. Government outlays for Desert Storm have already far outstripped ten years of spending on what the feds themselves describe as the greatest health threat facing the nation. In fact, for every $100 spent by the Pentagon this year, less than 60 cents is spent on AIDS. And that's not counting Desert Storm.

It's not just how much is being spent on the war, but how quickly it's being spent, that makes heads spin. In 1982, when medical experts were already convinced we had a catastrophe on our hands, just $8 million was allocated to AIDS. Not until 1988—almost a decade into the epidemic—did federal AIDS spending, including benefit programs, reach $1 billion.

Now even that paltry sum is in jeopardy. In the president's new budget, no new money after inflation is going to AIDS research, while military high tech will get a major boost. Even if Congress wanted to vote more AIDS dollars, its hands are, to borrow a metaphor, tied behind its back. October's budget agreement mandates that any increase in AIDS funding will have to come from cuts in other domestic spending.

That agreement had a devastating impact even before the war began. While forces were being built up in the Gulf, the $875 million Ryan White emergency AIDS care bill authorized last summer was butchered to $135 million. Meanwhile, the National Institutes of Health's AIDS research program has been limping along with thirty percent understaffing for two years.

No one expects we can emerge from even a short war without further domestic cutbacks, especially as the savings-and-loan crisis spirals out of control. And the impact of Desert Storm won't be just dollars and cents. Before the war we were already facing a shortage of doctors and nurses, particularly in the urban centers heavily hit by AIDS. The call-up of army reservists is exacerbating the problem: Every major hospital has lost staff.

A bloody ground war would also compound dire shortages in medical facilities. Hundreds of hospital beds in New York City alone—where patients can spend days on stretchers in hallways—have been promised to the Pentagon. Even the supply of blood products and organic drugs not easily replaced could be compromised.

What's already clear and hardly surprising is that the war will divert attention from AIDS and other domestic problems. ACT UP has been forced to practically pummel Dan Rather to get coverage. Americans killed by AIDS may outnumber Americans killed in Vietnam by nearly two to one, but how can the silent, gray war in the clinic compete with TV cameras built into the heads of missiles?

HYMN FOR THE UNSUNG

Ariel Dorfman

SOMEWHERE IN the Saudi Arabian desert, an American corporal is reading *Moby Dick*. He is reading Melville's novel, a newspaper reports, in order to "understand what drives people toward destructive obsessions," concentrating above all on Ahab, "how he kept after the whale"—and wondering if "he was like Saddam Hussein."

How typically American, I thought from my Third World perspective, this need to understand the enemy one is fighting—as American as his pathetic incapacity to achieve that understanding. Saddam as Ahab might fit neatly into the current interpretation of the Iraqi leader as a madman, irrationally pursuing his own downfall in spite of all warnings —but the corporal did not apparently seem interested in stopping to ask who the whale might be in this equation or what the whale might have done to Saddam, which parts of his body and mind had been devoured, to make him act with such abandon.

Because if Saddam is indeed Ahab, the clues to his present behavior might fruitfully be searched for in the past, a search that I doubt the corporal or his fellow Americans are particularly interested in. Instant amnesia seems to have infected the people of the United States as they devastate a country that a few months ago hardly any of them could find on a map. It is easier to conceive of Saddam as Satan—a personification of evil substituting for historical explanation. No need to ask what has been done to the Arabs—as to so many other Third World peoples—that

Ariel Dorfman is a writer who divides his time between his native Chile, from which he was exiled after the coup against Salvador Allende in 1973, and teaching in the United States at Duke University. Among his numerous books are *How to Read Donald Duck*, *Widows*, and *The Last Song of Manuel Sendero*. His piece originally appeared in the February 1, 1991, issue of the *Los Angeles Times*.

makes them feel so humiliated, enraged, threatened, alienated, that a tyrant such as the Iraqi leader can manipulate those feelings to turn himself into their representative. No need to ask why there is a power vacuum in the Middle East that this dictator, like others who will come, thinks he can fill. No need to remember that before this Ahab there was Mossadegh, an elected Iranian leader who nationalized oil and was overthrown with the help of the CIA in 1953. The autocrat who replaced him with a puppet was, of course, the shah. When the shah was in turn swept away by Khomeini's Islamic Revolution, Iraq was encouraged to arm itself to the hilt in order to contain the Iranian menace. Iraq expanded this mandate into a savage war, with America's blessing (and European and Soviet assistance), all human-rights violations and gassing of Kurds winked at, all condemnations blocked, until some years later when the U.S. ambassador would give Saddam Hussein the go-ahead for the invasion of Kuwait.

But what if Saddam is not Ahab?

How can it be that this young man who faces death so far from his home should be unable to catch even a glimmer of the possibility that Saddam might be the whale and that George Bush might in fact be an Ahab whose search for the monster in the oceans of sand and oil could end up with the ruin, not of the monster, but of those who were bent on its extermination?

Saddam Hussein, of course, is not unique as a monster. He is as monstrous as General Augusto Pinochet, who, having been brought to power by U.S. intervention against an elected democratic government, victimized my own people for seventeen years. And Iraq's aggression against Kuwait is as monstrous as the aggressions of the United States against Nicaragua and Panama, against Grenada and Vietnam, as monstrous as the Soviet invasions of Czechoslovakia and Afghanistan. And Saddam Hussein's lobbing of missiles at civilians in Israel is as monstrous as the Israelis' bombing of refugee camps in Lebanon.

For the corporal, or the American people, to understand Saddam Hussein in these terms, as one who has been selectively and conveniently demonized, would necessarily mean condemning their own country's complicity and participation in the pervasive evils of the world today. It would mean seeing the adventure in the Persian Gulf not as a struggle for democracy—which the United States has eroded all over the world by propping up friendly torturers—but as one more sad intervention in the affairs of a region that it knows nothing about, one more step toward the militarization of a world that should be disarming. It would mean denying America's own morality in a conflict that once again finds a superpower technologically assaulting a poor Third World country, no matter how well armed it may be. It would mean that the true connection of Iraq to Vietnam should be made: that the war in the Gulf is being used to refight the war in Indochina with far more lethal weapons—rewriting that American crisis and defeat, proving how it could have been won, having at last the "good war" the Pentagon has been seeking all these years with a singlemindedness that would have astounded even the crew of the *Pequod.*

These connections, alas, are not being made. Pursuing their reflection in the Gulf, Americans are blind to the true meanings of their actions. It is not, however, only their own image that Americans cannot decipher in the nightmare waters of this war.

Not far from the American corporal musing on *Moby Dick* there is an Iraqi corporal.

I know nothing about him, except that he breathes not many miles away and all too soon will be as close as a bayonet thrust, and not even that intimacy of combat will bring closeness or comprehension. It is the very fact that he is nameless, that he has no face, that no newspaper has told us his thoughts, that we have no way of knowing what *Moby Dick,* what Melville of his own culture, he reads in the darkness, what blindness of his own he is submerged in, the fact that his being is a blur that we must imagine; it is the stark fact of his very absence from our awareness that prepares his death. How easy to kill somebody we don't have to mourn because we never dared to imagine him alive.

I want neither Saddam Hussein nor George Bush to win the war in the Gulf. I wish that both of them could be defeated. But I anticipate that these two, Ahab and the whale, the whale and Ahab, George Bush and Saddam Hussein, will emerge unscathed, and that it will be their people who will have to pay for this absurd conflagration. It will be the two corporals who will pay, even if they survive, even if they are not shattered for life, they will be the ones, along with their children, who will pay endlessly for a war that nobody desires and that everybody seems so eager to fight.

Or is the world itself Ahab, suddenly gone mad?

THE ILLOGIC OF ESCALATION

(Statement of February 9, 1991)

Mikhail S. Gorbachev

The following are excerpts from the February 9, 1991, statement by President Mikhail S. Gorbachev of the Soviet Union on the war in the Persian Gulf.

THE DEVELOPMENTS in the Gulf zone are taking an ever more alarming and dramatic turn. The war, the largest during the past several decades, is gaining in scope. The number of casualties, including among the civilian population, is growing. Combat operations have already inflicted enormous material damage. Whole countries—first Kuwait, now Iraq, then, perhaps, other countries—are facing the threat of catastrophic destruction. . . .

The Soviet leadership reiterates its commitment, in principle, to the U.N. Security Council resolutions, which reflect the will of the majority of countries and the hopes of nations for a new world order that would rule out aggression and infringement on other countries' territory and natural resources.

However, the logic of the military operations and the character of the military actions are creating a threat of going beyond the mandate, defined by those resolutions.

Provocative attempts to expand the scope of the war, to draw Israel and other countries into it, thus giving the conflict another destructive dimension, the Arab-Israeli one, are also extremely dangerous.

Judging by some statements on a political level and those made by influential mass media organs, attempts are being made to condition people by both sides of the conflict to the idea of a possibility, and permissibility, of the use of mass destruction weapons. If this happened, the whole of the world politics, the world community in general, would be shaken to the foundations.

The only conclusion comes from historic responsibility, common sense and humaneness: to put to use all levers of a political settlement on the basis of the Security Council resolutions.

In this critical moment I appeal publicly to the Iraqi president, urging him to analyze again what is at stake for his country, to display realism which would make it possible to take the path of a reliable and just peaceful settlement. I shall immediately send my personal representative to Baghdad to meet President Hussein.

By taking these steps, we want, acting jointly with Arab and other Muslim countries, with European and Asian countries, with the United States in the first place, with all permanent members of the Security Council, not only to help overcome the state of war as soon as possible, but also to begin preparing a solid and equitable security system in that region. . . .

The security system should include, of course, the settlement of the Arab-Israeli conflict and the Palestinian problem. The countries of the region should play a decisive role in this process. Iraq should hold a worthy place in the postwar settlement. Its people cannot bear responsibility for the past developments. They deserve sympathy, compassion and support. . . .

I repeat that in order to make a breakthrough to peace in the Near and Middle East, it is necessary to put out the flame of war in the Gulf as soon as possible. . . . This is the most important thing now.

BOMBING BAGHDAD:
NO CAUSE FOR GUILT

Charles Krauthammer

H AVING PLAYED his Scud card, his oil-spill card, his oil-field-fires card, Saddam has little left in his hand. He has exactly three cards left: his Republican Guards, his chemical weapons, and Peter Arnett. The first two are useless so long as the United States refuses to oblige Saddam by launching a ground war.

Which leaves him with Arnett. Arnett, of course, is just shorthand for the Western press allowed into Iraq for the sole purpose of reading government-approved scripts and showing government-approved pictures of civilian casualties.

The press is one prong of Saddam's two-prong strategy for winning this war politically. Civilian casualties are the other. Saddam needs them both. Part I of his strategy, elaborated by Jim Hoagland last week, is to pile up Iraqi bodies. Saddam told U.S. Ambassador April Glaspie that America is too soft to withstand 10,000 losses. To date, Saddam has not inflicted 10,000 but 39. So his strategy shifts. He is now out to see whether America can withstand 10,000 *Iraqi* losses.

Saddam's strategy is one the Palestinians have perfected over the last decade: Provoke a fight, lose the fight, pile up the bodies and invite the press. That was the story of the Lebanon war of 1982, a war that the Palestinians provoked with years of unrelenting attack on civilians in northern Israel and which they won politically by successfully playing victim when Israel struck back. West Bankers then repeated this victory-through-victimization even more successfully with their highly telegenic *intifada.*

Charles Krauthammer is a contributing editor of *The New Republic* and a syndicated columnist. This column appeared in the February 14, 1991, issue of *The Washington Post.*

On the eve of this war, Arafat declared that he was in the same trench as Saddam. It is no surprise that his trench mate should have adopted the PLO technique for political victory in a losing war.

But political victory, in Iraq as on the West Bank, cannot be won without Part II: the press. Hence Arnett. Piling up bodies is not enough. Dead bodies are of no use unless they are on video. And not just any video. Iraqi TV would not be taken seriously.

When Iraq presses claims of victimization, the effect borders on the ridiculous. Iraq launches an unprovoked war of aggression—then claims to be aggressed against. It indiscriminately attacks Israeli civilians, boasts that it will turn Tel Aviv into a "crematorium"—then complains of attacks on its civilians. It scorns a dozen U.N. resolutions demanding that it withdraw from Kuwait—then Tariq Aziz complains that the Allied war effort has "far exceeded the mandate of the [U.N.] resolutions."

It is because Iraq cannot undertake a moral critique of anyone that it needs the Western press to do so for it. The Iraqis do not need Arnett's cameras. They are quite adept at video technology. What they need is for Iraq's suffering to go out under a New Zealand accent and a CNN logo.

A week ago, it was the milk factory, Iraq's only factory for infant formula, we were assured by Iraqi spokesmen. (A country that builds a dozen germ war, poison gas, and nuclear facilities can spare the change to build only one for infant formula, it seems.) Western cameras dutifully record the powdered milk strategically scattered about the ruins and, out front, that cleverly generic sign: BABY MILK PLANT. There is some dispute as to whether the place in fact turned out milk or biological weapons. Yet, by any moral calculus, if our intelligence indicated no more than, say, a one-in-five chance that it made biological weapons, the Allies had not just the right but the duty to destroy it.

And now, the first major civilian disaster of the war, the bombing of a Baghdad bunker packed with hundreds of civilians. With footage of this attack, Saddam's strategy gets under way. The resulting shock will increase pressure against the Allied war effort from the Arab street, the Soviets, the U.N. and American protesters.

How to meet the pressure? Not by restricting the press. Arnett and friends have every right to remain in Baghdad and pursue their story. Even in wartime, a free country may censor only military secrets, not disturbing pictures.

We meet the threat by exercising our critical faculties. One of the criteria for just war is proportionality of means to ends. The ends here are saving Kuwait from obliteration and the region from weapons of mass destruction. By any measure, casualties thus far have been proportional to that end. They have indeed been far less than one would have expected of a war against so vast a military machine as Iraq's.

The ultimate compliment to America's policy of discriminate targeting is given by the Iraqi military. It is moving military equipment and personnel into civilian areas for their safety. Richard Beeston of the London *Times* reported (after leaving Baghdad, mind you) that a local commander emerged to greet reporters from his headquarters—in a school. Saddam's interview with Arnett took place not in his bunker but in a safer place—a suburban bungalow.

And yet the exercise of one's critical faculties is one thing. Pictures of injured children is another. Civilian pain in war is a horror beyond words. But when a war is just, it must be faced with a kind of nerve. We demand of American soldiers on the front the nerve to risk their lives on our behalf. We, far to the rear and totally safe, have a reciprocal and far less onerous obligation to them: to keep our nerve in the face of Saddam's cynical strategy of broadcasting the carnage he has brought upon his own people.

That means not being panicked into demanding further restrictions, Vietnam-style, on the bombing. It means not rushing into a land war as a way of trading our dead for Saddam's. Saddam began the horror on August 2. He can end it tomorrow. So long as we scrupulously attack what we reasonably believe to be military targets, the bombing of Baghdad is a cause for sorrow, not guilt.

TOP GUN PARTY

Colman McCarthy

PENTAGON SMUGNESS, never in short supply even between wars, hit a sewer-line low when a smiling General Colin Powell said that his forces have "lots of tools. And I brought them all to the party."

War as fun time—Desert Storm becomes Desert Party—is a new twist in the business of organized slaughter. The general, speaking at a Pentagon briefing in late January, was obviously enjoying himself. He has been overseeing as many as 3,000 bombing runs a day, including B-52s cratering Iraq daily with 500 tons of high explosive and cluster bombs. For the Pentagon party-goers, overkill remains under-kill.

While flying over what another fun-loving general called "a target-rich environment down there," U.S. top guns know that the risks of being shot down are overwhelmingly small. The wild blue yonder is a tame blue yonder. In the first three weeks of the assault on Kuwait and Iraq, no U.S. plane had been downed in air combat. No Iraqi pilots—none—had attacked any U.S. forces.

It *is* a party—a drunken one turning sadistic. Relentless aerial bombardment—lately about as surgical as operating on a cornea with machetes—is a systematic destroying of Iraq's electricity, water, and sewage facilities. That, plus blowing up bridges and obliterating neighborhoods, is called "softening up" the enemy.

On February 12, waves of U.S. bomber pilots, confident they would face no firefights from Iraqi pilots and only minor antiaircraft threats, pulverized downtown Baghdad, with twenty-five major explosions

Colman McCarthy is a columnist for *The Washington Post*. This piece was published in the February 17, 1991, issue of *The Washington Post* under the title "The Coward's Air War."

turning buildings into rubble. On February 13, back the fearless warriors went, this time to obliterate with smart bombs what the Pentagon called an Iraqi "command bunker" but which the world now knows was sheltering hundreds of civilians trying to make it through another hellish night. Scores of noncombatants—women and children—were slaughtered.

Flacks for both war-obsessed governments immediately blamed the other side for the deaths of the civilians. The spin from propagandist Marlin Fitzwater—supported by no hard evidence—was that the evil Saddam was up to his old ruthless tricks by deliberately putting civilians in a military center. Whether he did or didn't, the seven U.S. spy satellites now in the Persian Gulf apparently had cataracts when eyeing the building's comings and goings. When trying to locate Iraqi military leaders, it turns out that smart bombs need dumb luck.

Regardless of what Saddam Hussein is doing to Iraqis, the sadistic ritual of daily bombing by the U.S. military is in keeping with its picking fights—in Grenada, Libya, and Panama—with enemies expected to be done in quickly. In those one-sided mini-wars, the Pentagon had lots of tools for the party. After a month in the Gulf, the United States is now involved in war for war's sake, war for the fun of it, war as a party that brings smiles to General Powell.

Which Iraqi citizens can say with any assurance that they are not part of the "target-rich environment"? After 73,000 sorties in a month, isn't it time for the United States to stop the bombing? Or is another aerial massacre of Iraqi women and children needed for the Pentagon to chill out? And another after that?

The civilians killed on February 13 were in a building across the street from a school and 100 yards from a mosque. Even if Saddam Hussein put families in it, an unanswered question is this: If that command bunker was so crucial strategically, why did a month pass before it was bombed? More than 67,000 sorties were made before February 13. Were U.S. pilots working up their courage to take out the big one?

They have been doing well on the little ones. According to a Reuters report of February 13, refugees fleeing Kuwait and Iraq to Jordan by bus said that two buses filled with civilians were hit by missiles from Allied planes. About sixty people were killed.

Picking off buses of poor people on desert highways shows the U.S. military at its most contemptible. It prefers, naturally, to put off a ground war, because there the threat of danger, despite reports of hunger and sickness among Iraqi conscripts, appears to be real. Safer to keep bombing from the air than shooting from the ground. With an impotent air force, Iraq has little defense against bombing raids. The U.S. policy of waiting them out becomes one of wiping them out.

After a month of obliterating Iraq, and now downtown Baghdad, the U.S. air war has been revealed as a coward's war.*

---

* Editors' note: As of mid-March, conclusive figures on Iraqi casualties were not available. After twenty-six days of war, Iraq's Deputy Prime Minister Saadun Hammadi said that Iraq had suffered 20,000 dead and 60,000 injured—civilian and military. But that was before the ground war began. While the U.S. military has refused to offer any hard estimates, Saudi sources believe that Iraq may have suffered a total of 85,000 to 100,000 military casualties. Other observers think that figure may be low, given the gap between the total number of Iraqis said to have been deployed in and around Kuwait (540,000), desertion rates as high as thirty percent (162,000), and total prisoners taken (perhaps 175,000). No one knows how many thousands of Iraqis, Kuwaiti hostages, and foreign guest-workers were killed in the carnage that took place on the roads leading out of Kuwait City in the war's final days, after President Bush rejected Iraq's offer to accept U.N. resolution 660 and to withdraw from Kuwait under international supervision. Nor do we know how many civilians may have perished in the aerial bombing of Iraqi cities that continued right up until Bush's announcement of a cease-fire the night of February 27. Civilian deaths in Iraq are expected to rise precipitously as the weather warms and disease spreads due to the lack of electricity, clean water, and sanitation.

The total number of U.S. dead, from combat and noncombat incidents, was 304, according to a report in *The Washington Post.*

IRAQ IS READY TO DEAL

(Radio Address of February 15, 1991)

Revolutionary Command Council

The following is a transcript of a February 15, 1991, Baghdad radio address attributed to Iraq's ruling Revolutionary Command Council, headed by Saddam Hussein, on a withdrawal from Kuwait. The text was provided by the State Department via the Foreign Broadcast Information Service.

HONORABLE ARABS, true Muslim believers, freedom-loving people around the world. Ever since the United States, Zionism, and the United States' imperialist Western allies came to realize that an Arab Muslim country, Iraq, was developing a force of its own, capable of being a counterweight to the imperialist-backed Zionism—a free, honorable force, resolved selflessly to tackle Zionist aggression and greed, and to reject imperialist hegemony over the region—the United States, Zionism, and all colonial powers who entertained hatred against Arabs and Muslims set about taking measures, making decisions, and waging campaigns of falsehoods and incitement against Iraq, with the object of thwarting the creation and development of this force, and isolating and punishing Iraq, because it has faithfully, determinedly, and efficiently gone beyond the limits set by the United States, imperialism, and imperialist forces for the states of the region.

The years 1988 and 1989 saw sustained campaigns in the press and other media and by officials in the United States and other imperialist nations to pave the way for the fulfillment of vicious aims.

The year 1990 saw these campaigns escalate feverishly and mount day by day. The aim was clear to us and to all conscious Arabs and true Muslims, as well as to all the free people who believe in freedom and justice in the world. The aim was to pave the way for destroying this nascent force and to tip the regional balance back in favor of the United

337

States, Zionism, and the imperialists—the balance that has been in place for many decades and that has prevented the Arabs from regaining their rights and the usurped and occupied lands in Palestine, the Golan Heights, and Lebanon.

It has also stood in the way of the Arab nation realizing its aspirations for revival, progress, and justice in the interest of occupying its deserved place in the world by virtue of its glorious history and its great contribution to human civilization.

In the early months of 1990, these campaigns intensified, expanded, and assumed a hysterical dimension, with daily incitements to hit Iraq, liquidate its leadership, and deprive it of the means to achieve a revival and progress. Along with other imperialist nations, the United States took a string of measures and made unfair decisions banning the export of whatever might contribute to Iraq's development and its scientific and industrial revival.

These decisions called for an effective economic blockade, including the cancellation of food contracts in March 1990. It was also clear that, in concert with the Zionist entity, the United States was preparing to hit Iraq's scientific and industrial facilities and liquidate its patriotic, believing leadership.

When the United States discovered that its plan, which largely rests on the Zionist military capability, fell short of achieving its evil aims, it brought into the conspiracy its hirelings, corrupt agents, and conspiratorial rulers in the region—the enemies of God.

Their role was to undermine Iraq's economy and then push Iraq to the brink of economic collapse.

In the meantime, the United States set about tightening up the network of the imperialist alliance in the interests of forging a political and military U.S.-Atlantic alliance with the aim of dealing a blow to Iraq and controlling the region, when the opportunity to achieve this aim presented itself with the lopsided balance represented in the Soviet Union becoming preoccupied with internal developments.

O Iraqis, O Arabs, O Muslims, O free men of the world. The events of August 2, 1990, in substance and goals, were not as portrayed by the U.S. and colonialist propaganda, or as were described by the traitorous rulers, followers of America. These events were a national, pan-Arab, and Islamic uprising against the conspiracy and conspirators—an uprising against injustice, immorality, corruption, and imperialist-Zionist-colonialist hegemony of the region, and against the plotters whose role in the U.S.-Zionist conspiracy became exposed.

Thus, the imperialistic-Zionist-Atlantic alliance revealed its true goals and intentions from the very first hours of those events. The alliance massed armies and forces, and organized the biggest and most malicious campaigns of misinformation, lies, and deception witnessed by the world in the modern age.

This oppressive and sly imperialist-Zionist-Atlantic alliance manipulated the United Nations to issue in unparalleled swiftness a series of unjust and unprecedented resolutions, although this body failed throughout several decades to fulfill the simplest demands of the Arab nation and preserve the simplest rights of the Arabs in Palestine, despite the clarity of the Arab right and the severity of the tragedy of the struggling Palestinian people, from which other Arabs, including the oppressed Lebanese people, have suffered.

This tyrannical alliance has forced its will on the world. It has pursued terrorist and extortionist tactics, as well as bribery, not to mention the malicious means of lying and deception found in the bag of tricks of imperialism, Zionism, and the colonial powers to pave the way for the aggression against Iraq.

O glorious Iraqis, O dear Arabs, O faithful Muslims, O free men and honorable persons throughout the world. The aggression that has been launched on Iraq, the courageous, proud, holy warrior, faithful, and patient country, is unprecedented in history. The entire history of mankind never records such an alliance in which the United States as well as two big powers participated—not to mention several other countries, thirty in number—against the holy warrior, courageous, and patient Iraq, whose population does not exceed eighteen million people. It is an evil, rancorous, malicious, and atheistic alliance against the bastion of faith and principles, against the center of freedom where the call for justice and fairness is made.

Over the past month, the United States and its allies, along with the Zionist entity, which has taken part in the aggression from the beginning, launched savage and destructive raids on the Iraqi people, on their economic, scientific, cultural and service property, and also on their religious centers and the sites of ancient civilizations in Iraq.

These raids are unprecedented in history in terms of the enormous firepower used and in terms of the means of killing and destruction used in a manner that contravenes the United Nations Charter, the false international legitimacy, and the new world order, which they wanted to use as an order for U.S.-Atlantic hegemony over the world.

The United States and the partners in the evil alliance, the planes that fire their missiles from a distance, and the long-range missiles, have dropped huge quantities of bombs and explosives on women, children, and old people in all Iraq's cities and villages, and even on the nomad bedouins in the desert.

They struck in a premeditated manner mosques, churches, schools, hospitals, civilian factories, bridges, main roads, telephone, electricity, and water centers, irrigation dams, cultural centers and sites in the country. They hit targets that have no connection any way whatsoever with the military effort or the military confrontation arena of which they have spoken.

Their latest crime was the ugly and dirty crime of the premeditated bombardment of a civilian shelter. They killed and burned hundreds of women, children, and old people. The aim of this unjust aggression was very clear, namely to proceed with the process of destruction that they desire and to punish the proud, free, and struggling Iraqi people, because they have chosen the road of freedom, independence, and glory, and have rejected humiliation, disgrace, and submission to the will of imperialism and Zionism.

The United States and its allies have waged a dirty and cowardly war against a courageous and faithful people. The history of peoples and nations and their fate are not decided by the material possessions of states and ruling regimes. How many strong and rich empires throughout history have fallen because they pursued the road of evil, cowardice, injustice, and decadence. This is the fate of tyrannical America and its decayed systems. It is the fate of Zionism and all the imperialist forces by the will of God.

Iraq has triumphed in this duel. It has triumphed because it has remained steadfast, courageous, faithful, proud, and strong willed. It has triumphed because it has maintained principles and the spiritual values inspired by the true religion of Islam and its noble heritage. Its material losses in this battle, despite their enormity, are small compared to its spirit of determination, its firm belief in principles, and strong determination to continue the course of renaissance and progress.

O dear Iraqis, O honest Arabs, O Muslims who truly believe in Islam, O honest and free men of the world. Proceeding from this firm and right feeling and this assessment of the nature of the showdown, and in order to rob the evil U.S.-Zionist-Atlantic alliance of the opportunity to achieve their premeditated goals, and in appreciation of the Soviet initiative conveyed by the envoy of the Soviet leadership, and in compliance with the principles outlined in leader President Saddam Hussein's initiative on August 12, 1990, the Revolutionary Command Council has decided to declare the following:

First, Iraq's readiness to deal with Security Council resolution No. 660

of 1990, with the aim of reaching an honorable and acceptable political solution, including withdrawal. The first step that is required to be implemented as a pledge by Iraq regarding withdrawal will be linked to the following:

A. A total and comprehensive cease-fire on land, air, and sea.

B. For the Security Council to decide to abolish from the outset resolutions 661, 662, 664, 665, 666, 667, 669, 670, 674, 677, and 678 and all the effects resulting from all of them, and to abolish all resolutions and measures of boycott and embargo, as well as the other negative resolutions and measures that were adopted by certain countries against Iraq unilaterally or collectively before August 2, 1990, which were the real reasons for the Gulf crisis, so that things may return to normal as if nothing had happened. Iraq should not receive any negative effects for any reasons.

C. For the United States and the other countries participating in the aggression, and all the countries that sent their forces from the region to withdraw all the forces, weapons and equipment which they have brought to the Middle East region before and after August 2, 1990, whether in land, seas, oceans, or the gulfs, including the weapons and equipment that certain countries provided to Israel under the pretext of the crisis in the Gulf, provided that these forces, weapons, and equipment are withdrawn during a period not exceeding one month from the date of cease-fire.

D. Israel must withdraw from Palestine and the Arab territories it is occupying in the Golan and southern Lebanon in implementation of the U.N. Security Council and the U.N. General Assembly resolutions. In case Israel fails to do this, the U.N. Security Council should then enforce against Israel the same resolutions it passed against Iraq.

E. Iraq's historical rights on land and at sea should be guaranteed in full in any peaceful solution.

F. The political arrangement to be agreed upon should proceed from the people's will and in accordance with a genuine democratic practice and not on the basis of the rights acquired by the Sabah family. Accordingly, the nationalist and Islamic forces should primarily participate in the political arrangement to be agreed upon.

Second, the countries that have participated in the aggression and in financing the aggression undertake to reconstruct what the aggression has destroyed in Iraq in accordance with the best specifications regarding all the enterprises and installations that were targeted by the aggression and at their expense. Iraq should not incur any financial expenses in this regard.

Third, all the debts of Iraq and countries of the region—which were harmed by the aggression and which did not take part in the aggression, either directly or indirectly—to the Gulf countries and to the foreign countries that took part in the aggression should be written off.

Besides, relations between the rich nations and poor nations in the region and the world should be based on justice and fairness in such a way that puts the rich nations before clear commitments regarding the realization of development in poor nations, and thus removes their economic sufferings.

This should be based on the saying that the poor have a share to claim in the wealth of the rich. Moreover, the duplicitous approach pursued in handling the issues of peoples and nations should be halted, whether this approach is being pursued by the United Nations Security Council or by this or that country.

A CRUEL HOAX

(Speech of February 15, 1991)

George Bush

The following are excerpts from remarks President Bush made February 15, 1991, to an audience at a Raytheon Company plant in Andover, Mass. Raytheon is the manufacturer of the Patriot missile.

I VIEW it as an honor to be here, to come to Raytheon, the home of the men and women who built the Scud-busters.

You know, earlier today maybe your hopes were lifted, maybe mine—mine were, and I think some hopes were lifted in downtown Baghdad with a statement. And I expressed earlier on regret that that Iraqi statement that first gave rise to hope in fact turned out to be a cruel hoax.

Not only was the Iraqi statement full of unacceptable old conditions, Saddam Hussein has added several new conditions.

And let me state once again: Iraq must withdraw without condition. There must be full implementation of all the Security Council resolutions. And there will be no linkage to other problems in the area.

And the legitimate rulers, the legitimate government, must be returned to Kuwait, and until a credible withdrawal begins, with those Iraqi troops visibly leaving Kuwait, the coalition forces, in compliance with United Nations resolution 678, will continue their efforts to force compliance with all those resolutions—every single one of them.

Compliance with the resolutions will instantly stop the bloodshed. And there's another way for the bloodshed to stop, and that is for the Iraqi military and the Iraqi people to take matters into their own hands and force Saddam Hussein, the dictator, to step aside and then comply with the United Nations resolutions and rejoin the family of peace-loving nations.

We have no argument with the people of Iraq. Our differences are with that brutal dictator in Baghdad.

Everyone here has a friend or a neighbor or a son or a daughter or somebody he knows in the Gulf. And to you let me say this, and to the American people, the war is going on schedule. Of course, all of us—all of us—want to see this war ended, the limited loss of life. And it can—if Saddam Hussein would simply comply unconditionally with all the resolutions of the United Nations.

But let me say this to you. I am going to stay with it, we are going to prevail, and our soldiers are going to come home with their heads high.

SOVIET PEACE PROPOSAL

(February 22, 1991)

The following are excerpts from the February 22, 1991, statement by Vitaly N. Ignatenko, a spokesman for President Mikhail S. Gorbachev, after talks between Foreign Ministers Aleksandr A. Bessmertnykh of the Soviet Union and Tariq Aziz of Iraq.

1. Iraq agrees to carry out resolution 660 of the United Nations Security Council, that is, to withdraw its forces immediately and unconditionally from Kuwait to positions they occupied on August 1, 1990.

2. The troop withdrawal will start the day after a cease-fire encompassing all military operations on land, sea, and in the air.

3. The troop withdrawal will be completed within twenty-one days, including a pullout from Kuwait City within the first four days.

4. Once the withdrawal has been completed, all U.N. Security Council resolutions will no longer be valid because the reasons for them will have been removed.

5. All prisoners of war will be freed and repatriated within three days after a cease-fire and the end of military operations.

6. Control and monitoring of the cease-fire and withdrawal of troops will be carried out by observers or peacekeeping forces as determined by the Security Council.

WHY MOSCOW WANTS TO
SAVE SADDAM

A. M. Rosenthal

IN ITS new move to regain political power in the Middle East, the Gorbachev government has one vital goal: the survival of Saddam Hussein.

Of course, that happens to be precisely the result that would be most dangerous for the United States and the Middle East. It would keep the whole region at arms, and soon enough, again at war.

Washington has not been rude enough to point out the conflict of interests. But as Saddam Hussein maneuvers to win the peace by accepting the Soviet "peace plan," it is easy to see what the Kremlin has at stake in his life and rule.

If he goes, through assassination or a political coup, which for a Mideast dictator is a temporary halfway house to extinction, Moscow will lose its only remaining ally in the area. Also: its best customer for weapons. Also: the military and political prestige it invested in Saddam Hussein for so long.

But if Saddam Hussein hangs on, the benefits to the Kremlin will be enormous, and continuing. Many Muslims loathe him, but those who adore him would correctly see the Kremlin as Saddam Hussein's savior.

Moscow would rebuild Iraq's armed forces. That would be a nice piece of business for the KGB and army generals with whom Mr. Gorbachev is allied.

With Saddam Hussein ruling in postwar Baghdad, the Soviet Union would be the only intermediary between him and enemies in Islam or the

A. M. Rosenthal, the former executive editor of *The New York Times*, is now a columnist for *The Times*. This piece, originally entitled "The Life of Saddam Hussein," appeared in *The Times* on February 22, 1991.

West. So without contributing a rifle or a ruble during the war, Mr. Gorbachev would influence the entire Middle East after the war.

But for the U.S.—no benefits, just trouble without end. As long as Saddam rules, the U.S. will have to keep large forces in the Middle East. The U.S. armed forces would be his hostage. Under Moscow's plan, Saddam would keep his army, planes, tanks and dictatorship. This is victory?

Every Arab nation that opposes him now would face his terrorism immediately, subversion always, domination eventually.

But his justification for existence would be the conquest and extermination of Israel and the Israelis. Americans like to think the Israeli army and air force can do anything. Maybe. But it took the full military and industrial power of the United States to face down the might of Iraq.

Saddam Hussein would live for the day when he would cross Jordan into Israel—by land, air or chemical missile. The Israelis would be fools if they sat and waited for him to come get them. They won't.

Now, for years President Bush and his secretary of state could not have been sweeter to Mr. Gorbachev. They praised him every hour on the hour, rounded up help for him. As for the Baltics—what Baltics?

But there goes President Gorbachev acting against American interests and any hope of a stable Mideast. The sorrow of it is we are surprised.

The "experts" in government, journalism and academia who made careers pandering to Mr. Gorbachev still talk of the danger of his being overthrown.

But the future is already the past. Mr. Gorbachev gave the Soviet Union an important measure of free expression—not free politics. But when he decided glasnost was endangering rather than promoting his goal of keeping the Soviet system alive, he cut back fast.

He was not pushed into it by "them"—some cabal of hard-nosed civilians and generals. He is them. Mr. Gorbachev has been overthrown already, by Mr. Gorbachev.

So the Soviet president finds it quite natural and appropriate to try to assert power in the Middle East.

The experts, including Mr. Bush and Secretary of State James Baker, never prepared Americans for that. They could not because they refused to see it themselves.

Washington talked itself into believing that Mr. Gorbachev was an essential partner in the new world order, whatever that is. But when Mr. Gorbachev moved, Washington was caught off guard. Then his new foreign minister contemptuously said it was not even Mr. Bush's business to reject the "peace plan"; a great partner.

But since the invasion of Kuwait, Mr. Bush has shown that he understands the danger of the killer of Baghdad. Perhaps Washington will look more clearly at the Kremlin now. Mr. Bush should tell the American people where U.S. interests conflict with Moscow's—as in the survival of Saddam Hussein. Then the logic and morality would be to keep up the air bombardment of Iraqi military targets until the dictator is finished and gone.

THE ULTIMATUM

(*Statement of February 22, 1991*)

George Bush

The following are transcripts of the February 22, 1991, statement made by President Bush in response to the Soviet peace proposal on the Persian Gulf, and a statement later by his spokesman Marlin Fitzwater.

T HE UNITED States and its coalition allies are committed to enforcing the United Nations resolutions that call for Saddam Hussein to immediately and unconditionally leave Kuwait.

In view of the Soviet initiative, which very frankly we appreciate, we want to set forth this morning the specific criteria that will insure Saddam Hussein complies with the United Nations mandate.

Within the last twenty-four hours alone, we have heard a defiant, uncompromising address by Saddam Hussein, followed less than ten hours later by a statement in Moscow that on the face of it appears more reasonable.

I say "on the face of it" because the statement promised unconditional Iraqi withdrawal from Kuwait, only to set forth a number of conditions, and needless to say, any conditions would be unacceptable to the international coalition and would not be in compliance with the United Nations Security Council resolution 660's demand for immediate and unconditional withdrawal.

More importantly and more urgently, we learned this morning that Saddam has now launched a scorched-earth policy against Kuwait, anticipating perhaps that he will now be forced to leave. He is wantonly setting fires to and destroying the oil wells, the oil tanks, the export terminals and other installations of that small country. Indeed, they are destroying the entire oil-production system of Kuwait. And at the same time that that Moscow press conference was going on and Iraq's foreign minister was talking peace, Saddam Hussein was launching Scud missiles.

After examining the Moscow statement and discussing it with my senior advisers here late last evening and this morning, and after extensive consultation with our coalition partners, I have decided that the time has come to make public with specificity just exactly what is required of Iraq if a ground war is to be avoided.

Most important, the coalition will give Saddam Hussein until noon Saturday to do what he must do—begin his immediate and unconditional withdrawal from Kuwait. We must hear publicly and authoritatively his acceptance of these terms.

The statement to be released, as you will see, does just this, and informs Saddam Hussein that he risks subjecting the Iraqi people to further hardship unless the Iraqi government complies fully with the terms of the statement. We will put that statement out soon. It will be in considerable detail, and that's all I'll have to say about it right now. Thank you very much.

CRITERIA FOR WITHDRAWAL

(Statement of February 22, 1991)

Marlin Fitzwater

FIRST, IRAQ must begin large-scale withdrawal from Kuwait by noon New York time, Saturday, February 23. Iraq must complete military withdrawal from Kuwait in one week. Given the fact that Iraq invaded and occupied Kuwait in a matter of hours, anything longer than this, from the initiation of the withdrawal, would not meet resolution 660's requirement of immediacy.

Within the first forty-eight hours, Iraq must remove all its forces from Kuwait City and allow for the prompt return of the legitimate government of Kuwait.

It must withdraw from all prepared defenses along the Saudi-Kuwait and Saudi-Iraq borders, from Bubiyan and Warba Islands, and from Kuwait's Rumaila oil field.

Within the one week specified above, Iraq must return all its forces to their positions of August 1 in accordance with resolution 660.

In cooperation with the International Red Cross, Iraq must release all prisoners of war and third-country civilians being held against their will and return the remains of killed and deceased servicemen.

This action must commence immediately with the initiation of the withdrawal and must be completed within forty-eight hours.

Iraq must remove all explosives or booby traps, including those on Kuwaiti oil installations, and designate Iraqi military liaison officers to work with Kuwaiti and other coalition forces on the operational details related to Iraq's withdrawal.

To conclude, the provision of—to include the provision of all data on the location and nature of any land or sea mines.

Iraq must cease combat air fire, aircraft flights over Iraq and Kuwait, except for transport aircraft carrying troops out of Kuwait, and allow coalition aircraft exclusive control over and use of all Kuwaiti airspace.

It must cease all destructive actions against Kuwaiti citizens and property and release all Kuwaiti detainees.

The United States and its coalition partners reiterate that their forces will not attack retreating Iraqi forces, and further will exercise restraint so long as withdrawal proceeds in accordance with the above guidelines and there are not attacks on other countries.

Any breach of these terms will bring an instant and sharp response from coalition forces in accordance with United Nations Security Council [resolution] 678.*

---

* Editors' note: Iraq did not comply with the U.S. ultimatum. The ground war began the night of February 23.

THE
FIRST CASUALTY

HOW THE MEDIA MISSED THE STORY

James Bennet

IT'S HARD to recall now that in the first days after Iraq invaded
Kuwait, sending any American troops—much less 430,000 of them—
to the Middle East never seemed inevitable. In fact, it didn't even seem
probable, since many lawmakers didn't like the idea. *The New York Times*
reported on August 3 that "Senator Sam Nunn . . . expressed the prevailing view on Capitol Hill when he said that the proper response
should be economic and political pressure and not military action."
When reports did discuss the possibility of military action, the emphasis
was always on air power, as in *The Washington Post* the following day:
" 'Carpet bombing is the phrase being used,' said one Pentagon official
familiar with the planning. . . . Military leaders have recommended
against sending U.S. ground forces to the Mideast." Why? Because "any
plan for using American troops on the ground in Saudi Arabia, Kuwait,
or Iraq chills military experts," explained a *Los Angeles Times* story on
August 5. "I think an economic boycott can be effective," said Caspar
Weinberger on *Nightline* the next day. "I think it would have to be backed
up by a naval blockade to be sure that that was working."

Even in the early hours of the deployment, there was more than a whiff
of potential disagreement over the type of force we should apply. *The
New York Times* again called on Nunn: " 'My hope is that we'll continue to
confine our role to protecting air bases and perhaps using American
troops to mine highways from Kuwait on which Iraq might send tanks
into Saudi Arabia, he said." But by the following day (same paper)
"congressional opinion swung solidly behind the president's action,"

James Bennet is an editor of *The Washington Monthly,* in whose December 1990 issue this article
originally appeared.

and none of the three national dailies mentioned above was able, evidently, to find someone to criticize either the president's goals or the means he'd chosen to achieve them—although forty percent of Americans disapproved of the deployment. Just two days before, the *Los Angeles Times* had explained that "Bush and his advisers are wary of any military option involving a confrontation with the Iraqi armed forces because they realize that it would run the risk of an enormous loss of life, not only of U.S. military personnel but also of U.S. civilians in the region." But now, and for the next crucial weeks of the buildup, the notion of "an enormous loss of life" almost vanished from that paper's pages.

You don't have to oppose the American troop deployment in the Middle East to worry about the singular absence of public debate—in the House and Senate, in the major papers, on TV—during those first few weeks. You just have to believe that good debate makes good policy. The initial deployment and its subsequent spectacular growth came as surprises: We progressed almost magically from a projected ceiling of 50,000 troops to nine times that number. Likewise, we faded from "The mission of our troops is wholly defensive" (George Bush's words) into trying "to ensure that the coalition has an adequate offensive military option" (George Bush's words). Meanwhile, the national dailies and *Nightline* provided blow-by-blow accounts and occasionally ran some tougher stories analyzing U.S. interests in the Persian Gulf and the president's goals—whether we were preparing to fight only for oil, whether it was feasible to push for Saddam Hussein's ouster. On the op-ed pages, there was some grumbling back and forth as to whether those goals were worth chasing. But there was almost no discussion in any of these influential, supposedly adversarial sources of news about the *means* the president had chosen and what human cost they'd entail.

For example, the *Post* editorialized in early September that all those American troops have to be in Saudi Arabia because "the circumstances in Iraq's case would make complaisance there intolerably costly. Suppose that the United States and the others had not sent troops and ships or shut off Iraq's trade." OK, let's suppose. If the *Post* had bothered to distinguish among those muddled alternatives, it might have found that they don't have to add up to "complaisance." Imagine that the U.S. had cut off Iraq's trade and, to contain Saddam (we were originally aiming for "wholly defensive" measures, remember), had sent ships and a) sent only a small "tripwire" force to Saudi Arabia, as other nations have done, or b) sent planes to Saudi Arabia, and only enough troops to protect them, since that nation has poor defenses. Or imagine that the U.S. had sent "no troops," but had relied on the naval embargo and on air power based on carriers and in Turkey, which has strong defenses of its own. It's easy if you try. For some reason, our national dailies and *Nightline* never did.

When Bush announced in early November that he was sending another 200,000 troops to the Gulf, the validity of the deployment—instead of the deployment itself—abruptly became news. Why were we risking so many lives? How could Bush be talking about taking the offensive? Congressmen were worried, columnists troubled, and reporters finally interested. But by then, we already had a quarter-million troops practicing offensive maneuvers in the desert who, according to the debate we were suddenly having, shouldn't have been there at all. Doing what many people now recognized was the right thing—reneging on Bush's new commitment and withdrawing some of the already deployed troops—would send dangerous signals to Saddam. As Al Haig, Henry Kissinger, and others pointed out, the horses had fled months before the press got excited about the idea of shutting the stable doors. Judging by a close reading of their coverage in the crucial first six weeks of the crisis, reporters for the *Los Angeles Times, The New York Times, The Washington Post,* and *Nightline* never asked the questions—Are any troops needed? If so, how many are enough? How many dead would be too many?—that would have jump started the national discussion that we at last began in November, maybe too late.

Of the three dailies, only one—the *Los Angeles Times*—published an editorial in the first six weeks that evaluated the size of the deployment. It's a doozy. "An anonymous Defense Department source is widely quoted as saying that contingency plans for the Persian Gulf could result in the insertion of up to 200,000 to 250,000 [U.S.] ground forces before it's all done," began the editorial on August 11. "These are sobering, not to say mind-boggling thoughts. Before they gain too much currency, it would be a good idea to freeze the frame and take a clear and realistic look at just what's being talked about." Ah, the omniscient voice of editorial reason, poised at last to tell it like it is. Read on:

> Predictions about world events are best avoided, especially in an area as volatile as the Gulf, but here's one anyway: Hundreds of thousands of American fighting men are not going to be put into the ferociously hostile environment of Saudi Arabia. That won't happen because (1) Congress would refuse to approve such a commitment; (2) the American people wouldn't support it; (3) the Saudis would not invite or tolerate it; (4) probably no senior military official would propose it;

and finally, (5) President Bush if for no other reason than that he faces re-election in 1992 would not request it.

Well. This is, of course, wrong. But that's not why it's so interesting. After all, the editorial writers weren't the only ones being suckered by the Bush administration, which planned to send a massive force from the very beginning of the deployment, according to reports published in *The New York Times* and the *Post* in late August—none of which noted that the press had been duped. On August 10 in *The New York Times*, R. W. Apple wrote of the estimate of 250,000 troops, "One of the handful of senior policy planners in the administration described that figure as preposterous." On the same day in the same paper, Michael Gordon pooh-poohed the idea of even 200,000. (The failure to take a more critical look at these numbers is surprising given that many of the same reporters had bought the fallacious "carpet-bombing" line at the beginning of the crisis. Gordon seemed to be expressing some frustration when he wrote the next day, after the official deployment figure had doubled almost overnight to 100,000: "The increased figure seemed less a reflection of a change in the Administration's plans, or its evaluation of the Iraqi threat, than a willingness among officials to discuss the size of the force with greater candor.")

The reason the editorial is interesting is that it hinted rather broadly that the *Los Angeles Times* thought a massive deployment of ground forces would be a lousy idea. In fact, it went on to urge, "Bush and his advisers ought to be making clear that the Arabian oil fields can be defended without involving American troops in an open-ended land war in the Persian Gulf. *The key to defending Saudi Arabia and nearby smaller states is air and naval power.*" [Italics added.] If Bush doesn't come clean, American support could "fade very quickly under the impact of horror stories suggesting that 250,000 American troops could be sent to fight a long and brutal desert war."

On August 22, the *Los Angeles Times* reported that the deployment "could grow to as many as 150,000 personnel." On September 3, it reported the force could grow to more than 200,000. Those new figures seem sufficient grounds for the editorial board to have revisited its earlier argument, either to announce that it had changed its collective mind or to attack the president's policy and push the air-and-naval-power alternative. The *L.A. Times* did neither. No *L.A. Times* reporter wrote a story critiquing the buildup or exploring other options (on the *Times* op-ed page—which did a much better job than the other papers in presenting a range of views—Edward Luttwak of the Center for Strategic and International Studies twice slammed the Bush approach). The other newspapers didn't pursue that story either. As late as September 12, *Nightline* managed to do an entire program dedicated to "A Critical Look at U.S. Persian Gulf Policy" that focused on the boycott and never critiqued the troop deployment.

In early September, the *Los Angeles Times* praised Bush for his "reasonableness" and "willingness to listen," and for "the George Bush style—on the slow side, on the cautious side, on the consensus side, on the pragmatic side." This about a man whose staff had misled the paper's reporters; who had made a monumental decision affecting the nation's future based on the advice of a handful of advisers; and who was pursuing a policy that the paper had called a "horror." Talk about appeasement.

O N N O V E M B E R 8, after the elections and while Congress was in recess, the consensus-building, slow and cautious Bush made the announcement that he was adding another 200,000 troops to beef up our offensive capability in the Middle East. That evening, Ted Koppel expressed some confusion: "I have a sense that we have taken sort of a major step forward from being . . . in a defensive posture to avoid an invasion of Saudi Arabia, to moving into a totally different kind of posture."

This shouldn't have come as such a shock, since for more than two months the nation's top dailies and *Nightline* had been running news that suggested American forces were preparing to attack, not only defend. Just as *Nightline* and the three papers never pointed out that the official size of the deployment was steadily ratcheting upward, none of them firmly came to grips with the fact that the initial line that the U.S. had deployed its forces for "wholly defensive" purposes had been crumbling from the get-go. *The New York Times,* at least, asserted in an editorial that "unilateral American military action may ultimately prove necessary." But in the first month and a half of the crisis, *The Washington Post* never went beyond endorsing defensive measures, and the *Los Angeles Times* declared, "Senator Sam Nunn . . . puts the issue clearly, leanly, and correctly: 'Our military mission is to defend Saudi Arabia.' Let's keep that in mind." Yet these papers never sounded the alarm as the true goals of the deployment became obvious.

There were clues everywhere that the mission was growing far beyond mere defense—clues like "In the early morning hours . . . troops practice offensive maneuvers" (*The Washington Post,* September 6); "Hostilities could also begin from the U.S. side" (*Los Angeles Times,* August 25);

"The question here has shifted from how well the United States and its allies would defend the Saudi kingdom to how well Washington and its allies might exercise an 'offensive option' to push the Iraqis out of Kuwait" (*The New York Times,* September 16); "The only thing keeping that [offensive readiness] from happening is the arrival of big U.S. equipment, particularly the M-1 tanks which are aboard these fast sealift ships and begin arriving next week" (*Nightline,* August 24). I could find no article in any of the newspapers and no discussion on *Nightline* that pulled the pieces together—the excessive numbers of troops, the offensive maneuvers the troops were practicing—into a description of what the administration was really up to.

On August 29, on *Nightline,* Dick Cheney told Sam Donaldson, "Well, again we'll come back to the proposition that our dispositions in the region are defensive. We're there to deter and to defend. . . . but we're not there in an offensive capacity, we're not there threatening Iraq." Those M-1 tanks slipped Donaldson's mind, evidently, since he didn't pursue the issue. Koppel's astonishment on November 8 was no doubt feigned, but he was making an important point: No one (including Koppel) had been telling the average American that it was part of U.S. policy to prepare to launch an attack. That was a strategy, by the way, that a majority of Americans opposed.

The closest anyone came, in the words of the *Los Angeles Times* editorial, to freezing the frame and taking a clear and realistic look at just what was going on was Michael Wines of *The New York Times,* who kicked off an August 19 story with this promising lead: "In only fifteen days, while Congress was scattered on summer recess and much of official Washington was on vacation, senior Bush administration officials have committed the United States to its broadest and most hazardous overseas military venture since the Vietnam war." Wines went on to point out that the administration had "deliberately kept vague" the length of the military commitment as well as the projected size of the force. He quoted Senator John McCain opposing the idea of a ground war, thereby—virtually for the first time among the three publications—introducing the concept of death into an analysis of the deployment: " 'We cannot even contemplate, in my view, trading American blood for Iraqi blood.' " And Wines quoted a dazed-sounding Senator Joe Biden on the dimensions of the force, saying he was "struck by the size of this. This is a big, big deal. . . . I never contemplated talk of 250,000 troops." There should be, Biden said, "not only some consultation, but some extensive debate."

But Wines came to the conclusion that since massive deployment was inevitable, we might as well lie back and enjoy it: "In the atmosphere of crisis, there is no evidence that extensive debate or consultations would have changed the American commitment in any way." He pointed out that "the pivotal decisions have been made by Mr. Bush and a handful of his top advisers," but offered this astonishing reassurance to those, like Biden, who worried about the absence of public discussion: "As the Vietnam experience proved, public debate and congressional action do not guarantee wise policymaking, several Bush administration officials and former government officials from the 1960s said in interviews."

When the United States first sent ground forces to Vietnam in March 1965, "You had overwhelming support in the public and the press," says Stanley Karnow, author of *Vietnam: A History.* "It's very hard to think of anyone—besides Izzy Stone—who objected." At the crucial moment in 1965, there was almost no dissent within the administration (Maxwell Taylor was the exception). Nearly eighty percent of Americans favored the move—partly because they didn't understand what it would entail, since Lyndon Johnson's spokesmen were pursuing "a policy of minimum candor." Sound familiar? The questions—What are we fighting for?—and the debate started when Americans began dying. If you believe that the United States should have fought the Vietnam war indefinitely, then you might consider that debate to have been unwise. Otherwise, you might wish it had started a little sooner.

A S   T H E Vietnam War progressed, Karnow argues, the press tended to trail public opinion, not the reverse. Johnson, watching Walter Cronkite report on the Tet Offensive, declared Cronkite would turn public support against the war. But by Tet, more Americans already were against the war than for it. Somehow, that news hadn't percolated up: "It was kind of like a wind tunnel, you know, with the press and the politicians talking to each other and not listening to anyone else," says Karnow. "Sort of like today, I guess."

Because no one pieced together the president's actual policy toward Iraq, throughout the first couple of weeks of the crisis the nation's leading newspapers couldn't help but overstate American support for the deployment. As the *Los Angeles Times* editorial quoted at length above makes clear, even Americans who closely followed the news (in fact, especially them, according to the polls) were tripping over each other to line up in support of a policy that was in fact not the one we were practicing. The pollsters were asking, as in a CBS News survey: "Do you approve of George Bush's decision to send U.S. troops to Saudi Arabia?" They weren't asking whether Americans approved of sending *250,000 of them* to Saudi Arabia. Robert Shogan of the *Los Angeles Times* was one of very few journalists to make this elementary distinction. On August 19, he wrote, "Bush enjoys overwhelming public support for his decision to send U.S. troops . . . but he does not have a blank check." (*Nightline* for the most part didn't concern itself with public opinion, although Representative Les Aspin did point out on the August 17 broadcast that "there is not, at this point, public support for using our military to invade Kuwait or to invade Iraq.")

Even taking the early poll results at face value, journalists—not just editorial writers or the flocks of hawkish columnists—repeatedly overstated the results. As late as August 24, by which time the size of the deployment and its offensive potential were becoming clear, E. J. Dionne led a story in the *Post* with: "After several weeks of nearly unanimous public support for President Bush's moves in the Middle East. . . ." The paper's own poll of August 10 had reported that, while most Americans support the president's "initial response," they "view the prospect of U.S. military engagement in the Middle East with a mix of skepticism, frustration, confusion, and outright fear." Sixty-eight percent said that the United States should not go on the offensive to liberate Kuwait. A *New York Times* poll published August 12 found that forty percent of Americans thought Bush was "too quick to send troops." In another *Times* poll conducted over a week later, that forty percent figure still held. By most standards, sixty percent doesn't qualify as "nearly unanimous support."

What Dionne probably meant is that support seemed unanimous among "opinion leaders"—that is, the people top journalists interview. His story featured those opinion leaders—what he called "small minorities on the left and the right"—who were "beginning" to dissent from the president's policy: Patrick Buchanan, Thomas Bethell, Ramsey Clark (all of whom dissented from the start). As another example, consider a story by Andrew Malcolm that ran in *The New York Times* on August 21. The teaser on the front page read, in part, "Little Dissent in U.S.: If war is in the offing, few Americans are voicing opposition." The headline declared: FEW FROM LEFT OR RIGHT PROTEST BUSH'S BIG STICK. "So far," wrote Malcolm, "the critics of American military involvement in Saudi Arabia have been few and soft-spoken." It quickly becomes obvious that the piece is not about "Americans" in general but about a certain type of American: opinion leaders, like Buchanan, Walter Mondale, Coretta Scott King, William Sloane Coffin, Jr. And in fact in the course of the story these people voice quite a bit of dissent, arguing in general for deterrence and a negotiated settlement—a policy drastically different from the one Bush was implementing.

It's at the bottom of the story, however, that we discover what "little dissent" really means, when Malcolm refers to the *Times* poll and dials up a couple of Americans with unfamiliar names. "Forty percent [of those polled] said the administration was too quick to send in the military and only forty-eight percent felt the government had tried hard enough to reach a diplomatic solution. . . . Deborah Huber, a twenty-one-year-old housewife in Wichita, Kansas, was among those in the poll with doubts. 'This is really hitting home for us,' she said in a subsequent interview. 'My husband's brother, David, is being shipped over on the twenty-fourth this month.' "

When it comes to matters of war and peace, the troubled Mrs. Huber is what *The New York Times* would call "unsophisticated." In an August 12 editorial, the *Times* assessed the president's efforts to rally support to his cause. Though Bush had demonstrated he was "a superb crisis manager," as a communicator he was stumbling. "A *New York Times* poll shows that while most Americans endorse the president's action, half do not comprehend the dangers. . . . Why must the U.S. again bear a disproportionate share of the burden of defending oil . . . ?" The *Times* understands, but too many Americans don't: "Sophisticated citizens know how much the world depends on Saudi oil. It's up to the occupant of the bully pulpit to educate ordinary citizens, including parents of those G.I.'s, to these harsh realities." In other words, the views of the Mrs. Hubers are supposed to be changed, not taken into account.

THAT EDITORIAL expresses an attitude that is certainly one source of the newspapers' repeated failure to give serious consideration to the opinions of the silenced forty percent. The attitude is summed up by the opposition of "sophisticated citizens" and "ordinary citizens, including parents of those G.I.'s." Editorial writers and reporters and the talking heads they interview are too sophisticated to have children in danger of being gassed, shot, or blown up. Although by November others were waking up to that issue, in the first six weeks of the deployment, of all the columnists—hawks and doves—venting their opinions on the crisis day after day on the national op-ed pages, only one—Mark Shields—raised it.

One day in August the celebrated op-ed by Alex Molnar, a marine's father who didn't think the president's goals in the Gulf were worth dying for, appeared shoulder-to-shoulder with, of all columns, one by A. M. Rosenthal, a leading hawk. It's interesting to compare their tones. Molnar: "I kissed my son goodbye today. . . . You have ordered him to Saudi Arabia." Rosenthal: "The likelihood is that Americans will die in the Middle East. . . . In decency to them and the people of the Middle East and in pressing self-interest, the United States must now think through and make clear two connected sets of war goals. . . . Saddam may still be able to kill thousands." If Molnar's tone struck many as melodramatic (and letters to the editor suggest that it did), Rosenthal's struck at least me as astonishingly breezy. The op-ed hawks purported to make their arguments out of common sense. The party line, as Rosenthal expressed it, was that "if Saddam is allowed to keep the missiles, poison chemicals, and nuclear potential . . . then one day he will murder far more people." The math is compelling, but it totally ignores—as almost all these columnists did—the possibility that other means than a ground war might accomplish the same ends. Without the pressure of knowing that your son or your brother-in-law could be among the "thousands," it becomes easier to overlook the "unsophisticated" question: "Couldn't there be a better way to do this?"

How else can you explain the total lack of interest the newspapers and *Nightline* expressed in the number of soldiers who might die? During the first weeks of the crisis, reporters occasionally referred to the prospective conflict as "bloody" or noted that "thousands" might be killed, but no one explored the question of what the war would actually look like. There were some clues, however. A doctor called up from the reserves told the *Los Angeles Times*, "There may never be another opportunity for me to see trauma cases like this." Without comment on page twenty-two, *The Washington Post* reported this chilling detail: "The department [of Veterans Affairs] has notified the Pentagon that it could make 9,200 [hospital] beds available within twenty-four hours, 18,321 within seventy-two hours and 25,000 within a month."

When thirteen American servicemen died in a plane crash in West Germany, the *Post* headline read: CRASH OF GULF-BOUND JET REVIVES GERMAN FEARS. The story ran on page thirty-three. Later, the *Post* did a longer piece on the families of the dead, offering this observation, "Treatment of the crash has been somewhat muted, partly because of uncertainty about whether the thirteen victims will become only an early and forgotten footnote in a much larger conflagration and perhaps partly because they did not die in the deserts of the Mideast." *The New York Times* ran about two inches of an inaccurate AP story: "Ten Die in Transport Jet Crash."

On September 5, Joshua Epstein, a Brookings Institution military analyst, held a press conference at which he presented a model that projected the number of divisions the United States would lose if it attacked Iraq. The *Los Angeles Times* wrote it up in a short piece at the foot of page six. The reporter asked government analysts to translate the division numbers into human terms: "They said Epstein's model implies that American and Saudi forces would suffer casualties of 32,000 to 48,000 troops." Hmmm . . . 48,000 . . . hey—that's close to one-quarter as many as we suffered in the whole Vietnam War! And Epstein predicted that a Mideast war would be over in *one month*. Seem like important news? Well, you probably never heard about it, because nobody else touched the story.

Also on September 5, CNN's *Crossfire* featured Richard Lugar and Les Aspin. Michael Kinsley pressed both guests to answer the question: "Is it worth 20,000 to 30,000 American casualties to get Saddam Hussein?" Both men—the chairman of the House Armed Services Committee and the ranking Republican on the Senate Foreign Relations Committee— said yes. Just for the record, here was Lugar's justification: "Finally we will come down to the point that if he exists and we're left out there in Saudi Arabia with our forces hunkered down, forever monitoring the situation, the casualties over the course of time will be greater or the loss of our national prestige and the whole world order will collapse in the process."

No newspaper or TV show picked up the story.

According to John Mueller, author of *War, Presidents and Public Opinion,* during the Korean and Vietnam wars, as casualties climbed from 100 to 1,000, support for the war dropped by fifteen percentage points; as casualties rose from 1,000 to 10,000, support decreased by another fifteen points. What would happen if U.S. forces suffered 20,000 casualties in the Middle East in a month-long war? "That would be catastrophic," he says. "That would be vastly more than were suffered in Korea in the first year. . . . I can even imagine impeachment." Unfortunately, like most journalists, pollsters haven't asked questions like, "Is it worth 20,000 to 30,000 casualties to get Saddam Hussein?"

THE REPORTERS who write "news analyses"—those who are supposed to bring a knowledge of history and a sense of proportion to bear on the news—are the ones who most let their readers down in the early weeks of the crisis. Generally based in Washington, these reporters tend to be those called on by the television talk shows to analyze events. Without exception in the first weeks, their analyses focused on the politics of the deployment and the view from D.C.: Could any cracks form in the president's domestic or international support? Does Scowcroft or Baker have the president's ear? What are the scenarios the military planners and armchair analysts think might be played out? Perhaps because these reporters don't have sand under their fingernails and some sense for which machines work, you never found yourself reading an authoritative analysis of the wisdom of the administration's *means.*

Nightline lagged far behind the print journals in this department. While the U.S. was in the first stages of building up its forces, ABC deployed Sam Donaldson to the Gulf, from where he was asked by the show's host, Jack Smith, if Iraqis really believed they could outfight Americans. "It's bluster, Jack," declared Donaldson. "The United States conventional forces are such that once they are brought to bear in this area, all of them —the sea power that we are amassing, the land power—B-52s, as you know, can come from Diego Garcia and elsewhere—we could, with conventional forces, level Iraq. I think there's no question about that."

The newspapers were a bit more thorough. At times, they served up analytical pieces on the president's goals like the ones Thomas Friedman of *The New York Times* produced in the early days of the crisis that aggressively compared the administration's rhetoric with our real, historical interests in the region. But more typical were pieces that suggested that the photos of aircraft carriers and tanks and the president's angry rhetoric had caused their writers to lose a little perspective, like this chest-thumping, navel-gazing August 20 "news analysis" by R. W. Apple: "The obituaries were a bit premature. There is still one superpower in the world, and it is the United States. . . . There is a rush of excitement in the air here. In news bureaus and Pentagon offices, dining rooms, and lobbyists' hangouts, the fever is back—the heavy speculation, the avid gossip, the gung-ho, here's-where-it's-happening spirit, that marks the city when it grapples with great events." Or when it grapples with itself.

A S I D E   F R O M journalists' lack of personal risk in a potential conflict, there are undoubtedly a number of reasons why stories appraising the size and strategy of the deployment didn't get written. For one thing, daily journalists rely on politicians to criticize other politicians' policies, and few in Congress had the guts to do that. For another, journalists can be patriots, too, and may have felt a duty to support the president's policy (whatever it was). On *Nightline,* Koppel and Barbara Walters invoked the administrative "we" in interviewing the Iraqi ambassador, and the *Los Angeles Times* editorialized on August 27 that it would be "bad policy" for Congress and the White House to start "quarreling over U.S. policy in the Middle East." Furthermore, criticizing the deployment could put you at some risk, since charges of "dual loyalty" (by Richard Cohen), "second guessing . . . to encourage Saddam" (by Jim Hoagland), "anti-Semitism" (Rosenthal), being "for Saddam" (William

Safire), and "appeasement" (just about everyone) were flying thick and fast. But whatever the reason, the "adversarial" press spawned by Vietnam let us down. The president's policy, right or wrong, left plenty of room for debate, and that room simply wasn't filled. When politicians close ranks behind a military action, journalists must have the intellectual independence and imagination to supply the critical counterweight on their own. If not, Americans will continue, over and over again, to find themselves crying over spilt blood.

On *Nightline* on November 8, Koppel discussed with his old mentor, Henry Kissinger, Bush's decision to double the size of the American forces in Saudi Arabia. After fielding several questions about the wisdom of the government's action, Kissinger grumpily observed, "America seems to specialize into putting 300,000 or more troops somewhere and afterwards starting to debate how important that is."

Koppel shot back: "Well, that's because there was never any opportunity to have a debate beforehand."

Later, Kissinger backpedaled a bit: "I'm not saying that shouldn't be —no, I'm not saying we shouldn't have a debate, but I'm saying that the debate must take into account what has already happened."

Koppel: "But what has already happened has happened without the benefit of the debate, that's precisely the point."

And whose fault, Ted, is that?

A MUZZLE FOR THE PRESS

Sydney H. Schanberg

"THIS WILL not be another Vietnam." That oft-repeated pledge by President Bush is his maxim for the war in the Persian Gulf. He and his men leave no doubt as to what it means, for they quickly explain that this time our troops will not have "their hands tied behind their backs." But there's an addendum to that promise which, though clear from the administration's acts, has not been spoken: "This time, the hands of the press will be tied."

So far it would appear from polls and general reaction that a lot of Americans are not displeased by the government's handcuffing of the press. We journalists are not a very popular bunch. Some people see us as whiny and self-important, and some even see us as unpatriotic because we take it upon ourselves to challenge and question the government in difficult times like these. I can't say we haven't invited some of this disapproval through occasional lapses from professionalism. But I don't think this suggests we should hunker down timidly now and wait for our ratings to rise. We are required to be responsible, not popular.

Let's look at what the administration has done to control and manipulate press coverage of this war and why it has done it.

First, the why. This is easy. The answer is Vietnam. Many politicians and senior military men cling tenaciously to the myth that the press, through pessimistic reporting, tipped public opinion and cost us the war in Vietnam. There's no factual support for this theory, but scapegoats

Sydney H. Schanberg, a columnist for *New York Newsday,* won a 1976 Pulitzer Prize for his coverage of the fall of Cambodia. His book on Cambodia became the basis of the movie *The Killing Fields.* His article was published, under the title "Censoring for Political Security," in the March 1991 issue of the *Washington Journalism Review.*

are useful when the historical evidence is painful. And that evidence suggests that a misguided and ill-conceived policy got America bogged down in a foreign war where the national interest was not fundamentally at stake. Eventually the public grew disheartened over the gap between the promises of success the White House kept making and the actuality of failure. Our losses, human and material, were what tipped public opinion.

This time around the White House isn't taking any chances. All reporters in the American portion of the Gulf war zone have to operate under a system of controls that goes far beyond anything imposed in any other modern war—unless you include Grenada and Panama, where reporters were essentially kept away from the action. Those were the dress rehearsals for the press muzzling in the Gulf—test runs, so to speak, to see if either the public or major news organizations would raise much of an outcry (they didn't).

The new controls go like this. To begin with, there is a list of security guidelines laying down the categories of sensitive military information (details of future operations, specifics on troop units, etc.) that the press cannot report because it might jeopardize American or Allied lives. No reporter has any objection to these restrictions. They are essentially the same ground rules the press abided by in World War II, Korea and Vietnam.

It's what has been added to these traditional ground rules, however, that constitutes the muzzle. First, the only way a reporter can visit a front-line unit is by qualifying for the "pool" system, whereby a handful of reporters represents the entire press corps and shares the story with everybody. Only a fraction of the reporters, mostly those from the largest news organizations, can qualify for the pools. The rest are permitted to forage on their own, doing rear-echelon stories, but the rules forbid them to go to the forward areas and warn that if they make the attempt they will be "excluded"—taken into custody and shipped back. (By February 12, as this article went to press, at least two dozen journalists had been detained in this fashion. In some cases their credentials were lifted, though returned later. One reporter, Chris Hedges of *The New York Times,* was grabbed and decredentialized by the American military for conducting what it termed "unauthorized" interviews without an escort. He had been interviewing Saudi shopkeepers along a road 50 miles from the Kuwaiti border.)

It gets worse. Though the pool reporters are allowed at the front, their visits are anything but spontaneous. The pools get taken only where the military decides to take them. They are accompanied at all times by an escort officer, even when interviewing troops, which means that truth and candor on the part of the interviewees often become instant casualties. When a pool gets back from its guided visit, all stories and footage must be submitted to a "security review"—a euphemism for censorship.

Of the two controls—the pool system and the review of stories for possible security violations—it is the former that is the more odious, for this is tantamount to prior restraint. If reporters can go only where their babysitters decide to take them and can stay only a short time, they have already been subjected to the ultimate censorship. Since they've been allowed to see nothing, what possible "secrets" can they be carrying? The system has worked all too well. The press has been crippled, rendered unable to provide the public with a credible picture of what war is like in all its guises. What has been delivered to the public instead are superficial brush strokes across the sanitized surface of war. Bombs fall remotely and perfectly, and no one seems to be bleeding.

The "security review" at the end of the pool process merely applies the final, harassing, delaying, cosmeticizing touches on the information and completes the subjugation of the press corps and, by extension, the public. In a typical incident, one of the censors had a problem with the word "giddy," the use of which he decided was a breach of military security. Fred Bruni of the *Detroit Free Press* had used the word to describe some young Stealth bomber pilots who were buoyant as they returned from their first combat mission. Without consulting Bruni, the censor changed "giddy" to "proud." No reality, please, not even when it's innocuous. When Bruni noticed the change, he protested and got the censor to accept "pumped up." Then the military, giving no reason, held the story for two days before sending it to the Detroit paper.

As anyone can see, the security issue is almost entirely a red herring. With very rare exceptions, the press has never breached any of the security rules—not in World War II, not in Korea and not in Vietnam. Barry Zorthian, who was the official spokesman for the United States Mission in Saigon from 1964 to 1968, said recently that though roughly 2,000 correspondents were accredited to cover Vietnam in those years and hundreds of thousands of stories were filed, only five or six violations of the security guidelines occurred. He recalled most of these as accidental or based on misunderstanding. To his knowledge, he said, none of them actually jeopardized any military operations or the lives of personnel.

Henry Kissinger, who has certainly shown no tolerance for press criticism, was asked on television the other day whether he could recall even one journalist breaching security in Vietnam. He replied: "I can think of

some reporting that jeopardized national security, but none in the field."
The reports he referred to were leaks out of Washington.

So it's all too clear that the current restrictions have nothing to do with
military security and everything to do with political security. Political
security requires that the government do as complete a job as possible at
blacking out stories that might lead to embarrassment or criticism of the
government or to questions from ordinary Americans about the war
policy. The press controls in the Gulf are preemptive strikes against the
possibility of such stories coming from the front.

But the control and manipulation of information has done something
else, too. It has debased the press.

Privately, some government officials have tried to justify the restraints
as a necessary counter-tactic against Saddam Hussein's strategy—i.e.,
his presumed belief that a prolonged war with steady casualties will
erode public support of the president. But a president who is seen to be
withholding information is also likely to lose public support over time. It
may sound corny, but our democracy relies on openness for its strength.
It's a messy system, often inefficient and clumsy, but it functions because
the public is included, not kept in the dark. It's worth reminding ourselves that the most supremely efficient systems in the world are dictatorships where the press is completely controlled.

When George Bush decided he wasn't going to let the press have a
front-row seat for this war, he was deciding against the public—even
though at this point many Americans not only seem unaware they're
being deprived of anything important to their lives but have even applauded the president's quarantining of the press. Again, the press can't
sit around chewing its nails over its popularity ratings. For better or
worse, with all of our fallibilities, we are the only professional independent witnesses who have an established role in our system. And we can't
abdicate that role, even if the public at some given moment in time
doesn't want to hear what we have witnessed.

As I write, more than 800 journalists have been accredited by the
military in Saudi Arabia, roughly eighty percent of them Americans or
working for American news organizations. Only about 125 have been
allowed into the pools. The rest can do other reporting but are officially
banned from the front lines. The press guidelines say: "News media
personnel who are not members of the official CENTCOM media pools
will not be permitted into forward areas. . . . U.S. commanders will
maintain extremely tight security throughout the operational areas and
will exclude from the area of operation all unauthorized individuals."

When a reporter at a Pentagon briefing asked if this meant that commanders had received an "operational order to detain reporters who show up unescorted out in the battlefield and remove them to the rear," the Pentagon spokesman, Pete Williams, replied: "There is a general order right now."

Contrast this with World War II, when General Dwight Eisenhower issued a quite different order, directing all unit commanders of the Allied Expeditionary Force to give correspondents "the greatest possible latitude in the gathering of legitimate news." The order went on: "They should be allowed to talk freely with officers and enlisted personnel and to see the machinery of war in operation in order to visualize and transmit to the public the conditions under which the men from their countries are waging war against the enemy."

Eisenhower's order went out on May 11, 1944, just before D-day. This makes the comparison with World War II even more appropriate, because President Bush and his men, in trying to erase the Vietnam image, have called upon Americans to think of the Gulf war as D-day at Normandy. Fine, Mr. President, call this war what you like, but please remember that American journalists were allowed to hit the Normandy beaches alongside the troops. And there were no Pentagon babysitters with them.

Also unlike World War II (and Korea and Vietnam), reporters are not being assigned to units and permitted to stay with them for extended periods. They're not even being allowed to fly on bombing missions in those planes where there is room. One such plane is the eight-engine B-52 Stratofortress. It flies in formations of three, each carrying roughly thirty tons of bombs. Such bombloads inflict a tremendous pounding over a wide area, and are usually directed at troop concentrations rather than buildings and installations. Military briefers in Vietnam called it carpet bombing, but the briefers in this war have bridled when reporters have used the phrase. Apparently carpet bombing has a harsh sound and must be deodorized.

In fact, there's a concerted attempt to try to edit out all reminders of Vietnam. It's hard to believe, but the Pentagon has gone so far as prohibiting the filming, or any news coverage at all, of the arrival of war dead at Dover Air Force Base, the main military mortuary. So much for the contention that the press restrictions are necessary for security reasons.

It's not that I don't understand the thinking behind the restrictions. There's hardly a government extant, ours or anyone else's, that wants people not under its control traveling to the front and witnessing a war and then telling everybody else about it—especially telling and showing the terribleness of war. Because the government fears that the terrible images might shape people's opinions.

This doesn't mean our politicians and generals are telling us a pack of lies. Not at all. They're just not telling us anything approaching a complete story. That's not their job as they perceive it. But it is the job of an independent press.

Which brings us, finally, to the issue of what the press has been doing for itself to try to reverse the new restraints. Darned little, sadly.

The break with this country's tradition of relatively open access to military operations began in Grenada in October 1983, when the Reagan White House kept the press out until the fighting was over. The major news organizations complained. To quiet us, the White House and Pentagon threw us a bone—the odious pool system. Oddly, we took it with barely a whimper. Then, on the first test of the system—the 1989 Panama invasion—pool reporters were barred from observing the military engagement all through the first and decisive day of fighting. The rest of the press corps, 500 strong, was virtually interned on a military base, even during the aftermath of the combat. As a result, we still have only the sketchiest picture of what took place and how many civilians and soldiers were killed.

And now we have our sanitized coverage of the war with Iraq. When the consequences of the press controls became obvious during the troop buildup prior to the war, a lawsuit was filed on January 10 in federal court in New York to overturn the restrictions on constitutional grounds. It was prepared by the Center for Constitutional Rights, an established civil liberties group, on behalf of 11 news organizations and five writers. The news organizations are for the most part small, liberal, alternative publications—*The Nation, In These Times, Mother Jones, L.A. Weekly, The Progressive, Texas Observer, The Guardian* and *The Village Voice*—plus *Harper's,* Pacifica Radio, Pacific News Service and writers E.L. Doctorow, William Styron, Michael Klare, Scott Armstrong and myself. Agence France-Presse, the French news agency, having been excluded from the press pool, has filed a companion suit.

All the major media organizations were aware of the lawsuit before it was filed, yet as I write, not one has joined it. The suit is about prior restraint of information, a constitutional issue that normally sets the television networks and leading newspapers into instant legal motion. I truly hope they will find their voices soon.

How to explain their inaction now? It's my belief that the press is still living with its own scars from Vietnam. And Watergate. We were accused, mostly by ideologues, of being less than patriotic, of bringing down a presidency, of therefore not being on the American team. And as a professional community we grew timid, worried about offending the political establishment. And that establishment, sensing we had gone under the blankets, moved in to tame us in a big and permanent way. These new press controls are, for me, a reflection of that move.

In late January CBS asked me to appear on "America Tonight" for a program on the press controls. Pete Williams, the Pentagon spokesman, agreed to appear opposite me, which created the potential for a good debate. Then the program's producer called. He said they had to dis-invite me because Williams had called back to say the Pentagon's chief counsel had ruled that no Pentagon official could appear with anyone associated with the lawsuit.

The producer explained: "Our feeling was, after much deliberation and discussion, that we felt there was greater value in getting the Pentagon spokesman on and confronting him and pressing him on the air than it was to get you on without the Pentagon. You can understand our position, can't you?"

I said yes, I understood it intellectually, but had he thought about the example, or even precedent, that CBS was setting? Here was CBS, arranging a program about press controls, and what does the network do? It agrees to accept government control over the selection of the other guest.

I asked the producer if he would open the program with an explanation to the viewers about how the participants got selected (Morley Safer was going on in my stead). The producer said he would raise the issue at the network. Then, a couple of hours later, he called to say they had cancelled the whole show and were instead going to use the time slot to do a straight news program on the Gulf war.

Some of you may wonder why you haven't heard more about the lawsuit before this. It's because, shamefully, Big Media have not only ducked the lawsuit, they have, by and large, failed to report it. For example, *The New York Times*, at this writing, has mentioned it only once, in two paragraphs at the end of a long piece out of Riyadh. Coverage in the rest of the major media has been almost as sparse. I hope this doesn't mean what it looks like.

That *Times* story, incidentally, said the press was chafing under the controls and that the military had been making vague promises about relaxing them. But the piece ended by saying that despite such talk, "there was no sign of change here."

How do the large news organizations explain their failure to do more than have meetings with, and send letters to, the Pentagon asking that the rules be softened—especially since the constant response is that the government isn't budging?

Floyd Abrams, a leading First Amendment lawyer who has become an unofficial legal spokesman for the establishment media, told the *New York Law Journal* that the leading news companies may have been reluctant to join the lawsuit because "there is a difficulty in prevailing in a facial challenge to the rules in the early days of the war." Does this mean they'll find their courage only if the war drags on and public opposition grows and then the media will run less risk of being called unpatriotic?

In the same *Law Journal* article, an in-house attorney at *The Times,* George Freeman, said: "We prefer to deal directly with the Pentagon during time of war rather than by what is a more protracted and adversarial way." That sentence speaks volumes about the independence of the press.

The lawsuit, boiled down, says the government's press controls are violative of the Constitution as regards freedom of the press and equal protection of the law. The relief it asks for is a return to the press ground rules of Vietnam, meaning voluntary observance of security rules and freedom of movement and access. The suit is not an anti-war document. Nor do I see it as a hostile act against our political and military leaders.

I see it, instead, as a necessary instrument of leverage which seeks to persuade the government that the suppression of information, for reasons other than national security or protecting the safety of our troops, is a departure from our traditions that will in the end corrode and weaken the public trust that presidents crucially need to govern.

This is no time for the press to cover a desert war by putting its head in the sand.

FREE TO REPORT WHAT
WE'RE TOLD

Robert Fisk

A COLONEL commanding an American air base in the Gulf last week decided to honor the pool reporters who had been attached to his fighter-bomber squadrons since the day the war broke out. He produced for each of them a small American flag which, he said, had been carried in the cockpits of the very first U.S. jets to bomb Baghdad. "You are warriors, too," he told the journalists as he handed them their flags.

The incident said a lot about the new, cosy, damaging relationship between reporters and the military in the Gulf war. So thorough has been the preparation for this war, so dependent have journalists become upon information dispensed by the Western military authorities in Saudi Arabia, so enamored of their technology, that press and television reporters have found themselves trapped.

For most journalists in the Gulf—and most of the Western armies—war is an unknown quantity, exciting as well as frightening, historic as well as deadly. The notion that this is a "just" war, a struggle between good and evil (as Messrs. Runcie and Bush would, respectively, have us believe) has presented us with a moral pretext for our presence. If Saddam Hussein is the Hitler of Baghdad—worse than Hitler in President Bush's flawed historical analysis—then it was inevitable that our reporting would acquire an undertone of righteousness, even romanticism.

As RAF fighter pilots took off from a Gulf airstrip a week ago, a young British reporter told her television audience that "their bravery knows no bounds." When ten U.S. Navy jets took off from the aircraft carrier

Robert Fisk is Middle East correspondent for *The* [London] *Independent* and the author of *Pity the Nation.* This article was published in the February 4, 1991, issue of *The Independent.*

USS *Kennedy* at the start of the war—in a campaign that we now know is also causing civilian casualties—a reporter for *The Philadelphia Inquirer* filed a pool dispatch from the ship describing how "Thursday morning was one of the moments suspended in time . . . paving the way for a dawn of hope." Journalists are now talking of Iraq as "the enemy" as if they themselves have gone to war—which, in a sense, they have.

The language is of the early forties, when Hitler's armies had reached the Pas de Calais and were poised to invade England. Journalists in uniforms and helmets are trying to adopt the *gravitas* of Edward R. Murrow and Richard Dimbleby. We are being prepared for "the biggest tank battle since World War II" and "the largest amphibious operation since D day [or Korea]."

This nonsense is as dangerous as it is misleading. When three of the largest Western armies launch their attack from the Muslim nation containing Islam's two holiest shrines, this is no time to draw parallels with the Second World War. If Ed Murrow were alive today, he would probably be among the reporters in Baghdad describing the effect of allied air raids. Nor is this the "dawn of hope." It may well be the start of renewed decades of hatred between the West and the Arab world. Yet our reporting does not reflect this.

It is not easy for journalists to exercise self-criticism when they are reporting history. And to cast doubt on the word of American or British officers in the Gulf is to invite almost immediate condemnation. Those of us who reported the human suffering caused by Israeli air raids in Beirut in 1982 were told we were anti-Semitic. Any expression of real skepticism about American military claims in the Gulf provokes a parallel accusation. Have we taken Saddam's side? Do we not realize that Iraq invaded Kuwait on 2 August?

There cannot be a reporter in Saudi Arabia who does not realize that Saddam Hussein is a brutal, wicked dictator who rules through terror. There can be no doubt about the savagery of his army in occupied Kuwait. Reporters who wander off to investigate military affairs in Saudi Arabia risk, at worst, deportation. The last journalist who did that in Iraq, Farzad Bazoft, was hanged. Long before Saddam invaded Kuwait, we were reporting on his cruelty—unlike the Saudis during the Iran-Iraq war, who were bankrolling his dreadful regime under the illusion that he was the savior of the Arab world.

Yet, almost three weeks after the start of the war, journalists have allowed themselves to be duped by the Western authorities, forced either to participate in pool reporting under military restrictions or to work independently at the risk of having their accreditation taken away.

In theory the "pool" means that the reports of journalists travelling with military units are available to all television networks and newspapers. In practice, it means that the only reporters officially allowed to witness events at "the front"—whether they be with the army, the navy or the air force—have their reports read and often amended by military censors.

It should be said at once that almost all ordinary soldiers are invariably friendly and helpful to journalists. It should also be said that there are journalists in the pool who are valiantly and successfully filing dispatches that describe the unhappiness as well as the motivation of soldiers at war, the boredom as well as the excitement, the mistakes as well as the efficiency. But many of their colleagues can claim no such record. Most of the journalists with the military now wear uniforms. They rely upon the soldiers around them for advice and protection. Naturally (and justifiably) fearful of the coming land war, they also look to the soldiers around them for comfort. They are dependent on the troops and their officers for communications, perhaps for their lives. And there is thus the profound desire to fit in, to "work the system," a frequent absence of critical faculties.

This was painfully illustrated last week when Iraqi troops captured the abandoned Saudi border town of Khafji. Pool reporters were first kept up to fifteen miles from the sighting and—misled by their U.S. military "minders"—filed stories reporting the recapture of the town. But when *The Independent* traveled to the scene to investigate, an American NBC television reporter—a member of the military pool—responded as follows: "You asshole; you'll prevent us from working. You're not allowed here. Get out. Go back to Dhahran." He then called over an American marine public affairs officer, who announced: "You're not allowed to talk to U.S. Marines and they're not allowed to talk to you."

It was a disturbing moment. By traveling to Khafji, *The Independent* discovered that the Iraqis were still fighting in the town long after the prime minister had claimed outside No. 10 Downing Street that it had been liberated. For the American reporter, however, the privileges of the pool and the military rules attached to it were more important than the right of a journalist to do his job.

The American and British military have thus been able to set reporters up against reporters, to divide journalists on the grounds that those who try to work outside the pool will destroy the opportunities of those who are working under military restriction—within it. That is why, when an enterprising reporter from *The Sunday Times* managed to find the Staffordshire Regiment in the desert last week, he was confronted by an angry British major accompanying the British press pool, who claimed that if he did not leave, "You'll ruin it for the others."

The "others," however, already have problems. When American correspondents on the carrier *Saratoga* quoted the exact words of air force pilots last week, they found that the captain and other senior officers deleted all swear words and changed some of the quotations before sending on their dispatches after a delay of twelve hours. On the *Kennedy,* news agency pool reporters recorded how fighter-bomber pilots watched pornographic video tapes to help them relax before their mission. This was struck from their report.

At one American airbase, a vast banner is suspended inside an aircraft hangar. It depicts an American Superman holding in his arms a limp, terrified Arab with a hooked nose. The existence of this banner, with its racist overtones, went unreported by the pool journalists of the base. A pool television crew did record U.S. Marine Lieutenant Colonel Dick White when he described what it was like to see Iraqi troops in Kuwait from his plane. His words are worth repeating: "It was like turning on the kitchen light late at night and the cockroaches started scurrying . . . We finally got them out where we could find them and kill them." These astonishing remarks went unquestioned, although there was certainly one question that was worth putting: What is the new world order worth when an American officer, after only three weeks of war, compares his Arab enemies to insects?

The unquestioning nature of our coverage of this war is one of its most dangerous facets. Many of the American television pool dispatches sound as if they have been produced by the military, which, in a way, they have. For the relationship between reporter and soldier here is becoming almost fatally blurred. Reporters who are working independently of the military have been threatened not just with the withdrawal of their accreditation, but also with deportation from Saudi Arabia—even though they willingly comply with all the security guidelines, which preclude the reporting of military details that could be of use to Iraq.

The system may be convenient for the military, but it is pernicious for the press. Reporters who worked in Vietnam are now describing official military briefings in Riyadh as even more uninformative than the notorious "five o'clock follies" in Saigon. This is supposed to be a war for freedom, but the Western armies in Saudi Arabia—under the guise of preserving "security"—want to control the flow of information.

There could be no better proof of this than the predicament of the French television crew who filmed the Khafji fighting at great risk to their lives, broke no security guidelines—and then had their tape confiscated because they were not members of the pool. In reality, the French were merely doing their job. If reporters were trusted to travel independently to the front, as they have done in so many other wars, obeying local military commanders, betraying no secrets, but taking responsibility for their own lives, the whole charade of pools and restrictions could be abandoned.

As it is, we probably do not yet appreciate how sad and humiliating is our acceptance of the present system. How are we going to justify what amounts to sycophancy if the forthcoming land battle turns into a blood-bath for the West? What excuses will we find for those uncritical reports? Generals will always blame the press for their failures, however much we bow to their rules. But when the bodies start coming home—when the West really begins to suffer—the public, whose support for this conflict is partly shaped by what it reads and sees on television, may not forgive us for our weakness in so humbly accepting those little flags handed out by the colonel.

WHAT IS THERE TO HIDE?

Walter Cronkite

WITH AN arrogance foreign to the democratic system, the U.S. military in Saudi Arabia is trampling on the American people's right to know. It is doing a disservice not only to the home front but also to history and its own best interests. Recent polls indicate the public sides with the military in its so far successful effort to control the press. This can only be because the press has failed to make clear the public's stake in the matter.

It is drummed into us, and we take pride in the fact, that these are "our boys (and girls)," "our troops," "our forces" in the Gulf. They are, indeed, and it is our war. Our elected representatives in Congress gave our elected president permission to wage it. We had better darned well know what they are doing in our name.

After World War II most Germans protested that they did not know what went on in the heinous Nazi concentration camps. It is just possible that they did not. But this claim of ignorance did not absolve them from blame: They had complacently permitted Hitler to do his dirty business in the dark. They raised little objection, most even applauded, when he closed their newspapers and clamped down on free speech. Certainly our leaders are not to be compared with Hitler, but today, because of onerous, unnecessary rules, Americans are not being permitted to see and hear the full story of what their military forces are doing in an action that will reverberate long into the nation's future.

The military is acting on a generally discredited Pentagon myth that

Walter Cronkite, the former CBS anchorman, has covered wars dating back to the Second World War. This article was originally published in the February 25, 1991, issue of *Newsweek;* he added the postscript especially for this book.

the Vietnam War was lost because of the uncensored press coverage. The military would do better to pattern its PR after its handling of the press in World War II, a war we won.

As in World War II, there should be censorship of all dispatches, film and tape leaving the battle area. The troops' security must be protected against inadvertent disclosures about particular weaponry, disposition of forces, tactical plans and the like. In World War II, most press material was sent by courier back to division headquarters where a designated intelligence officer cleared it for transmission back to the communications facilities. Usually this officer was a civilian called to wartime duty. In most cases, he was as concerned with the public's right to know as the military's right to certain secrets. In all cases, he was open to appeal by correspondents who thought their stories were being held up for political reasons.

We often won those arguments, usually by making the case that the enemy already had the information our army wanted to censor. Once in England the censors held up my report that the Eighth Air Force had bombed Germany through a solid cloud cover. This was politically sensitive; our air staff maintained we were practicing only precision bombing on military targets. But the censors released my story when I pointed out the obvious—Germans on the ground and the Luftwaffe attacking bombers knew the clouds were there. The truth was not being withheld from Germans but Americans.

With a rational censorship system in place, the press should be free to go where it wants when it wants, to see, hear and photograph what it believes is in the public interest. The number of correspondents wandering freely behind the lines must be controlled, but this was handled in World War II by the simple expedient of accreditation, and as long as this is applied liberally for established reporters of major organizations the public's rights are protected. Incidentally, war correspondents should be put in uniform. Regular military gear, without insignia and with a clearly identifiable "war correspondent" badge, worked well in World War II. Such gear, in most cases, was enough to assure transportation, food and shelter—and to identify the holder's noncombatant status in case of capture.

The military also has the responsibility of giving all the information it possibly can to the press and the press has every right, to the point of insolence, to demand this. The Gulf briefings are ridiculously inadequate. Why should we not be told what bridges have been hit? Don't the Iraqis know? Material from the briefings should be subject to the same censorship as battlefield reports. The reporters would get a much more candid appraisal of the fighting. The TV coverage would be delayed, but of what serious consequence is that?

It would be helpful if all sides agreed that live battlefield coverage is not an issue. The promise of such coverage was nothing but science fiction, despite our early experience of seeing Baghdad, Tel Aviv, and Dhahran under attack, live in our living rooms. But it simply can't be. Imagine the Iraqi commander monitoring American troop movements via CNN!

The greatest mistake of our military so far is its attempt to control coverage by assigning a few pool reporters and photographers to be taken to locations determined by the military with supervising officers monitoring all their conversations with the troops in the field. An American citizen is entitled to ask: "What are they trying to hide?" The answer might be casualties from shelling, collapsing morale, disaffection, insurrection, incompetent officers, poorly trained troops, malfunctioning equipment, widespread illness—who knows? But the fact that we don't know, the fact that the military apparently feels there is *something* it must hide, can only lead eventually to a breakdown in home-front confidence and the very echoes from Vietnam that the Pentagon fears the most.

POSTSCRIPT

This article was written just before the ground war began. The remarkable success of that operation may be used as an argument that the military restrictions on the press worked. This is as specious as claiming that, since all cats are animals, all animals are cats. The press restrictions had nothing to do with the victory.

The speed of the allied advance was so great and the war so suddenly over that the press restrictions were not tested adequately once the combat began.

We will never know whether they might have worked *to the military's satisfaction* if the war had been longer. We do know, however, that any system that prevented the press from reporting freely on all aspects of the conflict could not have served well a democratic people.

In fairness, the briefings improved as the battles unfolded, the military was tolerant of the independent television units that circumvented the rules to give us the first reports from liberated Kuwait City, and there were indications that the Pentagon was considering relaxing its pre-censorship by pool as the war went on.

In the months and years ahead we can hope that the military will understand better that the press is not anti-military in its attempt to fulfill the people's right to know and, for goodness sakes, that the public itself will join instead of criticize the press in the pursuit of that right so fundamental to the freedoms of the public itself.

TELEVISION AND THE INSTANT ENEMY

David Halberstam

EVERY DAY, I sit in my living room addicted to the television screen, watching the dazzling technology of this war—one covered live and in color by satellite.

This contrasts with the very early days of the Vietnam War, when there was only a handful of reporters in Saigon and the relatively rare TV reporters who showed up represented a minor journalistic presence. They were based in Hong Kong, came for short periods, worked much like print reporters and shipped their film to Hong Kong; from there it was sent to New York, where it competed for space on a fifteen-minute evening news show done in black and white.

How long ago that seems! Vietnam became our first TV war, and the networks soon went to color coverage, but without today's technology and its immediacy.

Contemporary technology is dazzling, offering rare, almost addictive, immediacy. "We should make our motto, 'We are the world, we are wired,' " a TV executive said recently, talking about his network's capacity for instantaneous coverage. What he meant was this: If we are there, the event is important; if we are not, the event is not.

That immediacy does not necessarily mean better, more thoughtful reporting; it is arguable that the lack of satellites and comparative slowness of the transmission process in the old days permitted the news

David Halberstam is the author of *The Making of a Quagmire, The Powers That Be,* and several other books, including, most recently, *The Next Century.* This article was published in the February 22, 1991, issue of *The New York Times* on the op-ed page under the title "Where's Page 2 in TV News?"

desks in New York to act less as prisoners of technology than they do today.

For if the technology has improved, then the editing function, the cumulative sense of judgment—the capacity of network news executives to decide what to use and how to use it, and how to blend the nonvisual and visual—has declined in precise ratio to the improvement in technology.

Film is more than ever an end in itself: To have the technology is to use it. The disparity between network news judgment and comparable cumulative print news judgment becomes steadily wider.

As I write, the cameras are at the ready. We await the imminent start of a ground war while the networks cover the scurrying back and forth of Iraqi envoys. America is at the point where small events are not merely covered but overcovered.

In general, the networks come too late to an important story, give us too little coverage in the days and weeks when the decision-making process is still unfinished (a good example is the appalling coverage of Senator Sam Nunn's hearings on the Persian Gulf) and too much once the shooting starts.

The coming of an hourlong news show, which would allow network journalists to do a better job explaining events, has been stillborn, and only ABC, with *Nightline,* qualifies as a network that gives us Page Two.

The lack of "space"—a twenty-two-minute news hole that has remained the same even as the networks' role in society has grown ever larger—and the obsession with film have produced something extremely serious: a pretense to internationalism (a network anchorman rushing off to cover a major foreign story), which is the gloss over an essential isolationism.

We are only beginning to understand how that isolationism affects a free society's capacity to develop a serious, thoughtful political agenda, foreign and domestic. The networks are not interested in foreign news as it represents constant, subtle, and evolutionary change in the world.

They are not interested because their executives, drawing upon immense amounts of polling, have decided that Americans are not interested in ordinary foreign news. They are, it appears, interested in foreign news only when it happens point-blank to Americans, preferably violently, thereby providing excellent footage.

Unfortunately, over a period of time, the decisions made in network newsrooms can dramatically alter the political attitudes of the nation, limit its attention span, trivialize its political debate, and diminish its capacity to create a genuine long-range political agenda.

One example is the poor job of covering Japan's economic challenge, because the Japanese, even if they produce cameras, cars, and VCRs, do not produce very much in the way of what is called action news.

An even more dramatic example of how TV's attitudes have affected American opinion and politics, and have thereby scrambled American attitudes, is found in American policy toward the Middle East—particularly the taking of hostages in Iran. It was not so much an overwhelming story (one with far greater consequences than appeared on the surface) as it was a rare foreign story with innate drama that TV could easily understand and could cover better and more quickly than print.

Television loved the story, and exploited it, magnifying events relentlessly. In turn, America was first fascinated and in time obsessed by these events. The lesson from the TV coverage seemed to be that the U.S., an immensely powerful country, had shown itself weak in dealing with a country many Americans considered a third-rate power.

That was not exactly true. We might have been momentarily unsure of what to do, confronting an extremely delicate new kind of foreign policy dilemma, but we were not weak. We were not watching the rise of a nation that was a greater power than the U.S., nor were we watching the coming of a power that in any important geopolitical sense threatened America.

We were involuntarily participating in an indignity, which, however unpleasant, is a very different thing—an indignity made infinitely greater because we covered it with such avidity. But because of the coverage—more accurately, the overcoverage—we became obsessed not with foreign policy, not with the Middle Eastern political balance, but with the evils of Iran and the Ayatollah.

By contrast, a truly important geopolitical event, the Iran-Iraq war—with arguably far greater political import for the world and the U.S.—was, by TV terms, a nonevent. It went on for eight years but was a distant struggle, fought between, as far as Americans could tell, two decidedly unlikable dictatorships.

Because they were dictatorships, opportunities to film were quite limited. It was a story that the print media did not cover particularly well (as compared, say, with their fine handling of Japan's economic ascent), but TV almost completely ignored it. To cover a story like this on TV demanded ingenuity, hard work and, perhaps worst of all, talking heads. Since there was no film, there was no story.

Thus, Saddam Hussein rose to power in a communications vacuum, with no small measure of American aid and assistance, and with Americans knowing and caring very little about him. Not surprisingly, because politicians respond to what is on people's minds, our government seemed little more aware of the danger posed by his rise.

As the media become lazy and careless, so does the government. There were, after all, no polls showing that the American people were bothered by Saddam Hussein's rise. In contrast to what we faced at the time of the Iran hostage crisis, what we faced as Mr. Hussein expanded his power was significantly more serious business.

Because of that, America's introduction to Mr. Hussein's threat to the Middle East has been abrupt and bitter: the coming of the instant enemy. That is a significant weakness of an America in which the prime source of information is ever more driven by an impulse to entertain, and where there is a lack of linkage between long-range political aims and objectives and truly deep support on the part of its people.

We have become terribly dependent upon an instrument of mass communications that feels that the cardinal sin is not so much to be inaccurate as to bore.

BRIEFINGSPEAK

George Black

Q: General, could you give us your sense of where Desert Storm stands right now?

A: Yes sir, we have an ongoing armed situation at this time and we're seeing some serious coalition force projection in the KTO. We have ID'd hostiles coming across and have taken a number of EPWs. I'm sorry, I can't give you any information about coalition KIAs, MIAs or POWs, and because of heavy SAM activity I can't give you any accurate BDA. But I do know that each of our men, and, of course, women, will be glad to get back on his, or her, APC or Humvee and get back to the KSA to sit down to a good hot MRE.

We have terminated battlefield preparation and significantly degraded the enemy's logistical sustainment capabilities. Sorties now number 127,000. We have rendered a number of his fixed wings inoperative and one helicopter is reported lased during an intercept while in hover status in Indian country. This kill is confirmed in a standard voice message from our Tomcat pilot: "Cold, cold, smoked the bitch." The enemy's aerial assets, then, are no longer a factor in the package, although surface engagements do continue at this hour between hostiles and friendlies.

We continue to aggressively pursue maritime interdiction and counter-Scud missions. The take from our intelligence platforms tells us that we have had optimum results against some very lucrative targets,

George Black is foreign editor of *The Nation* and a columnist for the *Los Angeles Times*. He is also the author of *The Good Neighbor: How the United States Wrote the History of Central America and the Caribbean*. This article was published as an editorial in the March 11, 1991, issue of *The Nation*.

though we still see a lot of potential out there. Put it another way, this is still a target-rich environment. We continue to lay down a steady volume of chaff and other ordnance in defense suppression operations against his Triple-A and other systems.

Between zero-five and zero-seven today allied smart bombs achieved very significant terrain alteration. Because of our belief in the sanctity of human life, we have attrited his main force in a surgical operation that has gone the extra mile to avoid collateral damage, though of course you're always going to break some eggs. We're particularly happy with the enhancement of favorable ground conditions as a result of the de-struct radius of the Maverick and the force multipliers on the Tomahawks. Coalition personnel-loss minimization remains positive. We've all heard rumors this morning, I know, of significant numbers of human remains pouches as a consequence of friendly fire, but that's a negative. I have no information to give you on that and I can't discuss why I'm not discussing it because then I'd be discussing it.

Ongoing templating of the theater by our AWACS lets us see how much terrain has been craterized and what percentage of the dictator's fixed assets still remains for our aviation elements to rubble-ize. Also, I'd just like to add a word here to say how proud we all are of our systems performance—the Patriot and Hellfire, as you know, have taken out much of the enemy's offensive capability, while the Stealth, Warthog, and Wild Weasel continue to transit his defensive alignments and allow us to diagram his intentions. Our pilots say there's so much traffic out there it's like standing on the median of the Interstate watching the hostiles scurry like cockroaches when the kitchen light is flipped on. As for our lead ground forces, they continue to haul ass and bypass, as our Pentagon greensuiters like to say, and they will be kicking some butt preparatory to cutting off the enemy's head.

Let me sum up then: Our game plan is right on schedule. We've been training for the Super Bowl for six months and now it's game time and we're already at the opposition's five-yard line. We told him to move it or lose it, and I'm happy to report that we're fighting on a level playing field. If he throws us a curve ball in terms of anything unconventional, we'll be ready to hunker down in a Mission-Oriented Protective Posture. But I feel comfortable that we're facing the bottom of his order and anything he throws at us we're going to hit straight into the bleachers. Could we drop the big one if this goes into extra innings? I'd like to refer you to the White House on that one.

We've been sent here by our commander in chief to do a job, and we're all good to go at this hour. I'm comfortable that we can get the job done and go home to commence building the new world order.

Q: General, in an essay I wrote in 1946, I said that the English language had become "ugly and inaccurate because our thoughts are foolish." I said that I believed words and meaning had parted company, and I also pointed out that "in our time, political speech and writing are largely the defense of the indefensible." Would you like to comment on that, sir?

A: I'm sorry, Mr. Orwell, I think I'd prefer not to get into that one since it might reveal too much about our intelligence capabilities.

THE AGONY OF
THE MIDDLE EAST

THE CRISIS OF THE ARAB WORLD

Fred Halliday

T HE CRISIS following upon Iraq's invasion of Kuwait is unique in the contemporary world, above all because of the multiple levels upon which it is being played out. In international terms, it is comparable to the major crises of the post-1945 period—Berlin 1948, Korea 1950, Suez 1956, Cuba 1962, the Arab-Israeli wars of 1967 and 1973. Yet it is distinct from, and more complex than, any of these. It is distinct because this crisis does not assume an East-West form, one of Soviet-American antagonism, and has in fact involved a significant degree of Soviet-American cooperation, if not complete agreement. It is more complex because in addition to its world dimension it has several other ones: It has provoked a crisis within the Arab world, between the bloc led by Iraq and that led by Saudi Arabia and Egypt; it involves to a degree never seen in modern times all three of the non-Arab states in the Middle East—Iran, Turkey, Israel; it is a crisis within the U.S. alliance, over the degree of military and financial support being given to the U.S.A. in the Gulf; it is also a crisis of the international economic system, given the importance of oil and the inflationary pressures which higher oil prices and increased military expenditures in the developed capitalist states have brought; finally, it is a crisis of the global political system, as reflected in the question of whether the United Nations can, or cannot, act to prevent evident breaches of its charter.

For the Arab world, in particular, this crisis marks a decisive moment,

Fred Halliday teaches political science at The London School of Economics and is author of several books, including *Arabia Without Sultans*. This article was published in the November–December 1990 issue of *New Left Review* under the title "The Crisis of the Arab World: The False Answers of Saddam Hussein." It originally appeared in *Le Monde Diplomatique*'s Arabic edition.

however the confrontation between Iraq and the West resolves itself. The Arab states have divided strongly in the past, as after the 1962 revolution in Yemen, and Sadat's visit to Israel in 1977. But this division gives the appearance of being deeper than any previous one: The invitation to Western armies by Saudi Arabia, and the alliance of several Arab states against Iraq, promises to strengthen the disunity of the Arab world. At the same time, the Iraqi action against Kuwait poses more clearly than at any time for nearly thirty years the question of Arab unity and of the unity of Arab politics in general. Iraq has captured Kuwait in the name of Arab unity, and no Arab state can be neutral or indifferent to this crisis.

This re-posing of the issue of the unity of the Arab world is evident in two respects. First, Saddam Hussein has revived the dynamic of secular Arab nationalism, with at its core the goals of Arab political unity and the redistribution of Arab oil wealth. For twenty years or more it has been widely assumed that this political program, which Nasser promoted in the 1950s and early 1960s, has failed: Its defeat was sealed in the defeat of 1967. Since the Iranian revolution it appeared that the initiative throughout the Middle East, including the Arab world, was in the hands of Islamist forces: They were the ones challenging imperialism, attacking established regimes, calling for the distribution of wealth, organizing the oppressed. Now the initiative has been retaken by the secular nationalists. Of course, Saddam uses Islamic language and poses as the champion of Islam. But everyone knows this is appearance only, a political camouflage. Saddam has been militantly opposed to Islamist politics within Iraq and outside. What he has effectively done by his action on 2 August is to steal their clothes and regain the leadership of radical politics in the region. This is one reason why Iran is so worried—it has lost the radical leadership.

The issue of unity is posed in a second respect, namely that of frontiers. One of the distinctive features of the Middle East as a whole—Arab and non-Arab—is the degree to which frontiers are regarded as irrelevant. Arab nationalists say the frontiers of the region are temporary and artificial creations. This is of course true, in that most of the boundaries were created by administrative decision, and usually under colonial rule in the early part of this century. But in itself this is not specific to the Middle East: Most of the frontiers in Europe and Africa are equally arbitrary and equally recent. What is at stake is not the issue of boundary definition—where geographically the frontier lies—but rather the question of whether the delimitation of states should be respected at all. What is distinctive about the Middle East, then, is the refusal of states to accept this delimitation. Interference in the internal affairs of other states is more pervasive in the region than anywhere else. Indeed, it follows from the logic of Arab nationalism that frontiers merely divide a political community that should be united.

This argument has been heard many times before: in the union of Syria and Egypt in 1958; in the various Libyan attempts at union; in the Syrian claim that it has a right to intervene in Lebanon; in the—ultimately successful—drive for Yemeni unity. What Saddam has done is to restate this case in a singularly stark way. Yet his ability to do so probably results from another more immediate trend, namely the questioning of frontiers in the aftermath of Cold War. When the communist regimes fell in Eastern Europe last year, lessons were quickly drawn: It was widely believed that dictatorships in the Middle East would also be vulnerable —and in particular Iraq. Many thought Saddam would share the fate of Ceausescu. But the fall of communism had another consequence, one that will take much longer to work itself through: namely, the revision on an international scale of frontiers for the first time since the end of World War II. Everyone knew that the division of the world into the existing system of 170 states was arbitrary, but since 1945 it has more or less been accepted. Until this year, there had been only one case of successful secession—Bangladesh in 1971—and only one of fusion—Vietnam in 1975.

The collapse of communism has altered this: as a result of the retreat of Soviet power, at least three states seem fated to disappear—East Germany and South Yemen have already done so, and it is probable that the third, North Korea, will in time be absorbed by a much stronger and more populous South Korea. At the same time, the possibility of secession, and of the emergence of new states, is also posed: in the U.S.S.R., where several of the fifteen republics are moving toward independence, and in some countries of Eastern Europe, most obviously Yugoslavia. In this perspective, the annexation of Kuwait to Iraq is not only an Arab matter but part of a broader global trend: it represents the coming together of a long-standing Arab drive for the fusion of states with the contemporary questioning of state frontiers derived from the end of Cold War.

If the Iraqi action against Kuwait therefore represents a revival of political goals present in the earlier period of Arab nationalism, it raises at the same time a number of difficulties for the Arab world as a whole, ones that will persist however the crisis is resolved. If Iraq survives the crisis, it will continue to promote these policies in the name of Arab nationalism. If Iraq suffers military defeat, there will be many in the Arab world who will continue to support the goals which Saddam has proclaimed. It is for this reason that the Iraqi action has aroused considerable support within Arab countries, many of whom, while disliking Iraq's internal and international policies, feel that Iraq embodies some of the goals of the revolutionary and radical nationalist movement so long kept on the defensive in the Arab world.

FOUR ISSUES in particular appear to be central to the Iraqi appeal in the Arab world: unification, redistribution of oil wealth, liberation of Palestine, resistance to imperialism. Amongst much of the population of the Arab world and amongst some of the intelligentsia, Saddam Hussein has found support because of his stand on these issues. The fusion of Kuwait with Iraq marks a step in the direction of Arab unity, with the removal of a boundary many regard as artificial and a colonial creation. The call for equal distribution of the oil revenues is an apparent attempt to resolve the fact that most Arab oil is found in countries with small populations, where conservative monarchies hold sway, and to reallocate this to the much larger oil-free countries. Saddam's stand on Palestine represents a break with the conciliation of much of the Arab world over recent years, a policy that seems to have done nothing to help weaken the Israeli position. As for external influence, the response of the West to the occupation of Kuwait seems to confirm that this remains a danger to all Arabs.

No one can doubt that the issues which Saddam is claiming to confront are real issues. The question is, rather, whether his solutions are the right ones, and whether they are likely to help to resolve these issues. Here there is room for considerable doubt, especially if the nature of Saddam's regime is taken into account. The Arab nationalist program of unity was linked, as in the time of Nasser, to the question of popular control and of democracy. In the case of Baathist Iraq, these considerations are absent. Baathist Iraq is a ferocious dictatorship, marked by terror and coercion unparalleled within the Arab world. Baathist ideology is overtly racist—toward Persians, Jews, Kurds. It is a regime that bears more resemblance to European fascism, in ideology and in its mechanisms of staying in power, than to a democratic or popular nationalist model. The internal character of Baathist Iraq affects any judgment of the kind of unity that regime achieves. There is all the world of difference between unity that comes about as a response to popular will and one that is imposed by military force: the recent instances of union in Yemen and in Germany are, for all their difficulties, democratic ones. That of Kuwait with Iraq is coercive, as is evident in the fact that no

Kuwaiti support for it could be mobilized, not even from Kuwait Baathists.

The redistribution of oil revenues within the Arab world is a priority, but not one that Iraq's action against Kuwait can solve. First, Iraq itself is not a poor country but has some of the largest oil reserves in the region. There is little justification for Iraq seizing the oil resources of Kuwait. Moreover, if economic benefit is the criterion, then the action itself has caused immense economic loss. Kuwait has, for the time being at least, been destroyed as a functioning economic entity, and hundreds of thousands of foreign workers and professional migrants have been driven out. Iraq itself has had to divert enormous resources to maintain its military machine. The boycott aside, it has to be imagined what is involved in keeping over one million men under arms in a country of seventeen million.

The question of Palestine explains much of Saddam's appeal but also contains the most cruel deceptions. Support for Palestine rests upon the argument that the Palestinian people are oppressed by Israel and denied the right to their own states. But Iraq has no right to claim to support the rights of any oppressed people, since it has treated the Kurdish minority within its own borders in a way similar to the Israeli treatment of the Palestinians. As violators of the rights of oppressed peoples, Iraq and Israel are comparable. Moreover, even in a strictly Arab context, Iraq's policy on Palestine has long been a two-faced one—promotion of division amongst Palestinian forces and inaction in practice, covered by demagogic militancy in words. Iraq, in common with Syria and Libya, has used its radical image to divide and weaken the Palestinians. Many of those Palestinians assassinated after calling for Arab-Israeli dialogue have been killed by Iraqi agents. Indeed one can conclude from past behavior that neither Iraq nor Syria would want to see an independent Palestinian state, unless they controlled it.

Iraq has also pushed the Palestinians into a maximalist isolation, one that denies the possibility of a two-state solution—the creation of a Palestinian state side by side with an Israeli one—and has undermined, by its recent actions, the creation of any significant links between Palestinian and opposition forces within Israel. The militaristic and chauvinist statements issued by Baghdad have only reinforced the most extreme Zionist sentiment within Israel and within the West . . .

Iraq's claim to be "confronting" imperialism has no more validity. Some of the supposed links between Iraq and the West are dubious: there is no evidence, despite Iranian claims, that Washington encouraged Iraq to invade Iran in 1980; nor is it sensible to argue that Iraq and the U.S.A. have colluded to divide up the Arab world between them through manipulation of this crisis. However, for all its anti-imperialist rhetoric, the Baathist regime in Baghdad has benefited on many occasions from the help of the U.S.A. This was most obviously the case, in 1987 and 1988, in the latter stages of the war with Iran, when the U.S. navy entered the Gulf and acted as an ally of Iraq. The U.S.A. also provided Iraq with military intelligence about Iran, derived from satellite photographs. Iraq now claims that prior to its occupation of Kuwait the U.S.A. was planning to attack it, and that U.S. diplomats encouraged Iraq to invade and so laid a trap for it. These are specious arguments. Most importantly, however, if the goal is to expel Western influence from the region, the action taken by Iraq has had the opposite result. . . . However the crisis ends, there is going to be a greatly enlarged permanent Western presence in the region for many years to come, indeed as long as the Gulf remains a major source of oil. Twenty years after the British withdrawal, Iraq has succeeded in bringing the imperialist forces back in.

The issue on which the Kuwait crisis confronts both the Arab world and the West is that of consistency. The West's policy has been rightly condemned for its inconsistency: for failing to take action, through the United Nations, against Israel while doing so against Iraq. Equally other cases of illegal intervention—Syria in Lebanon, Turkey in Cyprus, Morocco in the Sahara—have been passed over in silence. The United Nations has to adopt the same attitude to its allies as it has done to Iraq. Comparable condemnation of, and effective sanctions against, Israel are needed. It would, however, be mistaken to use criticism of Western hypocrisy to collude in what is a clear case of aggression by a fascist state.

The question of consistency also applies to Iraq. Iraq claims, among its other justifications for invading Kuwait, to be overcoming the "colonialist" legacy of division. Kuwait, it is said, was once part of Iraq and is now reunited with it. This is a dangerous argument. Most of Kuwait was never part of the vilayat of Basra. Moreover, if Kuwait is an artificial political entity, created by colonialism, so too is Iraq. By calling for the revision of frontiers, Iraq is opening up the possibility that its frontiers too will be subject to revision.

The modern state of Iraq, for all its claims to represent the ancient kingdom of Mesopotamia and the Abbasid state, is as much the creation of British imperialism as is Kuwait. This means that, whatever differences divide Arab states, they cannot be resolved by one state occupying the other and denying its legitimacy. The only long-term solution to the issue of legitimacy is for the governments of these states to acquire a democratic form, something neither Saddam nor the monarchs of the peninsula want to entertain. The alternative is that the same interventionist logic will be applied to Iraq: Iran, Turkey, Syria, Saudi Arabia could all make claims on part of Iraq. This alone should suggest that Saddam Hussein's answer to the Kuwait crisis is a false one. Let us hope that it will not also lead to tragedy through a war in which the Arab peoples, and especially the people of Iraq, will be the greatest losers.

THE BITTER FRUITS OF WAR

Rami G. Khouri

AMERICANS ARE shortsighted and naive to boast that Iraq is not going to be another Vietnam. Militarily, of course, they are right. However long this war lasts, there is little doubt that Iraq ultimately will be defeated.

Politically, however, the war with Iraq will be the granddaddy of all Vietnams. When the shooting stops, it won't be George Bush's coalition —that posse of desperadoes and bounty hunters—that will determine the political trends of the region. It will be the bitter, resentful grass-roots sentiments of hundreds of millions of Arabs.

I would estimate that three-quarters of the people of the Arab world stand with Iraq—not in support of its occupation of Kuwait, but in its confrontation with the United States. Every day that Iraq holds out against the United States and strikes against Israel, that grass-roots support for Iraq grows stronger. Even in the short term, this tremendous grass-roots pressure is likely to result in political turmoil throughout the region, including changes in regimes and leaders.

Understanding the contemporary frame of the Arab mind is essential to grasping the terms of reference within which we have viewed the mounting conflict with the United States.

The Arab world reached a historic turning point in the 1980s: People lost their fear. After the low-water mark of 1982, when the Palestine Liberation Organization and the Lebanese capital of Beirut were shelled

Rami G. Khouri is a Palestinian/Jordanian author and political commentator. He also hosts a weekly public-affairs talk show on Jordan Television. This piece is adapted from "America Will Reap a Festering Bitterness," which was published in the January 28, 1991, issue of the *Los Angeles Times*.

from the hills by Israel, supported by the U.S. Navy (which the high-minded Americans now seem to have conveniently forgotten) the Arab people were fed up. They had been so beaten down over the decades by their own autocratic leaders, by their inability to manifest their sense of pan-Arab unity, by their inability to do anything about Israel, by their inability to forge productive and honorable relations with the great powers, that they hit rock bottom.

Defeat seemed so total that renewal was the only way out. As elsewhere in the world, such as Roman Catholic Poland, large numbers of people turned to God when they gave up on the temporal order. From Jordan to Egypt, from Algeria to Lebanon, it was Islam that initially gave Arabs the strength to fight back.

Even though most Arabs didn't support the invasion of Kuwait, Saddam Hussein's fearlessness in standing up to our enemies, Israel and America, appeals to the new spirit of the Arab world—a spirit that says we'd rather die on our feet than live groveling on the ground.

Saddam Hussein is, of course, no Santa Claus. He is a rough man. He kills people ruthlessly. He has lived by the gun all of his life. Yet this unlikely, autocratic man has become the medium of a new Arab fearlessness that aims to cast off oppression and subjugation both from abroad and at home.

The great paradox of this conflict is that it is in precisely those Arab countries where the people have started to achieve democracy, where people are free to speak out and express themselves—such places as Jordan, Algeria, Tunisia, Sudan, Yemen, and among Palestinians—that the support for Saddam Hussein is so fervent and widespread. The United States is supported by only the mercantile autocracies. Egypt, as always, is an exception because of its obsequious political servitude.

Inconveniently for the West, the more free and democratic Arab countries become, the less sympathetic they will be to foreign designs for the region. The more Islamic and anti-Western they will become. Already, for example, the speaker of the House in the Jordanian Parliament is a member of the Muslim Brotherhood, which holds a plurality there. In Algeria, the Muslim Brotherhood has a majority of local assembly seats. In both places, however, their success has depended on playing within a pluralist framework and by democratic rules.

Saddam Hussein was not the chosen leader of these Arabs seeking a new order. Ironically, it was the Americans who made him so. After he invaded Kuwait, every Arab country, far from praising him, called on him to withdraw at once, and many Arab leaders undertook immediate and fervent diplomatic action to secure such a withdrawal. But the Saudis and the Egyptians panicked and called in the Americans.

The minute American forces landed in the region, the whole equation changed. The issue was no longer Iraq occupying Kuwait. It was Iraq standing up to the arrogant West, holding out for a solution to the many regional economic and political problems that plague us. For all of us now, Iraq symbolizes the willingness to get up off our knees and confront our enemies. And the longer Saddam Hussein drags out the war, the more he will elicit support and redeem the sense of humiliation felt by Arabs for years.

Arabs throughout the region were pleased that Iraq made good on its threat to hit Israel with missiles if the American-led coalition attacked Iraq. While the human and material damage from the missile attacks is relatively minor, the more important message to Israel is that its real long-term security cannot be based on occupying Arab lands, because eventually the Arabs will develop or acquire technologies that can send destructive weapons into Israel's heartland.

The West has money and high technology on its side. We have human nature and history on our side. That means we may lose the war, but we will inevitably win out in the years and decades ahead.

The thin veil of "Arabization" of this U.S. war through George Bush's ragtag, cash-register coalition won't succeed any more than did America's "Vietnamization" strategy. In time, no doubt, the last days of that Asian war will be replayed in our part of the world, with American helicopters lifting their ambassadors from the roofs of U.S. embassies throughout the region, perhaps with a few Arab leaders in tow, clinging for dear life and looking forward to exile in Hawaii.

If the United States wants to squander $150 billion and the lives of countless Iraqis to keep a bevy of corrupt, undemocratic autocrats in power and maintain by force of arms an inequitable and unstable political order that has failed the Arabs for three-quarters of a century, it will have no more success than did Jaruzelski in Poland or Ceausescu in Romania.

THE DECLINE OF PAN-ARABISM

Bernard Lewis

WHEN HE invaded Kuwait, Saddam Hussein broke two taboos, and the consequences of both violations will be far-reaching and probably permanent.

The first was the taboo on inter-Arab warfare. There have been many conflicts between Arab states during the past half century. These have occasionally led to border skirmishes—as for example between Algeria and Morocco, Libya and Egypt, North and South Yemen. There has, however, never been a full-scale invasion, occupation and annexation by one state of another, in defiance not only of the United Nations Charter, but also, in what is perhaps from an Arab point of view more important, of the Arab League Pact. Article V of the pact lays down quite explicitly that no member shall resort to force against any other member to resolve a dispute. Kuwait was a member in good standing of the League and, moreover, an ally and benefactor of Iraq.

In spite of Saddam's resort to pan-Arab appeals, his action against Kuwait was in fact a step in exactly the opposite direction—the primacy of state interests, with each individual Arab country pursuing its own concerns and policies, with little regard for the others. In other words, of the various role models that Saddam Hussein has from time to time named—Nasser, Saladin, Nebuchadnezzar—it is the last whom he follows most closely. The choice of this pagan tyrant is far worse than the "pharaonism" for which the Egyptians are sometimes denounced by

Bernard Lewis is professor emeritus of Near Eastern Studies at Princeton University and the author of numerous books, including *The Arabs in History* and *Semites and Anti-Semites*. This article is excerpted from "Who'll Win, Who'll Lose in the Gulf," which appeared in the February 20, 1991, issue of *The Wall Street Journal*.

their Arab brothers. This could well be the point of no return in the decline of pan-Arabism.

There is a striking parallel with the situation in Spanish America. After the ending of colonial rule, the English-speaking North American colonies were able to band together and form the United States. The Spanish-speaking South American colonies failed to do the same. The missed opportunity has not returned, and by now the states of Spanish America, in spite of their common heritage, have become different nations. It seems very likely that the Arab world will go the same way.

One of the reasons for the decline of pan-Arabism has been Arabs' increasing disillusionment with successive attempts to achieve it. All too often it seemed that the real objective of pan-Arab leaders was not so much unity as hegemony. Some chose a German model, each seeing himself as Bismarck and his country as Prussia, with a dominant role to play in the United Arab State. Others chose a revolutionary model and tried to displace their Arab fellow rulers by subversion.

By now, all of these states, however artificial in their origins, have become realities—each with a ganglion of interacting loyalties and interests and careers. Some of the states are by no means artificial, but represent ancient national and territorial entities that existed long before the arrival of the imperialists, and survived with their national identity unimpaired after the imperialists' departure. Obvious examples are Morocco and Egypt. Others are imperial artifacts, created by the European imperial powers for their own purposes and appearing for the first time as independent states after their departure. The most obvious example is Libya, an Italian creation still bearing a Roman name that the Italian Colonial Ministry gave it. Another, ironically, is Iraq.

When Saddam Hussein broke the taboo on inter-Arab warfare, he was reinforcing an existing trend. The second violation is much more important, because it was new and will certainly have far-reaching consequences: that is, the questioning of post-imperial frontiers. It has hitherto been generally accepted in the Middle East, as elsewhere in Asia and Africa, that whatever the misdeeds of the imperialists, it would be dangerous to question the borders they drew. It was agreed to respect these borders, since to question them would open a Pandora's box of conflicting claims and internecine warfare.

Saddam Hussein has opened that box. Kuwait as an entity has existed since the middle of the eighteenth century. It arose from the play of desert politics, and, as so often during the past millennia, it was recognized, not created, by an imperial power. The Romans, the Byzantines, the Persians and the Ottomans conducted their Arabian policies along similar lines. The frontiers of Kuwait were indeed drawn by British officials, but so were all the other frontiers of Iraq, except for the frontier with Iran, which was finally delimited by a Turco-Iranian frontier commission, with British and Russian observers, shortly before the outbreak of war in 1914. Iraq's northern frontier was long disputed, with Turkey claiming the districts of Mosul and Kirkuk. It was settled in Iraq's favor in 1926, when British pressure was brought to bear.

By rejecting the validity of the British-drawn frontier of Kuwait, Saddam Hussein has reopened all these questions. He has at the same time endangered almost every other frontier in the Mideast, including the frontiers between Syria and Lebanon, and between Egypt and its neighbors in Africa. Egypt has far stronger claims to both Libya and Sudan than Iraq to Kuwait. This argument also impugns the Palestine Charter of the PLO, which defines that country as the territory under the former British mandate. The choice is understandable, since the only previous independent states in Palestine were ruled by Jews or Crusaders, but the definition is undermined by Saddam's new doctrine.

The decline in pan-Arabism may also bring some advantage and some opportunity to Israel. If Arab states begin to reason in national rather than pan-Arab terms, some of them may come to the same conclusion as Anwar Sadat, when he decided that the interests of Egypt, if not of the Arabs, required a peace settlement. They may also see some value in the presence of a state that, being neither Arab nor Muslim, cannot threaten hegemony, Prussian-style, nor subversion, revolutionary-style, and which could even be a factor of stability when the inevitable American disengagement comes.

A regional role for Israel in the Middle East is no longer inconceivable, though it is still far from likely. What is much more likely is a greater role for the other non-Arab states, Turkey and Iran. The eclipse of Iraq, however temporary, will correspondingly increase the importance of Iran in the Gulf. If Iran's rulers continue to think in terms of national interests rather than Islamic revolution, that increase may become permanent. Turkey too may find itself obliged to abandon its long maintained policy of avoiding any involvement in Arab or Mideastern politics, and be compelled to play a more active part.

A FEW OF OUR FAVORITE KINGS

Dilip Hiro

L A S T   W E E K at the Carlton Club casino in Cannes, Sheikh Eyani, an adviser to Prince Faisal of Saudi Arabia, lost £8.8 million [about $17 million] at the roulette tables. He immediately wrote a check to settle two thirds of the debt. The story flatters every cheap caricature of the super-rich Arab princeling, and adds a new note of fiddling while the Gulf burns. But we need to recall one truth about the status quo Saddam Hussein threatens. The sheikh is in the casino because the Western powers put him there, and kept him there. When the dust of battle clears, a restoration of "business as usual" will mean more grotesque inequality, more resentment and, in time, another Saddam to voice the anger of the Arab poor.

The Gulf region contains sixty-six percent of the world's known oil reserves. Ensuring cheap access to this energy source for the West and Japan has formed a pillar of U.S. Middle Eastern policy since the Second World War. The others have been support for the state of Israel and hostility to Soviet influence. These aims have meant shoring up the widely despised ruling dynasties of Saudi Arabia and five smaller states: Kuwait, Oman, Bahrain, Qatar and the United Arab Emirates. Meanwhile, Western arms, trade and diplomatic muscle have allowed the oligarchs to freeze their lands' political life and strangle dissent at birth.

Until this month, the strategy had seemed to pay a handsome dividend. By summer 1990, the inflation-adjusted price of oil had dropped to the equivalent of its 1972 level. In short, a barrel of crude was as cheap

Dilip Hiro is the author of several books, including *The Longest War: The Iran-Iraq Military Conflict.* This article was published in the August 24, 1990, issue of *The New Statesman and Society.*

as in the days before the OPEC-led "oil shocks" of 1973–74 and 1978–79. Then Iraq turned against the principal quota-buster and price-cutter, its ally and banker in the war against Iran—Kuwait.

Even there, where the al-Sabahs ran the least vicious of the region's family businesses, the national assembly had been suspended for four years prior to the invasion. Of 1.9 million Kuwaiti residents, only 750,000 had citizenship rights. Of these, only 60,000 males were allowed to vote.

By way of compensation, all Kuwaitis enjoyed a lavishly funded welfare state with free health care and guaranteed male employment. Yet, the al-Sabahs, creatures of their British protectors until independence in 1961 and firm friends thereafter, found it hard to establish the legitimacy of their rule. Much of the opposition to them came from pro-Iranian Shiites; in 1985 one group tried to assassinate the emir. While calling for Iraqi withdrawal, the Teheran government has studiously failed to demand his return.

It was pressure from Saudi Arabia, also fearful of Islamic militancy, that helped push Kuwait into suspending its rudimentary parliament. The House of Saud has never bothered with such niceties. Yet the kingdom at the heart of "Operation Desert Storm," and so publicly embarrassed by the U.S. troops on its Arab soil, has courted and won American favor from the moment of its birth. The tribal leader Abdul Aziz ibn Abdul Rahman al-Saud finished his conquest of a swathe of former Ottoman lands in 1932. He worked fast: By 1933 the Standard Oil Company of California gained concessions for £50,000 in gold as an advance against future oil royalties. Thus he broke the regional pattern which had seen all concessions until then granted to British companies.

U.S. oil firms and their government have stood at the shoulder of the Saudi autocrats ever since. Their support has been reciprocated. After the Iranian revolution of 1979, King Khalid, "Protector of the Holy Shrines" of Islam, allowed the U.S. to store arms and ammunition on his territory. Saudi gratitude went further. During the Irangate scandal, Congress refused the Reagan administration funding for the Contra guerrillas in Nicaragua. So CIA director Bill Casey went to see the Saudi ambassador, who wrote a personal check for $1 million for the Contra account in Switzerland and promised another every month. And for a quarter-century, from 1962 to 1986, the oil minister Sheikh Ahmad Zaki Yamani belied his cartoon image as a blackmailer of motorists by seeking to protect Western interests in the Gulf.

Senior Saudi princes have made hundreds of millions of dollars from kickbacks on contracts given to Western firms. The pickings are richest in the field of weapons procurement, where the Saudis have spent on a grand scale since Western prodding led to the creation of the "Gulf Cooperation Council" in the early stages of the Iran-Iraq war. A recent package awarded to British defense companies amounted to £17 billion, the largest-ever single weapons deal. King Fahd's invitation to the infidel armies simply made visible a long history of mutual aid.

Yet even the despotic Sauds have cause to fear the instability that a Saddam, or a Khomeini, can arouse. The then king beat off demands for a constitutional monarchy from the progressive "Free Princes" in the early 1960s, and in 1979 Islamic republican guerrillas seized the Grand Mosque in Mecca. Fear of further discontent led the royal family to enforce Islamic law more strictly through the *Ulema* court of Koranic scholars. The rulers also promised an elected "constitutional assembly." Nothing came of it. But the standard torture of detainees by the *falaqa* (beating the soles of the feet), and occasional amputation or beheading for convicted criminals, remain all too real.

The smaller states now thrust into the front line all bear the marks of British influence. This dates from the late nineteenth century, when the opening of the Suez Canal led the Empire to protect each stage of the passage to India. Formal independence for all except Kuwait came in 1971. Informal control has never ceased. In Oman, the Foreign Office helped engineer the overthrow in 1970 of the ultra-orthodox Sultan Said by his son, Prince Qaboos. British military advisers continue to run the army, while U.S. forces have used harbors and airports since a pact with the sultan in 1980.

Other territories repeat the pattern of vast oil reserves, a tiny ruling class, a noncitizen populace of expatriates and susceptibility to outside pressure. The archipelago of Bahrain, with virtually no oil of its own left, is an exception. Its 400,000 population now depends on offshore banking and leisure facilities for the Saudi and foreign élites. Alone among Gulf states, it permits the legal consumption of alcohol. It also gives a home to the permanent U.S. forces in the Middle East. They occupy a naval base formerly used by the British.

The United Arab Emirates best displays the syndrome of shortsighted greed and foreign domination that so inflamed Saddam. With a minute native population (only one in eight of the 1.5 million inhabitants), the rulers of oil-rich Abu Dhabi, Dubai and Sharjah seem intent on pumping out as much of their 97.7 billion barrels of reserves as they can. With Kuwait, they helped drive down the price of crude and thus antagonized Iraq, which has about the same stock of oil but eighty times as many permanent mouths to feed.

In the last decade, Iran's Islamic purists, and now the pan-Arab nationalists of Iraq, have menaced the Gulf dynasties with the prospect of popular wrath. Both religious and secular radicals have denounced their corruption and enslavement to the West. Hardware and expertise from "decadent" America and Europe have indeed let the families dig their heels into the sand. Their oil wealth is no more fairly distributed now than in 1958, when the Saudis first bothered to separate the royal house's private income from the revenue of the state.

Washington and London have so far refrained for two reasons from pushing the monarchs toward political pluralism. First, it is much simpler to deal with six ruling families than the varied personalities and policies thrown up by a democratic system. Second, elected governments would feel the winds of Arab and Islamic militancy, and veer away from the West.

Whether Saddam is overthrown, or saves his skin by retreat from Kuwait, his Western enemies will face the first test of their attitude to political change in the Gulf. If a pan-Arab force were to occupy Kuwait with the Baghdad regime intact, the way would be open for a referendum on the fate of the monarchy. Yasir Arafat and Colonel Qaddafi suggested this option in their abortive peace plan.

But if, as now looks more probable, a bloody conflict ends in the downfall of Saddam, a grateful West would hastily restore Sheikh Jabir al-Ahmad al-Sabah to his palace. He has served the West well, and the Kuwait Investment Organization has plowed $100 billion into Western firms. (Its holdings include around ten percent of British Petroleum and Midland Bank.)

Restoration would be the scenario to please the Western nations most. Yet it would not solve the underlying problem: the fragility of the Gulf monarchies, which together possess sixty-six percent of global oil reserves. Whatever happens, they can never return to the era before 2 August 1990. This date will be seen by future historians as a milestone. It marks the beginning of the end for these remnants of feudalism in a region that until now has thrown an economic lifeline to the world's leading capitalist countries.

•

IN THE WAKE OF "DESERT STORM"

Scott MacLeod

NEVER HAD I felt so gloomy about the Middle East as I did recently after I spent an evening with King Hussein. The king probably knows the region, and certainly the Arabs, as well as anyone else, and he carries the burden of being conceivably the last of the Hashemite rulers. Until the Saudis took over the Hijaz, the region that includes Mecca and Medina, the king's clan was custodian of the Islamic holy places there for hundreds of years. His great-grandfather was the *sharif* of Mecca. Abdullah, his grandfather, helped lead the Arab revolt against the Ottoman empire and was rewarded by Britain with a new kingdom east of the Jordan River. Hussein, as a teenager, was at Abdullah's side when he was assassinated in 1951 at the Al Aqsa mosque in Jerusalem by a disaffected Palestinian. In 1958, a cousin, King Faisal of Iraq, was overthrown and murdered.

The king, who has led Jordan through many shaky periods for nearly forty years, is doing nothing to discourage the feeling that the entire region is headed for something dreadful. A week after American planes began bombing Iraq, Fouad Ayoub, a palace press officer I have known for many years, telephoned me at the Intercontinental Hotel in Amman. The king and Queen Noor, he said, would be giving an informal dinner that evening for a few cabinet ministers and some foreign journalists. Although the king is unhappy with much of the press coverage he receives, no other Arab leader makes as great an effort to deal with reporters personally, especially during times of crisis.

Scott MacLeod, *Time* magazine's Johannesburg bureau chief, was in the Middle East during the Persian Gulf crisis. This article was published in the March 7, 1991, issue of *The New York Review of Books*.

Hussein's palace is a collection of ordinary cream-colored villas and office buildings on top of one of Amman's many steep hills. Inside, in a reception room with old Damascene *mashrabiyah* paneling, we were offered fresh fruit juices, served in Hebron blown-glass tumblers. The king, when he finally appeared with his wife, was wearing a blazer over a dark turtleneck sweater. As we entered the dining room, we were told of reports that Iraqi Scud missiles were flying over Jordan on their way to Tel Aviv.

After a simple supper of Arabic *mezze,* the King invited us to ask questions. He looked sad and frustrated, although he never lost his temper as he gave us his long and measured replies. He expected a long war, he told us. He assumed that the might of the Allied forces was capable of dislodging Iraqi troops from Kuwait, but at a terrible cost. He was concerned about what Israel might do, but he seemed equally worried about an eruption of political unrest that would bring down Arab governments. When a British journalist pointed out that he had said nothing hopeful the entire evening, the king seemed to wince.

Saddam Hussein's confrontation with the U.S., which is how many Arabs view Operation Desert Storm, is tearing violently at the connections among nations and groups in the Arab world. Saddam has proved himself to be a radical seeking to destroy the status quo. Whatever the outcome of the war, his invasion of Kuwait and his refusal to yield to the immense power opposing him have deeply changed Arab politics. Shifts have already taken place in relations between Arab states, as well as in relations between the rulers and citizens in Arab states.

Current Jordanian politics provide some glimpse of what the consequences of the war may be, and, to me, they do not look very hopeful. Trends I have observed in Jordan and other parts of the Middle East during the last six months suggest that militancy and extremism will pose increasingly serious threats to moderation. Islamic fundamentalism seems to be gaining strength at the expense of the secular forces and ideologies that have until now prevailed in most Arab countries. As a result the prospects seem bleak that the war will eventually lead to peaceful settlements of the various disputes in the region.

Saddam Hussein is very popular in Jordan. This is one of the reasons why the king has increasingly supported Iraq against the Allies. For several months Jordanian officials had claimed that Jordan was neutral and had more or less abided by the U.N. sanctions against Iraq. But on February 6, the king bitterly condemned the attack on Iraq and charged that it was a "war against all Arabs and Muslims," intended to put the region under foreign domination. He gives his subjects the clear impression that he regards Saddam as a close Arab brother. Everywhere you go in Amman you come across posters showing Saddam alone or with the king. One widely displayed poster shows the king ceremoniously presenting Saddam with a gun. In the cafés men listening to Amman Radio cheer when the newscaster reports an Iraqi Scud missile attack on Israel or an Allied plane shot down by Iraqi fire. I can't think of a single one of my dozens of Jordanian friends, including those who have lived for years in the U.S. or Europe, who does not support Saddam. Hateful as he seems throughout the West and to the rulers in the Gulf themselves, Saddam, like no other leader since Nasser, speaks directly to the despair and powerlessness that many Arabs feel. That is particularly true now that he is seen in some Arab countries as standing up to the attacks of the United States and Europe in defense of Arab pride. His brutal invasion of Kuwait, for many Arabs, was forgotten on the day that American troops began arriving in Saudi Arabia.

Few Arabs in the richer Gulf states have any sympathy for Saddam, but a great many in poorer countries like Jordan do. In North Africa, anti-Western feelings set off by the Gulf showdown seem explosive, particularly in Algeria and Morocco. In Rabat, the capital of Morocco, on February 3 an estimated 300,000 people took part in the city's biggest political demonstration since the Suez crisis in 1956. Many of them displayed pictures of Saddam, despite the fact that their king, Hassan II, has sent about 5,000 Moroccan troops to join the Alliance. Well-informed recent visitors to Syria tell me that Saddam has a fair amount of popular backing there, despite President Hafez al-Assad's decision to join the Alliance.

Among the poorer Arabs, only the Egyptians seem ambivalent about Saddam. That is probably because they are preoccupied with their own serious economic problems and, in any case, they have never been enthusiastic about an Arab leader who is not an Egyptian. Tens of thousands of Egyptians who recently returned from working in Iraq have no illusions about his regime. Even so, two and a half weeks after the war began, Egyptian opposition groups, including the Muslim Brotherhood and various leftist political parties, issued a statement condemning the "brutal attack launched by the American and Allied Forces," which includes 45,000 Egyptian troops. Meanwhile, more than 50,000 Egyptians are reported to have been conscripted into Iraqi military service.

When no one else has been able to do so, Saddam offers many Arabs dreams of unity, with which they could finally achieve a respected place in the world; of prosperity, which could be brought about by an equitable distribution of Arab oil wealth;* of Israel's defeat, which would enable the Palestinians to have justice.

Shortly before January 16, I had dinner in Amman with Daoud Kuttab, a well-known Palestinian journalist who was visiting from Jerusalem. He recalled the powerful effect that Saddam, before the Kuwait crisis, had on Palestinians in the occupied territories when he threatened to "burn half of Israel." Throughout the *intifada,* Kuttab said, Palestinians watched as Israelis managed to carry on their everyday lives, going apparently unperturbed to the beach or to concerts. "Then this guy six hundred miles away makes a statement," Kuttab said, "and all of a sudden we see Israelis rushing out to get gas masks."

The desperation for change of some sort runs deep. Since the end of the Second World War, when most of the twenty-one Arab states became independent, not a single one has developed a stable working democracy, although there have been increasingly free elections in countries like Algeria and Jordan and some degree of press freedom in these and a few other Arab countries. Having been dominated by Turkish and then European governors for hundreds of years, Arab societies were susceptible to military dictatorship. Widespread popular demands for the destruction of Israel helped to give an element of popular legitimacy to dictatorships that otherwise would have enjoyed little or none. The central planning accompanying authoritarian rule has helped to produce economic stagnation in the poorer Arab countries.

To the West, Saddam's rule has been appalling. To ordinary Arabs, especially those who do not have to live in Iraq, his authoritarian style and his ruthless treatment of dissidents are not unusual. In any case, these Arabs don't look to Saddam as a model for government, but they are drawn to him by the way he addresses grievances over Israel or "Western imperialism" that are widely viewed by Arabs as being responsible for the retarded political development of their societies.

What gives Saddam his popularity, moreover, is not so much what he says as what he does. Like Nasser, he is a charismatic leader, but unlike Nasser, he does something besides talk. Arabs who have grown used to the fruitless wrangling over disputes involving, say, the Palestinians or Lebanon, were deeply impressed with how Saddam, after Kuwait's lead-

---

* Countries like Saudi Arabia and Kuwait, largely because of their natural oil resources, have had GNPs comparable with those of the U.S. and Western European countries. Countries like Jordan, Syria, Tunisia, Algeria, and Morocco, on the other hand, have had GNPs more closely resembling those of Eastern European countries.

Iraq, with a smaller GNP per capita than Saudi Arabia or Kuwait, is nonetheless a major oil-producing state that has done relatively little to share its wealth with poorer countries.

ers refused to consider his various demands concerning oil, simply snatched the country in a matter of hours. "I have always hated Saddam because I am a liberal," a Palestinian friend told me. "But he brings out the 'dictator' in me. Now I am all the way for Saddam. We Palestinians are drowning, and he is throwing us a rope."

Significantly, Saddam's popularity is at its highest now since the outbreak of war with the U.S.-led coalition. In view of the powerful forces arrayed against Iraq, many Arabs had assumed that Saddam would back down before the U.N.'s January 15 deadline for Iraq's withdrawal from Kuwait. The missile attacks on Israel convinced many Arabs that his efforts to link the Palestinian issue with Kuwait amounted to more than just talk.

In six short months, Saddam's moves have strongly influenced Jordanian politics, and not for the better. For one thing, there is the phenomenon of "intellectual terrorism," as a Jordanian intellectual I know calls it. The intensity and dogmatism of sympathy for Saddam frequently silence anybody who has a contrary opinion.

The West-Bank and Gaza Palestinians involved in the *intifada* were among the first to back Saddam. Palestinians in Jordan and elsewhere tended to be confused about whom to support, but they soon fell in with the sentiment of the *intifada.* Jordanians of Bedouin origin, the so-called "East Bankers," also quickly backed Saddam. They have always considered Iraq a friendly country, and have long harbored hostile feelings toward Gulf leaders, especially King Fahd of Saudi Arabia and the Emir of Kuwait, whom they view as having frequently humiliated their own, less wealthy monarch. Palestinians working in Kuwait came home to Jordan filled with bitterness toward Saddam. But it seems that most of them, partly as the result of the pervasive social pressure, reversed their view, at least in public.

Such is the fervor for Saddam that Jordanians who have slight misgivings about him are afraid to express them or, if they do, are told to shut up. A friend in Amman says that, in political conversations with colleagues, he cannot use the word "occupation" in reference to Iraq's occupation of Kuwait. If he does so, he is admonished and reminded that Iraq "embraced" Kuwait, or Kuwait is "the branch that returned to the tree."

Meanwhile the rise of the Muslim Brotherhood, which advocates an Islamic state, is a relatively new and politically far-reaching development in Jordan. A couple of years ago, few people paid the members of the Brotherhood much attention, in part because of the government's tight restrictions on all political activity. Now they are the most important political movement in the country, and are gaining more ground as the result of the crisis. Many Brotherhood members in Jordan are Palestinians, and the group has close links with the Hamas fundamentalist movement that has been active in the uprisings in Gaza and the West Bank. In its charter, Hamas calls itself the military wing of the Muslim Brotherhood in Palestine.

The Brotherhood began to gain more power in Jordanian politics in 1989. Economic stagnation led to the "uprising of the south," which included serious rioting in the city of Maan, traditionally an ethnic Bedouin stronghold for the regime. King Hussein was forced to relax his government's tight control of political activity, and he called the first elections since 1967. Unlike the conventional political parties, the Brotherhood had never been banned in Jordan and easily won the most seats. Nearly everybody I met in Jordan, including government officials, refers to the election as "the beginning of democracy."

Had the king felt inclined to oppose Saddam and back the U.S., he would have faced opposition both from the Brotherhood and from many of the Palestinians who make up at least sixty percent of Jordan's population of three million. The movement, with twenty-two members sitting in the eighty-seat lower house of the Jordanian assembly and ten other deputies who support it, strongly backs Saddam. (The forty-seat upper house is appointed by the king.) Seeing which way the wind was blowing, the king on January 1 appointed five members of the Brotherhood to his cabinet for the first time.

After the Allies attacked Iraq, the lower house approved a resolution calling "on all the Arab and Islamic nations to strike at American interests and the interests of those nations participating in the aggression against Iraq." Foreign Minister Taher Masri, who comes from a prominent family in the West Bank city of Nablus, left the assembly before the vote, which he was later quoted as saying was "unwise." The vote deeply embarrassed the king. All he could say afterward was that the parliament had "the right to express people's anger and frustration and despair." But it was obvious that popular opinion in Jordan was running dangerously ahead of his feelings; and in his speech on February 6, the king flatly declared, "We salute Iraq, its heroic army, its steadfast people."

I met Azzam Tamimi, the director of the Brotherhood's parliamentary office. He is an energetic young man in his mid-thirties, who spent five years studying physiology in England. His family is originally from Hebron, and a distant relative, Asaad Bayyoud Tamimi, is the Amman-based imam for an extremist Palestinian faction known as the Islamic Jihad. I found him in a cheerful mood. He still couldn't believe that the

Brotherhood actually held some formal political power in Jordan. "It's like a dream," he told me.

Jordan's laws have always conformed generally to *Sharia,* or Islamic law. The Brotherhood has achieved many of its legislative and administrative goals, such as lifting restrictions on political activists and abolishing interest rates for farmers and small businessmen. So the organization devotes much of its energies to the Gulf crisis and the *intifada.* Tamimi seemed to agree with other fundamentalists I met that Operation Desert Storm amounted to a new Western crusade against the Muslim faithful. He sees the war for Kuwait as nothing less than a struggle for power between Islam and Western civilization.

I found it hard to convince any Jordanians, whatever their political leanings, that the Allied forces went to war with Iraq in order to repel aggression. Tamimi subscribed to a popular theory I have often heard in the Middle East, that the U.S. used Iraq's invasion of Kuwait as a pretext to send a huge military force to the region to 1) smash Iraq's growing power, 2) protect Israel, 3) take control of the region's oil resources, and 4) crush the growing Islamic movements. "It is not a secret that we, as Muslims, look forward to eliminating the state of Israel," he said. "It seemed [to the U.S.] that Saddam, with his growing power, was becoming a real threat."

The attacks on Iraq have produced a disturbing increase in anti-Western feeling in Jordan. I asked Tamimi what the parliament meant when it called on Muslims to confront the West. He said Muslims were being called on to attack any American installation of a military or semi-military nature. However, the call seems to have been more rhetorical than practical. The Brotherhood, he said, did not have the means to attack any U.S. installations in Jordan. Some people, however, have begun staging attacks in Amman. Since January 16, gun shots were fired at a branch of Citibank. There was one small bombing and one attempted bombing at a branch of the British Bank of the Middle East, and the library at the French Cultural Center was burned down. At the same time, fundamentalists stepped up their rhetoric. A member of the king's cabinet, Religious Affairs Minister Ibrahim Zeid Keilani, who is a member of the Brotherhood, called in a televised sermon for a jihad "against America and its atheist allies until doomsday."

Since the Gulf crisis, Tamimi noted with pleasure, Jordan's television broadcasts have begun to reflect Islamic values more closely. "We have fewer Western-style films, and more films talking about Islamic history, war, and jihad," he said. "We also have documentaries on the role of the CIA, World War II. These are the things we would like our TV to show, instead of useless things like love stories and U.S.-made series like *Dallas*."

Tamimi told me that the Brotherhood had no problem with the king. The movement did not think that a monarchy was incompatible with its concept of an Islamic state and, in any case, its members believed in democratic means of change. But the ultimate goal was a great Islamic empire. "The Muslim community extends from the Atlantic Ocean to the Pacific Ocean," he said. "If the Muslim community was given the freedom to choose, it would choose to be re-united. We would be one Islamic unit." He said that he believed the borders dividing Muslims were drawn up by colonialists against their wishes.

What would be the advantage of one huge Muslim state? I asked. "Power," Tamimi replied without hesitation. "Power comes with unity. The United States is the greatest superpower now. Had it not had fifty united states, could it have that power?"

The first objective of power, he explained, was self-defense. "What is happening to us now—America and its Allies waging a devastating war against Iraq—is because we are divided and weak," he said. "The second thing is to be able to protect one's resources. The oil that is in Kuwait and Saudi Arabia does not belong to the Kuwaitis or the Saudis. It belongs to every Muslim in the world. Even the American Muslims. Who are the Saudis to enjoy the wealth alone, and have Muslims in Sudan starving to death?

"The third advantage," Tamimi continued, "is that when you are powerful, you can impress other nations. We, as an Islamic superpower, hope that we can spread our teachings to the world. Islam has to spread all over. Instead of people making fun of Islam or Muslims in the West, we would be able to provide the beautiful picture of Islam. What we can't tolerate is being prevented from conveying the message."

A significant effect of the crisis is the growing solidarity that has arisen between Jordan's Islamic fundamentalists and secular political groups, among them the Palestine Liberation Organization, Arab nationalists, and Communists. Hardly anywhere else in the Middle East have such diverse groups unified behind a cause. Nasser, the most powerful Arab nationalist so far, hunted down and imprisoned Egypt's Muslim Brotherhood. Shortly before the war started, Tamimi's group organized a protest rally of 15,000 people that included all the major factions in Jordan. They shouted slogans like "Use your chemicals, Saddam!" The group is also coordinating with the opposing factions in parliament.

Enmity toward the United States is the main factor behind the unity of the Brotherhood and its political rivals in Jordan. Before the Gulf crisis, the Brotherhood and most militant Muslims in the Middle East loathed Saddam, who, after all, is leader of a secular party, the Baath, and had waged a war against an Islamic republic. But Saddam during the last six months has openly sought fundamentalist support by calling for a jihad and by having the words *"Allahu Akbar,"* "God is Great," sewn into the Iraqi flag. As a result, he seems to be having surprising success in attracting Muslim sympathy. "What is in his heart is Allah's business," Tamimi told me. "But the [Islamic] rhetoric in his speeches leaves important marks on the Iraqi people and the Muslim world. When Saddam talks about a fight against the infidels, a war that is waged on behalf of Muslims, a victory that comes from Allah, we welcome that. I think he has proven to be credible and sincere."

The decision of Arab nationalists to join with fundamentalists is a sign of the nationalists' diminishing strength. The biggest loser, at least for the moment, seems to be Yasir Arafat and his policy of compromise. Not only has the PLO been losing political ground to Hamas in the occupied territories and to the Brotherhood in Jordan, but Arafat is in the position of having sought a compromise with the very forces that are now attacking Iraq, and that are portrayed as the enemies of the Arabs. As far as the Brotherhood and Hamas are concerned, Tamimi told me, "there is no compromise over any part of Palestine."

Although the PLO has thus far not officially altered its compromise policy, Tamimi believes that Arafat's program for a negotiated "two-state solution" seems to have come to a halt, especially after the failure of the dialogue between the U.S. and the PLO to yield results. "I hear many PLO activists talking about renouncing that policy," he said. "There is a growing trend within the PLO that the compromise policy is not going to work because the Israelis expressed more than once the view that they were not willing to give in to the Palestinians. I think the PLO is still strong, but Arafat as a leader is losing ground. He will lose more if he continues to insist on his political program. I hope to see them return to the PLO charter, which means struggle until the complete liberation of Palestine. But, personally speaking, I don't think Arafat is suitable as a leader anymore. If they want to continue being effective, I think they have to change their leader." In the short term, that would appear to be unlikely. Arafat, in fact, remains largely popular within the PLO's ranks. (The man long considered to be Arafat's likely successor, Salah Khalaf, also known as Abu Iyad, was assassinated in Tunis on January 15. The Tunisian authorities arrested as a suspect a PLO bodyguard who until last year had belonged to the Abu Nidal terrorist group, which is said to be backed by Iraq.)

I often heard in Amman that the king has never been more popular, thanks to his decision to go along with the strong sentiment in favor of Saddam. But the outlook for Jordan does not look promising. In the unlikely event that Saddam manages to face down the Alliance, the king will be carried away by militant political winds coming from Iraq. The crushing of Saddam, on the other hand, will cause deep disappointment among Jordan's people. Having had their hopes raised, they will feel growing despair and will harbor even stronger grudges against the U.S. and other members of the Alliance. Arabs in other countries will probably react in a similar way. The frustration will be compounded by the worsening economic situation in many Arab countries, especially in North Africa. Jordan's economy has been severely damaged already. Most of its exports went to Iraq, and its economy was also supported by remittances from Jordanians who have left their jobs in the Gulf since the crisis began with Iraq's invasion on August 2. After the war is over, moreover, Saudi Arabia and Kuwait will probably try to punish the king financially for his refusal to join in the Alliance by restricting his access to credits and oil.

Theoretically, after the war the king could serve as an intermediary between the U.S. and Arabs who sided with Iraq. But he is, I think, unlikely to rush forward with the kinds of moderate proposals that have generally characterized his efforts to solve Middle East problems. Many Jordanian officials I met in Amman seemed to think that an explosion of popular feeling could be averted if the West quickly and decisively took steps to solve the Palestinian problem after the end of the war. To them, that seems to mean forcing Israel to permit the establishment of an independent Palestinian state in the West Bank and Gaza. But they don't hold out much hope that this will happen.

One afternoon in late January, I had tea at the house of a cabinet minister I have known since 1985. As usual, the ground rules kept our discussion off the record. He was more discouraged than usual about the prospects of negotiating with Israel. Saddam's missile attacks, he believed, had the effect of boosting sympathy for Israel among Americans. Like many Jordanians, he was concerned that Jordan would get "dragged" into the Gulf war if Israel used Jordanian airspace to retaliate against Iraq. He was also concerned that Israel might use the crisis as a cover to expel thousands of Palestinians from the West Bank. Israel could seize a strip in the Jordan Valley, he said, "transfer" the Palestinians to it, and then withdraw across the river.

The minister, however, seemed most worried about what might happen on the streets of Jordan. "We are already in a difficult position," he told me. "The economy is in shambles. What if there are cries in the streets of 'Jihad!'? We don't know how we are going to handle it." But then he said he did know. "We would have to stop them," he said. "But we can't afford a clash between us and the people, especially not now."

Those anxious remarks may apply to the possible consequences of the war in a number of other Arab countries. The hopes of many Arabs for greater freedom from the perceived grip of the West, and from the control of their own governments, will, if they are strongly put forward, probably be suppressed by Arab police forces or soldiers.

THE PALESTINIANS AND THE GULF CRISIS

Rashid Khalidi

PALESTINIAN SUPPORT for Iraqi President Saddam Hussein's invasion of Kuwait on August 2, 1990, led many to believe that the Palestinians would suffer for supporting Iraq. The strong anti-Palestinian backlash in the United States, Israel, Egypt, and the Arab states of the Persian Gulf seemed to confirm this view. However, the Palestinian position on Iraq's invasion is much more nuanced, ambiguous, and equivocal than it has been portrayed. Thus, if the Palestinians continue to suffer from the effects of the Gulf crisis, it will be for reasons other than the stand they have taken on Iraq.

The keystone to the portrayal of the Palestinians as siding entirely with Iraq and against Kuwait is based on what took place at the Arab League meeting in Cairo on August 10. At the meeting, the PLO (Palestine Liberation Organization) reportedly voted against a resolution condemning the Iraqi invasion and supporting the deployment of American and other multinational forces to Saudi Arabia. This was a crucial moment in the crisis; only afterward was the Arab world openly divided over Iraq's invasion of Kuwait, and only afterward did the Arab states support an American presence in the region.

In fact, the PLO did not vote against the August 10 resolution. After the resolution was introduced, Egyptian President Hosni Mubarak asked only for the votes in favor—there were twelve—and then concluded the session refusing to allow amendments, discussion, votes against or abstentions. Three heads of state later claimed that Mubarak had pre-

Rashid Khalidi teaches modern Middle Eastern History at the University of Chicago, where he is associate director of the Center for Middle East Studies. This article appeared in the January 1991 issue of *Current History*.

vented them from speaking at the summit, and alternatives to the Egyptian-Saudi resolution were not presented for a vote. These included a PLO proposal that the Palestinians claimed had the approval of all parties, including Egypt and Saudi Arabia. The PLO said later that if Mubarak had allowed a vote, it would have abstained rather than voting against the resolution, since it opposed the Iraqi invasion of Kuwait but was unwilling to endorse a major United States military presence in the heart of the Arab world.[1]

This has also been the position of many Arab states, from Algeria, Mauritania, Tunisia, Libya, and Sudan in North Africa, to Jordan and Yemen in the Middle East. It also has many followers in countries like Morocco, Egypt and Syria, which voted for the resolution of August 10 and have sent troops to Saudi Arabia; it is even the position of some circles in Saudi Arabia itself.[2] For the Palestinians and other Arabs who have adopted this position, the Iraqi invasion, occupation and annexation of Kuwait is a great evil, but a massive American military presence in the region is an even greater evil.

In response to their stand, the Saudi government has inflicted particularly severe punishment on Jordan, Yemen, and Sudan. Citizens from these countries have been forced to return home from lucrative jobs in Saudi Arabia, and financial subsidies have been cut off. But the Palestinians and the PLO have felt the special ire of the Saudi government and its allies—Egypt, Syria, the Kuwaiti government-in-exile and the Gulf principalities. As of September 1990, the General Federation of Palestinian Trade Unions estimated that more than 56,000 Palestinians had left the Gulf, either because they had been expelled or because their work contracts were not renewed. Of these, an estimated 20,000 to 30,000 have returned to the Israeli-occupied West Bank and Gaza Strip.[3]

The Palestinians received this particularly severe treatment partly because they are weaker and more vulnerable than countries like Algeria and Libya, and are thus an easier target. But there are other reasons. The

[1] A "PLO Executive Committee Statement on the Gulf Crisis," dated August 19, made these assertions. It was published in Arabic by the *Palestine News Agency Bulletin* (Washington, D.C.), vol. 5, no. 26 (September 1, 1990).

[2] See David B. Ottaway, "Some Saudi Doubts about War Preparations Seep to Surface," *Washington Post*, September 20, 1990, pp. A25, A31; and Judith Caesar, "The War of Words in Saudi Arabia," *Washington Post*, October 10, 1990, p. A21.

[3] These figures were issued in a leaflet summarizing the results produced by an economic study group of the General Federation of Palestinian Trade Unions, reported in *The Jerusalem Post*, September 11, 1990. Estimates on returns to the occupied territories were made by Professor Saeb Ireqat of al-Najah University, presented at a seminar in Jerusalem on September 15, 1990, reported in *Al-Fajr*, September 16, 1990.

most important is that the Palestinians have been a crucial legitimizing factor in the Arab state system. The PLO's absence from the ranks of those supporting the Saudi Egyptian Syrian Gulf states coalition was seen by all these states as possibly undermining the domestic legitimacy of their overt alliance with the United States.

The Palestinian position on Iraq's invasion was profoundly ambivalent because virtually all Palestinians judged the invasion according to their own interests. On the one hand, the Iraqi invasion raised issues that are crucial to the political posture that the PLO has adopted in recent years, which is based on the acceptance of United Nations (U.N.) Security Council resolution 242. This resolution declares the inadmissibility of the acquisition of territory by war. On this basis, it calls for Israeli withdrawal from territories occupied during the 1967 Six-Day War, in return for a just and lasting peace. Most Palestinians, and certainly the PLO, believed that it would be inconsistent to champion such principles in the Arab-Israeli dispute but to deny them in the Iraqi-Kuwaiti conflict. The PLO thus repeatedly affirmed that it opposed the Iraqi occupation and annexation of Kuwait.[4]

On the other hand, the PLO and the Palestinians have long been preoccupied with Israel and the extensive support it receives from the United States. They are fundamentally opposed to anything that makes the Arab states more dependent on the United States and therefore less likely to support the Palestinian cause. For this reason, the PLO and several Arab states (notably Jordan, Yemen, Algeria and Sudan) tried to organize an Arab mediation effort that would settle the Gulf crisis and prevent American military intervention in Saudi Arabia.

The Palestinians' belief that the United States is "tilted" toward Israel is at the heart of the Palestinian reaction to the Gulf crisis. But other elements shape this belief as well. One important element is deep resentment at the failure of Egypt and the Arab states of the Gulf to use their influence with Washington to find a just resolution to the Palestine question. Many Palestinians make this criticism in even harsher terms. They accuse the oil-rich monarchies of the Gulf of caring only for staying in power with the help of their Western friends. They argue that these regimes purchase Western support by not allowing the embarrassing

---

[4]See the PLO Executive Committee statement on September 12, 1990, in which it reiterated its stand, in Arabic, in the *Palestine News Agency Bulletin,* vol. 5, no. 27 (October 1, 1990); as well as Yasir Arafat's speech to the Conference of Non-Government Organizations in Geneva on August 29, 1990, reported in *Al-Fajr,* op. cit.

Palestinian issue to become an irritant in their relations with the United States.

An undercurrent in this attitude is anger at the treatment skilled Palestinian workers have received in the oil-producing countries, where their efforts and those of other workers from Lebanon, Egypt, Jordan, and Syria have been essential in building modern infrastructures. Such estrangement between expatriate work forces and host governments exists to some degree in all the oil-producing countries, but it has grown particularly severe between the Palestinians and the Gulf states. This poor treatment explains in part the lack of sympathy among many Palestinians, and in much of the Arab world, for the cruel plight of the Kuwaitis.

Another factor in the Palestinian response to the crisis was a certain sympathy for Iraq among Palestinians and many others in the Arab world that preceded the invasion of Kuwait. This sympathy grew from despair over the failure of Arab efforts to resolve peacefully the conflict with Israel during the past few years, largely because of the intransigence of the Israeli government of Prime Minister Yitzhak Shamir and the complaisance toward the Israeli government of the administration of United States President George Bush. In a situation where the Palestinian *intifada* (uprising) has continued for nearly three years without effect and the leading "moderate" Arab states, notably Egypt, have been unable to affect American or Israeli policy, Iraq's belligerent posture appeared to be a viable alternative.

Despite such sentiments, the Palestinians had deep misgivings about an alignment with Iraq even before the invasion of Kuwait. In the past, Iraq has tried to control Palestinian policy in a heavy-handed manner. This was especially true in the mid-1970s, when it used dissident Palestinian factions like Abu Nidal's to launch murderous attacks on the PLO in order to force it not to advocate a compromise settlement with Israel. The Iraqi regime's harsh domestic policy has always been anathema to most Palestinians, who value freedom in their national movement, as seen by the open debates within the Palestine National Council, the Palestinian "parliament-in-exile."[5]

The situation inside the occupied territories, where the *intifada* had begun in December 1987, apparently weighed heavily in the PLO's decision to shift toward Iraq. Although the shift was symbolic, PLO

[5]For more on these debates see Alain Gresh, *The PLO: The Struggle Within* (London: Zed Books, 1985), and Helena Cobban, *The Palestinian Liberation Organization: People, Power and Politics* (Cambridge: Cambridge University Press, 1984).

leaders may have thought it was all that they could do in view of the disappointing American response to the PLO's peace initiatives in 1988.

Most disappointing was the Bush administration's decision soon after it took office not to move more quickly on the peace process than the Israeli government was willing to. Progress stopped completely once it became clear that the Bush administration was unwilling to force the pace or to penalize Israel, even when Shamir brought down his coalition government in March 1990, rather than go ahead with the provisions of his own peace plan. The Palestinians felt that the great sacrifices of the *intifada* and their attempt to meet American conditions for new negotiations had been in vain.

It was a clear sign of the direction events in the region were taking when an Iraqi-based Palestinian group carried out an unsuccessful attack on a Tel Aviv beachfront during the summer of 1990. The PLO, unwilling or unable to alienate Iraq, did not condemn the raid, a failure that allowed the Bush administration to break off the fruitless dialogue it had been pursuing with the PLO. This undermined the already dim prospects for negotiations and pushed the PLO further into the waiting arms of Iraq—which was undoubtedly one of the aims of the Tel Aviv attack.

H O W W I L L the Palestinians and the PLO fare because of their ambivalent response to the Iraqi invasion? The answer lies in three issues: (1) the direct impact of this crisis on the Palestinian communities in the Gulf and its direct and indirect impact on other Palestinian communities that are dependent on the Gulf; (2) the negative impact the crisis has had on perceptions of the PLO in the United States and Israel; (3) the possibility of linking the Palestinian-Israeli conflict and the Gulf crisis.

Although there are few reliable or recent figures on the size of the Palestinian communities in the Gulf, they are estimated at roughly between 500,000 and 600,000: more than 300,000 in Kuwait (before the Iraqi invasion); 150,000 in Saudi Arabia; and perhaps another 100,000 in the other Gulf states. While they were dwarfed in size by the Palestinian community of more than two million in Israel and the occupied territories and more than one million in Jordan, the Gulf Palestinians were the most prosperous Palestinian community.

Despite their status as noncitizens, whose continued prosperity and well-being were largely dependent on the goodwill of their hosts, the Palestinians in the Gulf did remarkably well for several decades. They became the nucleus of a new Palestinian entrepreneurial class made up of contractors, traders, bankers, and professionals; they were an important factor in Palestinian politics, funding and making up a large part of the various constituent groups of the PLO; and the modest remittances of tens of thousands of individual Palestinian expatriate workers played a major role in keeping the economies of the occupied territories and Jordan afloat.

The importance of these remittances was made clear during the economic slump of the mid-1980s, when oil-producing states suffered from a sharp decline in the price of oil. The recession devastated the economies of the occupied territories and Jordan, and contributed both to the *intifada* and to the unrest that led Jordan to reinstitute multiparty parliamentary elections. It is easy to imagine the impact wholesale expulsions of Palestinians from the Gulf would have on both these regions. Further damage would occur if individuals, charities, universities and other public bodies in the Gulf decrease their support for Palestinian institutions —a process that has already begun.[6]

The Palestinians' response to the Gulf crisis has also caused a shift in the way their cause is viewed in the United States and Israel. There is little question that, however inaccurately or incompletely the Palestinian and PLO positions have been conveyed in the media, the general impression of the Palestinians in these two countries has been negative. Iraq has been judged beyond the pale by virtually the entire range of respectable opinion, and the PLO has been described as little more than a stooge of the Iraqis, which has made it easy for those already opposed to the PLO to blacken its name further. The indiscriminate Palestinian popular support of Iraq in its opposition to the American military presence in Saudi Arabia made this task even easier and appeared to render superfluous a close reading of the Palestinian and the PLO response.

While there has probably been an erosion in support of the Palestinians in American public opinion, some skepticism is in order about the long-term impact of this erosion. The trends revealed in the Foreign Policy Association's 1990 poll, taken before the Gulf crisis, are extremely favorable to the Palestinians, with an absolute majority of the more than 5,000 respondents favoring a Palestinian state.[7] These are clearly long-term trends, and appear, moreover, to have been reinforced by the

[6]This is reported by the Union of Charitable Societies in the occupied West Bank, which described a considerable dropoff in funds from the Gulf in August and September 1990. "From the Field" (Chicago: Palestine Human Rights Information Center, 1990), pp. 3–4.
[7]The Foreign Policy Association's "National Opinion Ballot Report," issued in September 1990, found that out of 5,006 responses, fifty-eight percent favored a Palestinian state as a solution to the Palestinian question, as against thirty-two percent for various forms of autonomy, and four percent for Israeli annexation of the occupied territories.

strong reaction to the October killing of twenty-one Palestinians at the Temple Mount in Jerusalem.

As for Israel, the very sharp negative reaction among many Israelis to the pro-Iraqi demonstrations in the occupied territories would appear to be a setback for the Palestinians especially since some critics were Israeli doves. The condemnation by Palestinian leaders in these territories of Iraq's occupation and annexation of Kuwait two weeks after the invasion took place was ignored by many Israelis and did not alter the impression that the Palestinians stood firmly behind Iraq, including the threats by Iraqi President Saddam Hussein to use chemical weapons against Israel if Israel struck Iraq first.

A FINAL issue concerns the possibility of linking the Gulf crisis to the Palestinian-Israeli conflict. The heightened world interest in the region has certainly brought more attention to the Palestinians, as was seen by the strong international outcry over the Temple Mount incident. Had international attention not been on the Gulf and on an international role in resolving that crisis, the United Nations might have failed again to take action against Israel.

But more interesting than the international response to this crisis is the Arab world's response to the Palestinians as a result of the crisis. The speed of the United States response to the occupation of Kuwait, where its interests were involved, has been contrasted most unfavorably in the Arab world to its failure to respond vigorously to more than twenty-three years of Israeli occupation. Serious misgivings have begun to surface along these lines even in Egypt and Saudi Arabia, the pillars of the American alliance against Iraq.

Such misgivings were present in Saudi Arabia early in the crisis, but were ignored by most of the American media until many weeks later. Only at the end of October did *The New York Times* report that Saudi leaders had "second thoughts" about their confrontational attitude toward the PLO. The article noted that "what has become known as linkage is alive and well in many a Saudi mind"—a reference to the linkage that is stressed by many observers in the Arab world between Israeli occupation of Palestinian land and Iraq's occupation of Kuwait.[8]

The existence of such sentiments in influential circles in Saudi Arabia is a sign that they are nearly universal in the Arab world. However the

---

[8]See Youssef M. Ibrahim, "The Saudis' Quandary: To Persuade the Iraqis to Leave Kuwait. Is the Carrot or the Stick To Be Preferred?" *The New York Times*, October 24, 1990, p. A1.

Gulf crisis ends, the Arab world will hold the United States to a much stricter standard than ever before with regard to Palestinian rights. A conflict that initially appeared to have mainly negative consequences for the Palestinians and the PLO may create pressure toward a peaceful resolution of their conflict with Israel.

WAR AND PEACE IN ISRAEL

Robert I. Friedman

I FIRST HEARD of the Israeli progressive movement Peace Now in 1980, when I was a graduate student at the University of Wisconsin at Madison. One evening in a small apartment off campus, Tzali Reshef, then a young combat officer in the Israeli reserves and a Harvard-educated lawyer, eloquently argued that Israel's occupation of the West Bank and the Gaza Strip was immoral and was eroding the foundations of Zionism and democracy. "People who rule over another people cannot be free," he declared, adding that it was legitimate and necessary to publicly criticize the expansionist policies of the Israeli government. Reshef warned that a government that preferred building settlements across the green line (Israel's 1948 border) to the elimination of the historic conflict with the Palestinians was a government that was on a suicidal course.

In 1980, just three years into Menachem Begin's first term as prime minister, Reshef's message was bracing. Begin had already built dozens of ultranationalist settlements in the occupied territories, and most mainstream American Jewish leaders had either embraced the uncompromising policies of the Likud or were cowed into silence by the Israeli government, which maintained that public criticism of Israel gave aid and comfort to the enemy. In those days, it was important to hear prominent Israelis like Reshef say that the better part of valor was pro-

Robert I. Friedman is a staff writer for *The Village Voice* whose work appears in numerous other publications, including *The New York Review of Books, The Washington Post,* and *The Nation.* He is author of *The False Prophet: Rabbi Meir Kahane—From F.B.I. Informant to Knesset Member.* This article, originally titled "Israel's Peace Movement Calls for War," was published in the February 26, 1990, issue of *The Village Voice.*

test and demonstrations, and that American Jews could criticize Israel without being self-hating traitors.

Today, more than a decade later, under the shadow of the Scud missile attacks, it is clear that Peace Now has failed to stem the right-wing tide in Israel. Its goal seems farther away now than at any time in Israel's history. Though the movement once marshaled 400,000 demonstrators in the streets of Tel Aviv to protest Israel's complicity in the massacre of Palestinians at the Sabra and Shatila refugee camps in Beirut, it could barely muster several hundred people to participate in an anti-settlement rally on the eve of the Gulf war.

Peace Now's biggest problem has always been trying to sell a skeptical Israeli public on the notion that the Palestine Liberation Organization has reformed its terrorist ways and is ready to live in peace alongside Israel. Peace Now leaders rejoiced after the Palestine National Council voted in the fall of 1988 to recognize Israel. Following the PLO's diplomatic initiative, Peace Now explicitly called for negotiations with the PLO and the repartition of Palestine into sovereign Jewish and Palestinian Arab states.

At a Peace Now rally in Tel Aviv in June 1989, Amos Oz, Israel's most acclaimed author and liberal intellectual, cautioned against ignoring a historic opportunity to resolve the Palestinian conflict: "For decades, the Palestinian national movement took a frantic, extreme, and inflexible stance. It was undeterred by any form of slaughter, including the slaughter of its own people, and was not prepared to give up an inch. May God preserve the nation of Israel if it adopts a similar stance, now that the Palestinians are perhaps beginning to shake themselves free of the insane opinions which brought down on them, and upon us, a tragedy that has lasted for eighty years. May God preserve the nation of Israel from stepping straight into the shoes out of which the PLO is trying to step at this very moment."

Much to the consternation of Israeli right-wingers, Peace Now began to hold joint dialogue groups and press conferences with pro-PLO Palestinian West Bank leaders. Peace Now also brought Palestinians like Faisal Husseini—who is thought to be the PLO's highest ranking official on the West Bank—to Israeli towns and villages to preach a message of reconciliation.

If these activities assisted in breaking down stereotypes among Arabs and Jews, they also deepened the chasm between the right and the left in Israel, helping to transform the Jewish state into a bipolar society inhabited by hawks and doves. In blistering disputations, in speech after speech, and in angry manifestos, each side accused the other of leading

Israel to Armageddon. The left, however, seemed to be vulnerable to right-wing charges that it was fostering Israel's demise by naïvely encouraging peace talks with an organization the charter of which still calls for the Jewish state's destruction.

Not surprisingly, Peace Now reeled after Palestinians in the territories passionately embraced Saddam Hussein following the Iraqi dictator's invasion of Kuwait. Many Israeli doves reacted like spurned lovers. In a fit of political pique, prominent peace activist and Citizens Rights Movement Party Knesset member Yossi Sarid told Palestinians that he was not going to talk to them anymore so they should "forget my number."

"If one can support Saddam Hussein . . . maybe it's not so bad to support the policies of [Prime Minister Yitzhak] Shamir, [Housing Minister Ariel] Sharon, and [former Defense Minister Yitzhak] Rabin. In comparison with the misdeeds of Saddam Hussein, the sins of the state of Israel are as white as snow," he wrote in a now-notorious article for *Haaretz.*

Then two weeks ago, at a press conference in the Tel Aviv Hilton sponsored by the International Center for Peace in the Middle East, four of Israel's most distinguished peace activists not only announced that they were emphatically pro-war, but also called on the U.S.-led coalition to liquidate "the genocidal" regime of Saddam Hussein as "an essential condition toward achieving peace."

"Sometimes there are wars that are necessary to obtain peace. . . . Peace Now in Israel means war now!" declared Yael Dayan, a novelist and the daughter of the late Israeli war hero Moshe Dayan.

"There is a real, great difference between peaceniks and appeasers and pacifists," said Amos Oz, who even endorsed the use of tactical nuclear weapons if it means saving Jews from the mass destruction of chemical bombs. "In short, I'm a peacenik and not a pacifist. There is one thing worse than violence, and that is giving in to violence. . . . For a long time, we were used to being called 'traitors' by our countrymen [for promoting peace with the Palestinians]. Now we are likely to be called traitors by some peace-loving friends [in Europe and America] because of our position."

Oz's statement exploded like a cluster bomb inside America's sectarian liberal Jewish community. Especially repugnant to many American Jewish peace activists was Oz's allegation that favoring sanctions over saturation bombing is "appeasement." For Jews in particular, appeasement is a loaded word. It means selling out to evil as Neville Chamberlain did when he surrendered Czechoslovakia to Hitler at Munich in 1938. "Some Israelis are trying to say that if Hussein isn't beaten, the world is in danger [from another Hitler]," says Stanley Sheinbaum, a major benefactor of Peace Now, the publisher of *New Perspectives Quarterly,* and one of five American Jews who met with Arafat in Stockholm in December 1988. "The quantitative and qualitative difference between Hitler and Saddam is huge. So the word appeasement is not a relevant word. It is used by those who are trying to stir up a hysteria for very limited reasons."

For Oz, however, Saddam Hussein's threat to "burn half of Israel" echoes Nazi viciousness. "My impression is that Saddam Hussein would have been very happy to gain three or four months because, at least according to some experts, he was not very far from developing some sort of nuclear capability," Oz told me during a recent phone conversation from his home in Arad, an Israeli town in the Negev. "It may be fairly irresponsible to advocate giving him more time. We will never know until we actually have the details—but the very risk, the great danger that he might have [the bomb] gives me the creeps."

Oz says the "rift" with Sheinbaum and others in the Jewish peace camp is temporary. "I think that once the war is over—if it ends with the defeat of Saddam—then when it comes to the Palestinian issue we will be united. Because it is still the stance of myself and my colleagues [in Israel] that the two-state solution is the only feasible solution to the problem. On this I think there is broad consensus between myself and the peace movements in North America and Europe. . . . Let us not turn this disagreement [over the war in Iraq] into a theological split— into a typical left-wing, dogmatic, dramatic business. The essence of the consensus is the two-state solution, and we still stick to it."

But selling rapprochement with the Palestinians after the war will be an even stickier business than before. "Palestinians' support for Saddam Hussein has already made any future negotiating process more difficult," says Jonathan Jacoby, the Manhattan-based director of Americans for Peace Now. "It has become harder for Israelis to believe that the Palestinian people are ready to live in peace alongside a secure Israel, and it is important for all of us to consider the implications of the Palestinian response for our work."

Indeed, the PLO is apparently under intense pressure from the Palestinian rank and file to become more involved in the war on Baghdad's side. Lamis Andoni writes in the February 15 issue of the *Financial Times* that support within the mainstream PLO for a two-state solution "may be a casualty of this growing militancy." Citing moderate PLO officials, she says that there have been calls from most of the PLO factions— including those which have previously renounced such tactics—for reviving the armed struggle against Israel, and even launching terrorist attacks against Western targets.

Meanwhile, under the cover of war, Shamir is trying to destroy the last vestiges of Palestinian moderation in the occupied territories so that, after the dust has settled, the prime minister can claim that there is nobody but Palestinian extremists to talk to. In a preemptive strike on January 29, the Shamir government jailed Bir Zeit University philosophy professor Sari Nusseibeh, alleging—in leaks to the press, though not formally—that he had used his phone and fax machine to direct Scud missile strikes on Israel. The Oxford-educated Nusseibeh is a leading proponent of a two-state solution, who has worked intimately with Jewish peace activists. At the same time, he is reputedly a key political link to Yasir Arafat in the territories. Early on in the *intifada*, he was accused by Israeli security services of being one of the major coordinators of the rebellion as well as its paymaster, though he was never arrested or brought to trial.

Many in Israel believe Nusseibeh has been falsely accused by the Shin Bet, which does not have to present evidence in an open court in security cases. "The people in the military government say they have enough evidence to put him in jail for twenty years," says Nachum Barnea, an influential columnist for *Yediot Achronot,* Israel's largest newspaper. "I've heard so many lies from them, I don't know."

U.S. officials in Israel who are tracking Nusseibeh's case believe he was set up. "One view is that Israel is taking an opportunity to crack down" on Palestinian moderates now that the world is transfixed on the Gulf, said a U.S. diplomat in Israel. "The other is that they do have evidence. I think it's trumped up. Maybe Nusseibeh answered questions on the telephone, but *Haaretz* wrote that even [Defense Minister] Moshe Arens pinpointed Scud hits in media interviews."

But for Nusseibeh, who vigorously denies the allegations made against him, the smear of having spied for Iraq will haunt him long after he is released from prison, where he is now serving a three-month sentence under the Administrative Detention Act. The law, inherited from the British Mandate, allows the government to jail alleged subversives or terrorists without due process. "I'm ninety-five percent sure he's innocent," says Janet Aviad, a leader of Peace Now in Jerusalem who has worked closely with Nusseibeh. "But Sari is tricky. He might be saying one thing to me and something else to PLO agents in Cyprus."

Aviad had a long meeting with Nusseibeh just hours before he was arrested. "We had a sincere, open discussion in which we explained the huge delegitimization of the PLO and Palestinian leadership in the West

Bank and Gaza Strip that occurred in the last four to five months and steps that can be taken to change that. Sari was very anxious to help, but pessimistic."

Aviad says Nusseibeh argued that while Palestinians identify with Saddam Hussein, it doesn't mean that the PLO had changed its position on wanting a two-state solution. "It didn't wash," said Aviad, who concluded that the PLO's support for Saddam would continue to divide the Palestinian leadership in the territories from the Israeli left.

If Nusseibeh's rehabilitation will be difficult, what about the PLO? After all, when Palestinians in the territories climbed on their roofs to cheer the incoming Scuds, Israeli leftists ridiculed them in terms that brought applause—if not a few snickers—from the Israeli right, which has made a religion out of delegitimizing the PLO and Arafat. If much of the left doesn't trust the Palestinians anymore, why should the Israeli public?

I asked Amos Oz if perhaps the left should have given Arafat more credit for having recognized Israel, renounced terrorism, and signaled its willingness to enter into the Baker peace plan, which was scuttled by Shamir. Baker had proposed direct talks between Israel and Palestinian representatives from the occupied territories to discuss Palestinian elections.

"After the U.S. broke off talks with the PLO following the Abu Abbas beach raid last May, I wonder what choice Arafat had but to back Saddam Hussein," I said. "He had nothing to show for diplomacy and compromise. I wonder if he could have survived with his own people if he had sided with the American-led coalition?"

Making no effort to disguise his bitter contempt for the PLO, Oz replied: "I think the PLO had a choice and I think the PLO, for the umpteenth time, settled for the wrong option—morally wrong and practically wrong. It is tragic. . . . The Palestinians have the historical gift of putting their money on the dying horse and on the ugly horse. The Palestinian leadership was on the Nazi side during World War II. In fact, Palestinian headquarters was stationed in Berlin during those years. And then during the Cold War they sided with the Soviet bloc; and then even in internal Arab rifts they somehow always manage to be on the wrong side. Of course I have a lot of sympathy for the Palestinian people and I think they deserve a better leadership—but it's their business and not mine. . . .

"We Israeli peaceniks have not lost our faith in Israeli-Palestinian reconciliation despite sixty-something years of Palestinian refusal to recognize Israel's right to exist," Oz continued. "Then in [late 1988] the

Palestinian leadership recognized Israel's right to exist—and I was the first one to congratulate them and I regarded that as a historical breakthrough.

"[But] what did they expect—that all of Israel would be anxiously awaiting them with bunches of flowers the moment they uttered the words 'Yes, you have the right to exist as a state'? So this impatience in itself is a very worrying sign. I insist that the Palestinian people have another option—not to endorse Saddam, and to stick to their policy of [recognition] and to stand behind it for as long as it takes—and it may take years!"

For the foreseeable future, time appears to be on the side of Israel's truculent right-wing government, which is obsessed with achieving its vision of a Greater Israel. Even during the bleakest days of the Scud attacks on Israel, as many as 2,000 Soviet and Ethiopian Jews flew into Ben Gurion Airport, where they were handed gas masks and directed to absorption centers around the country. Many of these new immigrants are finding their way to West Bank settlements, where they join a movement that is systematically dispossessing an indigenous population of its land and water.

After the Gulf war, it is likely that the Bush administration will renew its pressure on Shamir to end his settlement enterprise and negotiate a land-for-peace deal with the Palestinians. Bush will need to make progress on the Palestinian front in order to satisfy his Arab coalition partners in one of the few viable currencies left in the Islamic Middle East—Palestinian nationalism. But Shamir is a genius at hunkering down. He has already begun to exploit the cleavages between the Israeli left and the Palestinians of the occupied territories.

This greatly complicates American postwar diplomacy in the Middle East. U.S. officials in Israel and Washington insist that the only way Bush will be able to push Shamir toward political compromise is if there is a significant and vocal Jewish opposition in the U.S. and Israel that supports the president. Without this support, AIPAC, working through Congress, will continue to paralyze the peace process.

But the Israeli left has been traumatized. The Palestinians' overwhelming support for Saddam Hussein appears to have taken the fight out of many left-wing peace activists. After years of courageously protesting against the occupation, agitating for Palestinian human rights, and risking physical attack from right-wing Jewish extremists, they feel a sense of anger and despair—as though the Palestinians have betrayed them. Wrote Yossi Sarid in *Haaretz:* "Now they are up on the roofs and like lunatics they yell 'Allah akbar' [God is great] and applaud the terrorist missiles raining down on our heads. . . . After the war, when 'Allah' is less 'akbar,' don't call me. . . . In the shelter, I don't have a phone . . . and in my gas mask, my breath comes with difficulty and my words are muffled.''

As Sarid makes clear, the Palestinians' rooftop warbling has sickened even Jewish progressives. If the Israeli public ultimately refuses to accept the Palestinians as legitimate peace partners, the Palestinians themselves will bear much of the blame. But so will the Israeli left for its paternalistic, self-righteous condemnation of the Palestinians for supporting Saddam. After twenty-two years of living under a humiliating occupation, Palestinian behavior may not be nice—but it is certainly understandable. The Palestinians and the Israeli left accuse each other of betrayal. In truth, however, it is peace that has been betrayed.

ON LINKAGE, LANGUAGE, AND IDENTITY

Edward W. Said

FROM THE moment that George Bush invented Desert Shield, Desert Storm was all too logical, and Poppy turned himself into Captain Ahab. Saddam Hussein, a dictator of the kind the United States has typically found and supported, was almost invited into Kuwait, then almost immediately demonized and transformed into a worldwide metaphysical threat. Iraq's military capabilities were fantastically exaggerated, the country verbally obliterated except for its by now isolated leader, U.N. sanctions given a ludicrously short run, and then America began the war.

Since 1973 the United States has wanted a physical presence in the Persian Gulf: to control oil supply, to project power and above all, recently, to refurbish and refinance its military. With his crude brutality no match for U.S. and Israeli propaganda, Saddam became the perfect target, and the best excuse to move in. The United States will not soon leave the Middle East.

The electronic war to destroy Iraq as a lesson in retributive power is now in full swing, the press managing patriotism, entertainment, and disinformation without respite. As a topic, civilian "collateral damage" has been avoided and unasked about; no one discusses how Baghdad, the old Abbasid capital, might survive the appalling rigors of technological warfare, or how the bombing of its water, fuel, and electrical supplies, which sustain four million people, is necessary to this "surgical" war (a

Edward W. Said is the Old Dominion Professor in the Humanities at Columbia University and has been a member of the Palestine National Council. He is the author of several books, including the forthcoming *Musical Elaborations* and *Culture and Imperialism*. This article was published in the February 11, 1991, issue of *The Nation* under the title "Ignorant Armies Clash by Night."

larger replay of Israel's destruction of Beirut). Few commentators have questioned the disproportion of 10,000-plus air sorties against a country roughly the size of California, or explained why a week into the war Iraq's air force, artillery, Scuds and major armored force still stand, or even how radio and television still work. That no one asks about the effect and placement of B-52 carpet bombing—a mass murder technique —is doubtless a psy-war achievement, but it is not a credit to the independent press.

It is curious, but profoundly symptomatic of the present conflict, that the one word that should be tediously pronounced and repronounced and yet left unanalyzed is "linkage," an ugly solecism that could have been invented only in late twentieth-century America. "Linkage" means not that there is but that there is no connection. Things that belong together by common association, sense, geography, history, are sundered, left apart for convenience' sake and for the benefit of U.S. imperial strategists. Everyone his own carver, Jonathan Swift said. That the Middle East is linked by all sorts of ties, *that* is irrelevant. That Arabs might see a connection between Saddam in Kuwait and Israel in Lebanon, that too is futile. That U.S. policy itself is the linkage, this is a forbidden topic to broach.

Never in my experience have nouns designating the Arab world or its components been so bandied about: Saddam Hussein, Kuwait, Islam, fundamentalism. Never have they had so strangely abstract and diminished a meaning, and rarely does any regard or care seem to accompany them, even though the United States is not at war with all the Arabs but very well might be, except for its pathetic clients such as Mubarak of Egypt and the various Gulf rulers.

In all the mainstream debate here since August 2, much the smallest component in the discussion has been Arab. During the congressional hearings that went on for two weeks in December, no significant Arab-American voice was heard. In Congress and in the press, "linkages" of all kinds went unexamined. Little was done to report oil-company profits, or the fact that the surge in gasoline prices had nothing to do with supply, which remained plentiful. The Iraqi case against Kuwait, or even the nature of Kuwait itself, liberal in some ways, illiberal in others, received next to no hearing; the point would not have been to exculpate Saddam but to perceive the longstanding complicity and hypocrisy of the Gulf states, the United States, and Europe during the Iran-Iraq war. Efforts were made to grapple with Arab popular rallying to Saddam, despite the unattractive qualities of his rule, but these efforts were not integrated into, or allowed equal time with, the distortions in American

Middle East policy. The central media failing has been an unquestioning acceptance of American power: its right to ignore dozens of United Nations resolutions on Palestine (or even to refuse to pay its U.N. dues), to attack Panama, Grenada, Libya, and also to proclaim the absolute morality of its Gulf position.

From pre-war television reports of the crisis I cannot recall a single guest or program that raised the issue of what right "we" had to get Iraq out of Kuwait; nor any exploration of the enormous human, social, and economic costs *to the Arabs* of an American strike. Yet on January 7, I heard a well-known "Middle East expert" say on TV that "war is the easy part; what to do afterward?" as if "we" might, in an afterthought, get around to picking up the pieces and rearranging the area. At the farthest extreme have been the unmistakably racist prescriptions of William Safire and A. M. Rosenthal of *The New York Times* as well as Fouad Ajami of CBS, who have routinely urged the most unrestrained military attacks against Iraq. The underlying fantasy strongly resembles the Israeli paradigm for dealing with the Arabs: Bomb them, humiliate them, lie about them.

From the beginning, when Arabs have appeared on television they have been the merest tokens: a journalist or two eager to show Arab failings and weaknesses (which were real and had to be pointed out); the Saudi or Kuwaiti ambassador, more enthusiastic about war than most Americans; the Iraqi ambassador, who defended the Husseinian view of the world with cautious amiability; the tiny group of Arab-Americans like myself whose position was neither with Iraq nor with the U.S.-Saudi coalition. Once, in the fifteen seconds I was given, when I began to elucidate an argument about the relationship between Iraqi aggression and American imperialism, I was cut off abruptly: "Yes, yes, we know all that."

Seen from the Arab point of view, the picture of America is just as constricted. There is still hardly any literature in Arabic that portrays Americans; the most interesting exception is Abdel Rahman Munif's massive trilogy *Cities of Salt*, but his books are banned in several countries, and his native Saudi Arabia has stripped him of his citizenship. To my knowledge there is still no institute or major academic department in the Arab world whose main purpose is the study of America, although the United States is by far the largest outside force in the Arab world. It is still difficult to explain even to well-educated and experienced fellow Arabs that U.S. foreign policy is not in fact run by the CIA, or a conspiracy, or a shadowy network of key "contacts." Many Arabs I know believe the United States plans virtually every event of significance in the Middle

East, including, in one mind-boggling suggestion made to me last year, the *intifada!*

This mix of long familiarity, hostility, and ignorance pertains to both sides of a complex, variously uneven and quite old cultural encounter now engaging in very unmetaphorical warfare. From early on there has been an overriding sense of inevitability, as if George Bush's apparent need to get down there and, in his own sporty argot, "kick ass" *had* to run up against Saddam Hussein's monstrous aggressiveness, now vindicating the Arab need to confront, talk back to, stand unblinkingly before the United States. The public rhetoric, in other words, is simply undeterred, uncomplicated by any considerations of detail, realism or cause and effect.

PERHAPS THE central unanalyzed link between the United States and the Arabs in this conflict is nationalism. The world can no longer afford so heady a mixture of patriotism, relative solipsism, social authority, unchecked aggressiveness, and defensiveness toward others. Today the United States, triumphalist internationally, seems in a febrile way anxious to prove that it is Number One, perhaps to offset the recession; the endemic problems posed by the cities, poverty, health, education, production; and the Euro-Japanese challenge. On the other side, the Middle East is saturated with a sense that Arab nationalism is all-important, but also that it is an aggrieved and unfulfilled nationalism, beset with conspiracies, enemies both internal and external, obstacles to overcome for which no price is too high. This was especially true of the cultural framework in which I grew up. It is still true today, with the important difference that this nationalism has resolved itself into smaller and smaller units. In the colonial period as I was growing up, you could travel overland from Lebanon and Syria through Palestine to Egypt and points west. That is now impossible. Each country places formidable obstacles at its borders. For Palestinians, crossing is a horrible experience, since countries that make the loudest noises in support of Palestine treat Palestinians the worst.

Here, too, linkage comes last in the Arab setting. I do not want to suggest that the past was better; it wasn't. But it was more healthily interlinked, so to speak. People actually lived with each other, rather than denying each other from across fortified frontiers. In schools you could encounter Arabs from everywhere, Muslims and Christians, plus Armenians, Jews, Greeks, Italians, Indians and Iranians all mixed up, all under one or another colonial regime, interacting as if it were natural to do so. Today the state nationalisms have a tendency to fracture. Lebanon and Israel are perfect examples of what has happened. Apartheid of one form or another is present nearly everywhere as a group feeling if not as a practice, and it is subsidized by the state with its bureaucracies and secret police organizations. Rulers are clans, families and closed circles of aging oligarchs, almost mythologically immune to change.

Moreover, the attempt to homogenize and isolate populations has required colossal sacrifices. In most parts of the Arab world, civil society has been swallowed up by political society. One of the great achievements of the early postwar Arab nationalist governments was mass literacy; in countries such as Egypt the results were dramatic. Yet the combination of accelerated literacy and tub-thumping ideology, which was undoubtedly necessary at some point, has proved far too longstanding. My impression is that there is more effort spent in bolstering the idea that to be Syrian, Iraqi, Egyptian, Saudi, etc. is a quite sufficiently important end, rather than in thinking critically, perhaps even audaciously, about the national program itself. Identity, always identity, over and above knowing about others.

Because of this lopsided state of affairs, militarism assumed too privileged a place in the Arab world's moral economy. Much of it goes back to the sense of being unjustly treated, for which Palestine was not only a metaphor but a reality. But was the only answer military force—huge armies, brassy slogans, bloody promises and, alas, a long series of concrete instances, starting with wars and working down to such things as physical punishment and menacing gestures? I speak superficially and even irresponsibly here, since I cannot have all the facts. But I do not know a single Arab who would disagree with these impressions in private, or who would not readily agree that the monopoly on coercion given the state has almost completely eliminated democracy in the Arab world, introduced immense hostility between rulers and ruled, placed a much higher value on conformity, opportunism, flattery, and getting along than on risking new ideas, criticism or dissent.

Taken far enough this produces an exterminism common to the Arabs and the United States, the notion that if something displeases you it is possible simply to blot it out. I do not doubt that this notion is behind Iraq's aggression against Kuwait. What sort of muddled and anachronistic idea of Bismarckian "integration" is this that wipes out an entire country and smashes its society with "Arab unity" as its goal? The most disheartening thing is that so many people, many of them victims of exactly the same brutal logic, appear to have identified with Iraq and not Kuwait. Even if one grants that Kuwaitis were unpopular (does one have to be popular not to be exterminated?) and even if Iraq claims to champion Palestine in standing up to Israel and the United States, surely the very idea that nations should be obliterated along the way is a murderous proposition, unfit for a great civilization like ours.

Then there is oil. While it brought development and prosperity to some, wherever it was associated with an atmosphere of violence, ideological refinement, and political defensiveness, it created more rifts than it healed. It may be easy for someone like myself to say these things from a distance, but for anyone who cares about the Arab world, who thinks of it as possessing a plausible sort of internal cohesion, the general air of mediocrity and corruption that hangs over a part of the globe that is limitlessly wealthy, superbly endowed culturally and historically, and loaded with gifted individuals is a great puzzle, and of course a disappointment. We all *do* ask ourselves why we haven't done more of what other peoples have done—liberate ourselves, modernize, make a distinctive positive mark on the world. Where is excellence? How is it rewarded? There are first-rate novelists, poets, essayists, historians, yet all of them are not only unacknowledged legislators, they have been hounded into alienated opposition. For an author today to write is perforce to be careful, not to anger Syria or the Islamic authorities or a Gulf potentate or two.

What seems intellectually required now is the development of a combination discourse, one side of which is concretely critical and addresses the real power situation inside the Arab world, and another side that is mainly about affection, sympathy, association (rather than antagonism, resentment, harsh fundamentalism, vindictiveness). Many of the Arab thinkers of what the historian Albert Hourani calls the liberal age, the late eighteenth to the early twentieth century, were reformers eager to catch up with developments in the West. We've had too much since then of thinkers who want to start from scratch and zealously, not to say furiously, take things back to some pure, sacred origin. This has given all sorts of pathologies time and space enough to take hold in the middle distance, now, with their structures left unscrutinized, while intellectuals go off looking for what *would* have been better, what *would* have been just, and so on. We need to know what it is about the present that we should hold on to, and how. What is just, why is it just, why should we hold on to it? We need odes not to blood and mythology or uprooted, mourned or dead plants but to living creatures and actual situations. As the novelist Elias Khoury says, we need a language that allows one to write neither of a discredited past nor of an immensely distant future.

The supreme irony is that we Arabs are *of* this world, hooked into dependency and consumerism, cultural vassalage, and technological secondariness, without much volition on our part. The time has come where we cannot simply accuse the West of Orientalism and racism—I realize that I am particularly vulnerable on this point—and go on doing little about providing an alternative. If our work isn't in the Western media often enough, for example, or isn't known well by Western writers and scholars, a good part of the blame lies with us. Hassanein Heykal, the great Egyptian journalist, has proposed a broadly focused pan-Arab cooperation authority for such things as development, coordinated industry, agriculture and the like. But we should also devote energy to an intellectual coordination effort that opens lines of communication among Arabs internally and externally with the rest of the world. The idea of equal dialogue, and rightful responsibility, needs to be pressed. The provincial and self-pitying posture that argues that a largely fictional and monolithic West disdains us ought to be replaced with the discovery that there are many Wests, some antagonistic, some not, with which to do business, and the choice of whom to talk to and how depends greatly on us. The converse is equally true, that there are many Arabs for Westerners and others to talk to. Only in this way, I think, will imperial America not be our only interlocutor.

If as Arabs we say correctly that we are different from the West, as well as different from its image of the Arabs, we have to be persuasive on this point. That takes a lot of work, and cannot be accomplished by a resort to clichés or myths. George Bush's idea that a new world order has to flow from an American baton is as unacceptable as the idea that Arabs can muster a big army led by a big tough hero and at last win a few wars. That is dangerous nonsense. Americans, Arabs, Europeans, Africans — everyone—need to reorient education so that central to common awareness is not a paranoid sense of who is top or best but a map of this now tiny planet, its resources and environment nearly worn out, its inhabitants' demands for better lives nearly out of control. The competitive, coercive guidelines that have prevailed are simply no good anymore. To argue and persuade rather than to boast, preach and destroy, *that* is the change to be made.

The war will be catastrophic and only distort the Arab world further. And there will be enough residual problems to start up another confrontation in the Middle East in a matter of seconds. We should be looking for political mechanisms with the Europeans and the nonaligned that would get a cease-fire and send everyone—including Palestinians—home. It is good to be reminded of that phrase by Aimé Césaire which C. L. R. James, that great champion of liberation, liked to quote: "No race possesses the monopoly of beauty, of intelligence, of force, and there is a place for all at the rendezvous of victory." This may be utopian idealism, but as a way to think about an alternative to conflicts that go from cultural hostility to full-scale war, it is both more inventive and practical than shooting off missiles.

PAX AMERICANA REDUX

KUWAIT IS LIBERATED

(Speech of February 27, 1991)

George Bush

The following is President Bush's February 27 address from the Oval Office announcing the liberation of Kuwait.

K U W A I T I S liberated. Iraq's army is defeated. Our military objectives are met. Kuwait is once more in the hands of Kuwaitis in control of their own destiny. We share in their joy, a joy tempered only by our compassion for their ordeal.

Tonight, the Kuwaiti flag once again flies above the capital of a free and sovereign nation, and the American flag flies above our embassy.

Seven months ago, America and the world drew a line in the sand. We declared that the aggression against Kuwait would not stand, and tonight America and the world have kept their word. This is not a time of euphoria, certainly not a time to gloat, but it is a time of pride, pride in our troops, pride in the friends who stood with us in the crisis, pride in our nation and the people whose strength and resolve made victory quick, decisive and just.

And soon we will open wide our arms to welcome back home to America our magnificent fighting forces. No one country can claim this victory as its own. It was not only a victory for Kuwait, but a victory for all the coalition partners. This is a victory for the United Nations, for all mankind, for the rule of law, and for what is right.

After consulting with Secretary of Defense Cheney, the chairman of the Joint Chiefs of Staff, General Powell, and our coalition partners, I am pleased to announce that at midnight tonight, Eastern Standard Time, exactly 100 hours since ground operations commenced and six weeks since the start of Operation Desert Storm, all United States and coalition forces will suspend offensive combat operations.

It is up to Iraq whether this suspension on the part of the coalition becomes a permanent cease-fire. Coalition, political, and military terms for a formal cease-fire include the following requirements:

Iraq must release immediately all coalition prisoners of war, third country nationals, and the remains of all who have fallen.

Iraq must release all Kuwaiti detainees.

Iraq also must inform Kuwaiti authorities of the location and nature of all land and sea mines.

Iraq must comply fully with all relevant United Nations Security Council resolutions. This includes a rescinding of Iraq's August decision to annex Kuwait and acceptance in principle of Iraq's responsibility to pay compensation for the loss, damage and injury its aggression has caused.

The coalition calls upon the Iraqi government to designate military commanders to meet within forty-eight hours with their coalition counterparts at a place in the theater of operations to be specified to arrange for military aspects of the cease-fire.

Further, I have asked Secretary of State Baker to request that the United Nations Security Council meet to formulate the necessary arrangement for this war to be ended.

This suspension of offensive combat operations is contingent upon Iraq's not firing upon any coalition forces and not launching Scud missiles against any other country. If Iraq violates these terms, coalition forces will be free to resume military operations.

At every opportunity I have said to the people of Iraq that our quarrel was not with them but instead with their leadership and above all with Saddam Hussein. This remains the case. You, the people of Iraq, are not our enemy. We do not seek your destruction. We have treated your POWs with kindness.

Coalition forces fought this war only as a last resort and look forward to the day when Iraq is led by people prepared to live in peace with their neighbors.

We must now begin to look beyond victory in war. We must meet the challenge of securing the peace. In the future, as before, we will consult with our coalition partners.

We've already done a good deal of thinking and planning for the postwar period and Secretary Baker has already begun to consult with our coalition partners on the region's challenges. There can be and will be no solely American answer to all these challenges, but we can assist and support the countries of the region and be a catalyst for peace.

In this spirit Secretary Baker will go to the region next week to begin a new round of consultations. This war is now behind us. Ahead of us is the difficult task of securing a potentially historic peace. Tonight though, let us be proud of what we have accomplished. Let us give thanks to those who risked their lives. Let us never forget those who gave their lives.

May God bless our valiant military forces and their families and let us all remember them in our prayers.

Good night and may God bless the United States of America.

ONWARD CHRISTIAN SOLDIERS

Lewis H. Lapham

> Saints should always be judged guilty until they are
> proved innocent.
>
> —*George Orwell*

DURING THE autumn advertising campaign meant to sell the
American public on the prospect of war in Iraq, President Bush
dressed up his gunboat diplomacy in the slogans of conscience and the
costume of what he was pleased to call "the new world order." First and
foremost, he had it in mind to prove to the lesser nations of the earth that
any misbehavior on their part (any sacking of cities or setting of commodity prices without express, written permission from Washington)
would be promptly and severely punished. Never, he said, would Saddam Hussein be allowed to receive any reward, profit, acclaim, benefit,
or honor for his trespass in the desert. No, sir, by no means, under no
circumstances, not while the United States still had soldiers and bombs
to send eastward out of Eden.

The president's righteousness waxed increasingly militant as the
merely political or commercial reasons for war proved inadequate to the
occasion. When the expedient arguments failed (the ones about the
price of oil, the preservation of American jobs and the American way of
life, the protection of Israel, the likelihood of nuclear war, etc.), Mr.
Bush shifted his flag to the higher ground of the moral argument, the
one about the American obligation to enforce the laws of God. Behold,
he said, the villainy of Saddam Hussein, an evil man committing acts of

Lewis H. Lapham is editor of *Harper's*. This essay is an amalgam of two pieces published in
Harper's: "Lines in the Sand" (October 1990) and "Brave New World" (March 1991).

"naked aggression" in what was once the innocent paradise of Kuwait. Know, O doubting world, that America stands willing to make the crooked straight and the rough places plain.

By October the president had tuned his rhetoric to the pitch of intransigent virtue given to the media orchestra by Saddam Hussein. Saddam was talking about "rivers of blood," about the will of Allah and a holy war against the foreign infidel. Mr. Bush was saying that "no price is too heavy to pay" to defend the standards of Christian behavior in a world already too densely populated with thugs. In late November, in an interview on CNN and still summoning the faithful to a twelfth-century crusade, Mr. Bush looked firmly into the television camera and asked what I'm afraid he thought was a shrewd and high-principled question: "When you rape, pillage, and plunder a neighbor, should you then ask the world, 'Hey, give me a little face'?"

The answer, regrettably, is yes. Of course you ask the world for a little face, not only for a little face but for as much face as can be had at the going rates. Why else did three American presidents persist in the devastation of Vietnam, at the price of 57,000 American dead, if not for the sake of what they defined as "America's credibility," "America's honor," "America's image in the world"? Why else did Mr. Bush invade Panama if not to prove that America's military prowess deserved the compliment of the world's fear and applause? Why else have we sent 400,000 troops to the Persian Gulf if not to outbid Saddam Hussein in the display of aggression?

Why else did Mr. Bush let slip the reins of Operation Desert Storm if not to ask of the world, "Hey, give me a little face"?

The phrasing of the president's question proclaimed his allegiance to the old world order, the one governed by force and the show of force. The autumn's diplomatic maneuvers made it clear that the White House meant to restore what used to be called the "Pax Americana."

By August 7, less than a week after Iraqi troops occupied Kuwait, the United States had mustered the largest military parade to be sent overseas since the Vietnam War. President Bush did his best to dress up the motive in the language of conscience and virtue. Explaining the national purpose to the American people, he said that the time had come for the United States "to stand up for what's right and condemn what's wrong, all in the cause of peace." His manner was that of a sincere and boyish scoutmaster, trying not to use too many big words, his earnest smile meant to convey an impression of goodness. A villain had arisen in the desert, a villain guilty of an "outrageous and brutal act of aggression," and the villain had to be punished. "America," the president said, "has never wavered when her purpose is driven by principle." He ended his speech by inviting his fellow countrymen to pray.

But pray for whom or for what? For a lower interest rate or the guarantee of unlimited gasoline at $1.17 a gallon? For the king of Saudi Arabia or the emir of Kuwait, both of them feudal monarchs renowned for their cowardice and greed? For the belief that all the oil in Arabia is somehow "our" oil? For the lost art of falconry and the practice of beheading a woman taken in the act of adultery?

On the day that he ordered advance elements of the 101st and 82nd airborne divisions into the Nefud Desert, Mr. Bush announced that he had "drawn a line in the sand." The phrase resounded with the bravado of schoolboy romance (possibly because lines in the sand have a way of being all too easily blurred or blown away), and the media obligingly portrayed Hussein as a bandit escaped from a B-movie or a lunatic asylum, as treacherous as he was violent, willing to wage war for the old Roman or nineteenth-century reasons—for the gold and the silk or the women and the slaves.

Between August and January the United States paid handsome bribes for the votes of the Security Council at the United Nations but otherwise listened as inattentively to the counsel of its nominal allies as George Will might listen to the political views of the wine steward in an Argentine restaurant in Santa Monica. The alliance put together in the Persian Gulf, with whichever kings or kingdoms happened to be free on waivers from OPEC or the Arab League, might as easily have been arranged by the late John Foster Dulles.

Careless of the costs, knowing little or nothing of the languages, history, or cultural traditions of the Middle East, confident that the war with Iraq would be won in a matter of weeks if not within hours or days, the makers of American policy assumed (as did Saddam Hussein) that their own moral equations somehow were synonymous with the laws of nature and the will of God.

In opposition to the incessant moralisms broadcast from the White House, a fair number of people in Washington, both in Congress and in the national media, offered tentative sketches of a world order that might not have been so easily understood by Saladin or Godfrey of Bouillon. They argued for patience, for the efficacy of economic sanctions, for an army under the command of the United Nations, for a coalition comprised of more or less equal interests, for the use of as little force as possible and then only as a defensive measure. They questioned the American capacity to balance the world on the scale of American justice or in the ledger of American commerce. From whom did we think we could borrow the money to pay for the imperial legions? Upon conquering the wicked city of Baghdad, whom did we hope to appoint to the office of proconsul?

The voices of doubt and restraint were lost in the din of the marching bands. Nobody in the Bush administration made the slightest attempt to imagine a future that didn't look exactly like the past. Nobody wished to understand the historical origins of Iraq's grievances, which have more to do with the British and Ottoman empires than with the United States. Nobody wished to restrain the predatory oil pricing that suits our own convenience. Nobody said anything about taking down the expensive military arsenals that we have so profitably sold to so many aspiring despots. Nor did anybody say much of anything about a decent settlement of the Arab-Israeli dispute, about alternative fuels and the management of the world's energy resources, about redistributing the wealth of the Middle East in some way that might promote the chance of peace.

By trying to preserve the illusion of a balance of power along the lines set forth by Lord Palmerston or Kaiser Wilhelm, Mr. Bush and his nostalgic friends in Congress and the Pentagon seek to comfort themselves with the cheerful news that they live in an orderly and coherent world, or at least in a world in which order and coherence remain within the range of the heaviest artillery.

The old world order assumes a distinction between naked and fully clothed aggression. On Sunday afternoons in Mozambique and Guatemala, law-abiding families vanish as abruptly from sight as did the law-abiding citizens of Kuwait, but they leave so quietly and so often that they offer no affront to the harmony of nations. Through the autumn ad campaign crying up the prospect of war with Iraq, the Bush administration made little mention of the thirty-three other wars currently in progress in the world. Nor did our media think to make the point that our own society assumes a norm of violence that would frighten all but the most remorseless Arab. No other modern nation, whether capitalist or socialist or Christian or Muslim, shares the American tolerance for crime. The indexes of murder and theft in the United States (i.e., aggression dressed in old sneakers as well as by Brooks Brothers and Bijan) dwarf the comparative statistics in England, Libya, France, Germany, and Iran. As with the old game of power politics, the rich man's aggression provokes less censure than the poor man's aggression, which suggests that Saddam's fault can be found not only with his tank captains but also with his tailor.

But the idea of a balance of power implies the existence of reasonably long-term interests and alliances, and in a world subject to sudden technological revolutions as well as to the bewildering movements of peoples, currencies, markets, oil spills, and fervent nationalisms, who can be sure that anything will remain the same from one week to the next? So many forces and allegiances have been let loose in the world, and the major powers find so many ways in which to combine and recombine, that even so subtle a statesman as Metternich would have been hard-pressed to change last year's enemies into next year's friends. What would have become of his certainties about Germany or Russia or the Polish frontier?

The fear of an ambiguous future in the aftermath of the Cold War gives rise to the wish for simplifications and a safe return to the past. Often on seeing Mr. Bush threaten Saddam with the scourge of war, I thought that he might be trying to substitute a lesser fear for a greater one, as if he would rather confront Iraq, no matter how despotic or heavily armed, than confront a world dissolved into anarchy, a world in which any terrorist with a crackpot dream of heaven can stuff an atomic weapon into an old suitcase and hold for ransom the life of New York or Washington.

Americans tend to think of foreign affairs in terms of sporting events that allow for unambiguous results. Either the team wins or it loses; the game is over within a reasonable period of time, and everybody can go back to doing something else. Much to everyone's regret, the events of the next twenty years seem likely to make nonsense of the sporting analogies. Too many powers can make their anger known to the world (if not at conference tables, then by means of an assassination or the poisoning of a reservoir), and the chains of causation have become much longer and more democratic than those conceived of by the Congress of Vienna. The crisis in the world will not resolve itself into a finale by Busby Berkeley and the chorus line at the American Enterprise Institute. If it isn't the Iraqis, then it will be the Syrians; if not the Syrians, then the Brazilians or the Lithuanians or the South Africans.

The pervasive intuitions of dread give rise to a confusion of feeling that makes it difficult to interpret such phrases as "the national interest" or to guess whether the voices prophesying war mean to signal an advance or a retreat. The presentiment of a terrible looming just over the horizon of the news seeps through the voices of people pleading for surcease and disengagement, who argue that the United States has wasted enough blood and treasure in the ill-conceived crusades of the past thirty years, that the country should retire to the fastnesses of its coasts and leave the rest of the world to its murdering corruption.

But where is it safe to hide? Odysseus could return from his wanderings to Ithaca, but the modern world doesn't provide the refuge of home islands. Who is not hostage to the interconnectedness of the AIDS virus and the radioactive wind?

Within the world's military headquarters I'm sure that innumerable officers have drawn contingency plans for all kinds of wars—wars against revolutions, proxy wars, diplomatic wars, wars in Yugoslavia and Korea, wars for oil and bauxite and grain, wars fought with conventional weapons, amphibious wars, air wars, ground wars, nuclear wars. But how large will these wars become, and how many people might have to be killed before the bugles sound the retreat? Nobody likes to discuss this question in public because it has become difficult to find either a sufficiently high-minded principle or an inescapable material interest on behalf of which several million people might think it glorious to sacrifice their children.

The vagueness is traditional. In August 1914 none of the Allied or Central powers could explain its reasons for going off to the First World War. Four years later, after ten million soldiers had died in the trenches, the governments in question still could not give a plausible reason for the killing. The best that anybody could do was to say that the war had been fought to end all wars, that its purpose had been to establish a "new world order" immune to the disease of power politics.

But who now expects the war in the Middle East to bring about a lasting peace or a better world? Who believes that the United States would risk annihilation to preserve a free and independent Abu Dhabi or the sacred anomaly of Israel?

Whether expressed in the Aesopian language of diplomacy or in the deployment of navies, the rules of power politics fail to take into account the number of people in the world who judge they have more to gain by the risk of war than by the prospect of negotiation. Most of the world is hungry, armed, and not much impressed by the rules of diplomatic procedure set forth with such earnest longing in the editorial pages of *The New York Times*.

Of the nations now buying weapons in the international arms markets, the majority must be considered young, both in terms of their existence as states (of the 159 nations represented at the U.N., nearly half have come into being within the past thirty years) and in terms of the average age of their populations. In the industrialized West the average age of the inhabitants continues to rise; in the Third World the demographics go the other way.

The passions of transcendence seize on the young, and as more and more nations suffer the anxieties and enthusiasms of youth, they can be expected to confuse the purposes of government with the freedom of individuals. The doctrines of nationalism hold that certain nations emerge from the chaos of history as objects of divine favor; the states that interpret those doctrines with the fervor of youth presumably will conduct their foreign affairs as if they were affairs of the heart.

Since the end of the Second World War—probably since the end of the First World War—the supposedly civilized nations of the world have been noticeably unsuccessful at transmitting to the next generation the public virtues of patience and self-restraint. They have distributed instead a more profitable line of private goods, among them visions of God and definitions of the higher truth, as well as cameras and transistor radios. Within the arenas of domestic American politics the romanticism of eager factions has dissolved the common interest into a multitude of special interests, all of them warring with one another for the available money and authority.

Over the next ten years I can imagine a comparable spectacle in the arena of international politics. Together with single-issue lobbies in Congress, I can conceive of single-issue nations dedicated to the proposition that their own flag, their own folk songs, and their own way of making fish soup constitutes a foreign policy. At the same time they will find themselves armed with weapons capable of inflicting vast Oedipal punishments on an older generation perceived to be obstructive and corrupt. Absent an imperial peace imposed on a recalcitrant world by parental fiat (a task for which the United States possesses a notable lack of talent), I find it hard to imagine a political order balanced by a squadron of gunboats. The more prosperous and settled a nation, the more readily it tends to think of war as a regrettable accident; to nations less fortunate the chance of war presents itself as a possibly bountiful friend.

The line Mr. Bush so boldly drew in so empty a desert was the line between profit and loss. To the capitalist sensibility, the geopolitics of money transcend the boundaries of sovereign states. The world divides, unevenly but along only one axis, between the nation of the rich and the nation of the poor. The frontiers run not only between Kuwait and Iraq but also between east and west Los Angeles; between black and white, north and south, surfeit and famine; between the first-class cabin of a Boeing 747 en route to London and the roof of a fourth-class train on the way to Calcutta. The Upper East Side of Manhattan belongs to the same polity as the Seventh Arrondissement in Paris; the yachts moored off Cannes or the Costa Brava sail under the flags of the same admiralty that posts squadrons off Newport and Palm Beach. The American or

Japanese plutocrat traveling between the Beau Rivage in Lausanne and the Ritz Hotel in Madrid crosses not into another country but into another province within the kingdom of wealth. His credit furnishes him with a lingua franca translated as readily into deutsche marks as into rials or yen or francs, buying more or less the same food in the same class of restaurants, the same amusements and the same conversation, the same politicians, dinner companions, newspaper columnists, and accordion music. The realm of money assumes the ecumenical place once occupied by the Catholic Church, and within this favored estate everybody obeys the same laws and pays homage to the same princes.

If the analogy has any truth in it, then the post–Cold War world begins to look like medieval Europe. The possessing classes are safely at ease behind the barbican of a high interest rate, assured of their salvation by the idols of a radiant technology, content among computers and fax machines and megatrends and cellular phones. On the other side of the walls, in the desolate slums of the Third, Fifth, and Sixteenth worlds, the nomadic mass of the heathen poor, otherwise known (in French policy journals) as "the terminally impoverished," tear at one another for bones.

But at what cost, and for how long, can the kingdom of wealth protect its comfort and preserve its cynicism? With what weapons and against how many enemies? Let George Bush draw a few more lines in the sand (along the border between Mexico and California, between Kennebunkport, Maine, and downtown Detroit), and who will pay for the ammunition?

Just as the breaking down of the Berlin Wall symbolized the failure of communism to make good on its promise of paradise regained, the American military presence in the Persian Gulf symbolizes capitalism's failure to redeem the same promise. If capitalism can sustain itself only by main force against increasingly hopeless odds, then how does it embody an intellectual or a spiritual triumph? Who explains the loveliness of the free market to the crowd in the streets of Rio de Janeiro?

The mechanics of the free market armed Saddam Hussein with the means to a murderous end. France sold aircraft to Iraq; the Soviet Union sold tanks and rifles; the Italians sold the equipment with which to manufacture weapons-grade plutonium; the Americans supplied food subsidies and export loan guarantees (in 1983); and the West Germans provided the poison gas.

Two days after the Iraqi army seized Kuwait, I found myself seated at lunch with an independent oil-well operator from Midland, Texas. West Texas intermediate crude oil had moved from $22 to $25 a barrel, and after buying the table still another bottle of champagne, the gentleman from Texas read aloud to the assembled company the telegram he sent that morning, only partly in jest, to Saddam Hussein: "Warm congratulations on your well-earned victory. Every good wish for your continued success."

The joke was funny because its logic was unanswerable. The capitalist ethic is rooted in the doctrine of the bottom line and the sanctity of the expedient price. Like communism, capitalism is a materialist and utopian faith; also like communism, it has shown itself empty of a moral imperative or a spiritual meaning. To the questions likely to be asked by the next century, the sayings of the late Malcolm Forbes will seem as useless as the maxims of Lenin.

A FALSE DREAM

Henry A. Kissinger

AMERICA HAS never been comfortable with fighting wars for limited objectives. World War I was cast as the war to end all wars; World War II was to usher in a new era of permanent peace to be monitored by the United Nations. Now, the Gulf war is justified in similar terms deeply embedded in the American tradition. In his speech of January 16 announcing hostilities with Iraq, President Bush described the opportunity for building a new world order "where the rule of law . . . governs the conduct of nations," and "in which a credible United Nations can use its peacekeeping role to fulfill the promise and the vision of the U.N.'s founders."

I have greatly admired President Bush's skill and fortitude in building the coalition. But the new world order cannot possibly fulfill the idealistic expectations expressed by the president; I doubt indeed whether they accurately describe what happened during the Gulf crisis.

American idealism was most eloquently formulated by Woodrow Wilson in his attempt to replace the ever-shifting alignments of the balance of power with an overriding common purpose. In Wilson's words, peace depends "not on a balance of power but on a community of power. . . . Nations agree that there shall be but one combination and that is the combination of all against the wrongdoer." In this view, the conduct of international affairs follows objective criteria, not unlike those of the law. All nations are expected to respond to challenges to international order from a common perspective and by united opposition.

Henry A. Kissinger was secretary of state in the Nixon and Ford administrations. This article originally appeared in the February 24, 1991, issue of the *Los Angeles Times* under the title "The Delicate Balance."

That hope was disappointed in the League of Nations and later by the United Nations. And not by accident. While every country has some interest in elaborating a concept that it can invoke in its own defense, the willingness to run risks varies with history, geography, power, in other words, with national interest.

Despite the near unanimity of U.N. decisions, historians will in all likelihood treat the Gulf crisis as a special case rather than as a watershed. An unusual set of circumstances combined to foster consensus. The Soviet Union, wracked by domestic crises and needing foreign economic assistance, had no stomach for conflict with the United States. But this does not mean that Soviet objectives in the Middle East in the postwar period will necessarily be identical or even compatible with those of the United States. China, though wary of superpower military action, sought to demonstrate the advantages of practical cooperation despite Tiananmen Square and ideological conflict. For Beijing considers Washington an important partner in China's determination to resist either Soviet or Japanese hegemony in Asia.

France was torn by conflicting emotions: concern over the reaction of the five million Muslims resident in France, its quest for preferential status in the Arab world and the desire to keep America linked to France should its nightmare of German resurgence come true. Thus, France for once resolved its ambivalences in favor of our view; but it would be unrealistic to treat a practical decision as a philosophic commitment. Among the permanent members of the Security Council, only Great Britain held views practically identical with those of the United States.

The Gulf states and Saudi Arabia saw their very survival at stake and were not much concerned with the principle invoked to safeguard their existence. Syria's President Hafez Assad has been in mortal conflict with Saddam Hussein for ten years preceding the Gulf crisis and will likely continue to struggle if Saddam remains in office after the war. As for Egypt, the rulers of the Nile competed with the rulers of Mesopotamia for 4,000 years before the doctrine of collective security was invented. The Persian-Arab conflict is of more recent vintage as history is measured in the Middle East; it is only 2,000 years old. This is why Iran will support the U.N. resolution only until Iraq is sufficiently weakened. After that Iran will probably continue its historical quest for dominance in the Gulf by pressuring America to leave.

Even during the current crisis the principle of collective security was not applied uniformly. Israel was urged nearly unanimously not to avail itself of its right of self-defense under the U.N. Charter despite unprovoked Iraqi missile attacks on Israeli civilians. The nations of the world seemed afraid that the Arab members of the coalition would change sides.

Finally, two special nonrecurring circumstances facilitated the creation of the global alliance. The first was the noxious character of Saddam Hussein. Another aggressor is unlikely to present so unambiguous a challenge.

The key element was American leadership—symbolized by the extraordinary set of personal relations between President Bush and world leaders. Without that American role, the world community would almost certainly have reached different conclusions.

None of this is to deprecate the extraordinary achievement of the administration in coalition-building. It is to warn against counting on being able to repeat this pattern in the future.

Most poignantly, American preeminence cannot last. Had Kuwait been invaded two years later, the American defense budget would have declined so as to preclude a massive overseas deployment. Nor can the American economy indefinitely sustain a policy of essentially unilateral global interventionism—indeed, we had to seek a foreign subsidy of at least $50 billion to sustain this crisis. Therefore, neither the United States nor foreign nations should treat the concept of the new world order as an institutionalization of recent practices.

Any reflection about a new world order must begin with noting its difference from the Cold War period. During the Cold War the principal fissure was between East and West. The ideological conflict led to a more or less uniform perception of the threat, at least among the industrial democracies which produce 72 percent of the world's GNP. The military and—for the greater period of time—technological predominance of the United States also shaped a common military policy. Economically, interdependence moved from slogan to reality.

The world into which we are moving will be infinitely more complex. Ideological challenges will be fewer; the danger of nuclear war with the Soviet Union will be sharply reduced. On the other hand, no one can know how well Soviet command and control arrangements for nuclear weapons will withstand domestic upheaval. Elsewhere, local conflicts will be both more likely and, given modern technology, more lethal. The collapse of the Soviet empire in Eastern Europe and the loosening bonds of the Western Alliance have unleashed nationalist rivalries not seen since World War I. The post-colonial period has spawned fanatical fundamentalist forces very hard for the comfortable, if not smug, industrial democracies to comprehend, much less to master. Economic rivalry among Japan, which is growing into superpower status, the European

Community, which is becoming increasingly assertive, and the United States will no longer be restrained by overriding security concerns. The confluence of these elements will characterize the new era as one of turmoil, and will require major adjustments in how we think about international relations.

United States policymakers face a number of imperatives:

- They must recognize that it is not possible to deal with every issue simultaneously. America must be selective, husbanding its resources as well as its credibility. Three levels of threat must be distinguished: those we must be prepared to deal with alone if necessary, those we will deal with only in association with other nations and those threats that do not sufficiently challenge American interests to justify any military intervention.

- They need to reexamine alliance policy and reallocate responsibility. Countries associated with us must be brought to understand that the United States' armed forces are not a mercenary force-for-hire. The special circumstance of the Persian Gulf left President Bush no choice except a disproportionate assumption of risk by the United States. As a general rule in the future, however, American military forces should be employed only for causes for which we are prepared to pay ourselves. That, in fact, is a good working definition of American national interest.

United States policymakers must recognize that the new world order cannot be built to American specifications. America cannot force feed a global sense of community where none exists. But it has an opportunity for creating more limited communities based on a genuine sense of shared purpose. This is why perhaps the most creative—if least well known—foreign policy initiative of the Bush administration is its effort to create a Western Hemispheric Free Trade Area, beginning with Mexico, Canada and the United States.

The list is illustrative, not exhaustive. In the end, the deepest challenge to America will be philosophical: how to define order. History so far has shown us only two roads to international stability: domination or equilibrium. We do not have the resources for domination, nor is such a course compatible with our values. So we are brought back to a concept maligned in much of America's intellectual history—the balance of power.

Of course it is possible to define the issue away by postulating the absence of clashing interests. I would welcome such an outcome, but find little support for it either in history or in the above analysis.

There is no escaping the irony that our triumph in the Cold War has projected us into a world where we must operate by maxims that historically have made Americans uncomfortable. To many Americans, the most objectionable feature of the balance of power is its apparent moral neutrality. For the balance of power is concerned above all with preventing one power or group of powers from achieving hegemony. Winston Churchill described it: "The policy of England takes no account of which nation it is that seeks the overlordship of Europe. It is concerned solely with whoever is the strongest or the potentially dominating tyrant. It is a law of public policy which we are following, and not a mere expedient dictated by accidental circumstances or likes or dislikes . . ."

A policy based on such concepts knows few permanent enemies and few permanent friends. In the current Gulf crisis it would avoid branding Iraq as forever beyond the pale. Rather, it would seek to balance rivalries as old as history by striving for an equilibrium between Iraq, Iran, Syria and other regional powers. In Northeast Asia it would seek to maintain equilibrium between China, Japan and the Soviet Union. In Europe, where the old balance has collapsed, the shape of its successor will depend on the outcome of the Soviet Union's internal struggles, especially on the Soviet capacity to continue its historic role in Europe.

These balances all need a balancer—a role the United States can no longer play entirely by itself and in some circumstances may not choose to exercise at all. But it needs criteria to establish priorities.

It is a paradox that no nation is in a better position to contribute to a new world order than the United States: it is domestically cohesive, its economy is less vulnerable to outside forces, its military capacity for the foreseeable future is still the world's largest and most effective. Our challenge is the price of success: triumph in the Cold War has produced a world requiring adjustment of traditional concepts. But the price of success is one for which most other nations would envy us.

THE PENTAGON'S NEW PARADIGM

Michael T. Klare

O PERATION DESERT Storm will constitute the new paradigm for U.S. military action in the 1990s. While prior models for overseas combat assumed that American forces would be fighting the Warsaw Pact in Europe or revolutionary guerrillas in Central America, the new model envisions periodic encounters with well-armed regional powers like Syria or Iraq. Such conflicts, as shown by Desert Storm, are likely to be high-speed, high-tech affairs entailing the unrestrained use of America's most capable and sophisticated weapons. In essence, we will be taking weapons designed for a war with the Soviet Union and using them against the rising powers in the Third World. To distinguish such encounters from both the "high-intensity combat" expected from a war in Europe and the "low-intensity warfare" experienced in Central America, Pentagon officials are using the term "mid-intensity conflict" (MIC) for regional clashes of this type.

Although at present there is no obvious candidate for the "next Iraq" to provoke U.S. military intervention, the perceived risk of mid-intensity conflict is likely to persist for many years to come. Many other Third World nations harbor hegemonic ambitions that could someday lead to a collision with the United States, and a good number of these aspiring powers also possess large arsenals of modern weapons—including, in some cases, weapons of mass destruction (i.e., chemical, nuclear, or biological munitions). So long as these rising powers are viewed in Washington as possible threats to America's global interests, U.S. forces

Michael T. Klare is associate professor of peace and world security studies at Hampshire College in Amherst, Massachusetts, and defense correspondent for *The Nation*. This article was excerpted from the May 1991 issue of *Technology Review*.

will remain poised for further regional conflicts on the model of Desert Storm.

The perception that the current era would be dominated by mid-intensity engagements was already widespread among senior military leaders at the very onset of the 1990s. Fearful that the Cold War's end would produce incessant calls for reductions in U.S. military spending, Pentagon officials were ardently seeking a significant overseas threat to replace the Warsaw Pact as the main justification for retention of a large military establishment in the post–Cold War era. All-out war with the Soviet Union has become less and less likely, and sustained counter-guerrilla warfare in Latin America appears to enjoy limited public support. The threat posed by emerging Third World powers, however, seems to arouse considerable anxiety among civilian leaders—especially when the powers involved are believed to possess nuclear and/or chemical weapons. Encouraged by a favorable climate in Congress, the Department of Defense began reshaping U.S. forces for the MIC mission in January 1990—six months before Saddam Hussein ordered the takeover of Kuwait.

Adoption of a national security posture based on MIC has many obvious attractions for the U.S. military—not the least of which is the fact that it provides a rationale for the retention of large, high-tech forces in the Pentagon lineup. With the rapid disappearance of the Warsaw Pact, there appears to be little need for such forces in Europe, and the anti-narcotics and counterinsurgency operations underway in Latin America will be conducted by the Green Berets and other lightly armed infantry forces. By emphasizing the risk of mid-intensity engagement with well-armed regional hegemons, however, the Defense Department can plausibly rationalize the retention of armored and mechanized units of the type now being withdrawn from Europe.

"There was a time when conflict in developing countries conjured up a vision of simple, low-tech warfare that would not require sophisticated weapons," Admiral Carlisle A. H. Trost observed in 1990, but "that time has passed." Today, "developing countries are armed with 'First World' weapons. Proliferation of chemical weapons, growing access to nuclear weapons capability, and proliferation of cruise and ballistic missiles, submarines and high-performance tactical aircraft mean that virtually any nation . . . can bring capable and deadly weapons to bear." This being the case, Trost argued, "the fundamental defense issue for the United States in the foreseeable future is to maintain a military posture that protects our interests and those of our allies from a diversity of regional threats," including those posed by heavily armed local powers.

The adoption of MIC as the central thrust in U.S. strategic policy has another major attraction for U.S. officials: It invests us with a military *mission* that appears worthy of our continued superpower status. Knocking off Manuel Noriega of Panama may have provided a degree of satisfaction for a day or so, but no one can truly claim that the incarceration of Noriega represents a cause as illustrious as the containment of Soviet expansionism over a forty-year period. With the Cold War's end, many U.S. leaders perceived a significant "mission gap"—that is, the lack of a global military mission comparable in scale and importance to the policy of containment. And American leaders clearly crave such a mission: As suggested by General Colin Powell of the Joint Chiefs of Staff, "We have to put a shingle outside our door saying 'Superpower Lives Here,' no matter what the Soviets do, even if they evacuate from Eastern Europe." Now, with Operation Desert Storm and the adoption of an MIC-oriented strategy, U.S. leaders can claim that America has found a way to justify that "shingle."

No one has more enthusiastically embraced this new global mission than President Bush himself. When Iraq is finally vanquished, he told Congress in his 1991 State of the Union address, we "will have sent an enduring warning to any dictator or despot, present or future, who contemplates outlaw aggression." Yes, he admitted, America will be forced to bear a disproportionate share of the burden of delivering this message. But, he argued, this is to be our special calling: "Among the nations of the world, only the United States has had both the moral standing, and the means to back it up. We are the only nation on earth that could assemble the forces of peace."

And so, we have once again found a mission in the world. But while wrapped in moralistic finery, the new U.S. posture also carries with it some important geopolitical advantages that are not being ignored by U.S. policymakers. Many of the areas considered most significant from an MIC perspective also harbor vital sources of critical raw materials— especially oil—whose possession and control in the years ahead will unquestionably provide vast strategic benefit to those nations involved. By serving as the self-appointed "guardian" of these critical assets, it is argued, the United States can assume for itself a dominant role in world affairs. As suggested by Senator John McCain in 1990, "Our friends and allies are even more dependent on global stability and the free flow of trade than we are." Thus, by providing a substantial capacity for military intervention, American forces "will remain the free world's insurance policy"—and our allies had better not lose sight of this fact!

Whether motivated by a wish to retain large military forces or a desire to serve as the "free world's insurance policy," the U.S. commitment to an MIC-oriented posture will have profound consequences for the United States in the years ahead. To prevail in future conflicts of this sort, we will clearly have to maintain a mammoth military establishment, on a par with that sustained throughout the Cold War period. To do this, moreover, we will have to keep military budgets at peak Cold War levels, thus eliminating any hope that a significant "peace dividend" can be garnered from the Cold War's end. And because U.S. forces are likely to be permanently stationed in remote and inhospitable locales like Saudi Arabia, we can expect a progressive decline in voluntary military enlistment—thus prompting vigorous calls from Congress and the Pentagon for early restitution of the draft.

The adoption of an MIC-dominated strategy also raises deeper questions about America's future world role. President Bush has spoken frequently of his quest for a new world order based on international cooperation, and many Americans have taken heart from inspiring images of this sort. But Washington's concomitant desire to serve as the world's preeminent superpower and to suppress all major challenges to regional stability could result in interventionary behavior of a sort that will alienate many of our friends and divide the world community. A belief in the efficacy of force as a response to belligerent local regimes could also diminish the effort put into nonproliferation and other prophylactic measures designed to curb the spread of sophisticated weapons. There is good reason, therefore, to question the wisdom of adopting an MIC posture and of rebuilding the U.S. military along these lines. Before proceeding in this fashion, we should examine the genesis of MIC doctrine and weigh its purported benefits.

F O R A L L of its potential significance, the focus on mid-intensity warfare is a very recent phenomenon. Throughout the 1980s, U.S. military planning was dominated by two primary concerns: a hypothetical high-intensity conflict (HIC) in Europe, and the proliferation of low-intensity conflict (LIC) in Central America. To prepare for the former, President Reagan authorized the expenditure of billions of dollars on the modernization of U.S. nuclear and nonnuclear forces; to prepare for the latter, the White House ordered a huge buildup of America's "power projection" capabilities—aircraft carriers, amphibious assault groups, light infantry units, and the special operations forces. Little effort, however, was devoted to preparation for mid-sized conflicts that fit into neither of these categories—either because the problem was not considered significant, or because it was assumed that existing HIC and LIC capabilities would suffice for any other type of conflict that might erupt.

As the 1980s drew to a close, however, many military analysts began to pay increased attention to the military threat posed by emerging Third World powers. Although Pentagon rhetoric retained its emphasis on the Warsaw Pact and the threat of guerrilla warfare, it was becoming increasingly evident that a war in Europe was the least plausible of contingencies and that the lightly armed forces intended for LIC encounters in Central America would be cut to ribbons by a heavily armed regional power like Syria or Iraq. As a result, a number of analysts began to press for a reassessment of U.S. strategic assumptions and for the development of military doctrine for full-scale combat with these emerging powers.

Essential to the arguments of these analysts is the view that MIC is not just LIC writ large, but a new type of ballgame entirely. A good way to appreciate the difference between LIC and MIC is to compare Operation Just Cause, the December 1989 invasion of Panama, and Operation Desert Storm, the current U.S. engagement in the Persian Gulf. In Panama, the United States faced a glorified police force of perhaps ten thousand men equipped with zero tanks, no missiles, and only four (propeller-driven) combat planes; to overcome this paltry force, Washington committed an estimated 25,000 infantry troops. In Iraq, by contrast, the United States faced a battle-tested army of one million men equipped with some 5,500 tanks, 700 modern combat planes, and a vast supply of guided missiles; to overpower this potent force, Washington deployed nearly 500,000 combat troops backed by some 1,800 aircraft and 150 warships.

The clear distinction between these two encounters reflects the growing differentiation between the smaller and poorer Third World countries like Panama and the dozen or so regional powers that have acquired large arsenals of modern weapons along with a capacity to produce nuclear and/or chemical munitions. Included in this select group of emerging powers are Argentina, Brazil, Egypt, India, Iran, Iraq, Israel, Pakistan, South Africa, Syria, Taiwan, Turkey, and the two Koreas. These nations are obviously not in the same league as the two existing superpowers, but, in comparison to most other Third World states, stand out as formidable military leviathans.

So long as the Soviet Union was seen as the single overwhelming threat to U.S. national security, the potential threat posed by these Third World leviathans was largely ignored by American policymakers. Indeed, in their efforts to secure regional allies for the global struggle against the

Soviet bloc, U.S. officials established formal or informal alliances with many of these countries—often providing them with modern arms and war-making technologies in the process. And while the bulk of such aid went to close U.S. allies like Israel and South Korea, Washington also provided sophisticated scientific and technical gear to Iraq and other Soviet-allied nations in the hope of diminishing their dependence on Moscow.

As the perceived severity of the Soviet threat began to decline, however, U.S. strategists began to place much more emphasis on the threat posed by emerging Third World hegemons. "In the years ahead," observed the Commission on Integrated Long-Term Strategy (a high level study group formed by the Department of Defense and the National Security Council in 1988), "many lesser powers will have sizable arsenals." Included in the capabilities of these "lesser powers" would be growing supplies of chemical weapons, ballistic missiles, and, in some cases, nuclear arms. Such capabilities, the Commission warned, "will make it much riskier and more difficult for the superpowers to intervene in regional wars," and, as a result, "the U.S. ability to support its allies around the world will increasingly be called into question."

Because any impediment to U.S. intervention in the Third World was considered anathema by the former security officials (including Henry Kissinger) who participated in this study, the Commission called for a significant expansion of America's capacity to conduct intensive, high-tech wars in non-NATO areas. "We must diversify and strengthen our ability to bring discriminating, nonnuclear force to bear where needed in time to defeat aggression," the Commission argued. In the Third World, this means "versatile, mobile forces, minimally dependent on overseas bases, that can deliver precisely controlled strikes against distant military targets."

Enunciated too late in the Reagan period to have much influence on military policy, this perspective seems to have had an early and decisive influence on the strategic outlook of the Bush administration. The president himself introduced this theme in his first major address on national security affairs. "Coping with a changing Soviet Union will be a challenge of the highest order," he observed in May 1989. "But the security challenges we face today do not come from the East alone. The emergence of regional powers is rapidly changing the strategic landscape." Of greatest concern is the fact that "a growing number of nations are acquiring advanced and highly destructive capabilities—in some cases, weapons of mass destruction, and the means to deliver them." In response, he argued, we must intensify our efforts to curb the spread of advanced weapons, and, where necessary, "we must check the aggressive ambitions of renegade regimes."

This notion of "renegade regimes" armed with sophisticated weapons became a major theme in administration rhetoric in the months ahead, especially after the collapse of communist regimes in Eastern Europe signalled the approaching end of the Cold War. Bush continued to stress the overwhelming threat posed by Soviet forces until the very end of 1989, but in early 1990, with the Warsaw Pact in disarray and the Soviet economy in shambles, the emergence of well-equipped Third World adversaries like Iraq and Syria came to be viewed by the president as the *preeminent* threat to U.S. security.

In accordance with this outlook, the Department of Defense began to articulate a new approach to national security. Thus, in his first annual report to Congress, Secretary of Defense Dick Cheney warned that while there has been much improvement in European security, "we must also recognize the challenges beyond Europe that may place significant demands on our defense capabilities." In response to these challenges, he affirmed, the United States must adopt strategies "that rely more heavily on mobile, highly ready, well-equipped forces and solid power-projection capabilities."

In the months that followed, Cheney and his associates began to convert this precept into formal Pentagon policy. In February 1990, Cheney approved a top-secret Defense Policy Guidance statement covering the years 1992–97 that reportedly ordered the services to place far less emphasis on the Soviet threat and far more emphasis on preparing for clashes with emerging Third World powers. Although details of the document have not been made public, reporters who have been briefed on its contents indicate that it calls for a phased reduction of U.S. forces in Europe and for the simultaneous creation of a large, multi-division strike force based in the United States and intended for rapid deployment to distant Third World troublespots—just the sort of force, in fact, that was rushed to the Persian Gulf in the aftermath of Iraq's invasion of Kuwait.

In consonance with Cheney's directives, each of the service chiefs— the chiefs of staff of the Army and Air Force, the chief of naval operations, and the commandant of the Marine Corps—issued similar guidance documents to their own cadres. Thence, in a series of statements, documents, and position papers, the senior military leadership hammered out a new strategic doctrine for U.S. military forces in the 1990s— a doctrine built around the concept of mid-intensity conflict in the Third World. And, while still rough in some places, this doctrine was already well developed by August 7, when President Bush ordered U.S. forces to prepare for a major confrontation with Iraq.

A T   T H E   heart of this new MIC doctrine is the belief that U.S. efforts to protect its vital overseas interests will inevitably provoke clashes with the emerging powers of the Third World. "Changes in Europe and the Soviet Union do not promise a tranquil world nor an end to threats to American interests around the globe," an Air Force "white paper" affirmed in June 1990. Of particular concern is the emergence of regional powers "working their own agenda," and equipped with large quantities of modern weapons. This combination of "emerging threats to national security interests [and the] proliferation of sophisticated weapons . . . presents new challenges for U.S. military forces," the Air Force noted. *"The likelihood that U.S. military forces will be called upon to defend U.S. interests in a lethal environment is high. . . ."* (Emphasis added.)

A remarkably similar outlook was provided in April 1990 by General Carl E. Vuono, the chief of staff of the U.S. Army. "Because the United States is a global power with vital interests that must be protected throughout an increasingly turbulent world," he argued, "we must look beyond the European continent and consider other threats to our national security." Foremost among these threats is the emergence of regional powers equipped with sophisticated weapons. "The proliferation of military power in what is often called the 'Third World' presents a troubling picture. Many Third World nations now possess mounting arsenals of tanks, heavy artillery, ballistic missiles, and chemical weapons." The United States "cannot ignore the expanding military power of these countries," Vuono noted, and thus "the Army must retain the capability to defeat potential threats wherever they occur." Ultimately, *"this could mean confronting a well-equipped army in the Third World."* (Emphasis added.)

Running through all of these documents is the conviction that the United States—and the United States alone—can serve as the world's protector against aggressively minded regional powers in the Third World. "There will be no substitute for the leadership that the United States has provided to the West," Vuono affirmed in January 1990. "No other Allied or friendly nation has, or is likely to develop, the necessary economic, political, and military power to replace the United States in that role." As suggested earlier, it is through this very capacity to resist regional hegemons that America's continued superpower status can be assured—or so say the proponents of an MIC-oriented posture. "There is absolutely no substitute for decisive, clearheaded American leadership," former Assistant Secretary of Defense Richard Armitage avowed in August 1990, at the onset of the Gulf crisis. "Those who so recently predicted America's imminent decline must now acknowledge that the United States alone possesses sufficient moral, economic, political, and military horsepower to jump start and drive international efforts to curb international lawlessness."

The new military paradigm also holds that when the United States is actually provoked to battle by a hostile Third World power, it should use military force in a timely and decisive manner. To prevail in future clashes with such adversaries, the Air Force noted in June 1990 (a mere two months before the Iraqi invasion of Kuwait), "U.S. forces must be able to provide a rapid, tailored response with a capability to intervene against a well-equipped foe, hit hard, and terminate quickly." The need, in sum, is for "fast, agile, modernized conventional capabilities."

In examining these and other statements of this sort, it quickly becomes apparent that the Pentagon game plan for MIC is consciously intended to overcome the "mistakes" of Vietnam (as seen by U.S. military officers) and thereby to ensure a decisive American victory. From the military's perspective, the principal U.S. error in Vietnam was to apply American firepower gradually, in the mistaken belief that the enemy would be inspired to sue for peace at an early level of escalation; instead, it is argued, the North Vietnamese took advantage of this "gradualism" to build up their own capabilities and thereby neutralize U.S. strength. Rather than repeat this miscalculation in future encounters, current U.S. doctrine calls for the fast, concentrated application of American firepower in order to destroy enemy capabilities and crush his will to fight.

One can, of course, draw other lessons from Vietnam—for instance, about the need for political clarity and cohesion when commiting a democracy to a grinding conflict abroad. But it is the aversion to gradualism that has governed U.S. war plans in the Persian Gulf. "If we go to war," Desert Storm General H. Norman Schwarzkopf observed in November, "I am going to use every single thing that is available to me to bring as much destruction to Iraqi forces as rapidly as I possibly can in the hopes of winning victory as quickly as possible."

Other U.S. commanders, making frequent references to Vietnam, have offered similar views. "Many of us here who are in this position now were in Vietnam, and that has left a profound impact on our feelings about how our nation ought to conduct its business," explained General Charles A. Horner, the commander of U.S. Air Force units in Saudi

Arabia. "We think that war is a very serious business and it should not be dragged out in an effort to achieve some political objective."

Central to the notion of winning these engagements quickly is the belief that every advantage in U.S. technology and firepower should be employed so as to stun, cripple, and defeat enemy capabilities. The army of the future "must be lethal," General Vuono wrote in 1990. "Lethality results from quality soldiers . . . equipped with weapons that are superior to those of any adversary and available in numbers adequate to defeat potential enemies." General Schwarzkopf accentuated this point in September when discussing U.S. plans for a war with Iraq: "We would be using capabilities that are far more lethal, far more accurate, and far more effective than anything we've ever used."

The implications of all this is clear: There will be no gradualism in these encounters, no restraints on the concentrated application of U.S. firepower. The president himself underlined this precept in his much-quoted November 30, 1990 press conference on developments in the Gulf: "Should military action be required, this will not be another Vietnam; this will not be a protracted, drawn-out war. . . . If one American soldier has to go into battle, that soldier will have enough force behind him to win, and then get out as soon as possible. . . ."

From these maxims have come the U.S. battle plan in the Gulf, and from them will emerge the defining military doctrine of the 1990s. Adoption of this doctrine will have an enormous impact on U.S. foreign policy, lodging the United States in an antagonistic relationship with rising Third World powers and inviting a military response to disagreements that will inevitably arise. The MIC doctrine will also govern the future organization of U.S. forces and the development and procurement of military hardware in the years ahead.

In line with emerging military doctrine, senior American officers began, in early 1990, to hammer out a blueprint for the combination of arms and combat forces that would best serve U.S. needs in the mid-intensity conflicts of the future. Progress on this effort had not proceeded very far by August 2, when Iraqi forces invaded Kuwait and provoked the current crisis in the Persian Gulf. Since then, Pentagon officials have speeded up development of the MIC master plan, while improvising parts of it in Saudi Arabia. Full implementation of this blueprint by the United States will undoubtedly provide Washington with a strong and versatile capacity for the prosecution of mid-intensity conflicts in the years ahead. The price of this capability will, however, be staggering. Paying for the Persian Gulf conflict and all of the new weapons sought by the Department of Defense (and by allies like Israel and

Egypt) will encumber the U.S. Treasury and the U.S. taxpayer for years to come, and consume resources desperately needed to rebuild American cities, rehabilitate U.S. industries, and restore damaged ecologies. These costs will not be shouldered with equal equanimity by all Americans, and could provoke opposition from those who feel unfairly burdened by the steady erosion of domestic programs and benefits.

Added to all of this is the risk of recurring U.S. military involvement in Third World power struggles that could escalate into major regional conflagrations. When you adopt a strategic doctrine whose basic premise is that you are likely to come into conflict with emerging powers that are "working their own agenda" (as the Air Force put it), and that consequently you may wind up "confronting a well-equipped army in the Third World" (as suggested by General Vuono), then you will be predisposed to view overseas incidents—like the Iraqi takeover of Kuwait—as a clear case of regional aggression that must be met with decisive military action—as was in fact the U.S. reaction just four months after Vuono uttered his prophetic words. This is not to say that the January 1991 U.S. offensive against Iraq was planned *before* the invasion of Kuwait, or that U.S. forces were spoiling for a fight; rather, it is to suggest that adoption of an MIC-oriented doctrine will tend to produce a militant response to certain overseas developments, and lead to the early initiation of military action when it is believed that vital American interests are at stake.

We have heard the president speak fervently of his dreams for a new world order based on international cooperation and the peaceful resolution of conflict. Many Americans, and many other peoples, share similar hopes. But a policy based on the early initiation of military action by the United States, designed to demonstrate the continued validity of our superpower status (while advancing America's geopolitical and economic interests), is not likely to result in a cooperative world order but rather in a new Pax Americana in which U.S. soldiers are the principal instrument of regional stability. We may receive certain benefits from this arrangement, but we are also likely to pay a heavy price in blood, and in the continued decline of our cities, our non-military industries, and our natural environment.

WHY WE NEED TO
POLICE THE WORLD

Anthony H. Cordesman

IRAQ LOST the war because of Saddam Hussein's military incompetence and the shock of the Allies' excellence. Iraq was doomed because its backward-looking forces clashed with America's new military culture and competence. The bad news is that if the military budget is cut in accordance with present plans, that competence will suffer and our ability to resist aggression will be hurt.

America's new military culture is exemplified by General Colin L. Powell and General H. Norman Schwarzkopf. It is apparent in virtually every field grade officer involved in operational planning and combat. It is based on our defeat in Vietnam, catastrophes like our intervention in Lebanon in 1983, and on awareness that U.S. strategy, tactics, and forces had to be restructured to enable us to compete with the Soviet Army's vastly superior mass.

It stems from the knowledge that the U.S. entered Vietnam emphasizing vastly superior numbers, firepower, rigid tactics and a separation among the services and service branches. It is based on the realization that short tours for combat commanders to meet promotion requirements were no substitute for leadership by officers who stayed and fought with their troops.

It is based on the view that formal doctrine and set-piece exercises in which the "enemy" was always easily defeated were no substitute for practical exercises. Each service forced commanders to cooperate with other services, and exercises were toughened up: the "enemy" fought as

Anthony H. Cordesman teaches national security studies at Georgetown University and is a military analyst for ABC News. This article appeared on the op-ed page of *The New York Times* on February 28, 1991, under the title "America's New Combat Culture."

a probable foe would and was more experienced than the forces undergoing training.

The culture recognized that we had fought much of the Vietnam and Korean wars using books written in World War II. So the military wrote a new book, the air-land battle.

The new strategy stressed initiative, agility, depth of operation, and synchronization of all four services and their branches. New tactics stressed avoiding battles of attrition and accepting risk, using night and poor-weather operations, attacking enemies' specific vulnerabilities and keeping the battlefield "fluid" through continuous operations so that foes would be kept off balance and forced to move in desired directions.

The new culture implied a new civil-military relationship. This unwritten bargain said the military would never again willingly fight a major war if it did not have full political support, if it could not use all its force to win quickly and decisively, if gradual escalation and political bargaining deprived it of the ability to maintain momentum and if politicians tried micro-management.

Saddam Hussein, unaware of all this, made fatal political judgments. He believed the U.S. would not risk war and, if it did, could be put off by threats of the kinds of losses that defeated it in Vietnam. He believed the U.S. was too weak to lead an anti-Iraq alliance.

Iraq enjoyed air and missile supremacy in its war with Iran. Its low-technology air force lacked training and experience in air-to-air combat, fluid combined operations and precision targeting and bombing. In the Gulf war, the Allies won total air supremacy. They then decisively attacked Iraq's land forces in detail.

Iraq had almost complete superiority in reconnaissance and intelligence during the Iran-Iraq war. But long before the Gulf war began, the U.S. established an air and naval defensive screen over Saudi Arabia that left Iraq virtually without reconnaissance and intelligence. When the war began, Allied reconnaissance aircraft and deep reconnaissance patrols moved into Iraq. Their ability to monitor movement at night and in poor weather gave the Allies nearly perfect vision over the battlefield.

The Iraqis had a huge advantage over Iran in artillery numbers, range, and munitions. Iraq's fixed defenses held off the Iranians long enough to bring in sizable amounts of artillery. The Allies had fewer weapons, but superior targeting and many aircraft to provide close support.

Iraq's strong forward defenses—minefields, razor wire, berms, dugouts, buried tanks, thousands of anti-infantry weapons—delayed or halted Iran's human waves. When Iran penetrated Iraq's defenses, Iraqi tanks and armor rushed in. Limited Iraqi forces could hold a broad front.

The Allies first concentrated on a narrow area of Iraq's front, penetrated quickly and leapfrogged Iraqi positions by air, then struck to the west of Iraq's main defenses. The Allies seized and kept the initiative, moving faster than the Iraqis. The Iraqis lost cohesion, were forced in the direction the Allies desired and could never deal with the fluid battlefield. The Allies bypassed Iraq's main forces and froze them in place with air power.

In the Iran war, while Iraq had command, control, and communication weaknesses, Iran was inferior and its forces were politically divided. In this war, the Allies destroyed most of the Iraqi command and communications system in a week.

Every tenet of the Allied air-land battle worked. The system functioned at a level of perfection virtually unknown in the fog of war.

As for the bad news, under military budget plans, the U.S. will cut its forces by twenty-five percent over the next five years. This will put many professionals who won this war out of work. Many of our technological assets will be gone—perhaps much of our readiness as well. If this goes on, we will be unable to refight our last war, much less the next one. Any effort to check future aggression will be threatened.

Like it or not, the U.S. is the only nation that can assemble and project enough power to meet any aggressor. While Americans may not want to be the world's policeman, they must consider what it could be like to live in a world without any policeman at all.

WHAT WILL THIS WAR MEAN?

Marcy Darnovsky, L. A. Kauffman, Billy Robinson

H OW ARE we to understand this war?
  Emotional responses come easily and powerfully: outrage, disgust, horror, grief. These reactions are unambiguous, and they move us to protest.

But around and within those certainties lie perplexities and confusions. The slogans we chant in protest are unsatisfying because they seem so incomplete. Is blood really being spilled primarily for oil? What's the real agenda of this war, and is it hidden or right on the surface; is the Gulf war born of capitalism's triumph in the Cold War, or is it a desperate move by a declining empire? What *exactly* is at stake, globally and domestically? We say that we want the troops home now, and we mean it, but couldn't the consequences of a short war—a green light for more U.S. military adventures—be as deadly as those of a long one? How stable and how deep is popular support for the war in the United States?

These questions and confusions are due, in part, to the fluidity and indeterminacy of the war itself, and to the sense that so much is up for grabs. George Bush has evidently decided that hot war is the best post–Cold War bet—a gamble that will change the world. As the commander in chief and a small circle of his buddies roll the dice, many thousands of lives are being snuffed and millions more turned inside out; global balances of power are shifting; new economic arrangements, new pat-

Marcy Darnovsky, L. A. Kauffman, and Billy Robinson are members of the Bay Area *Socialist Review* editorial collective. This essay is excerpted from "Warring Stories: Reading and Contesting the New Order," which appeared in the 91/1 issue of *Socialist Review*.

terns of political influence, new modes of social control, and new forms of resistance are emerging.

But our perplexities also arise from the inability of any existing critical or theoretical framework to fully explain this conflict. Some of the assumptions, categories, and concepts that have become dear to the left clearly don't work—for example, the notion that since Vietnam "the American people" won't support large-scale military operations anymore. Others—like the notion of "imperialism"—are only slightly more helpful, for they obscure much of what seems distinctive about this conflict and the changed world in which it is occurring.

Our sense is that this is a multifaceted war, irreducible to any single cause, slogan, or agenda. It represents a complex breaking apart and coming together of recent histories of power, identity, and meaning.

FOR MANY on the left, the first impulse is to frame this war in economic terms. It's an obvious move: The presence of large amounts of oil in Iraq, Kuwait, and Saudi Arabia means that the immediate economic interests of the advanced capitalist countries are engaged in a way that they never were in the Falklands, Grenada, or even Vietnam. The huge scale of Kuwaiti oil wealth invested in the United States—especially in the strategic but troubled financial sector—provides another economic dimension. Moreover, a variety of economic indicators—like the huge profits that the major oil companies have racked up since the inception of the crisis, or the jump in Raytheon stock since the first Patriot missiles were launched—illustrate quite neatly and dramatically the cozy, interdependent relationship between capitalism and war; the intermingling, in this case, of blood and oil.

Another economic explanation for the war focuses on what's been called Pentagon capitalism or the permanent war economy. The war against Saddam Hussein showcases weapons smart and dumb, high-tech and low, and gives the Pentagon and military contractors a winning argument for new weapons systems and new rounds of subsidies.

But the dimensions of the conflict that a strictly economic interpretation misses may be as important as the truths it captures. There is a gap between the scale of the economic interests involved and the scale of the war—and hence a crucial intellectual and political challenge to make sense of what fills that gap. Certainly, economic factors alone cannot explain what has made this war such an easy sell to the U.S. public. We need to understand the jumbled mix of stakes and desires—factors not easily reducible to economic terms—that have helped this war garner such broad, though possibly shallow, support.

• • •

GEORGE BUSH has declared repeatedly that this war is designed to defend and consolidate the new world order, "a world where the rule of law, not the law of the jungle, governs the conduct of nations." It's obvious enough that this new world order is not an order framed in the interests of Africans, Latin Americans, or the ordinary people of the Middle East. Behind the talk of a new world order is a contest to determine the balance of power in the post–Cold War world—a contest among the supposed victors of the Cold War, the advanced capitalist countries.

Whatever else the Bush administration is doing in the Gulf, it seems to be staking out a place for an economically declining United States vis-à-vis the economically ascendant but largely demilitarized European Community and Japan. When Bush declares that this war will not be another Vietnam, he is pointing in part to the decade-long attempt to reassert U.S. power. In the face of the country's economic slide, its vast military machine will maintain the position of the United States as a crucial, irreplaceable player in the global games of power. A U.S. victory in the Persian Gulf—whatever that means—would assure the United States a central place at the world's bargaining tables alongside the new great powers, Germany and Japan.

This scenario of Great Powers fighting it out over global spoils clearly echoes classic left theories of imperialism. But labeling the present conflict as an "imperialist war" can obscure the transformations that have taken place in recent decades in the relations of power, domination, and exploitation between and within North and South.

The topography and character of power in the North has shifted profoundly. There is no longer any single imperial center, no key military-economic power; instead we are witnessing something like "flexible specialization" of imperial power, with economic and military functions being divvied up among the states of the North.

The nature of the South, and of resistance from it, has also changed in recent years. "The Third World" was always an oversimplified category, lumping all non-Western peoples and states together indiscriminately as if their "non-Westernness" were the only significant thing about them. Over the last several decades, as political developments such as the industrialization of key Pacific Rim countries, the formation of the OPEC oil cartel, and the rise of regional military powers like Iraq have widened the differences *among* the countries of the South, the category "Third World" has become increasingly ill-suited to describe global realities.

At the same time, this war takes place against the backdrop of the decline of the politics of Third World national liberation; the last twenty years have witnessed the destruction from without or self-destruction from within of a distressing number of such movements. The near-total withdrawal of the post–Cold War Soviet Union from its role as protector, sustainer, or exploiter of movements of national liberation has also dramatically changed global equations of power, helping to create the vacuum that George Bush and Saddam Hussein have been battling to fill.

Political discourse has yet to catch up with the new configurations of power and domination; there is a pressing need to reconceptualize this new landscape and to develop a new language for talking about it that draws on the insights of earlier theories without becoming imprisoned by their terms.

And nowhere is this need more critical than in the imperative to speak morally and lucidly in support of the simultaneous claims for a Palestinian national self-determination and Israeli national security. What does the discourse of Third World national liberation help illumine here and what does it obscure? What other truths about the nature of nationalism must we learn in order to come to terms with the realities of the Israelis and the Palestinians, situated within the bloody histories of imperialism, fascism, colonialism, and genocide? To "press for a just solution" from some viewpoint abstracted from historical involvement is simultaneously necessary and inadequate; to plunge into history is to risk entrapment in a horrifying web of fear and hatred, cynically exploited on every side.

IN MANY important respects, this war is also about the construction and reproduction of "Americanism," a national identity which is more invented and less stable than that of any other advanced capitalist country. U.S. identity has more to do with ideology—that is, certain interpretations of the "American founding," or images of the United States as the "moral" and "democratic" exemplar—than with a shared culture, history, or tradition. This ideological character of U.S. identity explains in part the presence of competing conceptions of Americanism in this country. (The peculiar contest between pro- and anti-war demonstrators over who may properly lay claim to the flag is one such example.) Where but in the United States would it be possible for people to characterize unpopular activity as "un-American"—an absurd concept when translated into any other national context. The effort to reconstitute and impose a new variant of this old "Americanism" is a crucial element of this war, one that helps explain the present widespread support for the conflict.

For forty years, Cold War anti-communism gave the United States a crucial ideological and discursive basis for shared identity, incorporating a range of accounts of both what Americans *were* (God-fearing, benevolent, democratic, committed to the rule of law) and what they were *not* (mindless, power-hungry, totalitarian). The discourse of anti-communism put together a complex and seemingly coherent ensemble of principles that linked U.S. power and American identity. While this ideology was increasingly contested during and after the 1960s, it retained significant cultural and political potency up until the fall of the Berlin Wall.

Part of what we see taking place in and around the Gulf war is the beginnings of a post–Cold War, post–anti-communist American identity. This discourse-in-formation is full of slippages and contradictions; it is incomplete, not yet coherent, and appears open to contestation from many fronts.

To the extent that there's an overall recipe for this emerging identity, it seems to contain some familiar ingredients: part moral crusade, part racist invocation of an "Other," and part reassertion of the U.S. role as a global power. The dimension of "moral crusade" comes into play in the oft-repeated simile of the conflict: Saddam Hussein as another Hitler.

For Bush and all the spin doctors in his camp, this is a great storyline. It's short, memorable, fits into a sound bite, and is, in superficial terms, plausible enough to be widely accepted. It plays into the long-standing ideological rationale of U.S. imperial ambition: the Americanist quest for a moral identity through virtuous conquest of evil, the sense of a people pursuing its self-interest while collectively embodying some transcendent ideal.

It would be a mistake not to acknowledge just how well this story is working and how widely it's being accepted. But focusing on its constructedness—its status as story rather than fact, and the cultural desires and needs it successfully taps—makes it possible to begin thinking more clearly about both how to challenge it and how to develop effective counter-stories for the anti-war movement to tell.

The emerging American identity is also being constructed by means of opposition—opposition, in this case, to "Others" marked by the color of their skin and the alleged strangeness and irrationality of their culture. The anti-Arab, Crusade-like character of this war is vicious and dangerous, not only in the most obvious sense, but also because it suggests the degree to which the emerging post–Cold War Americanism is placing racism at its very core.

This racism has the potential to be both like and unlike older racisms. It shares the virulence of the racism of the U.S. past, kindling a hatred of Arab-Americans reminiscent of lynchings and cross-burnings. It also stands in continuity with the "subtler" racism of the domestic triage policies of the Reagan-Bush era, policies that have consistently attacked and sharply eroded living conditions for people of color over the last decade.

However, this emerging racism may be less stable than previous racisms. The figure of General Colin Powell evokes an uneasy, self-conscious attempt at the highest level to incorporate African-Americans into the "Self" while defining Arabs—and Arab-Americans—as the "Other." But this trick would require considerable sleight-of-hand. The now-widespread expression "people of color" speaks to the increasing tendency of African-Americans, Latinos, Asian-Americans, and others both to stress shared experiences of racism and to celebrate culture and community across ethnic divides—creating new social resources for contesting the racist dimension of the new Americanism.

It takes little imagination to see that poor people of color stand to lose the most by this war—both in the bombed cities of Iraq and the inner cities of the United States. Not only will this war take many of the best and brightest young men (and women) of color, who are disproportionately represented in U.S. ground forces; but the enormous economic costs of this war—and the anticipated orgy of military spending and weapons programs that is likely to follow in its wake—will exacerbate the already staggering U.S. fiscal crisis, the brunt of which will be borne by women and people of color.

The third major ingredient in the U.S. identity under construction in and around the Gulf war is the rehabilitation of the United States' now-eroded position as a world power. The reestablishment of this position carries more than material importance; it has symbolic and discursive weight as well. Since at least the Second World War, U.S. global power has been an important part of the hegemonic U.S. identity—an element of that identity that many people in this country claim and assert. But as the costs at home of remaining a power abroad becoming increasingly evident, the psychic satisfactions of identifying as a global "leader" seem already to be fading.

The ongoing attempt to recalibrate U.S. identity in the post–Cold War era raises many questions and suggests both danger and opportunity. Who is included in this particular Americanism, and who excluded?

What spaces remain for competing versions of U.S. identity? What resources might identity politics—the efforts of women, people of color, gays and lesbians, and others to build a politics out of shared experience—provide for contesting not just the terms of U.S. identity, but the placement of American nationalism itself at the center of that identity?

MORE LIKELY A NEW WORLD DISORDER

William Pfaff

A NEW world order has been promised for after the Gulf war. The prudent man, however, would wager on a new disorder.

George Bush and his advisers have not yet described the new order of which the president has spoken. Mr. Bush has said only that he envisions international conduct based on the rules of law and a larger role for United Nations peacekeeping. It seems reasonable to say that Washington has only begun to think about this matter.

Policy in Washington characteristically follows the speechwriter's phrase. To promise a new world order seemed a good idea last August. What the promise meant waits to be explained.

The promise was easily made because new orders are familiar terrain for an American people whose national experience began in the Enlightenment ambition to establish a "novus ordo seclorum." Mr. Bush's proposal is in the direct line of American reformist internationalism, begun with Woodrow Wilson's invention in 1917 of the principle of universal national self-determination, and then of the League of Nations. After that came Franklin Roosevelt's Atlantic Charter in 1941, promising "Four Freedoms" to the people of the world, and after that the United Nations, an American idea.

However, this is a policy tradition which rests on a fallacy, the uncritical transposition of national to international experience. It assumes that an association or coalition of the world's nations can represent the will of

William Pfaff is the author of several books, including *Barbarian Sentiments: How the American Century Ends.* He is a regular contributor to *The New Yorker* and a columnist for *The International Herald Tribune* and the *Los Angeles Times.* This essay is an amalgam of two of his *Los Angeles Times* columns, "More Likely a New World Disorder After this War" and "An Immense and Costly Success," published on January 30, 1991, and February 20, 1991, respectively.

the world's peoples; hence that an assembly of governments provides a form of world democracy and can claim the legitimacy of world opinion.

Abroad, there is a different idea about the new world order. It is widely thought to be one in which the United States, the "only superpower," would act as world policeman to defend democratic interests. A French commentator foresees this new order "forbidding, in the name of the rights of peoples, repression in the Baltic states as well as (Syria's) annexation of Lebanon." This seems deeply unrealistic, for four reasons.

The American public is most unlikely to end the war in the Gulf with any appetite for launching other wars elsewhere, "police actions" or not, which do not directly serve essential U.S. national interests. The experience of this war is more likely to promote isolationism than internationalism.

Second, the European powers and Japan, which—with notable exceptions—have made no great military contribution to the Gulf effort, would not seem candidates to join similar American-led "police actions" in the future. They seem likely to object to a world order-keeping arrangement in which the issues and actions are unilaterally determined by Washington—as has been essentially the case for the Gulf.

A third problem is the indebtedness and relative decline in industrial competitiveness of the United States, which diminishes its ability to lead. The United States' global leadership today rests chiefly upon military power. Europe and Japan meanwhile possess economic and industrial resources of much greater competitive value in a world released from the East-West military confrontation.

Finally is the problem of the United Nations. The vast majority of U.N. members are unrepresentative governments, class- or interest-bound oligarchies or dictatorships, or outright despotisms. On the U.N. Security Council, two of the five permanent members are single-party dictatorships with abominable records of human rights abuse. The Security Council seems scarcely the suitable agency for establishing world democracy and respect for human rights.

This is one reason why the United States and other democracies have in the past ignored U.N. resolutions or exercised their veto. America will cooperate with the United Nations in the future when U.N. decisions coincide with or advance the policies of the democracies. Washington is likely to pay greater respect to international law than in the recent past, but it certainly will not renounce its right to determine policies unilaterally. There is nothing surprising in this. However, it is not what people expect from a new world order.

It may be doubted that there will be such an order. The world in the future may prove less orderly than it was when frozen by Cold War. Rather than providing the paradigm for a new international order, the Gulf war may provoke further disorder.

We too easily neglect the fact that this affair was not a product of individual ambition or the policy of a single nation, Iraq, but had cultural and historical sources in Europe's domination of Islamic society from the time of the Dutch conquest of Indonesia in the seventeenth century and Britain's conquest of Moghul India in the eighteenth. The rage that Saddam Hussein exploits—and the late Ayatollah Khomeini, and Muammar Qaddafi—has its origins in more than three centuries of foreign domination.

Since the late 1940s, four Islamic states have struck back—Indonesia against the Dutch, Algeria against France, Egypt under Nasser at Suez and under Sadat in the 1973 attack on Israel, and Iran under Khomeini. The Gulf war was a fifth such effort. Only a fool would think it the last.

It is very difficult to believe that there can be an "orderly" resolution of the tensions that now exist not only between the Islamic countries and the West but also between all the impoverished or failing societies and the privileged nations. The gap between them grows deeper.

Who can believe that people who experience mounting anarchy, impoverishment and renewed national and communal irredentisms in the Balkans, the Soviet Union, and South Asia can be given pacification and "order" by a coalition led by the United States—even if it were a coalition acting in the name of the United Nations? The idea of a new world order is not ignoble. However, an idealism that rests on illusions is itself an illusion.

But where are we then? There are two approaches possible to the postwar Middle East, but only one is a probability, which is that we go back to much the situation as before. Iraq will be stricken from the power balance for a decade or so. The influence of Syria, Iran, and Turkey will be enlarged. Egypt and Saudi Arabia will be stronger political actors, but still American clients. The influence of Islamic fundamentalism throughout the region will be much enhanced. The Palestinian-Israeli struggle will be more envenomed than ever.

A Palestinian settlement is, in principle, possible—in practice remote. The Bush administration would dearly like one. However, the war has hardened extreme commitments on both sides. The idea that Israel would yield territory for a Palestinian state, or the Palestinians, or Jordanians, accept the removal of Palestinians to Jordan, with Jordan renamed "Palestine"—what this Israeli government apparently wants—seems more unlikely than ever.

The optimistic approach to the postwar Middle East could be called the neocolonialist one. It holds that the West has a duty, interest and opportunity to remake the Middle Eastern order by garrisoning the region and intervening in active support of governments whom the West approves (among whom, until very recently, Iraq would have been numbered).

One can also hear intervention justified by the contention that, politically, Islamic society is inherently corrupt and vicious, having "century after century" been led by "hater-killers"—to employ the expressions of Mr. A. M. Rosenthal of *The New York Times.*

A characteristic statement of the optimistic view says that "intervening to restore Kuwait carries with it the contrary obligation not to withdraw afterwards, but to garrison the region. Not as an act of imperialism, and even less for oil, but out of confidence in the West and its democracy, proving that superior force now means peace."

A still more robust British commentator, in London's *Sunday Telegraph,* assures us that "power in the Middle East *does* flow out of the barrel of a gun, and henceforth it must be ours rather than theirs."

There certainly is something to be said for that, but not only in the Middle East. The observation about power and guns was originally Chinese and continues to fit China very nicely. The Middle East was not a very peaceful place even when the Europeans ran it. Two world wars were waged in Syria, Palestine, Egypt, Libya, and the Maghreb, which Europeans started, not the Arabs, conducting their campaigns on Arab territory and drafting Arab auxiliaries to fight for them.

The European powers took the Arab Middle East away from the Ottoman Turks by war. Afterwards, between the world wars, there was a relatively quiet period, except for the Rifs fighting Spanish and French colonial forces, the Senussi fighting the Italians in Libya, and the Palestinians fighting the Jewish settlers moving into Mandate Palestine. There were, however, no high-tech Arab-Israeli wars, no Iran-Iraq slaughter, and terrorism was a minor phenomenon.

One can certainly make a case for neocolonialism. But why bother? The people advocating it saw their countries lacking the courage of their convictions when those countries did rule the Middle East, and they do not have the political weight today to try to reimpose it.

Britain scuttled from Palestine (and India), leaving chaos behind, and was pushed out of its other colonies under constant pressure and the drumbeat of criticism from the United States—the leading force in the decolonization of precisely those parts of the world, Iraq, Lebanon, Vietnam, and Cambodia, where American governments have since intervened militarily to "save" the natives from communism and "disorder."

Let us try to be realistic about what is to come in the Middle East. The United States is not going to garrison and run the region, even if this administration wished to do so—of which it shows little sign. Moreover, the American attention span is short and something will soon push the Middle East low on Washington's agenda.

The United States will become more implicated in Arab affairs than in the past. It may acquire base agreements or leave a small permanent force in the Persian Gulf. This actually is probably not a good idea because it would perpetuate the enmity of those who would see even this as neocolonialism, while it would lack the ability to make a real difference in how the region develops.

The future of the Middle East is not really susceptible to fundamental change through outside intervention. The political culture of the place is too dense, the history too rich for that. The future, unfortunately, is likely to prove very much like the recent past, possibly rather worse. That is the real reason for criticizing this war. It has been an immense and costly success, whose result will prove only that the mills of God grind slowly, and brook little help from man.

WHAT A WONDERFUL WAR

Robert Scheer

WHAT A wonderful war.
Or so it seemed that Saturday afternoon in front of the mall with people of every age, if not every color, happily waving their American flags, sporting yellow ribbons, and eliciting the approving roar of automobile horns. People where I live, in the shadow of John Wayne Airport, surrounded by high-tech defense industries and Marine air bases, really liked this war. But it wasn't just here, in conservative Orange County, California, that the war played so well. Most Americans loved it. Why not? The TV was good, the body count low, and the enemy bad.

George Bush pronounced Saddam Hussein another Hitler and suddenly we tasted the panache and valor of World War II. Forget that Hitler was at the helm of the world's strongest economy and that Iraq couldn't even produce aluminum tank parts. Or that Hitler had conquered mighty industrial France while Iraq had been checked by Third World Iran. Don't confuse the thing being sold for the thing itself.

For the purposes of advertising copy, which is what modern government is all about, Saddam was just perfect for the part. He was about to build a nuclear bomb, according to the president and his men, even though Iraq's efforts to do so were extremely primitive and at least a decade behind Brazil's own similar program, according to the March 1991 issue of the *Bulletin of the Atomic Scientists*. But no matter, the image stuck. Hussein, certainly evil by any standard, would make a world-class

---

Robert Scheer is the author of several books, including *How the U.S. Got Involved in Vietnam, With Enough Shovels: Reagan, Bush and Nuclear War,* and most recently, *Thinking Tuna Fish, Talking Death: Essays on the Pornography of Power.* Since 1976 he has been a national correspondent for the *Los Angeles Times.* He wrote this essay especially for this book.

devil. Much better than Panama dictator Manuel Noriega or those characters down in Grenada whose military base turned out to be a commercial airfield.

And Kuwait the perfect heroine to be saved. Prior to this war most Americans couldn't have found Kuwait on a map if their lives depended on it. Expertise didn't rise rapidly afterward. Few seemed aware that Kuwait had been a British protectorate until 1961 and that Iraq's leaders, including those who were strongly pro-Western, had long claimed Kuwait as part of their country. Or that Kuwaitis make up less than one quarter of their country's population and that only about two percent had any serious connection with power.

Suddenly Kuwait was blessed as a plucky outpost of the Free World despite the Kuwait blockade of Western oil following the Six-Day War and its cozy relation and extensive arms deals with the Soviet Union. Nor did it matter that the U.S. had no treaty offering protection to this pumping station of a country despite our sudden discovery of its vital importance to our security.

Future historians will have to sort out just how this morality play got going but suddenly Kuwait's mistake in backing Iraq in its war against Iran, only to be betrayed afterwards, was treated not as shameful opportunism gone awry but rather as another bold chapter in the struggle for human rights.

Even sober-minded world leaders jumped on the bandwagon proclaiming the liberation of Kuwait a sacred international obligation. Of course the joker was that this international obligation be borne almost totally by the U.S. Not by Japan, France, and Germany, all of whom are far more dependent upon Mideast oil than the U.S. Just why this country, which did not have a predominant economic interest in the region, should bear the predominant military burden was never explained.

For Americans the normal resistance to being used so shamefully was mitigated by a line of credit from those nations who did have the most to lose. We became the mercenary troops for the oil sheikhdoms as well as Japan and Germany, and the locals here didn't mind because they once again confused military with economic prowess.

No better illustration of our pathetic economic weakness despite, or more likely because of, our military strength occurred on the day Iraq accepted Gorbachev's peace proposal. Once proud Citicorp, the largest American banking company, announced that a thirty-five-year-old Saudi prince had become its biggest shareholder through a $590 million investment. The bank was desperate for cash and this Saudi kid, only a distant cousin of the king, bailed them out. Now that's power without a gun. But probably any of the four thousand Saudi princes and princesses, the people who own the country we saved, could have done the same. Shouldn't these guys at least be required to pay our troops some huge bonus for keeping them in business?

These nagging questions didn't even come up in most of the circles I visited because the entire war seemed free of serious cost. And it was great fun. There was a grand indifference to Iraqi death. It became hip to like weapons once again and the analogy with Nintendo could not be overdrawn. McLuhan lives. Weapons with built-in TV cameras give the idea of living room war a whole new meaning. Is the day far off when you can push a button at home and kill some wogs abroad? Friends admitted that they found the video war thrilling and addictive.

Not me. I don't like those weapons. Tell me again why over a month of bombing, surgically or not, a civilian population doesn't qualify as terrorism. Come on, terrorizing the population was one of the prime goals of those tens of thousands of sorties; to turn the population of Iraq against Saddam. The goal might be noble but the means were the same as in hijacking a commercial aircraft, treating civilians as combatants.

And what about "carpet bombing" troops senseless with fuel-air explosives that suck out the air and shake the earth with the power of a small nuclear explosion? In what way is this a moral act superior to using chemicals against troops? I have had a ground eye view, in Southeast Asia and in the Middle East, of surgical strikes. If you're on the receiving end it just seems outrageous to argue that weapons of mass and ultimately indiscriminate destruction are all right if they're high tech and Western.

One stark legacy of this war is a further blurring of the line between military and civilian targets and a denial of the moral underpinnings of the war against terrorism. That cause was also not helped by our sudden embrace of the government of Syria as an "ally" when only months before we had branded them the chief backers of terrorism in the world.

If the goal of the war was, as Bush often stated, a new world order beginning with peace and stability in the Middle East—forget it.

For openers: You cannot have stability when a small group of people are sitting on a huge pot of gold and their neighbors are mostly broke. The liberation of Kuwait and the protection of Saudi Arabia and the Emirates heightens rather than settles the main contradictions in the region.

Does the liberation of Kuwait require nothing more than the return of the emir and the rest of the royal family back to power? And if the emir permits the Parliament, which he suspended in 1986, to resume its work will it still represent only the 60,000 eligible male voters out of a population of two million? Non-Kuwaitis made up eighty percent of the country's work force but had no rights or possibilities of citizenship. Even their children who were born in Kuwait had no claim on citizenship. Should the "freeing" of Kuwait once again validate this feudal reign? Is it off the wall to have suggested that a U.N.-supervised election for all Kuwaiti residents be part of the liberation package? Or will it be enough that the Western companies that have been hustling for reconstruction deals since the first day of the Iraqi invasion get their contracts signed?

Sorry to have to bring it up, but what about the price of oil? The West, led by the U.S., has pressured the Saudis and Kuwaitis to produce enough to hold prices down. As a result, and despite decades of scare headlines about oil blackmail, the price of oil has not kept up with the cost of finished high-tech industrial goods and pharmaceuticals. This low price explains our failure to obtain energy independence through conservation and alternative fuels. The incentive has just not been there.

Should the price of oil be low as the U.S. insists? That has been acceptable to the Arab countries with a lot of oil and a small population but not to those with many mouths to feed. The price of oil and in particular Kuwait's undermining the OPEC price by cheating on its quota was the original source of Iraq-Kuwait tension.

Rest assured that the power of the oil-rich sheikhdoms to set prices will be rudely challenged again no matter who rules the populous states of Iraq and Iran. Surely one Saudi nightmare has to be that the Egyptians who by the millions replaced Pakistanis, Palestinians, and others who fled the kingdom will tire of doing the dirty work and want to share more directly in the riches. After all, Egyptians, as representatives of a far older civilization and with a modern army might chafe at the houseboy role laid out for them by the Saudi princes. The Saudis clashed with Egypt over Yemen in the '60s and they are just going to have to cut a deal with one of the larger Arab states for protection when the Yankees go home.

Unpleasant truth two: the forces that gave rise to Saddam Hussein will continue beyond his defeat and even his death. New Arab leaders will emerge espousing the cause of pan-Arabism and citing the memory of Saddam along with that of Egypt's Nasser. The massive show of technologically superior military power by the West will impress in exactly the opposite way than intended. The American public thrilled to the display of firepower as if it were a manifestation of high culture. But a different and very long historical memory will be nourished in the Arab world where the war will be viewed as yet another crime of Western imperialism.

I remember being in the streets of Cairo the day Nasser resigned in ignominy after his huge and expensively equipped military was so soundly and suddenly defeated by the Israelis. Millions of Egyptians, uncoerced, rushed into the streets weeping and begging that Nasser return to power. He is today still the Arab world's greatest modern martyr. Weeks later I was in Israel interviewing the men who had led that nation to victory. They assured me that an era of peace was now at hand for them within their new secure borders. It didn't happen. Peace with Egypt, such as it is, came about only decades later when Israel withdrew to its original side of the Sinai. And peace with the rest of the Arab world, we all know now, is hardly at hand.

The point is that the Arabs as a people are hurting and the definition of victory and indeed leadership involves lowered expectations. Saddam will eventually be judged a hero by most on the Arab street for the same reason that Nasser was—he dared to stand up to the West.

Which brings up a third unpleasant truth: The West is not loved. This should be obvious given a history of carving up the region along state boundaries convenient to the French, English, and eventually the U.S. The TV image of British officers briefing on the progress of the campaign to liberate Kuwait might be seen differently by those who remember Sir Percy Zachariah Cox, the British high commissioner in this part of their empire, who whipped a red pencil out of his pocket and simply sliced Kuwait off from Iraq.

The West fought a war to prevent Arab control of the Suez Canal and supported Israel in the second, 1967, canal war. The West and the U.S. have been cozy with Israel and seem relatively indifferent to the fate of the Palestinians. The reasoning that says it is horrible for Iraq to move into Kuwait but acceptable for Israel to invade Lebanon or to seize the West Bank and Gaza will be lost on most Arabs.

The U.S. intervention in the Gulf puts the Arab-Israel conflict in our face. We have empowered U.N. resolutions with renewed importance. The burning post-victory question throughout the Mideast will be: What about those other U.N. resolutions, particularly U.N. resolution 242 which stipulates Israeli withdrawal from the occupied territories and the need for "a just and lasting peace"?

Because it suited his short-term purposes Bush wrapped his Gulf intervention in the U.N. flag without any serious national debate about what this step towards world government means. Where I live the big slogan used to be "Get the U.S. out of the U.N. and the U.N. out of the

U.S." Has all that changed? Or do we just use the U.N. when it suits our purpose? Is it like the World Court which we chose to ignore when it condemned the U.S. mining of Nicaragua's harbors?

What is the lasting principle of Operation Desert Storm? Are we bound only by those U.N. resolutions that affect oil-rich countries? Will we intervene only when other countries are willing to pay the bill because oil is involved? Will we intervene in a resource-poor country if it's only a matter of genocide as in Cambodia or Uganda in the past?

The good news is that we have blundered onto a new stage of international involvement. It will be much more difficult to ignore genocide or other forms of cruelty as they occur in the future. But if this comes to mean Pax Americana in which the U.S. attempts to adjudicate every dispute it will prove a disaster.

The alternative is simple but difficult to implement: genuine international cooperation in which we and our forces play only a minority role. If we can't accept this lesser position because of domestic American politics then we should retreat from building a new world order, at best a dangerous proposition once embraced by Hitler, and just let it evolve naturally.

The lesson of previous efforts to police the world's hot spots should be clear. No matter how one-sided the battlefield victory, the political results will be messy in the extreme. In the bars and at church socials later they will ask who really won and what did they win? There will never be a clean moment of victory and exultation because, once again, the goals of war are not clearly defined. The hand waving the flag will slow, the jaw will slacken and the bright moment of Saddam's defeat will be tarnished by a complex reality which we can barely comprehend, let alone control.

Further Reading

Abdalla, Ahmed. "Mubarak's Gamble." *Middle East Report,* January–February 1991.

Abdulghani, Jasmin M. *Iraq and Iran. The Years of Crisis.* Baltimore: Johns Hopkins University Press, 1984.

Abir, Mordechai. *Saudi Arabia in the Oil Era: Regime and Elites; Conflict and Collaboration.* Boulder, Colo.: Westview Press, 1988.

Ahmad, Eqbal. "Nightmare Victory?" *Mother Jones,* March–April, 1991.

Ajami, Fouad. *The Arab Predicament: Arab Political Thought and Practice Since 1967.* Cambridge: Cambridge University Press, 1981.

_____. "The Summer of Arab Discontent." *Foreign Affairs,* Winter 1990/91.

al-Khalil, Samir. *Republic of Fear.* New York: Pantheon Books, 1990.

Armstrong, Scott, et. al., eds. *The Chronology: The Documented Day-by-Day Account of the Secret Military Assistance to Iran and the Contras.* New York: Warner Books, 1987.

_____. "Saudis' AWACS Just a Beginning of New Strategy." *The Washington Post,* November 1, 1981.

Assiri, Abdul-Reda. *Kuwait's Foreign Policy.* Boulder, Colo.: Westview Press, 1990.

Bates, Greg, ed. *Mobilizing Democracy: Changing the U.S. Role in the Middle East.* Monroe, Maine: Common Courage Press, 1991.

Batatu, Hanna. *The Old Social Classes and the Revolutionary Movements of Iraq.* Princeton: Princeton University Press, 1978.

Berman, Paul. "The Gulf and the Left." *The Village Voice,* October 23, 1990.

Bill, James. *The Eagle and the Lion: The Tragedy of American-Iranian Relations.* New Haven: Yale University Press, 1988.

Blair, John M. *The Control of Oil.* New York: Pantheon, 1976.

Blumenthal, Sidney. "The CIA and the War Debate: Whose Agents?" *The New Republic,* February 11, 1991.

Borosage, Robert. "The Peace Movement: Countering Bush's Gambit in the Gulf." *The Nation,* September 24, 1990.

Caesar, Judith. "Saudi Dissent: Rumblings Under the Throne." *The Nation,* December 17, 1990.

Childers, Erskine. "The Use and Abuse of the United Nations." *Middle East Report,* March–April 1991.

Chomsky, Noam. *The Fateful Triangle: The United States, Israel and the Palestinians.* Boston: South End Press, 1983.

———. "Nefarious Aggression." *Z Magazine,* October, 1990.

Commission on Integrated Long-Term Strategy to the Secretary of Defense. *Discriminate Deterrence.* January, 1988.

Committee Against Repression and for Democratic Rights in Iraq. *Saddam's Iraq: Revolution or Reaction?* Revised edition. London: Zed Press, 1989.

Congressional Research Service. *Oil Fields as Military Objectives: A Feasibility Study.* Prepared for the House Committee on International Relations, August 21, 1975.

Cordesman, Anthony. *The Gulf and the Search for Strategic Stability.* Boulder, Colo.: Westview Press, 1984.

———, and Abraham Wagner. *The Lessons of Modern War, Vol. II: The Iran-Iraq War.* Boulder, Colo.: Westview Press, 1990.

Crystal, Jill. *Oil and Politics in the Gulf: Rulers and Merchants in Kuwait and Qatar.* Cambridge: Cambridge University Press, 1990.

Day, Arthur. *East Bank/West Bank: Jordan and the Prospects for Peace.* New York: Council on Foreign Relations, 1986.

Dorman, William A., and Mansour Farhang. *The U.S. Press and Iran: Foreign Policy and the Journalism of Deference.* Berkeley: University of California Press, 1987.

Draper, Theodore. *A Present of Things Past: Selected Essays.* New York: Hill and Wang, 1990.

Eveland, Wilbur Crane. *Ropes of Sand: America's Failure in the Middle East.* New York: W. W. Norton, 1980.

Falk, Richard. *Revolutionaries and Functionaries: The Dual Face of Terrorism.* New York: E. P. Dutton, 1988.

Ferguson, Thomas. "The War's Inevitable Fifth Horseman." *The New York Times,* February 3, 1991.

Friedman, Thomas L. *From Beirut to Jerusalem.* New York: Farrar, Straus and Giroux, 1989.

Fromkin, David. *A Peace to End All Peace: Creating the Modern Middle East, 1914– 1922.* New York: Henry Holt and Company, 1989.

Ghareeb, Edmund. *The Kurdish Question in Iraq.* Syracuse: Syracuse University Press, 1981.

Haim, Sylvia G., ed. *Arab Nationalism: An Anthology.* Berkeley: University of California Press, 1962.

Halliday, Fred. *Arabia Without Sultans.* London: Penguin, 1974.

Halpern, Manfred. *The Politics of Social Change in the Middle East and North Africa.* Princeton: Princeton University Press, 1963.

Hameed, Mazher A. *Arabia Imperilled: The Security Imperatives of the Arab Gulf States.* Washington, D.C.: Middle East Assessments Group, 1986.

Helms, Christine Moss. *Iraq: Eastern Flank of the Arab World.* Washington, D.C.: The Brookings Institution, 1984.

Henderson, David R. "Do We Need to Go to War for Oil?" CATO Institute Foreign Policy Briefing, October 24, 1990.

Hiro, Dilip. *Holy Wars: The Rise of Islamic Fundamentalism.* New York: Routledge, Chapman and Hall, Inc., 1989.

_____. *The Longest War: The Iraq-Iran Military Conflict.* New York: Routledge, Chapman and Hall, Inc., 1991.

Hudson, Michael C. *Arab Politics: The Search for Legitimacy.* New Haven: Yale University Press, 1977.

_____, ed. *The Palestinians: New Directions.* Washington, D.C.: Center for Contemporary Arab Studies, Georgetown University, 1990.

Ibn Bayyan, Hayyan. "Open Letter to Saudi Arabia." *The Nation,* April 4, 1981.

Ismael, Tareq Y. *The Arab Left.* Syracuse, N.Y.: Syracuse University Press, 1984.

Kedourie, Elie. *Arab Political Memoirs and Other Studies.* London: Frank Cass, 1974.

Khadduri, Majid. *The Gulf War: The Origins and Implications of the Iran-Iraq Conflict.* New York: Oxford University Press, 1988.

_____. *Independent Iraq: A Study in Iraqi Politics from 1932 to 1958.* 2nd ed. London: Oxford University Press, 1960.

_____. *Republican Iraq: A Study in Iraqi Politics Since the Revolution of 1958.* London: Oxford University Press, 1969.

_____. *Socialist Iraq: A Study in Iraqi Politics Since 1968.* Washington, D.C.: The Middle East Institute, 1978.

Kimche, Jon. *The Second Arab Awakening: The Middle East, 1914–1970.* New York: Holt, Rinehart and Winston, 1970.

Kinsley, Susan. "The Kurds: Persecuted Throughout the Region," *Human Rights Watch #1,* Winter 1991.

Klare, Michael. "Fueling the Fire: How We Armed the Middle East." *Bulletin of the Atomic Scientists,* January–February, 1991.

_____. "The Superpower Trip: Policing the Gulf—and the World." *The Nation,* October 15, 1990.

Kolko, Gabriel. *Confronting the Third World.* New York: Pantheon Books, 1988.

Kwitny, Jonathan. *Endless Enemies.* New York: Congdon and Weed, 1984.

Lacey, Robert. *The Kingdom: Arabia and the House of Sa'ud.* New York: Harcourt Brace Jovanovich, 1981.

Lamb, David. *The Arabs: Journeys Beyond the Mirage.* New York: Random House, 1987.

Laqueur, Walter Z. *Communism and Nationalism in the Middle East.* London: Routledge and Kegan Paul, 1956.

Lewis, Bernard. *The Arabs in History,* 2nd ed. New York: Harper and Row, 1967.

————. *The Middle East and the West.* New York: Harper and Row, 1964.

Lockman, Zachary and Joel Beinin, eds. *Intifada: The Palestinian Uprising Against Israeli Occupation.* Middle East Report and South End Press, 1989.

MacShane, Denis. New York: "Gulf Migrant Labor: Working in Virtual Slavery." *The Nation,* March 18, 1991.

McLachlan, Keith, and George Joffe. *The Gulf War: A Survey of Political Issues and Economic Consequences.* The Economist Intelligence Unit Special Report no. 176. London: The Economist, 1984.

McNaugher, Thomas L. *Arms and Oil: US Military Strategy and the Persian Gulf.* Washington, D.C.: The Brookings Institution, 1985.

Ma'oz, Moshe. *Asad: The Sphinx of Damascus.* New York: Weidenfeld & Nicolson, 1988.

Marr, Phebe. *The Modern History of Iraq.* Boulder, Colo.: Westview Press, 1985.

Matar, Fuad. *Saddam Hussein; The Man, the Cause, the Future.* London: Third World Center for Research and Publishing, 1981.

Middle East Report. *Crisis in the Gulf.* Resource packet. Washington D.C., 1990.

Middle East Watch. *Human Rights in Iraq.* New Haven: Yale University Press, 1990.

Miller, Judith, and Laurie Mylroie. *Saddam Hussein and the Crisis in the Gulf.* New York: Times Books/Random House, 1990.

The Minority Rights Group. *Migrant Workers in the Gulf.* London: Minority Rights Group, Ltd. Report No. 68.

Mortimer, Edward. *Faith and Power: The Politics of Islam.* New York: Random House, 1982.

Mosley, Leonard. *Power Play: Oil in the Middle East.* New York, Random House, 1973.

Pfaff, William. "Islam and the West." *The New Yorker,* January 28, 1991.

Quandt, William B. "The Middle East." *Foreign Affairs: America and the World,* 1990/91.

————. *Saudi Arabia in the 1980's.* Washington, D.C.: The Brookings Institution, 1981.

Safran, Nadav. *Saudi Arabia: The Ceaseless Quest for Security.* Cambridge: Harvard University Press, 1985.

Said, Edward W. *Covering Islam: How the Media and the Experts Determine How We See the Rest of the World.* New York: Pantheon, 1981.

———. *Orientalism.* New York: Pantheon, 1978.

Sampson, Anthony. *The Seven Sisters.* New York: Viking, 1975.

Sawdayee, Max. *All Waiting to be Hanged: Iraq Post Six Days War Diary.* Tel Aviv: Levanda Press, 1974.

Schanberg, Sydney H. "Censoring for Political Security." *Washington Journalism Review,* March 1991.

Seale, Patrick. *Asad: The Struggle for the Middle East.* Los Angeles and Berkeley: University of California Press, 1989.

Sherry, Virginia. "Kuwait Before—and After?" *The Nation,* November 5, 1990.

Sick, Gary. *All Fall Down: America's Tragic Encounter with Iran.* New York: Random House, 1985.

Sid-Ahmed, Mohamed. "The Gulf Crisis and the New World Order." *Middle East Report,* January–February, 1991.

Sluglett, Peter. *Britain in Iraq, 1914–1932.* London: Ithaca Press, 1976.

———, and Marion Farouk-Sluglett. *Iraq Since 1958.* London: Kegan Paul, 1988.

———, and Marion Farouk-Sluglett. *Iraq Since 1958: From Revolution to Dictatorship.* Revised edition. London: I.B. Tauris, 1990.

Stone, I. F., "War for Oil?" *The New York Review of Books,* February 6, 1975.

Stork, Joe. *Middle East Oil and the Energy Crisis.* New York: Monthly Review Press, 1975.

Taubman, Philip, Robert Hersey, Jr., and Judith Miller. "U.S. Aides Say Corruption Is Threat to Saudi Stability." *The New York Times,* April 16, 1980.

Tucker, Robert W. "Oil: The Issue of American Intervention." *Commentary,* January, 1975.

Utovich, A. L., ed. *The Middle East: Oil, Conflict, and Hope.* Lexington, Mass.: Lexington Books, 1976.

Viorst, Milton. "The House of Hashem." *The New Yorker,* January 7, 1991.

———. "Report from Baghdad." *The New Yorker,* September 24, 1990.

Wallach, Janet and John Wallach. *Arafat: In the Eyes of the Beholder.* New York: Lyle Stuart, 1990.

Weissman, Steve, and Herbert Krosney. *The Islamic Bomb.* New York: Times Books, 1981.

Winestone, H. V. F., and Zahra Freeth. *Kuwait: Prospect and Reality.* London: Allen and Unwin, 1972.

Woodward, Bob. *Veil: The Secret Wars of the CIA, 1981–1987.* New York: Simon & Schuster, 1989.

Wright, Robin. *Sacred Rage: The Wrath of Militant Islam.* New York: Simon & Schuster, 1985.

Yergin, Daniel. *The Prize.* New York: Simon & Schuster, 1991.

Zahlan, Rosemarie Said. *The Making of the Modern Gulf States.* London: Unwin Hyman, 1989.

Permissions Acknowledgments

Grateful acknowledgment is made to the following for permission to reprint previously published material:

Amnesty International USA: Report on Iraq/Occupied Kuwait. Copyright © 1990 Amnesty International Publications. Reprinted by permission.

Current History: "The Palestinians and the Gulf Crisis" by Rashid Khalidi from the January 1991 issue of *Current History* magazine. Copyright © 1991 Current History, Inc. Reprinted by permission.

Ariel Dorfman: "Hymn for the Unsung" by Ariel Dorfman from the February 1, 1991, issue of the *Los Angeles Times*. Reprinted by permission of Ariel Dorfman.

The Economist: "Kuwait: How the West Blundered" from the September 29, 1990, issue of *The Economist*. Copyright © 1990 by The Economist Newspaper Limited. Reprinted by permission.

Harper's Magazine: "Onward Christian Soldiers" by Lewis H. Lapham from the October 1990 and March 1991 issues of *Harper's Magazine* and "Why We Are Stuck in the Sand" by Christopher Hitchens from the January 1991 issue of *Harper's Magazine*. Copyright © 1990, 1991 by *Harper's Magazine*. All rights reserved. Reprinted from the October 1990, January 1991, and March 1991 issues by special permission.

Hill and Wang, a division of Farrar, Straus & Giroux, Inc.: Adaptation from "American Hubris" from *A Present of Things Past* by Theodore Draper. Copyright © 1990 by Theodore Draper. Reprinted by permission of Hill and Wang, a division of Farrar, Straus & Giroux, Inc.

The Independent: "Free to Report What We Are Told" by Robert Fisk, published in *The Independent* on February 4, 1991. Copyright © 1991 *The Independent*. Reprinted by permission.

Institute for International Economics: "Sanctions Work: The Historical Record" by Kimberly Elliott, Gary Hufbauer, and Jeffrey J. Schott (Original title: "The Big Squeeze: Why the Sanctions on Iraq Will Work") from the

Index

Micah L. Sifry is Middle East editor of *The Nation,* and has written widely on the region for numerous publications. He also specializes in American domestic politics. He holds a B.A. in Politics from Princeton University, and an M.A. in Politics from New York University. He lives and works in New York City.

Christopher Cerf is an author, editor, and an Emmy- and Grammy Award-winning contributor to *Sesame Street.* Among his many books are *The Experts Speak* (with Victor Navasky), *The Pentagon Catalog* (with Henry Beard), and *Small Fires: Letters from the Soviet People to Ogonyok Magazine* (co-edited with Marina Albee). He is a graduate of Harvard University and a former senior editor at Random House.